THE PICARESQUE

Hispanic Issues

HISPANIC ISSUES
VOLUME 12

THE PICARESQUE

TRADITION AND DISPLACEMENT

GIANCARLO MAIORINO

◆

EDITOR

UNIVERSITY OF MINNESOTA PRESS
MINNEAPOLIS   LONDON

The editors gratefully acknowledge assistance from the Program for Cultural Cooperation between Spain's Ministry of Culture and United States' Universities; the College of Liberal Arts and the Department of Spanish and Portuguese at the University of Minnesota; and Renaissance Studies, the Comparative Literature Program, and the Department of Spanish and Portuguese at Indiana University.

Published by the University of Minnesota Press
111 Third Avenue South, Suite 290, Minneapolis, MN 55401-2520
Printed in the United States of America on acid-free paper

Library of Congress Cataloging-in-Publication Data
The picaresque : tradition and displacement / Giancarlo Maiorino, editor.
        p.   cm. — (Hispanic issues; v. 12)
    Includes index.
    ISBN 0-8166-2722-3 (hc : alk. paper). — ISBN 0-8166-2723-1 (pb : alk. paper)
    1. Picaresque literature, Spanish—History and criticism.   2. Spanish fiction—Classical period, 1500–1700—History and criticism.   I. Maiorino, Giancarlo, 1943–   II. Series.
PQ6147.P5P53   1996
863'.08709—dc20   95-32079

Hispanic Issues

For
Howard Mancing
and
to our Italo-Spanish encounter
at Butler University

Contents

◆ Introduction
Renaissance Marginalities

Giancarlo Maiorino

I

The issue of picaresque marginality in Renaissance culture is one that brings up matters of distance as well as of depth at the periphery of canonical literature, which drew new strength from the authority of the classics. Vis-à-vis the centrality of humanist epics (Petrarch), panegyrics (Leonardo Bruni), and treatises (Leon Battista Alberti), the antihumanist core of the picaresque was parodic at heart, and found more congenial sources in Boccaccesque *novelle*, which had started a rich tradition of their own throughout Europe.

The range of literary genres between the opposition canonical/anticanonical found a counterpart in the commensurate spectrum of linguistic sources and styles. Much literary history, in fact, is validated by the history of words. The same year that Christopher Columbus sailed westward, Antonio de Nebrija addressed Queen Isabella of Castille in the prologue of his *Gramática de la lengua española* (1492): "Siempre la lengua fue compañera del imperio." With the blessings of political authority, language and canonicity joined forces in an iron-fisted pact. At the center of Spanish culture, Diego de San Pedro had humanistic models in mind when he constructed his *Cárcel de amor*. Its publication coincided with the acceptance of Castilian as the imperial language. Six years later, however, Alfonso Martínez de Toledo published *Arcipreste de Talavera* (1498), a satire of love that imitated the rhythms of vernacular speech. Both styles merged in Fernando de

Rojas's *La Celestina* (1499). In the humanistic spirit, Juan de Mena wrote the epic poem *Laberinto de Fortuna* (1444) as a Spanish equivalent to the *Aeneid.* Almost a century later, Juan de Valdes wrote *Diálogo de la lengua* (1535); it was a model of refined conversation in which writing was subordinated to speaking; and the hope was that no gap would exist between the two. Such literary "sources" notwithstanding, the picaresque also drew from an array of folkloristic materials such as tales, proverbs, anecdotes, and *refranes.* They had worked their way into forms of expression which edged between written and unwritten poetics. Amid that literary landscape, unwritten poetics thrived at crossroads where artists responded to the latent energies of unofficial culture, which included the genres of everyday life such as letters, confessions, sermons, diaries, and hybrid genres that existed outside official culture. The novel was the one genre whose closeness to life in the raw and society in the making would never tire of breaking down the boundaries between fiction and nonfiction. That culture included the heterogeneous voices of a readership which was informal, unassuming, and often congenial with the writer's own mind set. With an eye to current interests in "implied readers" and "reception aesthetics," Renato Poggioli, Walter Ong, Wolfgang Iser, Hans Robert Jauss, and Mikhail Bakhtin have taught us that such a readership could be unruly, provocative, and ever expanding. For sure, it made its presence felt in the world of art, which responded with unprecedented blends of fact with fiction.[1]

Between 1550 and 1559, the countergenre of the picaresque asserted itself. *Lazarillo de Tormes,* in fact, presents an urban society of paupers whose fundamental task is to survive in the thick of a derelict existence. Without any doubt, the picaresque countered the canonical standard of literary and materialist imperialism. By the middle of the sixteenth century, therefore, the languages of *historia* and *intrahistoria* (to borrow the term from Miguel de Unamuno) were active in arts and letters as nowhere else in the rest of Europe. *Hidalgos* and affluent noblemen faced *pícaros* and indigent people at a socioeconomic divide that culture at large neither could nor would bridge.

The emergence of novelistic and dramatic texts in the wake of *La Celestina* and *Lazarillo de Tormes* exposed—if it did not take to task—the literature whose entrenched predominance made the picaresque "peripheral." By now, however, we have learned that Renaissance texts are important for what they leave out as much as for what they present. Throughout the fifteenth century, the literature and anthropology of Humanism, whose sociopolitical agenda was rooted in privilege and prejudice, created monumental figures whose virtual character was exempt from the trials and tribulations of existence. It suffices to remind ourselves that Baldassar Castiglione's *Il Cortegiano* outlines a most selective picture of society. The court in fact lodged the very core of those "happy few" who so fascinated Jacob Burckhardt, Walter Pater, and W. B. Yeats. But Yeats himself felt that the Renaissance was the invention of an elite, and its texts were bound to raise the fundamental question: What was their currency amid the population at street corners and in marketplaces? Successful merchants and courtiers aside, what did such a literature say about common people? Above all, how much of culture and society did the paradigm of humanist textuality ignore? At the court's—or *palazzo's*—doorstep, however, there were artisans, peasants, soldiers, and merchants who made such a refined existence possible by stocking up goods and providing services through the back door. Because of their "inferior" birth and faith within the official culture of catholic Spain, *conversos* were "marginalized" in the midst of their own productive peers in the very places of business. Since they stood at the ground floor of society's *vertical* structure, they bodied forth the supporting base of the socioeconomic pyramid. By any objective standard, their number, their tasks, and their economic weight were not peripheral at all. So approached, the very concept of marginality proved to be at once ironic and deceptive. As the sixteenth century unfolded, the cultures of Reformation and Counter-Reformation could not but take notice of the need to reach out toward the lower levels of society. In their own ways, Erasmus, Montaigne, and picaresque authorship popularized artforms more responsive to the pulse of life and the broader spectrum of a human nature whose complexity Niccolò Machiavelli lodged between the poles of *verità effettuale* and *verità ideale*. The humanist was bound to become humane, well in the spirit of Boccaccio's opening words in the *Decameron: "Umana cosa è*—It is human."

At the ground floor, however, one would also find *pícaros*, beggars, thieves, prostitutes, and an array of less than productive people who have always been kept away from, and ignorant of, whatever was taking place on the upper floors. The economic dependence of such a destitute humanity was endemic. And scholarship has found its parasitic condition to be typical of picaresque textuality. As such, parasites can live at the center while remaining peripheral, as it actually happened to Lázaro de Tormes when he became *pregonero* in Toledo.[2] We thus confront another aspect of marginality, whose sociology drew an inner ring within its own periphery. As Michel Sèrres has taught us, the parasite is "the tactician of the quotidian." And much picaresque quotidianity was parceled out to urban residence in the city's underside; its hovels, ghettoes, *chabolas*, and *barrios*. The world, that is, of *la mala vida* in its several variations: *picaresca, rufianesca, germanesca, celestinesca*. We roam here with Andreuccio amid Boccaccio's Malpertugio neighborhood in Naples (*Decameron* II:5); the ill-famed quarters of Rinconete and Cortadillo; and the *escudero*'s ghostly lodgings in a district crowded with prostitutes. Indeed, the unthinkable reverse of those monumental cities that Renaissance utopianism represented in literary texts (Leonardo Bruni's *Panegyric to the City of Florence*), pictorial perspectives (Luciano Laurana's *Architectural Perspective*), and actual city plans (Bernardo Rossellino's Pienza). It was only in places of habitation—whether they be roadsides or universities—that *pícaros* could, and did, undertake educational processes. The parodic nature of the picaresque could not but reflect such a nomenclature, which was at once spatial, social, and economic. Even the link between poverty and criticism, whether it be literary, historical, or a combination of both, somehow echoes the dualism center-periphery. Once he decided to undertake his monumental study, *Capitalism and Material Life*, Fernand Braudel conceded that he was shifting from the noble, magisterial, and exalted history of Martin Luther and François Rabelais to the economic history of the Medicis and the Fuggers; a kind of history of minor resonance, still undeveloped, and the object of many a prejudice (*Afterthoughts* 4–5).[3] A line was drawn between "epic" and "picaresque," ideology and praxis. Yet, it goes almost without saying that Medician praxis was by no means typical of the ordinary lifestyle of people at large. It is not by accident that modern parlance refers to Medician gestures as acts of extraordinary generosity made possible by extraordinary wealth. To a great extent, "bourgeois" thus defines an upper middle class whose materialist credentials affect its lack of genealogical luster. This study, instead, focuses on the picaresque borderline; its relevance is minor only in terms of aristocratic and mercantile standards of outstanding affluence.

At the edge between begging and earning, work and theft, the *pícaro* has been called a "half outsider," much as "outsiderism" has been found to be constitutive of the genre itself.[4] Outsiderism thus stood opposite canonicity, whose texts ignored the marginalized periphery where the rest of humanity lived; and the "rest" was quantitatively the "most." One need not be ideologically minded on the trail of Marxist and post-Marxist experiences to realize that the *padre di famiglia* and *il cortegiano* were the tip of the social iceberg. In many ways, most humanity was submerged well below the cresting wealth of the upper class. Submerged forms cannot be seen, and it would be difficult to take notice of them, let alone to speak about them. And that was the case with common people caught up in the practice of everyday life. Such an *infrahumanidad* did not write about itself, for the simple fact that it had neither the means nor the education. For its part, the dominant class was determined to let that state of things endure. And endure it did. Most *pícaros* never crested above anonymity and survival. But one *pícaro* did. Although he could not uproot social injustice, Lázaro de Tormes headstarted a novelistic discourse that would change the very notions of canonicity and marginality forever.

Once humanist idealism no longer could conceal its theoretical makeup, more empirical artforms began to assert their presence. After the turn of the sixteenth century, Ludovico Ariosto let madness have the best of chivalric heroes; Francesco Guicciardini vindicated the *particolari* of reality against Machiavellian abstractions; and Giovanni della Casa wrote rules of conduct for middle class people who met standards of "mediocrity" rather than excellence. Culture at large began to move toward the life-sized, which humanist textuality had kept at the margins of society. Slowly, arts and letters began to reach out toward the practice of existence below historical magnitude and heroic deeds. The picaresque thus gained height and grounds. It was the marginality of the ordinary man, what Michel de Certeau has called the common and anonymous hero, who is the "murmuring voice of societies. In all ages, he comes before texts. He does not expect representations . . . the increasingly sociological and anthropological perspective of inquiry privileges the anonymous and the everyday" (vii). At its picaresque juncture, the common and anonymous hero did get a chance at representation, which forced authorship to bring to literature a new set of images, events, and ideological assets. Much picaresque narrative centered on the day-to-day-ness of habit and practical routine, which could be paraphrased by the title of Braudel's book *The Structure of Everyday Life*. Marginal materials became a central focus of attention, and daily practice provided a rather objective measure of the book's subtitle, "The Possible and the Impossible." In order to encompass culture at large, Braudel found it necessary to bring together a number of *parahistoric* languages such as food, housing, money, clothes, luxury, and tools. In the study of everyday life, therefore, historians and semioticians shared parallel, if not outright similar, methodologies. It seems as if modern historians had been making a subtextual critique of humanist idealism vis-à-vis picaresque empiricism.[5] By weighing "the possible" at every step of his painful journey out of indigence, Lázaro de Tormes would learn that, for low-born wretches like him, outsiderism would always edge on outsiderism itself. The dialogics of marginality would find no resolution in qualitative changes of any major consequence.

On anthropological grounds, Victor Turner also understood that liminality could signal permanence instead of, or in addition to, transience. He thus defined liminality as a state in itself; it could be diachronic as well as synchronic. When popular acclaim called Mateo Alemán's *Guzmán de Alfarache* by the shortened *El Pícaro*, titology itself proved the point; the picaresque had undergone evolution as well as settlement. And evolution took place within the Hispanic tradition as well as across the European continent. Drawing from anthropological lessons, Gustavo Pérez-Firmat maintains that the concept of liminality is a *position* that designates "the spatial relationship between a center and its periphery."

Whatever its nature, liminality "occupies the periphery in relation to a contextually determined center" (xiv). The two terms thus share interchangeable characteristics. But marginality is more sociologically bound, and it has a greater literary currency—from Jacques Derrida to Barbara Hernnstein Smith and Paul Julian Smith. At any rate, both terms emphasize reciprocity and relationship, which the picaresque enacted through binary oppositions: rich/poor, integrated/marginal, country/city, money/power of rank, master/servant. Dualisms of that sort added to the parodic nature of the genre, whose textuality called for subtextuality. Equally relevant are Carlos Fuentes's comments on denotation and connotation. Denotative texts such as pastoral novels and novels of chivalry were no more than anachronistic prolongations of medieval textuality. By contrast, picaresque literature was connotative inasmuch as it marked a rupture of the epic order; it foregrounded a transgression "of the previous norm while, all the time, supporting itself on what it is violating" (20).

On social and literary grounds alike, the picaresque was rooted in the center-periphery dialogics. As a matter of fact, the anti-canonical novel and its canonical counterparts stood in a relationship of copresence. Synchronicity could best be expressed through the image of a "bush" rather than the traditional "ladder." The Renaissance revival of ancient forms raised the problem of generic productivity, for while some forms were successfully revived— Sannazaro's pastoral *L'Arcadia*—others fell into a state of sterility—Petrarch's Roman epic *Africa*. On contemporary grounds, the tragicomedy *La Celestina* had followers, but it did not signal the beginning of a generic proliferation comparable to that of *Lazarillo de Tormes*. Instead of strict evolutionary sequences, therefore, one could rely on the biological imagery of the bush branching out in different directions at the same time.[6] And two of those new branches were the essay and the novel. Such a configuration fits— and echoes—the *allopatric theory*. Allopatric means "in another place," and the theory maintains that new species arise and are cut off from their parental group as well as from the periphery of the ancestral core. In the nomenclature of family evolution, the short story was indeed a precedent to the novel. The periphery plays a role in defining progress, whose dynamics are liable to leaps and changes. David Fishelov writes that marginality includes genres "below" the "high" genres, but also above them, that is to say, avant-garde literature (48–49). According to this definition, the rise of the novel would indeed be allopatric, for it was not only lateral but also ground-breaking. On the down side of that line of reasoning, we must remember that the parasitic side of the picaresque tends to perceive society as a stable construct quite inimical to transformations. To that extent, even picaresque texts written by *conversos* would not fit the modern concept of minor literature, which is actively political.[7]

II

Picaresque marginality, therefore, implied neither exclusion nor alienation; nor did it pave the way for any Cervantine insufficiency.[8] Instead, it fostered dialogism. Its voices were echoed throughout the ever-present, but as yet unchartered, landscape of a low-life society teeming with human mediocrity and afflicted by economic indigence. That humanity found temporary relief in carnivalesque exuberance, which artists such as François Rabelais and Pieter Brueghel have popularized. While Mikhail Bakhtin has highlighted the cornucopian affluence of Renaissance culture in *Rabelais and His World*, the picaresque foregrounded its reverse, that is to say, an unredeemable poverty of purse and thought that in fact was all too permanent for most people. My opening essay sets up the broader landscape, and the most inclusive social condition, of the population at large. My focus is on the sixth *tratado* of *Lazarillo de Tormes*, in which young Lázaro undertakes an unprecedented climb toward economic and literary achievements. His approach to work and love bridged the economic gap between cost of living and standard of life. He promotes his *buena fortuna* by relying on work as much as on love, which he treats as a materialistic means of investment. His long-term project would lead him out of social waywardness and into the very heart of Toledan economy.

In the second essay, George Shipley reminds us that a life without sex makes for a very dull story and that sex did play a role among Lázaro's *fortunas* and *adversidades*. As a matter of fact, sex affected both; marriage promoted Lázaro's good luck, but his *ménage-à-trois* also led to Vuestra Merced's threatening inquiry. And neighborly *malas lenguas* unveiled both the manifest and covert aspects of the business of sex, which is sustained through the picaresque texts included in this collection. Such a thematic concern links periphery to center, exercising a leveling effect that tends to merge the two topographies together.

My opening comparison of *Lazarillo de Tormes* and Velázquez's *The Waterseller* is meant to illustrate the literary argument. At the same time, however, it is an apt introduction to the third essay in this volume, which draws from expertise in literature and art history. Janis A. Tomlinson and Marcia L. Welles in fact have joined forces in the interdisciplinary essay on *Lazarillo de Tormes* and Murillo's *Four Figures on a Step*. While upholding the thematics of love under the guise of transgressive sexuality, this essay takes its start at the divide between what Paul Julian Smith has termed "pictorialism" and "representation," another boundary pairing that sets communality against isolation, and spatial context against fragmented spaces.

Quite literally, interdisciplinarity closes up on the pages of a single text in the fourth essay by Luis Beltrán, who takes up a reading of Francisco Delicado's *La Lozana andaluza,* published in Venice between 1528 and 1530, shortly before the writing of *Lazarillo de Tormes*. Like her male counterpart, Lozana belongs to the same world of human and moral destitution that thrived in the underbelly of the Renaissance. And she would pave the way for a whole lineage of *pícaras* who secured their survival by exercising the world's oldest profession. The text intertwines written word and visual illustration (*mamotreto*). By focusing on the "author's author" and the divide between typography and sexuality, the essay centers on the erosion of mimesis as it accommodates a sustained process of incarnation meant to reconcile clashes between the demands of immanence and longings for transcendence. Under such pressures, the narrative often degenerates toward excess and outright grotesque effects. The marginality, that is, of unproportional forms which betray an authorial standpoint that is willfully antihumanistic. By any standards, the picaresque shift of gender is not a pleasant one. Lozana's ugliness, in fact, is of a pathological kind, even though clients and admirers alike find her noseless face attractive. At once opportunistic and commercial, the sexual thematics toys with less-than-charming variations. At once unadorned and undisguised, sexuality flaunts its hedonistic and mercantile attributes.

Shifts in gender lead us to the fifth essay by Nina Cox Davis, whose titological emphasis on "Breaking the Barriers" sets the stage for the appearance of the female *pícara* in López de Ubeda's *La pícara Justina* (1605). Some reservations notwithstanding, the sexual reprobate of *La Lozana andaluza* was transformed into a virgin sinner (Friedman 87). For male *pícaros*, maternal heritage was transferred to women who would serve them as wives to be pandered or prostitutes to be pimped. But the iconoclastic *pícara* Justina tested that homosocial economy. In the process, such a breaking of barriers undermined male-bound discourse. Whether casual or deliberate, the upshot singled out the political potential of the picaresque.

In picaresque ontology, marginality could not be conquered through spatial shifts, whether it be in the city of Toledo and Seville, at the other side of the Alps, or across the oceans. It could only be conquered through social ascent, which proved to be ever more elusive. Deficient productivity and social conservatism slowed down the path-breaking teleology of the journey, and reliance on proverbs and *exempla* injected retrospective wisdom into the narrative. The conspicuous presence of such forms of authority betrayed the 'marginal' status of a genre whose own novelty was ill at ease within the traditional hierarchy of writing.[9] Undaunted by Foucauldian doubts about the very substance of "What is an Author" as well as Barthean pronouncements about the "Death of the Author," the sixth essay by Carroll B. Johnson takes up the matter of author and authorship in the canonical paradigm of the genre, *Guzmán de Alfarache*. By centering on the borderline between the humanistic heritage of an integrated Self and the premodernist constitution of a rather disjointed and antihumanistic Other, the essay focuses concerns with canonicity and marginality on authorship, which links literary production to Guzmán's experiences with the powerful and the powerless. Even in matters of authority, economics play an important role. Etymologically speaking, Vico reminds us, *auctor* derives from the Greek *autos*. Its Latin equivalent gives *proprius*, which also means property. In a socioeconomic nutshell, therefore, the very concept of authority stands at the borderline of literary and economic production.

Concerns about authorship and discourse as well as economics and heritage come together in the seventh essay by Edward H. Friedman, whose study of narrative space in Quevedo's *Buscón* draws together several strands introduced in the previous essays. While paying attention to criticism couched in the spirit of Poststructuralist counterreadings, Friedman centers on the reciprocity that the development of institutions and individuals brought to public and private spheres of social influence. At the same time, he is careful to highlight the unbridgeable *difference* between experiences stretched out over the oceans and the persistence of personal habit at the core of the protagonist's selfhood. Like Lázaro de Tormes, El Buscón has inherited undesirable genes, is determined to pursue amelioration, and finally accepts social determinism in the spirit of failure rather than under the aegis of some sort of "conversion." The narrative space of the picaresque thus accommodates the ironic alternatives of idealistic fictions and confessional textuality.

The eighth essay by Manuel Durán takes a diachronic leap by scouting picaresque elements in the works of Cervantes. In the same breath, Durán draws an analogy between the invention of the picaresque and Christopher Columbus's voyage. Both explored unknown territories, and both were followed by periods of uncertainty and doubts. Marginality thus drew a kind of macrocosmic perimeter, which Quevedo extended to the New World. Yet, it took less to charter the new continent than to exhaust the outer reaches of the picaresque, which is still unfolding before our eyes. Its microcosmic reach, however, touched on Lázaro and Guzmán, both of whom could only afford omelettes made, like their corrupted societies, of rotten eggs. The literary background of *Guzmán de Alfarache* harks back to *La Celestina*, in which Pleberio sees life as a trap. It caught mice, thieves, and any poor soul who tried to be part of the social system without having armed himself with predatory fangs. Because of the dominant indigence of too many people, that trap divided wealth from starvation, the have from the have-not. It made cruel selections, and delivered a devastating punishment in the second *tratado* of *Lazarillo de Tormes*. As a matter of fact, the trap could be taken as a central symbol of the picaresque at large. Sorting out thematic and stylistic differences, the essay outlines the extent to which such a heritage reached Cervantes, who found in the picaresque a viable source of imitation and emulation.

The ninth essay by Anne J. Cruz extends the picaresque outreach to filial rogues on British islands where authorial paternity included the names of John Awdeley, Robert Greene, and Thomas Nash. As he migrated from Spain, the *pícaro*'s lot improved; his marginality, in fact, often stemmed from "middle-class" affluence and respectability, which paved the way for a more rewarding future. Outside Spain, the picaresque took on features that reflected local conditions and indigenous traditions. Because of that heterogeneity, Anne Cruz explores variants without altering her approach to the Spanish model. Although her focus centers on the issue of poverty and social mobility, she brings up the protean character of picaresque marginality. Since it invaded the rest of the Continent in a major way, picaresque production made the very concept of marginality burst at the seams, before much modernity would set it right at the center. Whether at the center or at the borders, poverty and exploitation stood at the core of the picaresque. Recently, Peter N. Dunn has written that *Lazarillo* "makes us stare at" rather than raise "the issue of poverty." The *pícaro* in fact accepts poverty as a central, not marginal, condition of the world (294–95). Since indigence was there to stay, a kind of double jeopardy ensued. Whenever the *pícaro* "settled" into a better condition of life, the presence and contiguity of beggars and vagrants would keep on reminding him of the instability of his *buena fortuna*. The *caso* launched against Lázaro de Tormes is an appropriate reminder of that vulnerable condition (Dunn 305). At that point, marginality defined a state of being rather than a threshold.

In the tenth essay, Howard Mancing offers a definition of the genre. It would seem that any attempt at defining the picaresque genre is at least paradoxical. Yet, the essay sorts out generic diversity—comic biography, fictional autobiography, realistic and/or satiric novel—and social pluralism—a servant to many masters, a delinquent, a beggar, a social climber. Drawing on recent genre theory and major studies of the picaresque that have flourished during the past thirty years, Mancing has singled out predominant criteria for defining the genre; sociological, thematic, formalist. Other approaches notwithstanding, criticism has rallied around two poles: exclusivist and mediated. That dualism in turn engendered subcategories—from antipicaresque to pseudopicaresque. In the 1970s, a new generation of studies yielded excellent works, which, however, were not committed to the matter of definition. Having accepted the idea that genres change and evolve, which is explicitly stated by Alastair Fowler and Fernando Lázaro Carreter, Mancing takes that thesis one step further. At the gate of picaresque nomenclature, he offers his own "protean" definition.

III

At the very end of *Writing in the Margin,* Paul Julian Smith concludes that

> the particular significance of Spain and its Renaissance writers might be as an example of persistent and irreducible marginality. For Spain is the "woman" of European culture. She is excluded from the main currents of political and cultural power, scorned for her supposed emotionalism and sensualism, and pitied for her lack of that serene classicism or rationalism which once presented itself as the ideal. (204)[10]

At the center of Renaissance culture, one would find the heroic past, whether it be mythic, classical, or relatively modern. The center is a world of exemplary achievements and impeccable precedents. At the humanist center, the high genres shaped contemporaneity into virtual and metahistorical figures—the Courtier, the Prince. Amid such a transcendental topography of the mind, ancient Greeks and Italian humanists offered answers and solutions, instead of asking questions or testing the process of existence (Lukács 31). And they knew it. In fact, Castiglione himself wrote *Il Cortegiano* in the defensive mode of an apology. Moreover, he let one of his courtiers raise the issue of an inductive, and experiential, process of learning. The perfect Courtier "without defect of any kind" is endowed with grace as a gift of nature or the gods. "But as for those who are less endowed by nature and are capable of acquiring grace only if they put forth labor, industry, and care, I would wish to know by what art, by what discipline, by what method, they can gain this grace." At the center, an uncanonical question was raised.

> "I am not bound," said the Count, "to teach you how to acquire grace or anything else, but only to show you what a perfect Courtier ought to be." (41)

The "protonovelistic" question was asked, but it could not be answered without undermining the whole fabric of humanist perfection, which was postulated as nothing short of an epiphany. At the margins, the new form of the novel unraveled a "genre-in-the-making" crowded with less than perfect characters to say the least. Once the novelistic mode gained strength, topographies of perfection yielded to the itinerant and interactive chronotope of the road, which shaped much of the *pícaro*'s experience from Tormes and Salamanca to Toledo and Seville.[11] Contemporaneity, Mikhail Bakhtin reminds us, has been a "subject of representation only for the low genres. Most importantly, it was the basic subject matter in that broadest and richest of realms, the common people's creative culture of laughter." At first, *Lazarillo de Tormes* was read as a comical text. Yet, comicity could gauge the "distant destinies of literature's future unfolding" (Bakhtin, *Dialogic* 20, 33).

Marginality vis-à-vis the canonical armature of Italian Humanism stirred imitations in Spain, from Sannazaro's pastoralism to Castiglione's courtiership. Well into the sixteenth century, however, Italian Humanism fell prey to its own canonicity; originality was stifled, while much talent and learning were wasted in making canons even more canonical than Aristotle and Horace would have suspected. Torquato Tasso's best "epic effort" went into correcting his *Gerusalemme liberata* in light of orthodox standards that led him to rewrite epic, which he called the *Gerusalemme riconquistata*. It may not be accidental that the centrality of humanist poetics slowly dried out originality in Italy. Boccaccio was the first great short story writer, but the novel developed in Spain. Likewise, Petrarch's epistolarity often verged on essayistic ontology, but it was Michel de Montaigne who created the essay in France. They all capitalized on Italian lessons amid cultures less burdened by tradition and theory. At the margins, questions that would prove crucial to modernity were raised. The novelist asked, "How does one shape a life?" (Guillén 156). And the essayist echoed, "How does one shape a thought?" (Maiorino 92). Instead of engaging themselves in endless—and often pointless—debates as to whether any legitimizing authority could be found among the ancients, Old and New Christians alike found more freedom in the literature that exchanges with other European cultures brought to Spain since the early fifteenth century.[12] Montaigne and picaresque writers proceeded to create new forms, however tentative they were about the value and legitimacy of their own novelty. At the margins, popular culture and unwritten poetics shouldered experimentation. With the oncoming culture of the Baroque gaining grounds, consensus tested rule, certainty yielded to indeterminacy, and conformity made room for innovation. All those tendencies went into the making of the picaresque, which bridged the gap between the early and the late sixteenth century. In fact, synchronic variety, diachronic complexity, and protean genes are traits typical of the picaresque, even though its definition compounds the uniqueness of each individual work.

"After all, the boundaries between fiction and nonfiction, between literature and non-literature and so forth are not laid up in heaven" (Bakhtin, *Dialogic* 33). So Mikhail Bakhtin has been telling us. In the humanist heaven of flawless models, the future had to be shaped as a complete and perfected memory of the past. But down on earth, by roadsides and market places at the periphery of *accademie, studioli,* and patrician palaces, the everyday practice of life unraveled at the other side of perfection. At the periphery of wealth, privilege, and culture itself, the majority of people faced existence with all its uncertainties and open-endedness. With a laugh or a grimace, picaresque voices were heard everywhere. They made sure that literature, art, and culture itself would always keep one step ahead of memory, and never tire of taking one more step into the future, which came to be—warts and all.[13]

Notes

1. A fuller quotation is reported by Juan Luis Alborg in his *Historia de la literatura española: Edad Media y Renacimiento* (1: 291). The term "unwritten poetics" was coined by Renato Poggioli in his discussion of the modern novel in *The Spirit of the Letter* (345). Rosalie Colie adds that "from 'real' literature as opposed to criticism and theory, of course, we recover what is far more important, the *unwritten* poetics by which writers worked and which they themselves created" (29–30). For the idea of the audience as the writer's own fiction, see Walter Ong. On the concept of implied reader, see Iser's classic, *The Implied Reader: Patterns of Communication in Prose Fiction from Bunyan to Beckett*. On reception theory, I refer to Hans Robert Jauss, *Toward an Aesthetic of Reception*. On the novel as an open genre close to reality, see Bakhtin (*Dialogic* 38–40). On linguistic and textual experiments, I draw from Rivers (44–45, 57–58, 66–67).

2. This is Harry Sieber's thesis in *Language and Society in Lazarillo de Tormes*. On Sieber's approach, see Roberto González-Echevarría (10–11).

3. Such a dualism reflected two projects, one by Lucien Febvre, which death interrupted, and the other by Braudel, which produced *Capitalism and Material Life 1400–1800*.

4. Claudio Guillén introduced the term "half-outsider" (80); and Rosalie Colie insisted on the picaresque's commitments to "outsiderisms" (94). Just to clarify the near-centrality of picaresque outsiderism from a sociological standpoint, it ought to be noted that Lázaro is a parasite as well as a conformist. And Alexander Blackburn tells us that "the pícaro is a conformist with little antisocial tendencies in the affirmative sense. He yearns to enter society, implicitly accepting social values no matter how hostile to his dignity they have proved to be." Loneliness for "the literary pícaro is the loneliness of an individual isolated *within* society" (19–20).

5. This constitutes the field of investigation in his *The Structure of Everyday Life: The Limits of the Possible* (Preface, 31) and *Afterthoughts on Material Civilization and Capitalism* (6–7).

6. On the biological model, see Stephen Jay Gould.

7. See Gilles Deleuze and Félix Guattari (especially 16–17). Three characteristics are singled out: (1) minor literature doesn't come from a minor language; it is rather that which a minority constructs within a language; (2) everything is political; (3) everything takes on a collective value.

8. E. C. Riley has focused on the "marginality" of Cervantes, who "wavered between a frankly stated pride in his literary achievements and a sense of poetic insufficiency" (5–6).

9. Paul Julian Smith writes in this connection: "the rhetorical frame thus suspends teleology . . . the art precedes the artist, but it is itself subject to their practice of it" (104).

10. Before the Hispanist, Mikhail Bakhtin wrote: "In the high genres all authority and privilege, all lofty significance and grandeur, abandon the zone of familiar contact for the distanced plane (clothing, etiquette, the style of a hero's speech and the style of speech about him). It is in this orientation toward completeness that the classicism of all non-novel genres is expressed" (*Dialogic* 20).

11. The concept of chronotope, as the dynamic and interactive coexistence of time and space, was introduced by Mikhail Bakhtin, who has linked it to the

picaresque in *The Dialogic Imagination: Four Essays.* In the appended Glossary, Michael Holquist so defines chronotope: "Literally 'time-space.' A unit of analysis for studying texts according to the ratio and nature of the temporal and spatial categories represented. The distinctiveness of this concept as opposed to most other uses of time and space in literary analysis lies in the fact that neither category is privileged; they are utterly interdependent. The chronotope is an optic for reading texts as x-rays of the forces at work in the culture system from which they spring" (425–426).

12. On matters of Renaissance experiments, see Rivers 39–72.

13. The initial impetus for this volume grew out of the conference titled, "Renaissance Displacements: The Enduring Marginality of the Picaresque," which was held at Indiana University in Bloomington, March 12–14, 1992.

Works Cited

Alborg, Juan Luis. *Historia de la literatura española: Edad Media y Renacimiento.* Madrid: Editorial Gredos, 1966.

Bakhtin, Michael. *The Dialogic Imagination: Four Essays.* Austin: Univ. of Texas Press, 1981.

———. *Rabelais and His World.* Cambridge: Harvard Univ. Press, 1968.

Blackburn, Alexander. *The Myth of the Picaro: Continuity and Transformation of the Picaresque Novel. 1554–1954.* Chapel Hill: Univ. of North Carolina Press, 1979.

Braudel, Fernand. *Afterthoughts on Material Civilization and Capitalism.* Baltimore: Johns Hopkins Univ. Press, 1977.

———. *The Structure of Everyday Life: The Limits of the Possible.* New York: Harper and Row, 1979.

Castiglione, Baldassar. *The Book of the Courtier.* Trans. C. Singleton. New York: Anchor Books, 1956.

Certeau, Michel de. *The Practice of Everyday Life.* Berkeley: Univ. of California Press, 1984.

Colie, Rosalie. *The Resources of Kind: Genre-Theory in the Renaissance.* Berkeley: Univ. of California Press, 1973.

Deleuze, Gilles, and Félix Guattari. *Kafka: Toward a Minor Literature.* Minneapolis: Univ. of Minnesota Press, 1986.

Dunn, Peter. *Spanish Picaresque Fiction: A New Literary History.* Ithaca: Cornell Univ. Press, 1993.

Fishelov, David. *Metaphors of Genre: The Role of Analogies in Genre Theory.* University Park: Pennsylvania State Univ. Press, 1993.

Friedman, Edward H. *The Antiheroine's Voice: Narrative Discourse and Transformations of the Picaresque.* Columbia: Univ. of Missouri Press, 1987.

Fuentes, Carlos. *Don Quixote; or, The Critique of Reading.* Austin: Univ. of Texas Press, 1976.

González-Echevarría, Roberto. "The Life and Adventures of Cipión: Cervantes and the Picaresque." *Cervantes.* Ed. Harold Bloom. New York: Chelsea House, 1987.

Gould, Stephen Jay. *Ever Since Darwin: Reflections in Natural History.* New York: Knopf, 1977.

Guillén, Claudio. *Literature as System: Essays towards the Theory of Literary History.* Princeton: Princeton Univ. Press, 1971.

Iser, Wolfgang. *The Implied Reader: Patterns of Communication in Prose Fiction from Bunyan to Beckett.* Baltimore: Johns Hopkins Univ. Press, 1974.

Jauss, Hans Robert. *Toward an Aesthetic of Reception.* Minneapolis: Univ. of Minnesota Press, 1982.

Lukács, Georg. *The Theory of the Novel.* Cambridge: MIT Press, 1971.

Maiorino, Giancarlo. *The Cornucopian Mind and the Baroque Unity of the Arts.* University Park: Pennsylvania State Univ. Press, 1990.

Ong, Walter. "The Writer's Audience Is Always a Fiction." *PMLA* 90 (1975): 9–21.

Perez-Firmat, Gustavo. *Literature and Liminality: Festive Readings in the Hispanic Tradition.* Durham: Duke Univ. Press, 1986.

Poggioli, Renato. *The Spirit of the Letter.* Cambridge: Harvard Univ. Press, 1965.

Riley, E. C. *Don Quixote.* London: Allen and Unwin, 1986.

Rivers, Elias L. *Quixotic Scriptures: Essays on the Textuality of Hispanic Literature.* Bloomington: Indiana Univ. Press, 1983.

Sèrres, Michel. *The Parasite.* Baltimore: Johns Hopkins Univ. Press, 1982.

Sieber, Harry. *Language and Society in "La vida de Lazarillo de Tormes."* Baltimore: Johns Hopkins Univ. Press, 1978.

Smith, Barbara Herrnstein. *Contingencies of Value: Alternative Perspectives for Critical Theory.* Cambridge: Harvard Univ. Press, 1988.

Smith, Paul Julian. *Writing in the Margin: Spanish Literature of the Golden Age.* Oxford: Clarendon Press, 1988.

Turner, Victor. *Fields, Dramas, and Metaphors: Symbolic Action in Human Society.* Ithaca: Cornell Univ. Press, 1974.

Unamuno, Miguel de. *Our Lord Don Quixote.* Princeton: Princeton Univ. Press, 1976.

◆ Chapter 1
Picaresque Econopoetics: At the Watershed of Living Standards

Giancarlo Maiorino

I

At the divide between the waning of feudalism and the birth of capitalism, orations on human dignity, praises of folly, seafaring discoveries, and mercantile adventurism set off outbursts of human ingenuity. Merchants in Florence and elsewhere, Jules Michelet wrote at an early stage of Renaissance criticism, upheld a religion that found "in gold its real presence and in letters of exchange its eucharist."[1] It was the "other" Renaissance of commercial pursuits that made ambitious individuals proud, powerful, and appreciative of the advantages wealth could bestow on lineage and society.

At the beginning of early modern Europe, the sociology of wealth quantified its influence through an array of paintings, ledgers, account books, and art objects as well as literary, historical, and ecclesiastic texts. While "signifiers" such as "labor," "price," and "profit" are not just mercantile, concepts of value, utility, and effectiveness have been artistic and economic for the longest time. *Seme*, in fact, means "word" and "coin." Even people could be "of base coinage"; like gold, they could be adulterated.[2] As a matter of fact, the very word-concept "classical," which has set a major standard in Western culture, stems from the appropriate usage of language among educated citizens who belonged to the first-class taxpayers, whereas *proletarius* did not pay taxes (Aulus Gellius, *Noctes Atticae* xix, 8, 15). Canon-making and cultural standards were thus geared to economic and social criteria (Curtius 249–50).[3] In a significant way, therefore, mimesis was "econo-mimesis."[4] In the wake of studies on the Protean complexity of the Renaissance, scholarship has highlighted the impact of economics on the cultural syncretism of the age through such topics as "Venetian and Dutch *Elites*," "Art and Accounting," "The Embarrassment of Riches," "The Poetics of Accumulation," and "Cultural Aesthetics."[5]

Antiquity favored affluence over indigence, and so did Humanism in Florence and elsewhere. Below the veneer of aristocratic wealth and mercantile prosperity, however, the majority of the population lived in abject poverty. Paganism and Christianity took the poor to be a familiar presence on street corners and in marketplaces. Because its social depth and range were significant, poverty was recognized, but no remedies were proposed. Throughout the early Middle Ages, society was entrenched along the divide between *maiores et potentiores* and *minores et infirmiores*. After the tenth century, a tripartite structure ordered society into *oratores, bellatores*, and *imbelle vulgus*. Physical work and mechanical arts were held in low esteem vis-à-vis intellectual and moral strength. The humanists did not openly test that assumption. In Spain, the picaresque mindset did not either, but it did expose a society whose class divisions left no doubts about who was privileged and who was exploited. If the new novelistic mode did not call for open revolt, it nevertheless singled out an unfair state of things. To foster awareness was a first step toward provoking indignation, which in turn could lead to change. But it would take centuries for that process to shake the status quo (MacMullen 86–87, 118, 127). Economic power and class discriminations were thus crucial to marginality, picaresque or otherwise. *Popolo grasso* and *ricos hombres*, in fact, knew how to guard their wealth, and they did it with a vengeance (Huppert 17). At best, indigence was to be alleviated, but not eliminated.

Introductory remarks of this sort make it clear that *Homo ludens, Homo loquens,* and *Homo oeconomicus* shared a common vocabulary long before the Renaissance, and research could not but follow suit. Sociologists have explored the psychological and aesthetic range of the philosophy of money, and historians have found in consumerism a point of entry into processes of cultural change.[6] Along Mediterranean shores, the 'golden century' drew strength from the "cycle of gold" that financed it. Any golden age, in fact, must rest on gilded foundations if it is to have a lasting impact on society.[7] Since it became a marker of individual and collective "fashioning," wealth—or lack thereof—affected what could be called econopoetics, which this essay takes to describe deficient negotiations between economic signs and noneconomic verbal signifiers in *Lazarillo de Tormes* (1550–54?).

While focusing on the autobiographical life of a single individual from birth to adulthood, the picaresque text exposes bankrupt aspects of sixteenth-century culture in Spain, where the Christian Reconquest set up a mindset whose outlook on economics was substantially different from Italian or Dutch mercantilism. Once the Old Christians emerged victorious, the socioeconomic context of the Iberian peninsula retained Arabic and Jewish ascendancy on matters of agriculture, trade, and business. To them, one ought to add Italian merchants and bankers. And many Spanish businessmen who excelled at their trade used wealth to acquire estates and become noblemen in the manner of landed aristocrats. By so doing, they dried out the ranks and power of their own middle class. While the wealth coming from the New World kept dreams of grandeur alive, the ruling classes kept on despising any sort of manual or commercial labor. Their unproductive supremacy was bound to tumble. And it did. At the opposite pole of purity of blood and contempt of money and labor, there emerged the picaresque. To put it in terms of New Historicism, this study explores artworks embedded into a network of material practices which called on will, guts, and wits to face the relentless assaults of poverty.

In his lifelong study of the picaresque, Francisco Rico has found in the technique of "point of view" the "unifying principle" of plot, meaning, and narratology (91–92).[8] Likewise, my approach to *econopoetics* makes poetics primary to interpretation, while economics represents a distinctive "point of entry" into a reading of the text that pays equal attention to aesthetic and social relationships. Especially in the antiheroic mode of lifestyles at the margins of affluence, the picaresque borrowed from the traditions of chivalry and Humanism as much as it relied on parody to stir a

better awareness of the societal makeup. Compromises and reversals of that sort reached depths that Italian texts never dared to
probe, even though the Spanish art of thieving was paralleled on
Italian shores by writings on the related "art of lying."

In spite of gold and goods coming from overseas, too many
royal policies proved to be disastrous to commerce and agriculture. In their rubble, the ranks of beggars, *pícaros,* and vagrants
grew almost out of control. Alongside the aristocracy, humanist
elites, and a small middle class, there also thrived a "sub" or "under" culture of *pícaros,* thieves, and adventurers that would crowd
Cervantes's *Novelas Ejemplares* and the Golden Age stage of Lope
de Vega and Tirso de Molina. Even conservative estimates
counted *pícaros* by the thousands everywhere. And among all
Spanish cities, Mateo Alemán called Seville the *Babilonia de pícaros.*

In the empirical form of a novelistic journey from Salamanca,
the city of law and learning, to Toledo, the city of business and
trade, *Lazarillo de Tormes* presents the growth of a social outcast
whose ambition is to build a better future for himself. Since picaresque "success" thrives more on standards of mediocrity than
excellence, the text deals with a blindman's boy who succeeds in
becoming town crier. His growth would not produce another tale
of rags-to-riches in either the epic or the chivalric mode, but it
would tell a story of human survival more typical of life-as-is.[9]
The new genre thus presented urban paupers, alienated middle-
class *conversos,* and individual stories whose self-preservation
was spurred and defended by hook and by crook.[10] Although
roguery was part of the European scene at large, the socioeconomic depth and artistic output of picaresque life in Spain was
unique. Around the middle of the sixteenth century, the life of the
underprivileged made inroads into the art and literature of Spain,
where a *"crítica vulgar"* under the aegis of *"lo insignificante"* offset
the traditions of epic and chivalry (Castro, *Cervantes* 121). As
Sancho Panza later put it,

> "There are only two families in the world, my old grand-
> mother used to say, the *Have* and the *Have-Nots.* She was
> always for the *haves,* and to this very day, my lord Don
> Quixote, the doctor would rather feel the pulse of a *Have*
> than a *Know." (Don Quixote* II: Chapter 20)[11]

By setting forth ideas about poverty that already had concerned Erasmus, writings such as Juan Luis Vives's *De subventione pauperum* called for a sharing of basic goods with the poor. Contacts between economics and the picaresque quickly revealed gaps between the affluence of the aristocracy and the destitution of the working classes—not to mention the underemployed. Since the bourgeoisie had been disintegrating at the periphery of the other two groups,[12] the novel voiced long-standing contrasts that were socioeconomic at heart.[13] In their midst, Lázaro de Tormes spent much of his youth growing out of *lacería*.

With ease, *Lazarillo de Tormes* would validate the Bakhtinian emphasis on the "prosaic intelligence" and the "prosaic wisdom" of a vulgar discourse that stood as a counterpoint to more privileged genres (Morson and Emerson 308). Picaresque and Cervantine characters believed that "stealing was a free trade," much as they relished "gipsy language" and "thieves's slang."[14] And one need only add that, before the emergence of the picaresque, *La Celestina* gave tragicomic form to the concept of life as mere doing. In addition to literary precedents, picaresque literature included *poesía cancioneril, teatro primitivo, refranes glosados, diálogos*, as well as continuations and imitations of *La Celestina*; all in all, a *literatura desesperanzada* that fostered a rather pessimistic vision of human life (Villanueva 91, 136–37). At the periphery of ingrained privileges, poverty had spread as a social disease throughout Europe, and tales of utter destitution were popular everywhere around the middle of the sixteenth century. However bright the veneer of imperial grandeur, almost half of the population was poor in Spain (Herrero 876–79). While playing a role in the emergence of the picaresque, data of that sort quantified a dejected humanity whose presence was conspicuous throughout Europe. The poor had to remain poor, even though some attention was invested in turning a sympathetic eye toward them. After all, it was economically advantageous that they survive and be strong enough to work.

In the vocabulary of social distribution, the picaresque text was probably the first to call attention to the oppressed humanity of *infrahombres*.[15] The humanity, that is, of *mozos, pícaros,* and cheap manpower, not to mention thieves, criminals, *picardía,* and *vida buscona;* a low-life world where *jerigonza, nombres germanescos,* and slangs of all sorts gained currency. Picaresque novels, Michel Butor would remind us, exposed "les entrailles, les dessous, les coulisses de la société—the guts, the underside, the margins of society" (96). Hence the dilemma: what kind of language would such a humanity speak? It certainly was neither humanistic nor courtly, let alone chivalric. Instead, it was more likely a vernacular counterlanguage replete with colloquialisms, preliterate jargon, *refranes,* and the *vox populi* of proverbial phrases. The type of linguistic brew that was more Erasmian—from *Adagia* to *Colloquia*—than Ciceronian. This essay aims at reconciling the New Historicist emphasis on unheroic subjects with the uniquely Spanish notion of *intrahistoria.* Instead of a microhistory, however, I focus on the prototype of the picaresque. While centering on the economic marginality of poor Spaniards whose lives were shaped by survival, my approach sets out to balance the ever widening gyre of contextuality—which draws from New Historicism, cultural anthropology, and interdisciplinary approaches of sorts—with aesthetic matters of form.[16] From food and lodging to fashion, money, and manners, econopoetics brings together an array of different languages, which are reciprocally paraliterary and paraeconomic. For Barbara Hernnstein Smith, the traditional tendency to exclude economic factors from works of art and literature mystifies their very nature. And the picaresque could certainly prove that exclusions of that sort would have the effect of defining the genre out of existence (33).[17] My treatment of econopoetics in *Lazarillo de Tormes* centers on the waterseller chapter, whose threshold function will be highlighted through a comparison with Velázquez's painting of the same subject (Figure 1).

II

Lázaro becomes a waterseller in the sixth chapter of *Lazarillo de Tormes.* At first, he takes up the task of mixing colors for a painter. But he soon quits because that job made his life very hard. In the cathedral of Toledo a priest then gives him the job of water carrier. Lázaro discharges his duties successfully. He pays the priest an agreed amount of money and keeps the rest for himself. After four years, he has saved enough to buy clothes and a sword. At that

Figure 1. Diego Velásquez, *The Waterseller of Seville* (1619–20). Apsley House, London. Courtesy Bridgeman/Art Resource, New York.

point, he decides to quit his job and try for better luck. Age-wise, he is a restless youth whose socioeconomic ascent begins with the instruments of the trade: a whip, four jugs, and a donkey. So equipped, he sets out to carry water around town. Yet he never calls himself *aguador.* During those four years, however, the tempo of life picks up. The vaguely achronological "by now" and "one day" of the boy's earlier tasks echoed medieval practices, which divided the day along religious zones such as "at dawn," "about noon," or "toward sunset." That was the beggar's time at street corners familiar to blindmen and their servants. Neither time nor space could be of their choice, for they had to be "where" and "when" alms were more likely to be given. By contrast, the young water carrier pays the priest thirty *maravedís* every day, keeps the rest, and works for himself on Saturdays. His daily chore sets a money-yielding pace; time itself is about to become a clock-measured commodity. Lázaro thus learns to discipline talent, initiative, and the dynamics of his environment into a profitable routine. He saves money and gains confidence in himself; however meager his earnings, he can set ambitious goals. Money brings regularity to the narrative, while savings introduce some vestiges of wealth. Yet, the appearance of prosperity would not yield substantial possessions.

The job of waterseller gives Lázaro security. But security could not remain his life project. In the commercial city of Toledo, in fact, the *escudero* taught him that one's life had to be guided by a set of principles. Once Lázaro understood that he had to pursue a version of honor within reach of his *buena fortuna,* the economic makeup of the chapter turned around. Jugs and whips faded into the background:

> I did so well at the job that after four years of careful saving I had enough to dress myself very decently in second-hand clothes; I bought an old fustian jacket and a worn coat with braided sleeves and a vent. I also got a cloak which had had a fringe once, and an old sword made when they used to make them at Cuéllar.(76)[18]

If he still appreciates the fact that it took him four years of careful saving to buy second-hand clothes, one must surmise that Lázaro's ensuing prosperity has been rather limited. His experience points back to the *escudero,* whose pathetic demeanor carried the stamp of economic bankruptcy. The text thus brings to the fore disjunctions between "cost of living" and "standard of life." The former is meant to provide for basic needs. At the periphery of affluence most humanity kept on struggling with cost of living. Amid low-life society, cost of living sets up compensations based on exploitation rather than fairness. And all sorts of political, psychological, and religious pressures were brought to bear on the acceptance of such a disparity. By contrast, standard of life points to a lifestyle that makes cultural values almost as primary as subsistence itself. In a minor—if not parodic—key, Lázaro reaches, or at least he thinks he has reached, that qualitative threshold at the end of the sixth chapter. Thereafter, he would try to convince himself that his good luck has drawn cost of living and standard of life into a profitable—if not honorable—equation.

For Lázaro de Tormes, standard of life represents the future. For the *escudero,* instead, it symbolizes loss. In fact, he enters the narrative long after his standard of life fell by the wayside. The economy he bodies forth is out of currency, and his rhetoric of wishful affluence folds under its own insubstantiality. Lázaro, instead, begins to invest in the future. Weekly earnings and weekend overtime draw a line between dependence and self-sufficiency. Yet, he could buy only second-hand clothes, a worn-out cloak, and an old sword. Earlier in the fourth chapter, he was given an old pair of shoes that lasted only one week. Nevertheless, he got to know what it meant not to walk barefooted and what it would take to wear shoes once again. Consumable items of that sort demanded a steady income. As always, advantage had a price. The symbolism of shoes in folklore and literature (*Libro de Buen Amor*) points to sexual favors, which would be given at the price of moral taxation by the end of the last *tratado*. If Lázaro gets old stockings from the archpriest, we can bet that the same provider would offer his wife plenty of shoes!

Increases and depletions of Lázaro's *buena fortuna* are part and parcel of a novelistic project that set much of the action within reach of water. Actually, he was born by the river Tormes—"mi nacimiento fue dentro del río Tormes." Having traded amniotic for fluvial waters, so to speak, the journey downstream transforms him neither into a leader of people nor a valiant knight. Along the way, however, he would learn just about everything one could want to know about matters of indigence.

To draw on current levels—if not kinds—of narrative, the picaresque text would fall outside the *grand récit* of a totalizing and idealized concept of history. Yet, it could be counted among those *petites histoires* that historians and cultural anthropologists—from Natalie Zemon Davis and Stephen Greenblatt to Carlo Ginzburg, Piero Camporesi, and Michel de Certeau—have linked to anecdotes and the practice of everyday life.[19] Amid artworks one would assign to the province of *grand récit*, Velázquez's *Las Lanzas* (or the *Peace of Breda*) stands out. Conversely, his *Waterseller* fits the unheroic context of *pequeño intrahistórico*.

Whereas Lázaro's ambulatory job takes water to people, youths and adults gather around Velázquez's old man. He bestows lifegiving liquid in a room where two jugs are set on a table flanked by a bench. Since the composition is foreshortened, a sense of spatial closure draws viewers into a communal space at the edge of the large water jug. While it is just a commodity in the novel, water involves the archetypal transmission of life in the painting, where the waterseller stands out as the embodiment of an almost archetypal task.[20] His gaze does not betray senescence, and there is nothing temporary about him; above all, his posture projects the solemn stability of ritual. Whereas it serves commercial exchanges in the novel, water involves a higher form of transaction in the artwork. The old man holds the bottom of the goblet and the youngster secures his grip on its stem; generations thus join hands. Dictionaries of Renaissance symbols tell us that the purity of glass pointed to intellectual and spiritual clarity. The goblet stands as a transparent point of conjunction between young and old. A kind of eucharistic act is performed, if we only think of contemporary proverbs—"People of Toledo, people of God, water belongs to him, and we only sell it"—or Juan Luis Vives's words: "Your drink shall be . . . that natural liquor prepared by God for all living creatures in common - pure, clean water." While passages from Matthew and Psalms speak of water as fountain and source of human experience, Francisco de Quevedo and the moralist Damián de Vegas insisted that heaven was waiting for those who would give a glass of water to one who thirsts (Wind 103; Moffitt 10).

Velázquez's pot-bellied jug is of plain clay, and its shape introduces the waterseller's own figure. Correspondences of that kind make the human face itself appear to be "stilled from within"

(Steinberg 282). Under somber lighting effects, the artwork reveals a subdued interplay of clay glazed and unglazed, of wrinkles and flesh, of wood and fabrics, and of a miracle-bestowing goblet. Carrier and vessel are bound together into the portrait of an activity that foregrounds the waterseller's story. By ignoring urban settings and commercial equipments, the artist has painted a rather bare and yet sheltering environment in which objects are as crucial to meaning as human presence itself; one is a function of the other, and both of them shoulder the representation of a humanized reality.

Whereas macrohistory acts out narratives which recount pasts of epic grandeur, microhistory is linked to the description of current events and prosaic, if not altogether petty, attitudes of mind. Emphasis is placed on situations that tend to "equalize" people and things. At their static worst, we confront texts that simplify individualism and edge on genre. By yielding an array of details in excess of what is appropriate to the economy of the narrative, texts of that sort create "still life" conditions. Velázquez's painting, however, avoids such a pitfall. Even a cursory comparison with his own *bodegones* makes it clear that *The Waterseller* foregrounds a view of human values bent on praising dignity rather than depravation, and intensity rather than insignificance. The pictorial economy of details is as axiomatic as it is crucial to the implied narrative. If one were to argue that description debases human beings to the level of inanimate things, then one could trust that Velázquez "redeemed" the descriptive mode; he did not start with *things,* but with *people.* At their most constructive, picaresque artworks take on a kind of "narrative grandeur," which one could indeed find typical of what has been called the epic of the *infrahombre.* Readers and viewers are thus moved to reflect on moral and ethical aspects of human existence.

Since it is full of water, the jug responds to external heat by exuding moisture. At spots where drops and runnels make its thick impasto seem almost transparent, the clay partakes of the goblet's brilliance. Condensation thus couches beauty in forms which call to mind the forthcoming passion (baroque or otherwise) for the evanescent—from snow flakes to air bubbles. At the same time, the jug's horizontal crevices echo the wrinkles on the old man's forehead, just as blemishes on the smaller jug repeat the rough texture of his cheeks. Man and jug meet through the handle, which makes the mimesis of reality more direct by foregrounding the utilitarian function of clay ware. At the same time, tears in the old man's cloak heighten fullness and consumption. In the painter's hands, even forms of stillness, Mikhail Bakhtin might agree, could be chronotopic. With ease but without banality, pictorial surfaces unfurl textures which weave a life-giving image.

The large jug rests on a bench that sets it apart from the rest of the composition. Its small neck and heavy size disqualify it as an object apt to expedite distribution. On the table, the smaller pitcher with a wider neck and a clay cup on its top proves to be a more practical dispenser of fluids. One vessel is unique in Velázquez's *oeuvre,* and it works as a pivot between here and there, quotidianity and archetype. The other is of a stock that appears on kitchen and dinner tables from *Christ in the House of Martha and Mary* (1618) and the *Old Woman Frying Eggs* (1618) to *Christ at Emmaus* (1620–21). The coarseness of the clay jug clashes with the elegant goblet he hands to the youngster. Task, thought, and posture are so transparently wholesome that the goblet seems to mirror a humane clarity of heart. That refined piece of craftsmanship is strikingly different from Velázquez's usual glassware. While *Three Men at the Table* (1618–19) and *Bacchus-Borrachos* (1628–29) show cheap tumblers, *The Waterseller* makes a qualitative leap. With pride, common laborers in Pedro de Guzmán's *Los bienes del honesto trabajo* (1614) could "drink from the work of their hands" (Wind 101–2). A daily task thus turns into an act that exudes wholesome maturity. It would be safe to guess that thoughts about wealth, profit, or career-oriented ambitions have never made a dent in the old *aguador*'s sense of social responsibility. Subtly, the artist has juxtaposed the economics of the trade, which demands efficient utensils, to an archetypal blueprint. The old man does not deal with merchandise, and he seems to have forsaken profit. For sure, he has relinquished the 'competitive' evil of goals and ambitions tailored after, and against, other people.

While focusing on expectation and magnanimity, the crystal-clear goblet heightens a still moment replete with past, present, and future. We look at a life-giving transparency. Liquidity itself has been dissolved into a mental contemplation on the meaning of water as the very sustenance of life. Silence enfolds a virtual narrative apt to pour wisdom into the naive emptiness of youth. Such a potential for story telling seems to make a case for ekphrasis in reverse. The picture, in fact, is emblematic in a literary sense, much as language has corporealized itself into the silent people of *intrahistoria.* Ordinary individuals of that sort are more familiar with facts than performances, much as they speak in songs, maxims, and legends of a kind which the old man would pass on to the youth.

Proverbial forms voice the ethical underpinning of folklore, which reflects the more stable aspects of popular culture (Gramsci 189–90).[21] It suffices to add that picaresque texts are studded with maxims. The *ciego* relies on the long-standing symbolism of wine and horns to set up the plot. Economics motivates his journey toward Toledo, and proverbial wisdom justifies it; a hard man in fact can give more than another who does not have anything to give. Selfishness of that kind is unknown to the old waterseller, and it points to that border line where the indigent humanity of *intrahistoria* edges on more affluent counterparts. On moral and economic grounds, proverbial wisdom tends to spur conformity, which would reinforce Lázaro's gregariousness.

As a literary image, the jug's full shape harks back to grain bins and maternal wombs at the beginning of the novel, which also highlights shoes, cloaks, bread, sausages, cow's feet, and the priest's glorious bunch of onions. Such an array of things and goods belongs to what the nomenclature of art has called "rhopography." Its etymon, *rhopos,* points to trifles and small wares that cultural aesthetics has parceled out to the realm of triviality.[22] By contrast, unimportant things are of little interest to artists interested in "megalography," which depicts objects symbolic of gods, heroes, and memorable deeds. With an eye to economic matters, "megalography" finds a parallel in Xenophon's *Oeconomicus,* which defines lavish public expenditures. The virtue of *megaloprepeia* is thus unthinkable in the picaresque, and Norman Bryson insists that rhopography ought to remind us that "all men must eat; there is a levelling of humanity, a humbling of aspiration before an irreducible fact of life, hunger" (61). Hunger makes objects functional; spoons, knives, glasses, and plates imply touch, hands, and mouths. Activities of that sort would be just as familiar to Murillo's destitute youths, who are forever engaged in eating grapes and watermelons (*Two Boys Eating Fruit* [1670s]).[23] The world of rhopography was bound to proliferate. Laurence Sterne's *Tristram Shandy* includes a "chapter on things," and Honoré de Balzac would divide his human comedy into three categories: men, women, and things. Things thus began to take on human qualities; in turn, humans were ever more dependent on materialist goods. Realism, in fact, refers to res, that is to say, to things. Etymologically speaking, realism is "thing-ism" (Levin 33–34, 193).

Cow's feet, innards, and tripe punctuate the prosaics of *Lazarillo de Tormes,* which rejoices in the depiction of eating scenes known as *bodegones* and *bamboccianti* in contemporary painting. Usually, the *pícaro* was an errand boy—*esportillero* or *ganapán*—who hung around kitchens and other places of consumption, ready as he was to carry packages, take on odd jobs, and seize any opportunity— however underhanded—that might yield food or money.[24] Their world often was contained at the far edge of stoves and dinner tables, where darkness dimmed historical events and perspectival space. Velázquez's own *Old Woman Frying Eggs* is a *bodegón* in which the youth holds a watermelon and a water pitcher. Time is culinary, and the two frying eggs mark the seconds that separate the raw from the cooked. By contrast, stark details in *The Waterseller* deny the possibility of an "eating scene." Everybody stands as if expected to stage an event extraneous to the casualness of "dining time." The transfer of water is linked to acts that are passive for the youth, acquisitive for the adult, and dispensational for the old man. Such archetypal thematics, Miguel de Unamuno would comment, seem to draw from "los abismos sub-históricos, bajo la historia" (49–50). It is a ritual that outlasts human generations without changing people's lot.

At a higher pitch of privation, Velázquez's water jug calls to mind a literary counterpart in the third *tratado,* where Lázaro shared bread and cow's feet with his master:

> He asked me to get the water-jug and when I brought it it was as full as when I had come back from the river. That told me quite clearly that he hadn't eaten very much that day. We drank and went to bed very happily. (57)[25]

Toothpicks are in order after food consumption, and water is part of that activity. Food calls for a drink; starvation does not. Quickly, therefore, Lázaro understands that his master has not had a meal. At an earlier occasion and in spite of evidence to the contrary, Lázaro presumed that an *escudero*'s jug would contain wine: "'Agua es,—me respondió. Bien puedes beber.'—'You can drink this,' he said. 'It's water'" (52, 33). That correction foregrounded utter indigence, while the sword upheld an obsolete world of appearances at variance with life. In fact, Lázaro found in the *escudero*'s purse neither a copper coin "ni señal que la hubiese tenido mucho tiempo—any trace of one having been there for a very long time" (58, 39). The water's undisturbed stillness is of a kind akin to still lifes in the French and Italian sense of *nature morte* and *natura morta*. Actually, the ghostlike existence of the *escudero*, whose nobility is bygone and whose wealth is out of currency, is itself a kind of "lifeless nature." To that extent, swords, toothpicks, and water jugs could be read as *fragments ideologiques*.[26] The jug foregrounds an implied narrative; rather than denying human presence, it calls forth the *escudero*'s haunting insubstantiality. As a result, the tempo of the story slows down to motionlessness, which echoes the mental inanity of the *escudero*'s worn-out existence (Blanchard 276–77). The narrative thus moves from effects to causes. The jug is full because the empty purse could not buy food. For the *escudero*, description earmarks the breakdown of potential action, which is instead implicit in Lázaro's own surprise. In one case, water points to inanity and sterility; it is the stillness of the deathlike. For the boy, that very stillness is taken as a negative pause in the unfolding process of life's travails.

As a servant to the *escudero*, Lázaro gears his concept of time to hunger. Having met his new master in the morning, he measures time against the expected routine of "shopping" for lunch and dinner. Hours pass by, but neither lunch nor dinner is mentioned. Time thus stretches out hopes and delusions. To justify himself, the *escudero* reverses the orderly routine of food consumption: "Pues, aunque de mañana, yo había almorzado y, cuando así como algo, hágote saber que hasta la noche me estoy así. Por eso, pásate como pudieres, que después cenaremos—Well, although it was quite early, I'd already eaten. If I eat early, you'd better know that I don't have anything else until nighttime. You'll have to make do as well as you can. We'll have supper later on" (32, 51). Master and servant are playing cat-and-mouse. The "provider" tries to mask his inability to provide for his servant by "displacing" the time of biological needs. When stomachs are not fed, the narrative stealmates into an ominous silence. The very absence of sounds reduces existence itself to a kind of life-threatening wait that puts human potential on hold, as if the future could not come to pass. Hunger reduces time, space, and the world itself to nothing more than the expectation of food. Wits, honor, hopes, memories, and human personality lose all relevance vis-à-vis hoped-for food. At that point, Lázaro and his master are reduced to the animal-like state of predators whose whole being could respond to nothing but the call of hunger.

In the ontological nomenclature of the picaresque, eating time plays a major role, marking as it does the materialist heartbeat of existence. Once lack of nourishment is exposed, the ontology and stylistics of literary art strikes close equivalences between words and things. Whether it be the jug in the literary text or in Velázquez's painting, language thrives on forms of such simplicity that image, writing, and expression seem to defy the very concept of fiction. To that extent, goblet and jug offset the objectual deceptiveness of the stone-bull episode at the end of the first *tratado*. Whereas the mousetrap signals the presence of goods, unused water denies them. Having reached a state of utter indigence, the text exposes the futility of people whose social standing has to deny starvation, however irrefutable its evidence. By the same token, such "descriptions by default" are quite typical of the picaresque parody of conspicuous consumption. With a passion, literary stylistics mixes taxonomic with rhetorical codes. The first selects items to be foregrounded for description's sake; the second chooses strategies of denotation, connotation, and significance that thicken the symbolism of the narrative. In the picaresque mode, exchanges between the two are at once effective and recurrent. Since men of honor would neither beg nor steal, the outcome is all the more predictable. Just as he wanted sex but could not buy it, so did the *escudero* end up eating a cow's foot his servant had begged for.

Recent scholarship has focused on the unsavory vicissitudes that hunger has imposed on the poor. Throughout the sixteenth century, a cluster of texts outlined the effects of famine from Italy to Poland. Behind the ambiguous and ominous term "refuse," in fact, there lurked instincts that preyed on corpses and dung; there were no limits to abomination, so much so that the remains of *Buscón*'s father were linked to the taking of the Holy Sacrament (Camporesi 86–87). Literally and symbolically, the economics of food consumption were an apt, if pitiless, barometer of societal conditions.[27] While the *escudero*'s toothpick is no more than a gestural afterthought in the wake of a meal he never consumed, Lázaro finds comfort in the memory of bits of food. Although no semantic field other than food and sex can claim a more euphoric vocabulary (Jeanneret 8–9), picaresque rhopography breaks down discourse through a rhetoric of loss; food and sex are equally deficient in it. However much hunger could not ennoble the praxis of life at its most basic, Marco Antonio de Camos resorted to human anatomy to justify social order (*Microcosmia* 1595). Faith was lodged in the head and royalty in the heart; veins and nerves stood for nobility; legs and feet carried merchants, artisans, and farmers. The poor, in turn, were reduced to nails, hair, and human debris that fed on edible waste (139–46).[28] Because food defines humanity in itself as well as in relation to life at large, picaresque diets are indicators of cultural status. After a reading not of Rabelais or Perrault but of picaresque poverty, one ought to surmise that Louis Marin's "food for thought" would be strictly verbal among most *pícaros* who never made it to Toledo. In Segovia, there were people who would gladly "breakfast" on nominatives by "swallowing the words" (95, 97). Instances of that sort are introduced in the third chapter of *Lazarillo de Tormes*, where the penniless *escudero* feeds Lázaro words instead of meals he craves for more than his servant.

Master and servant, in fact, inhabit a house apt to lodge the dead rather than the living.[29] We need only mention that Benedetto Croce called the picaresque "l'epica della fame," a label that set parodic correlations between megalography and rhopography, the epic and the novel.[30] On novelistic matters of *romanzi della fame*, onions as big as oranges constitute the staple diet of Sicilian fishermen in Giovanni Verga's *I Malavoglia* (*The House by the Medlar Tree* 1881). The nineteenth-century *verista* novel, in fact, updated picaresque toils.[31] They all shared stylistic and thematic traits that weighed on food intake, whether it be actually eaten or just conjured up by the imagination. And trade between what Italo Calvino has called the dialectic of *sapore* and *sapere* has been central to a genre as privative or cornucopian as the novel.

The ritual integrity of Velázquez's *aguador* stands out even more forcefully if one sets it against the literary narrative. In Toledo's cathedral, a greedy priest gives Lázaro the job of waterseller; with ease, men of the cloth would turn into dubious *mercaderes; hombres de negocio* and *hombres de iglesia* often were one and the same.[32] Just as easily waters were parted between business and religion. To make things worse, doubts have been shed on representations of "pristine" and good-natured watersellers. Equations between *aguadores* and *moriscos* were negative, and so they would remain in Lope de Vega's *El anzuelo de Fenisa* and Cervantes's *gente baja* (*Don Quixote* I: 21). Emphasis was placed on genealogical falsification, name changing, and efforts at furtive assimilation (Shipley, "Lazarillo de Tormes" 250). A Cervantine nobleman, Don Tomás de Avendano, took up "the trade of water-carrier" in Toledo. "With a single load of water he could wander about the city all day long, looking at the silly girls."[33] Prejudices aside, that menial job was just a few notches above begging.

By and large, watersellers were unsavory characters closer to Velázquez's own *Drinkers* (also called *Borrachos* 1626–28),[34] which José Ortega y Gasset has read as a Titianesque bacchanal that has been turned "into drunken debauch. Bacchus is a fraud. There is nothing more than what you can see and touch." To that extent, Velázquez paved the way for the "administrative era in which, in place of Dionysus, we speak of alcoholism" (Ortega y Gasset, *Velázquez* 97; Braudel, *Structure* 23–24, 27–29). Because he is not a fraud, the old *aguador* would keep on living the same way. He is a symbolic image of the enduring, and yet stagnant, "infra-economy" of material life. His time frame is one in which the reliability of ritual takes precedence over the instability of gains and losses.[35] In a substantial way, the *aguador* bodies forth a concept of personality rooted in a culture where individualism is equated with one's given role in society. Man could not yet conceive of himself as an individual except through communal "otherness" (Manrique de Aragon 42). Much as deities were trivialized, Velázquez bestowed dignity on common people; the heroic became common, and the ordinary grew into prominence. Although he lived at the fringe of the urban world he never thought of entering, the waterseller could not be found among the swelling ranks of Sevillian *picardía*, which rounded its beggars and cutpurses by the slaughterhouse or in nearby San Lucar de Barrameda. At that point in the narrative, old and young watersellers did not, and could not move away from the routine of everyday life; to borrow from Miguel de Unamuno, "el suceso del día, de cada día, es para el hecho de siempre . . . el hombre de cada día esta naciendo diariamente." Measured against standards of social climb and conspicuous consumption, it was indeed the average life—*vidita*—of an ordinary man—*hombrecito* (Ortega y Gasset, "Sobre el cultivo" 9: 907; Braudel, *Mediterranean* 2: 740).[36]

In a way, Lázaro is forced to mystify his origins as much as he has to demystify reminiscences about the *escudero*'s ghostlike nobility and empty claims. Societal myths are measured down to the "realistic" potential of a dispossessed soul out to secure some sort of civilized living for himself. At that threshold, we ought to recall Claudio Guillén's comments on picaresque role-playing, which compels the *pícaro* to "compromise and live on the razor's edge between vagabondage and delinquency. . . . He becomes what I would call a 'half-outsider'"(80). Actually, that boundary condition unravels through stages. In the first two chapters, Lázaro lives at the edge of survival. Even though he has become street-wise, his lack of mental sophistication emerges in the third *tratado*, where he fails to conceptualize the literal reference to the "dark house" in the episode of the funeral cortege. Since he is determined to dress up his societal "other," Lázaro changes jobs and breaks away from the simple existence of Velázquez's waterseller. He reaches a point where economic choice and societal constraints lock horns, and the ensuing narrative would teach him the limits of both.[37] Once he invests his earnings in buying worn-out apparel, his hard-gained "affluence" turns into another form of poverty. As a result, existence shapes itself as a deficient, if not outright negative counterpart of affluence. Later, Miguel de Unamuno asked a significant question: "What zeal can a worker show as he fashions toys for the sons of the rich merely so as to earn bread for his own children, who have no such toys to play with?" (302). That was a rather middle-class question grown out of a world of production that remained quite foreign to picaresque parasitism. Survival could not, and did not, empower anybody to test the "destination" of goods. For most people, work was aimed at sustenance rather than improvement, much as zeal stemmed from need rather than competence. As a waterseller who provided a service as old as humankind, Lázaro could have lived comfortably at the fringe of bureaucracy and business. Because he rejected work limited to survival, the youth gave up a job and much of his upbringing with it. His father had been working at the mill for fifteen years, and only a transgression halted that routine. In his son's case, circumstances drove him out of agricultural milieus. Two processes converged: one of social integration and the other of moral debasement.

Part and parcel of Lázaro's growth is a new sense of monetary precision and critical judgment. In the first two *tratados*, time is linked to acts of theft, whether they involve a piece of sausage or a few breadcrumbs. The appearance of money, however, alters the *mozo*'s behavior: "cuanto le mandaban rezar y le daban blancas, como él carecía de vista, no había el que se la daba amagado con ella, cuando yo la tenía lanzada en la boca y la media aparejada; que por presto que él echaba la mano, ya iba de mi cambio aniquilada en la mitad del justo precio ("when people asked him to say prayers and gave him *blancas*, as soon as they offered the coin I grabbed it, popped it into my mouth and handed him a half *blanca*. However quickly he stretched out his hand I had already halved the value of the offering") (10, 29). First of all, half *blancas*, whole *blancas*, and *maravedís* immediately point to immaterial goods that could be gained by means of equally immaterial services. Unlike food, money could be halved, doubled up, stored, and exchanged with ever-varying speed.[38]

By paying the priest thirty *maravedís* every day, Lázaro the waterseller introduces a clock-paced concept of time, which quickly becomes a commodity linked to the sequence *ganancia-recaudo-ahorre-compre* (earning-collecting-saving-buying) (Sieber 76). However pedestrian its way, the picaresque echoes an eventful shift. Rather than being linked to living experiences, time is divided into measurable units. That development replaced events that could be framed by approximation—*à-peu-près*—with models of conduct that subordinated time, work, and money to precise standards of evaluation. Whether on pagan or Christian grounds, the Deity was assumed to have created through numbers, weights, and measurement. Before the Renaissance, however, nobody bothered to implement those principles in the world of material existence. Lázaro is thus able to discipline the dynamics of his environment into a profitable routine. He saves money and gains confidence in himself; however meager his earnings, he has grown to a point where he could entertain ambitious projects; chance gives way to plan. Money brings regularity to the narrative; a steady income calls for a stable job in a place where picaresque mobility comes to a halt. While saving rushes in some "potential" for wealth, the appearance of prosperity would not yield substantial benefits.

Individual growth under the aegis of economics thus pivots around the concept of self-reliance. Ironically, its point of origin could be traced back to Lázaro's experience with the stone bull in the first *tratado*. The very fact that a blind beggar would teach self-reliance set the "educational process" on a rather slippery footing. It was imperative that "el mozo del ciego un punto ha de saber más que el diablo" (8). Literally and symbolically, the blindman could not but refer to a world of darkness where survival itself is nestled in the "darkened" pit of loss and privation. Because the world of darkness is irremediable by definition, self-reliance teaches Lázaro to outwit his master, even though society will prove to be crowded with legions of people blind at heart whose standards of survival would be ever more difficult to meet. In the sixth *tratado,* self-reliance shifts toward income-yielding work. As such, the devil's standard is both pervasive and unspoken. Once work, service, and income steer Lázaro's socioeconomic lot toward a kind of primitive marketplace economy where the evil of exchange proves to be a blessing, Lázaro finds that work empowers him to pursue values at bay of any *ciego*'s reach. In a rather contradictory way, trade imposes the burden of regularity and efficiency on one's lifestyle; "in the name of work" is preferable to "in the service of." The power of earning money by means other than begging and theft belongs to a devil unknown to the *ciego*. The *hombre de bien* is good and respectable also because he is a money-earning individual. Steady work and a legitimate job free self-reliance from the scourge of both alms and gifts.

At this point, we ought to bear in mind that money makes its appearance in the picaresque text sooner than one might expect. The blindman, in fact, "destas sacaba el grandes provechos con las artes que digo, y ganaba más en un mes que cien ciegos en un año—made a lot of money from these tricks and earned more in one month than a hundred blind men usually do in a whole year" (9, 28). Yet, all that money has no impact on his lifestyle. Master and servant keep on fighting over crumbs by the wayside, and the canvas bag shows evidence of little food and nothing else. What about all that money? By counting money, master and servant activate a "battle of wits" at once attractive and inconsequential. Once he hires Lázaro, the *ciego*'s intake of *maravedís* dwindles because his *mozo* cheats him by switching half *blancas* for whole ones; and he gets away with it. Although theft as exchange succeeds, there is no evidence that money could change anyone's lot. Strife is between paupers; the biggest crust of bread is carried off by the one who begs best (Unamuno 409). Support for that downtrodden condition falls back on folkloristic *cuentos*. It is a pivotal moment in the narrative, one that would lead to Lázaro's appointment to the office of *pregonero*. His hopes come through, but at a price. Slowly, he would settle into a complacent routine whose goal is to maintain *el estatismo de su estado* (Prieto 30–33). Yet, the *caso* launched against him spurs the present toward a troublesome future. While updating adversities, the *Prólogo* also promises a follow-up. From an economic as well as a literary standpoint, the picaresque steered away from the indefinite, if not outright fabulous, past of romance.

To be a *hombre de bien*, Lázaro must avoid jobs that call for manual labor. Once he understands that words could earn him an income, Lázaro sets out to become a *Homo loquens*. Hence, he breaks free of archetypal models. Although he could flaunt only worn-out clothes, his readers would not lose sight of him for generations to come. Once he makes it clear that his life's goal is other than his humble job, the economic makeup of the sixth *tratado* turns around. Jugs and whips fade in the background. The spatial gives way to the temporal, which sets up the value-loaded pace of "everyday—*cada día*" work. As soon as he adjusts to the pressures of money-yielding time, Lázaro's conduct becomes *cronoeconómico*. While his daily routine is restricted to the socioeconomic confines of *intrahistoria*, no reference is made to the larger historical—if not macrohistoric—framework. The nameless author, in fact, did not date his autobiographical experience, except for the final reference to Charles V's entrance in Toledo (either in 1525 or 1539).

Hard work aside, Lázaro can buy only second-hand clothes, a worn out cloak, and an old sword. New forms of investment are called for. Although weekly earnings and weekend overtime draw a line between freedom and dependence, all he could show for four years of hard work is old stuff. Selling water is neither profitable nor honorable. Means and goals are disjointed. Hypothetically speaking, the *escudero* predicted that minor noblemen would pay with a sweaty doublet for his services. The barter of things prevailed over the exchange of money. Lázaro, instead, earns wages and makes profits on the side. Determined as he is to seek prosperity, he sets out to change jobs and break the archetypal life cycle of Velázquez's waterseller. For the old *aguador*, selling water was not just a job; it gave him identity, personal pride, and social respect. For Lázaro, instead, it is an economic task that he judges in strictly economic terms. He wastes no time in sizing up the limits of that humble job, which allows him to buy clothes and a sword meant to sketch out an image appropriate to his wished-for role in society. Whip, jugs, and donkey give way to the purchase of objects apt to fill symbolic needs. Money thus trades the necessary for the aesthetic. If we think of Karl Marx's remarks that money changes "representation into reality and reality into mere representation," then we could agree that Lázaro is on his way to shift from the factual reality of waterseller toward the "representation" of himself in light of values he has inherited from the *escudero*. Whereas the *aguador*'s healthy activities at the level of cost of living are reflected in the unblemished condition of jug and goblet, the incipient pursuit of standards of life begins with the acquisition of old and worn-out items, which echo the ruinous state of the *escudero*'s alleged real estate back in Valladolid. Objects symbolic of a higher social standing betray the volatility—and vulnerability—of the very concept of standard, which could be neither defined with precision nor upheld with confidence. One variable was money, whose valuation and devaluation made the standard itself liable to continuous redefinitions. In a significant way, therefore, standards of life tend to measure frustration as well as success.[39] If we reflect on the analogy drawn between the novel's claim to represent reality and money's claim to represent things of enduring value, then we might agree that both claims shortchange fiction and reality alike. Lázaro's money, in fact, is invested at the periphery of the *aguador*'s reality as well as the periphery of the *escudero*'s anachronism. Much of Lázaro's earnings still are based on gifts and exchanges, his would-be *provecho* as a modern *mercader* turns out to be as misleading—if not outright fictitious—as the *escudero*'s land-based wealth of times past. In light of such precedents, his ambitious plans are uncertain. Money could not buy the future, and the past had become worthless.

At night, the town crier has plenty of time to think about moral payoffs which neither wine nor sleep could ease; nevertheless, everybody teaches him that money moves people. He is neither a critic nor a reformer of society, but a survivor and an opportunist. The final words in the seventh *tratado* tell us that the *pregonero* has reached the peak of his *buena fortuna*. The *Prólogo*, however, makes it clear that his luck has been called into question. Once the indictment is launched against him, Lázaro falls prey to the wider circularity of *Fortuna*'s rise and fall. At the top of the ladder, his steadfast growth stalls, and he begins to slip down.[40]

Yet, it is in the sixth *tratado* that Lázaro transcends the wanderer, the jester, and the have-not. He thus takes notice of his environment, whereas the Sevillan *aguador* of Velázquez did not (Alter 6). Segovia and Toledo were manufacturing towns, and it was through Seville that precious metals from the New World were pouring into Europe. While chapters of human history followed the migratory rhythm of gold and silver across the oceans, there were social enclaves which held on to the timelessness of archetypal lifestyles. Mythic resistance and economic adventurism stood side by side, much as the primeval stability of "material life" was set against the mercantile growth of "economic life." Material life is rooted in the steady pace of daily routines that have remained unchanged for centuries. For Américo Castro, that is the history that only needs to be "described;" it refers to the mere facts of living, the plain linen of life without embroidery. What is at stake here is the lives of people whose existence rests on elementary motivations—physiological, psychic, and economic.[41] Within boundaries of that sort, economic matters could not exceed the cost of living, which set strict limitations on the life of *pícaros*, beggars, millers, and water carriers old or new. Their menial tasks are typical of an economy that is oriented neither toward production nor surplus goods, but toward the satisfaction of elementary needs. As Antonio de Guevara wrote at that time, "It is a privilege of villages that those who dwell in them have flour to sift, a bowl for kneading, and an oven for their baking."[42] At such a basic level, existence relies on those economic institutions that restrict human potential to survival. As the third *tratado* unfolds, Lázaro's need to find a master tests the materialist core of cost of living. Quickly, the narrative makes it clear that the servant has to provide for himself as well as for his master, who is bound to play a twofold role in the youth's growth. While he introduces Lázaro to a world of values, the unity-duality of master and servant proves that utter poverty still treasures a kind of hierarchical order. Antona Perez, in fact, believed that his son would not stand a chance in life unless he served someone, even as hopeless a character as a blind beggar. To be himself, Lázaro needed a master, and his ascent in society traded one form of dependence for another. Medieval ideology called for man to earn only what was necessary to let him live in his given place. Any gain in excess of need was a sign of greed—*turpe lucrum*. In light of that doctrine, Lázaro's meager savings as waterseller foreshadow doom, exceeding as they do the cost of living.

Cost of living becomes problematic the moment it is linked to lifestyles that rest on cultural values. Lázaro reaches that threshold in the sixth *tratado*. Thereafter, he tries to convince himself that his *buena fortuna* has drawn cost of living and standard of life into a favorable equation; although needs measure the first and achieve-

ments the second, they are both materialistic. Yet, the latter gives
goods a metaphorical depth which could be at once humanizing
and dehumanizing. As a water carrier, Lázaro lived on the ground
floor, as it were, of material life. But he found that the bottom level
was neither comfortable nor satisfactory. Through care and calcu-
lation, he thus proceeded to set standards of life for himself. To set
Lázaro's choice in historical perspective, we ought to turn to one of
Don Quixote's "educational" axioms: "I tell you, Sancho, that no
man is worthier than another unless he does more than another"
(*Don Quixote* I: Chapter 18). That lesson may have fallen on deaf
ears in the Cervantine text, where the *hidalgo* alone "did" more
than most to "make himself"—*hacerse*—into a better Other. But
such a self-creating impulse was absent in pre-Cervantine fiction.
In the picaresque mode, however, the *mozo* from Tormes made
himself into a better Other; if not as *pregonero*, certainly as author.
That his "worth" was ultimately deficient should not diminish his
achievement. Even the undistinguished Don Quijano the Good,
after all, denied Don Quixote and regained sanity. Such different,
and yet parallel, ascents shed light on Renaissance polarities;
courtly versus picaresque, anachronistic versus contemporary.
Whereas Lázaro espoused values that were concrete and led to
specific actions, Don Quixote never stopped charging windmills.
In the elementary marketplace of basic services, the waterseller,
whether he be a pictorial image or a literary figure, operated
within a socioeconomic enclave that ushered in a rather independent, though narrow, sense of self-reliance. The old *aguador* had always known that; young Lázaro, instead, was in search of social
status. He based his future on the stability of societal structures
whose authority was institutional. However pegged to a legitimate job, Lázaro's self-reliance would remain largely parasitic. It
was the "Other" that validated the self, whose fortunes were
bound to remain at risk.

In the immemorial time of myth, man thrives on nature; in the
remembered time of human experience, he exploits the mechanisms of civilized society. Lázaro's surname—*sobrenombre*—stems
from a river; it is a place-name. His roots are linked to water, which
would yield temporary as well as permanent benefits. Whether it
be in literary texts or ritual codes, water stands for life-sustaining

values. By contrast, wine remains a carrier of shame, income, and punishment. Wine caused Lázaro's early beatings, but wine also healed him. From *El Buscón* to *La Hija de Celestina,* the antigenealogy of parental indignity often is linked to wine consumption. And the *ciego*'s prophecy about wine spells trouble for Lázaro.

With an eye to spatiotemporal coordinates, the chronotope of the road exhausts its itinerant potential in the sixth *tratado.* The *escudero*'s lesson at last bears fruit, even though the *pregonero* would not further his career amid the hypocrisy and corruption of Toledan society. By growing into a writer, however, he would break free of everyday mediocrity, reaching out toward that *sublime du quotidien* that disrupts routine to the advantage of transcendence. Questions of meaning vis-à-vis picaresque quotidianity at last touch on central aspects of literary fictions somehow aimed at "realism." Tomé Gonzales's work as a miller who provided for his family year in and year out ended the moment he was caught stealing. Hence, "fue preso, y confesó, y no negó, y padeció persecución por justicia—they arrested him, and he confessed, denied nothing and was punished by law" (5, 25). The verbal sequence strings out three complementary actions whose conciseness points to John and Matthew. A tone of stoic endurance couples theft with a sense of inevitability that plagues the social landscape of poverty. In a rather parodic mode, the indignity of theft is diminished by the steadfast acceptance of punishment. Later on, Lázaro's own routine of waterseller exhausts the "literary potential" of such an insignificant practice. Miller and waterseller make it clear that transgression and transcendence are part and parcel of picaresque teleology. From the very beginning, the text mixes literalness with literariness.

At the fountainhead of picaresque textuality, sheer descriptions of life-as-is tend to be negative. Tomé, the *escudero,* the *fraile de la Merced,* and the *buldero* suggest that the praxis of life could not support itself without sliding toward degeneration one way or another. In Tomé's case, criminality edged on incredulity when Antona told the *ciego* that his son was "hijo de buen hombre, el cual por ensalzar la fe había muerto en la de los Gelves—the son of a good man, who had been killed for the greater glory of the Faith at the battle of Las Gelves" (7, 27). Before Cervantes, therefore, "mills" needed not be just mills. Like stone bulls and old stockings, they all upheld ambiguity. On Sanchopanzesque matters of unidealized existence, Miguel de Unamuno wrote that "fear and only fear made Sancho see—makes the rest of us simple mortals see— windmills where impudent giants stand . . . those mills milled bread, and of that bread men confirmed in blindness ate" (57). The sixth *tratado* thus ends with a self-aggrandizing, though wishful, sense of materialist transcendence, which glorifies the power of privilege and protection (Parret 18–19, 168–69). Although nurtured in poverty of body, aesthetic consciousness and literary creation could not fail to set Lázaro's mills of the mind in motion.

From beginning to end, Mateo Alemán insists that Guzmán de Alfarache began as a *pícaro* and ended as *maestro pícaro*. In his case, the writer tells his *discreto lector* "lo que hallares no grave ni compuesto, eso es el ser de un pícaro." As a matter of fact, the verb *picardear* calls for random appreciations on matters of literary taste, which the *pícaro* would just as well extend to conduct: "Las tales cosas, aunque seran muy pocas, picardea con ellas."[43] It is, in other words, a life deficient in direction as much as in ideology. Lázaro de Tormes reaches that stage in the sixth *tratado*, where the job of waterseller teaches him discipline and points to a safe harbor. He trades indigence for sufficiency. Perhaps unbeknownst to himself, Lázaro faces up to ideology. His decision to give up his job made of *picardear* an intransitive verb, which he replaced with ameliorative pursuits.

III

Velázquez's old waterseller wears a humble and tattered jerkin. Lázaro, instead, buys a second-hand cloak. Sinners and criminals, so we are told, wore a *jubón de azotes* as sign of punishment; and Lázaro's father had worn one. In light of the *caso* hanging over his head, one might wonder whether Lázaro would ever wear a new cloak or rather something more appropriate for a *pregonero* who had been Tomé Gonzales's son back in Tejares and who would walk criminals to their punishment in Toledo. Although the life of criminality was not a choice for Lázaro, the picaresque offered fertile grounds to the epidemic *humus* of delinquency.

Among people involved in some kind of economic service, the miller and the *buldero* body brought forth pathological aspects of work ethics; they cannot keep their greed under control. Amid picaresque *infrahumanidad*, honesty often is shortchanged. But one could bet that the old waterseller in Velásquez's painting is an exception. To borrow from Miguel de Unamuno on matters of lifestyles based on humility, there exists a sublime form of activity that converts work "into prayer" for "the greater glory of God." The painter captured that spiritual commitment when he painted his old *aguador*. Below that standard, Sancho is encouraged to be the first in "his craft," so as to make of work a point of honor that could dignify "the artisan." At that point in the narrative, we could surmise that Lázaro discharges his job with honesty and efficiency, but in the name of materialist profit rather than God's greater glory. At the fountainhead of picaresque textuality, sheer descriptions of life-as-is tend to be negative. And it could not be otherwise, since the social mimesis at stake here is the life of ethical and material poverty. Tomé the *escudero*, the *fraile de la Merced*, and the *buldero* suggest that the praxis of life could not support itself without degenerating one way or another. Perhaps the very notion of common men leading common lives under the guidance of ordinary values is itself a fiction. For sure, the picaresque test could not endorse that premise. Its socioeconomic structures, in fact, are based on strife between production and consumption, ingenuity and parasitism. It is thus indicative that as soon as the arts began to deal with econopoetics, Renaissance artists concerned themselves with the novel as well as with pastorals, utopias, romances, and fables. At the very time that economic concerns became ever more paramount, such "unnovelistic" textuality relished forms of socioeconomic escape against forms of socioeconomic success.

As a *pregonero*, Lázaro would stand at the right side of the law, even though he could not keep too far from criminals. Actually, they never lost sight of each other (Cros 178, 189).[44] Even more than his heir Buscón, Guzmán was privileged with formal education. It included "latino, retórico y griego—a good Latinist, Rhetorician, and Grecian," and his goal was to become a churchman. But things turned out otherwise. He ended up in prison, where he set out to write his *memorias*. Learning was prominent in the *pícaro's carrera de vivir.* Yet, it would not yield social and materialist benefits in the tradition of Florentine Humanism. Somehow, the more punishing circumstances of *vivir* had the best of education. Only the written texts of *pícaros'* lives survived. None of them grew to establish himself as either a scholar or a civic leader. Once human nature began to respond to the trials of growth, time castigated people to an extent that humanist treatises on merchants (Alberti) and courtiers (Castiglione) bypassed. Whereas the Italian humanists presented virtual figures whose potential was never tested by life, the picaresque put the learning of Guzmán and Buscón to the test of existence. They could never afford the leisure of scholarship in the *studiolo.* Instead, they had to write in prisons or lonely rooms where criminality and indignity afforded them a downgraded version of *otium's* privileged idleness. None of them emerged victorious, but they all survived.

For sure, Lázaro was bound to dress up for better "employment." The elementary field of primeval facts made room for deeds that would yield greater profits. To put it in terms of Clemente Pablos, the barber who sired Buscón, Lázaro was about to trade a mechanical for a liberal art; at least he so believed. Yet, we all know that Clemente Pablos was executed by his own relative, Alonso Ramplón, the hangman. And Alonso never claimed that his trade was more than a mechanical art, whose equipment of "cordeles, lazos, cuchillos, escarpias y otras herramientas del oficio—rope, nooses, knives, meat-hooks and other tools of the public executioner's trade" (162, 142) made a compelling case for rhopography at its crudest.

When all is said, is Lázaro's divestiture as a waterseller an ominous premonition? Wine earned him the first beating. Would his rise to the *oficio* of town crier charged with the sale of wines be prophetic of greater punishments? While the bureaucratic title of *pregonero* refers to function rather than origin, Lázaro's surname is rooted in nature, which he tries to leave behind. Nominally at least, the town crier would be appointed by the king, who is mentioned at the end of the book. But Toledans would never forget that he came from Tormes. Short of either epiphanic or fateful rescues, his ascent would be bound to flow downstream amid muddled waters.

Notes

1. *Histoire de France* (Paris, 1898), vol. vii; as translated in Wallace Ferguson's *The Renaissance in Historical Thought: Five Centuries of Interpretation* (Cambridge: Houghton Mifflin Co., 1948) 176.

2. On classical precedents, see Victor Ehrenberg, *The People of Aristophanes: A Sociology of Old Attic Comedy* (219) and Fernand Braudel, *The Structure of Everyday Life: The Limits of the Possible* (3). On the more archetypal grounds of pre-verbal cultures, Giambattista Vico has made an observation whose semiotic implications are important: "Since its has been demonstrated that the first gentile nations were all mute in their beginnings, they must have expressed themselves by gestures or by physical objects having natural relations with their ideas. They must have used signs to fix the boundaries of their estates and to have enduring witnesses of their rights. They all made use of money. All these truths will give us the origins of languages and letters, and thereby of hieroglyphs, laws, names, family coats of arms, medals, money, and of the language and writing in which the first natural law of the gentes was spoken and written" (*The New Science* par. 434).

3. Having noted that such a standard was upheld by Sainte-Beuve, Curtius noted: "What a tidbit for a Marxist sociology of literature!"

4. In his exemplary study, Marc Shell writes that his "book seeks to understand dialectically the relationship between thought and matter by focusing—for reasons I shall now consider—on economic thought and literary and linguistic matters" (2).

5. See Peter Burke, *Venice and Amsterdam: A Study of Seventeenth-Century Elites;* Basil S. Yamey, *Art and Accounting;* Simon Schama, *The Embarrassment of Riches: An Interpretation of Dutch Culture in the Golden Age;* Richard Halpern, *The Poetics of Primitive Accumulation: English Renaissance Culture and the Genealogy of Capital;* Patricia Fumerton, *Cultural Aesthetics: Renaissance Literature and the Practice of Social Ornament.* Stephen Greenblatt finds the same complexity at work on more focused matters of Renaissance individualism: "There is no such thing as a single 'history of the self' in the sixteenth century, except as the product of our need to reduce the intricacies of complex and creative beings to safe and controllable order" (8).

6. On sociological grounds, I refer to the paradigmatic scholarship of Georg Simmel, *The Philosophy of Money.* Richard Goldthwaite writes that the historian ought "to look outside his discipline at some of the larger problems of cultural history—at the wellhead of demand and at the nature of material culture; and with a different perspective of this kind he can perhaps reorient his own research on purely economic problems to raise new questions that will—at last—get him out of the greatest gaps that divide the disciplines in Renaissance studies" (2: 39).

7. Within the province of cultural aesthetics, in fact, Fernand Braudel and the French school of the *Annales* have set money and business at the core of historical studies. For a comprehensive analysis of the *monde Braudellien* vis-à-vis historiographical method and economic factors, see J. H. Hexter (61–148) and Hayden White's discussion of the *Annales* in *The Content of the Form: Narrative Discourse and Historical Representation* (32–45). On matters of Spanish historiography, Américo Castro has warned against Braudel's concentration on "economicomaterialistic reasoning." Although important, the "historicomaterialistic vision" could not account for the unifying forces that made the Reconquest possible. In fact, "the eco-

nomic dimension came later; it was not the primary and unifying 'logos'" (*Spaniards* 5–6).

8. Peter Dunn takes structural elements such as "I," the various "others," and Vuestra Merced to "serve as points of entry into the text" (91). Susan Sniader Lanser has spearheaded an encompassing notion of point of view, and her detailed study of the matter opens with a chapter in which she proposes "A Philosophy of Point of View" (11–63).

9. With a Marxist outlook on the whole concept of the Renaissance, Agnes Heller has consistently set the ideal against the real within the humanist tradition itself: "Everyday life was at least as important a *theme* of Renaissance thought as the problems of ontology, epistemology, art, or ethics; more accurately, there was a constant and fruitful interaction between those 'technical' matters and the study and analysis of daily life. The former were, for the most part, an outgrowth of the examination of the latter" (157–58). For Heller, Montaigne, Bacon, and the development of science and technology were representative of the age's adherence to the practice of life.

10. I paraphrase here Elias L. Rivers, whose concise but clear pairing of two counter-genres, the pastoral and the picaresque, is worth quoting: "The two different sets of fictional conventions underlying these two works constitute a perfect binary opposition. The Spanish pastoral romance, deriving from Garcilaso's eclogues and Sannazaro's *Arcadia* (1504), present a utopian world of shepherds, who, with a readily accessible and seldom-mentioned diet of natural foods such as acorns and cheese, devote themselves to a leisurely life filled with music and with dialogues about love; the shepherds are courtiers in disguise, placed in an idealized world of natural art, which is free of social and economic pressures. Conversely, the Spanish picaresque novel, with roots in exemplary (*ex contrario*) folktales about sly tricks and deceptions, presents an urban society of paupers who, under the constant pressure of hunger and economic necessity, learn to defend themselves by hook and crook, trying to rise in a harsh world of free enterprise" (66–67).

11. "Dos linajes sólos hay en el mundo, como decía una abuela ma, que son el tener y el no tener; aunque ella al de tener se atenía; y el día de hoy, mi señor Don Quijote, antes se toma el pulso al haber que al saber."

12. For historical background, J. H. Elliott writes that Spain was unique because it lacked a "middling group of solid, respectable, hardworking *bourgeois* to bridge the gulf between the two extremes . . . The contempt for commerce and manual labour, the lure of easy money from the investment in *censos* and *juros*, the universal hunger for titles of nobility and social prestige—all these, when combined with the innumerable practical obstacles in the way of profitable economic enterprise, had persuaded the *bourgeoisie* to abandon its unequal struggle, and throw in its lot with the unproductive upper classes of society" (305–6).

13. As Walter L. Reed puts it, "Thus in the literary history, the literary politics, and the literary sociology of sixteenth-century Spain one can see similar structures, structures of polarization with a relatively weak middle between the two extremes. I would argue not that these structures are a direct cause of the early Spanish novel but that they are homologous with the form of the novel in a culturally significant way. They both reflect and produce the structure of the Spanish picaresque, where divine transcendence and human degradation conspire against the middle estate of man. They also mirror and project the structure of *Don Quixote*, where an incor-

rigible idealistic imagination keeps colliding with an incontrovertibly material world. In these novels and in this society, it is a game of both ends against the middle. And it is in the book itself, that mechanically reproduced and privately consumed text of uncertain authority and value, that these extremes are brought most intriguingly together" (35). A while ago, a pioneer in the interdisciplinary study of the sociology of art, Arnold Hauser, wrote that Cervantes wavered "between the justification of unworldly idealism and of wordly-wise common sense" (2: 147).

14. I draw here from Cervantes's "Rinconete y Cortadillo," *Exemplary Novels* (New York: Penguin Books, 1982) 94–95.

15. The term has been popularized by Pedro Salinas in *Ensayos de literatura hispánica* (72). To set such a social level within the context of Renaissance society at large, it could be helpful to point to Stephen Greenblatt's *Renaissance Self-Fashioning: From More to Shakespeare,* which centers on a higher middle-class plateau, where none of the figures he analyzes "inherits a title, an ancient family tradition or hierarchical status that might have rooted personal identity in the identity of a clan or caste. With the partial exception of Wyatt, all of these writers are middle-class" (9).

16. On the subject of New Historicist criticism, I refer to the programmatic collection of essays assembled by H. Aram Veeser, *The New Historicism* (xi, xiv). On strictly picaresque matters, José Antonio Maravall recommended back in 1976 that "a study of the picaresque novel in relation to the rapidly advancing precapitalist spirit has yet to be done" (40).

17. The full passage reads: "The recurrent impulse and effort to define aesthetic value by contradistinction to all forms of utility or as the negation of all other measurable sources of interest or forms of value—hedonic, practical, sentimental, ornamental, historical, ideological, and so forth—is, in effect, to define it out of existence; for when all such utilities, interests, and other particular sources of value have been subtracted, nothing remains" (33).

18. Quotations from *Lazarillo de Tormes* are from the edition by Everett W. Hesse and Harry F. Williams; translations are from *Two Picaresque Novels* with page numbers indicated in the text.

"Fueme tan bien en el oficio que al cabo de cuatro años que le usé, con poner en la ganacia buen recaudo, ahorré para me vestir muy honradamente de la ropa vieja. De la cual compré un jobón de fustán viejo, y un sayo raído de manga tranzada y puerta, y una capa que había sido frisada, y una espada de las viejas primeras de Cuéllar."

19. Gene Brucker gives a retrospective overview on that historical school, to which he contributed his *Giovanni and Lusanna: Love and Marriage in Renaissance Florence:* "The story of Giovanni and Lusanna fits into a genre of historical writing, microhistory, that has recently achieved some notoriety in the discipline" (vii–viii). Other noteworthy examples of the genre that have recently appeared include Carlo Ginzburg's tale of the Friulian miller Menocchio (*The Cheese and the Worms,* 1980), Natalie Zemon Davis's account of the footloose peasant Martin Guerre, and Judith Brown's poignant story of the nun Benedetta and her tribulations in a Tuscan convent.

20. On more strictly literary grounds, Paul Julian Smith has drawn a parallel distinction between the inclusiveness of pictorialism and the fragmentariness of representation in *Writing in the Margin: Spanish Literature of the Golden Age* (78–88).

The critic would consider Francisco Rico's *The Spanish Picaresque Novel and the Point of View* as one that enforces a humanistically unifying, validating, and authentic point of view (81). See also John F. Moffitt (5).

21. In his treatment of the "nocion del 'popular' en literatura," Maurice Molho refers to, and paraphrases, Gramsci on matters of popular literature (*Cervantes* 18–19).

22. Patricia Fumerton writes that "trivial" is "my general term for an analytic of the fragmentary, peripheral, and ornamental addressed at once to the context of historical fact and to the texts of aesthetic artifact" (1).

23. By way of contrast, such edible items were foreign to the geometric and textured theatricality of those untouchable still lifes that Francisco de Zurbarán or Juan Sánchez Cotán have made us familiar with. For "spiritual" interpretations of these still lifes, see Edwin Mullins's comments (19–21) and Bryson (60–69).

24. Marcelin Defourneaux so describes such activities: "A degree above those who lived by begging came the *pícaros*, who, with the aid of a little work sufficient to keep them from the offence of vagabondage, applied themselves to scrounging and petty theft; such as the *pinches de cocina* (scullions), who could always find enough to feed themselves and their friends plentifully at the expense of the kitchens where they were employed, and the *esportilleros* (street porters and errand boys), who being responsible for delivering to the homes of customers goods of all kinds, pinched anything that could be hidden easily under their clothes. Alongside them were the peddlers (*buhonero*), a calling carried on for some time by Estebanillo after being, he says, 'degraded' from his status of pilgrim, and investing his capital in the purchase of knives, combs, rosaries, needles, and other shoddy wares, which he sold in the streets of Seville, an obligatory stage in every picaresque life" (219).

25. "Pidiome el jarro del agua, y díselo como lo había traído. Es señal que, pues no le faltaba el agua, que no le había a mi amo sobrado la comida. Bebimos, y muy contentos nos fuimos a dormir como la noche pasada" (38).

26. The French term was used by Louis Marin (*Etudes* 91).

27. On specific matters of literature, see Alban K. Forcione (98).

28. See also Javier Herrero, "Renaissance Poverty and Lazarillo's Family: The Birth of the Picaresque Genre" (882).

29. On hunger in the picaresque, see Pedro Salinas, *Ensayos de literatura hispánica*. Joaquín Casalduero wrote: "En los tres primeros tratados, la crueldad de la vida, la avaricia, el orgullo son solamente la modulación del mismo tema: el hambre. Lazarillo no es nada más que el punto donde a través de varias representaciones converge la misma necesidad de subsistencia, esa necesidad que siente la humanidad de conservarse" (65).

30. On Croce's comments on *Lazarillo de Tormes* and *La Celestina*, see Benito Brancaforte (118–24). Until 1948, Marcel Bataillon maintained a similar thesis in his lectures at the university, but then gave priority to the theme of *honor* (see *Pícaros y picaresca: La pícara Justina*).

31. On food in the Italian novel from Alessandro Manzoni to Primo Levi, see Gian Paolo Biasin, *I sapori della modernità: Cibo e romanzo*. D. H. Lawrence wrote a couple of essays on Verga, and he so commented on *I Malavoglia*: "There is too much, too much of the tragic life of the poor, in it. There is a sort of wallowing in tragedy: the tragedy of the humble. It belongs to a date when the 'humble' were al-

most the most fashionable thing. And the Malavoglia family are most humbly humble. Sicilians of the sea-coast, fishers, small traders—their humble tragedy is so piled on, it becomes almost disastrous. The book was published in America under the title of *The House by the Medlar Tree* (273).

32. See Maurice Molho, *The Politics of Editing* (*Introducción* 35, 42); George A. Shipley, "Lazarillo and the Cathedral Chaplain: A Conspiratorial Reading of *Lazarillo de Tormes*, Tratado VI" (231); Harry Sieber, *Language and Society in "La vida de Lazarillo de Tormes"* (78).

33. *The Illustrious Kitchen Maid*, in *Six Exemplary Novels* (Great Neck, N.Y.: Barron's Educational Series, 1961) 261.

34. An excellent essay on the sixth *tratado* is George Shipley's "Lazarillo de Tormes Was Not a Hardworking, Clean-Living Water Carrier" in *Hispanic Studies in Honor of Alan D. Deyermond: A North American Tribute.*

35. To put it in Georg Lukács's critical terms, such images of primeval simplicity would confirm that "biological and sociological life has a profound tendency to remain within its own immanence" (90).

36. To expand on the socioeconomic conditions of classes of manual workers, the *aguador* shared with many a lifestyle of subsistence, as Erich Fromm clarifies for us: "Although there were always some who had to struggle hard to earn enough to survive, by and large the guild member could be sure that he could live by his hand's work. If he made good chairs, shoes, bread, saddles, and so on, he did all that was necessary to be sure of living safely on the level which was traditionally assigned to his social position. He could rely on his 'good works,' if we use the term here not in its theological but in its simple economic meaning" (43–44).

37. On the relationship between economics and sociology, see Stephen R. G. Jones (10–11).

38. Having divided the text into two parts, each containing three *tratados*, Joaquín Casalduero made the fourth *tratado* pivotal inasmuch as it stressed "el aumento de movilidad, el tempo rápido que va a introducir en la segunda parte" (63).

39. On the connection between frustration and realism, see Jon Romano, *Dickens and Reality* (94). On the representation of objects in Balzac and Dickens, see John Vernon, *Money and Fiction: Literary Realism in the Nineteenth and Early Twentieth Centuries* (75–79).

40. George A. Shipley writes that Lázaro's story "is more exactly the chronicle of an initiation into a vile and degraded world. He represents as an arrival in safe port and, later, as a rise to a pinnacle of satisfaction what is scarcely more than a lateral move of incorporation into the debased city of man in the fallen world" ("The Critic as Witness" 179–80).

41. It is worth quoting Castro's assessment of description: "This is life with a minimum of significance, devaluated life—when compared with the lives of those people who created the great cultures of the earth. In this, as in all questions of value, there is gradation. The lowest level corresponds to groups now called primitive, groups that have arrived at dead ends of human self-realization and who mark time down the centuries. For such life as this description is quite adequate . . . There are no deeds or triumphs of any sort to incite the children of the future. Such primitive peoples may, in effect, be thought of as residing at the end of blind alleys, as excluded from the broad avenues of future possibility available to others" (*Idea* 293).

42. *Menosprecio de corte y alabanza de aldea* (Madrid: Calpe, 1967) 71–72. I follow the translation and commentary in José Antonio Maravall, *Utopia and Counterutopia in the "Quixote"* (Detroit: Wayne State Univ. Press, 1991) 45.

43. *Guzmán de Alfarache* edición, introducción y notas de Francisco Rico (Barcelona: Planeta, 1983) 94.

44. Cros refers here to the social and moral frontiers of the picaresque.

Works Cited

Alter, Robert. *Rogue's Progress: Studies in the Picaresque Novel.* Cambridge: Harvard Univ. Press, 1965.

Bataillon, Marcel. *Pícaros y picaresca: La pícara Justina.* Madrid: Taurus, 1969.

Biasin, Gian Paolo. *I sapori della modernità: Cibo e romanzo.* Bologna: Il Mulino, 1991.

Blanchard, Marc Eli. "On Still Life." *Yale French Studies* 61 (1981): 276–277.

Brancaforte, Benito. *Benedetto Croce y su crtica de la literatura española.* Madrid: Gredos, 1972.

Braudel, Fernand. *The Structure of Everyday Life: The Limits of the Possible.* New York: Harper and Row, 1979.

———. *The Mediterranean and the Mediterranean World in the Age of Philip II.* Vol. 2. New York: Harper and Row, 1972.

Brucker, Gene. *Giovanni and Lusanna: Love and Marriage in Renaissance Florence.* Berkeley: Univ. of California Press, 1986.

Bryson, Norman. *Looking at the Overlooked: Four Essays on Still Life Painting.* Cambridge: Harvard Univ. Press, 1990.

Burke, Peter. *Venice and Amsterdam: A Study of Seventeenth-Century Elites.* London: T. Smith, 1974.

Butor, Michel. *Essais sur le roman.* Paris: Gallimard, 1969.

Calvino, Italo. *Sotto il sole del giaguaro.* Milan: Garzanti, 1986.

Camporesi, Piero. *Bread of Dreams: Food and Fantasy in Early Modern Europe.* Cambridge: Basil Blackwell, 1989.

Casalduero, Joaquín. *Estudios de literatura española.* Madrid: Gredos, 1973.

Castro, Américo. *The Spaniards.* Berkeley: Univ. of California Press, 1971.

———. *Hacia Cervantes.* Madrid: Taurus, 1967.

———. *An Idea of History: Selected Essays of Américo Castro.* Ed. S. Gilman and E. D. King. Columbus: Ohio State Univ. Press, 1977.

Cros, Edmond. *Mateo Alemán: Introducción a su vida y a su obra.* Salamanca: Anaya, 1971.

Curtius, Ernst Robert. *European Literature and the Latin Middle Ages.* New York: Harper and Row, 1953.

Defourneaux, Marcelin. *Daily Life in Spain in the Golden Age.* New York: Praeger Publishers, 1970.

Dunn, Peter. "Reading the Text of *Lazarillo de Tormes*." *Studies in Honor of Bruce Wardropper.* Ed. D. Foz, H. Sieber, R. TerHorst. Newark: Juan de la Cuesta, 1989.

Ehrenberg, Victor. *The People of Aristophanes: A Sociology of Old Attic Comedy.* New York: Schocken Books, 1962.

Elliott, J. H. *Imperial Spain, 1469–1716.* New York: St. Martin's Press, 1963.

Ferguson, Wallace. *The Renaissance in Historical Thought: Five Centuries of Interpretation.* Cambridge: Houghton Mifflin Co., 1948.

Forcione, Alban K. *Cervantes and the Mystery of Lawlessness: A Study of El casamiento engañoso y El coloquio de los perros.* Princeton: Princeton Univ. Press, 1984.

Fromm, Erich. *The Fear of Freedom.* London: Routledge and Kegan Paul, 1950.

Fumerton, Patricia. *Cultural Aesthetics: Renaissance Literature and the Practice of Social Ornament.* Chicago: Univ. of Chicago Press, 1991.

Goldthwaite, Richard. "The Economy of Renaissance Italy. The Preconditions for Luxury Consumption." *I Tatti Studies. Essays in the Renaissance.* Vol. 2. Florence: La Nuova Italia, 1987.

Gramsci, Antonio. *Antonio Gramsci: Selections from Cultural Writings.* Ed. D. Forgacs and G. Nowell-Smith. Cambridge: Harvard Univ. Press, 1985.

Greenblatt, Stephen. *Renaissance Self-Fashioning: From More to Shakespeare.* Chicago: Univ. of Chicago Press, 1984.

Guevara, Antonio de. *Menosprecio de corte y alabanza de aldea.* Madrid: Calpe, 1922.

Guillén, Claudio. *Literature as System: Essays towards the Theory of Literary History.* Princeton: Princeton Univ. Press, 1971.

Halpern, Richard. *The Poetics of Primitive Accumulation: English Renaissance Culture and the Genealogy of Capital.* Ithaca: Cornell Univ. Press, 1991.

Hauser, Arnold. *The Social History of Art.* Vol. 2. New York: Vintage Books, 1951.

Heller, Agnes. *Renaissance Man.* London: Routledge and Kegan Paul, 1978.

Herrero, Javier. "Renaissance Poverty and Lazarillo's Family: the Birth of the Picaresque Genre." *PMLA* 94 (1979): 876–79.

Hexter, J. H. *On Historians.* Cambridge: Harvard Univ. Press, 1979.

Huppert, George. *After the Black Death: A Social History of Early Modern Europe.* Bloomington: Indiana Univ. Press, 1986.

Jeanneret, Michel. *A Feast of Words: Banquets and Table Talk in the Renaissance.* Chicago: Univ. of Chicago Press, 1991.

Jones, Stephen R. G. *The Economy of Conformism.* Oxford: Basil Blackwell, 1984.

Lanser, Susan Sniader. *The Narrative Act: Point of View in Prose Fiction.* Princeton: Princeton Univ. Press, 1981.

Lawrence, D. H. *Selected Literary Criticism.* New York: Viking Press, 1956.

Lazarillo de Tormes. Ed. Everett W. Hesse and Harry F. Williams. Madison: Univ. of Wisconsin Press, 1969.

Lazarillo de Tormes. Two Picaresque Novels. Trans. Michael Alpert. Baltimore: Penguin Books, 1969.

Levin, Harry. *The Gates of Horn: A Study of Five French Realists.* New York: Oxford Univ. Press, 1963.

Lukács, Georg. *The Theory of the Novel.* Cambridge: MIT Press, 1971.

MacMullen, Ramsay. *Roman Social Relations: 50 B.C. to 284 A.D.* New Haven: Yale Univ. Press, 1974.

Manrique de Aragón, Jorge. *Peligrosidad social y picaresca.* San Antonio de Colonge: Hijos de J. Bosch, 1977.

Maravall, José Antonio. *La literatura picaresca desde la historia social (siglos XVI y XVII).* Madrid: Gredos, 1986.

———. *Utopia and Counterutopia in the "Quixote."* Detroit: Wayne State Univ. Press, 1991.

Marco Antonio de Camos. *Microcosmia: Gobierno universal del hombre cristiano, para todos los estados y cualquiera de ellos.* Madrid, 1595.

Marin, Louis. *Etudes Semiologiques.* Paris: Klincksieck, 1971.

————. *Food for Thought*. Baltimore: Johns Hopkins Univ. Press, 1989.

Marx, Karl. "Economic and Philosophical Manuscripts," in Erich Fromm, *Marx's Concept of Man*. New York: F. Ungar Publisher, 1968.

Moffitt, John F. "Image and Meaning in Velázquez's Water Carrier of Seville." *Traza y Baza* 7 (1979): 5.

Molho, Maurice. *Cervantes: Raíces Folklóricas*. Madrid: Gredos, 1976.

————. *Introducción al pensamiento picaresco*. Salamanca: Anaya, 1972.

Morson, Gary Saul, and Caryl Emerson. *Mikhail Bakhtin: Creation of a Prosaics*. Stanford: Stanford Univ. Press, 1990.

Mullins, Edwin. *Great Paintings*. New York: St. Martin's Press, 1981.

Ortega y Gasset, José. "Sobre el cultivo de la demótica." *Obras completas*. Vol. IX. Madrid: Revista de Occidente, 1971.

————. *Velázquez, Goya, and the Dehumanization of Art*. New York: W. W. Norton, 1972.

Parret, Herman. *Le sublime du quotidien*. Paris: Hades, 1988.

Prieto, Antonio. *Ensayo semiológico de sistemas literarios*. Barcelona: Planeta, 1972.

Reed, Walter R. *An Exemplary History of the Novel: The Quixotic versus the Picaresque*. Chicago: Univ. of Chicago Press, 1981.

Rico, Francisco. *The Spanish Picaresque Novel and the Point of View*. Cambridge: Cambridge Univ. Press, 1984.

Rivers, Elias L. *Quixotic Scriptures: Essays on the Textuality of Hispanic Literature*. Bloomington: Indiana Univ. Press, 1983.

Romano, John. *Dickens and Reality*. New York: Columbia Univ. Press, 1978.

Salinas, Pedro. *Ensayos de literatura hispánica*. Madrid: Aguilar, 1958.

Schama, Simon. *The Embarrassment of Riches: An Interpretation of Dutch Culture in the Golden Age*. New York: Knopf, 1987.

Shell, Marc. *The Economy of Literature*. Baltimore: Johns Hopkins Univ. Press, 1978.

Shipley, George. "Lazarillo and the Cathedral Chaplain: A Conspiratorial Reading of Lazarillo de Tormes, Tratado IV." *Symposium* 37 (1983): 231.

————. "Lazarillo de Tormes Was Not a Hardworking, Clean-Living Water Carrier." *Hispanic Studies in Honor of Alan D. Deyermond: A North American Tribute*. Ed. S. Miletich. Madison: Univ. of Wisconsin Press, 1986. 247–56.

————. 'The Critic as Witness for the Prosecution: Making the Case against Lázaro de Tormes." *PMLA* 97 (1982): 179–80.

Sieber, Harry. *Language and Society in "La vida de Lazarillo de Tormes."* Baltimore: Johns Hopkins Univ. Press, 1978.

Simmel, Georg. *The Philosophy of Money*. London: Routledge and Kegan Paul, 1978.

Smith, Barbara Herrnstein. *Contingencies of Value: Alternative Perspectives for Critical Theory*. Cambridge: Harvard Univ. Press, 1988.

Smith, Paul Julian. *Writing in the Margin: Spanish Literature of the Golden Age*. Oxford: Clarendon Press, 1988.

Steinberg, Leo. "José López-Rey, Velázquez: A Catalogue Raisonné of His Oeuvre, with an Introductory Study." *Art Bulletin* 47 (1965): 282.

Unamuno, Miguel de. *Our Lord Don Quixote*. Princeton: Princeton Univ. Press, 1976.

Veeser, H. Aram. *The New Historicism*. London: Routledge and Kegan Paul, 1989.

Vernon, John. *Literary Realism in the Nineteenth and Early Twentieth Centuries*. Ithaca: Cornell Univ. Press, 1984.

Villanueva, Francisco Márquez. *Espiritualidad y literatura en el siglo XVI*. Madrid: Alfaguara, 1968.

White, Hayden. *The Content of the Form: Narrative Discourse and Historical Representation*. Baltimore: Johns Hopkins Univ. Press, 1987.

Wind, Barry. *Velázquez's Bodegones: A Study in Seventeenth-Century Spanish Genre Painting*. Fairfax: George Mason Univ. Press, 1987.

Yamey, Basil. *Art and Accounting*. New Haven: Yale Univ. Press, 1989.

◆ Chapter 2

"Otras cosillas que no digo": *Lazarillo's* Dirty Sex

George A. Shipley

APOLOGIA PRO VITA SUA: "MALAS LENGUAS NO [SÍ] NOS DEJAN HABLAR" ("Badmouthers don't [do] let us talk")

It stands to reason that sex should raise its ugly head in *La vida de Lazarillo de Tormes, y de sus fortunas y adversidades* ("The Life of Lazarillo de Tormes, and concerning His Misfortunes and Adversities"). The text is lively and true-to-life even where it is most stylized, and a Life and Times without sex makes for an improbable story, and a dull one. The narrator in this case, what is more, "confesando yo no ser más sancto que mis vecinos" ("confessing that I am no more holy than my neighbors") purports to present the "entera noticia" ("full account") of an unsaintly life.[1] Certainly some sex should be expected among the *fortunas y adversidades* of a ne'er-do-well who is, on his claim, no better than his neighbors and whose neighbors are, by his account, not saintly in the least.

The anonymous author of this text took care to make his narrator as low a creature as conceivably could rise to the occasion of penning so clever a document as the two of them challenge us to read. Claiming to have begun his life not far removed from the muck of Salamanca's low life, then to have stumbled into it, then to have struggled for the better part of a lifetime to climb out to the precarious security of a situation that is only a marginal improvement, the narrator indeed would have an incongruously clean story to tell if his ups and downs had not included all manner—or at least a variety of manners—of sex.

What we take to be a short novel is for its narrator a document of a different sort. It appears to be his calculated defense against well-armed neighbors who can drum him from their midst if ever they take that resolve. Because of Lázaro's involvement in a current and scandalous *caso* they have an immediate cause sufficient to justify a move against him. Furthermore they have an abundant pretext in their accumulated, if incomplete, testimony concerning his past. "Malas lenguas," he complains, "que nunca faltaron ni faltarán, no nos dejan vivir, diciendo no sé qué y sí sé qué"(132) ("Badmouthers, who never were lacking and never shall be, don't let us live, saying I don't know what all, and I do know what all"). The hounded narrator's account of his upbringing, in consequence, is designed aggressively to bad-mouth his neighbors, even as it claims his assimilation into their community. The text Lázaro pens is in a manner of speaking his own abridged but potentially expandable pretext, designed to anticipate and counter his detractors' current claims.[2] It works by deflecting, mimicking, replicating, and reflecting the charges of his attackers, utilizing evidence and tactics of persuasion consistent with a practiced town crier's practice. We might think of his ploy as a rhetorical equivalent of that subterfuge of our own time called the preemptive reaction strike: the narrator insinuates that the protagonist's *amigos y señores* have shaped him into the ethical pervert he is. They have rewarded him from start to finish, in small ways, for doing their bidding; who, then, is to blame for his life?

What veteran reader of ironic and satiric literature will be surprised to discover that the business of sex operates manifestly and covertly as a powerful thematic motif in Lázaro's narrative? The narrator continues to use sex, as he says Lazarillo had done, to satisfy his superiors. But now he permits, encourages, facilitates, regulates, and profits from the commerce, as he had not always done, and sex—writing about it and threatening to write about it—has become a means for Lázaro to arrest the pretensions of his neighbors. To save his situation Lázaro, the narrator, sheds light, a little light, obliquely, on his own dark sexual history (or pretends to do that); but he also depicts it all as resulting from the domineering perversity of his betters, who after all made him the crier he is.[3]

The greatest ironic imaginings that preceded *Lazarillo* in Spanish literary history, the *Libro de buen amor* and *La Celestina*, make much use of the leveling power of sexual representation and innuendo.[4] So too do Lázaro's literary heirs, beginning with Mateo Alemán and Francisco de Quevedo, and also Miguel de Cervantes. About sexual matters in *Lazarillo*, however, little was written until recently, and no one took much note of the slight. The diminutive Lazarillo gathered most of readers' and commentators' attention, and he generally was judged an innocent and a victim whose exploitation moved many readers to sympathy unnuanced by skepticism, uninformed by irony. The rascal Lázaro escaped scrutiny for a long time. The refocusing of attention on the narrator of the text, advanced in Spain first and principally by Francisco Rico, and by Fernando Lázaro Carreter, and in this country earlier by Claudio Guillén and then by Stephen Gilman, Harry Sieber, and others, made possible the discovery of the narrator's guile, evidenced in round-about nastiness of many kinds concealed in more or less esoteric allusions and significant ellipses.[5] These close readings remain fundamental; collectively they reveal the patterned and systematic interrelation of many bits of text the significance of which was obscure so long as they were regarded as incidental bits of amusement. The bits, we are learning, are rather threads; and the threads are interwoven according to principles of design more intricate than discreet readers imagined. In the continuing process of recovery of obscured significance we see that sexual references are to be found, if not everywhere in our text, in many places, beginning, end, and middle. It seems they are as patterned as other parts of the text's expressive system, into which they are integrated. Just where are they found, how do they function, and for whom?

Reading Lázaro's Lips

It is increasingly possible, because decreasingly it is considered unseemly, to describe and discuss these matters. They are again attracting the attention that we imagine both Lázaro and his author, for their separate purposes, must have hoped they would attract, and their study is fostered by a social and professional climate more favorable to their discussion than formerly. The findings are diverse, the assessments sometimes contradictory and often disputed. Consequently this field, where a dozen scholars have sunk test holes, is marked now by a few rich discoveries, some rubble, a number of empty shafts, and many disputed claims. These last provoke considerable nay-saying along with some willful short-sightedness.[6]

What some see in the text, others allege is not there. Occasionally it is suggested that the dirt lies embedded in the eyes of its beholders, who project it enlarged onto the screen of the text. This is a predictable and normal charge and not rarely a justified one; we will be able to draw useful conclusions from it. But we must not allow charges so easily raised, and so regularly defensive and evasive (and never, to my knowledge, closely reasoned or carefully questioned) to settle the issue. The possibility that readers might be engaged in transplanting sexual innuendoes from their minds into the text is worth considering, for it can help us refine our understanding of the unusual way, the possibly corrupting way, that this text provides readers some of the *agrado* ("pleasure") and *deleite* ("delight") that the narrator in his Prologue promises.

Let us veteran scholars admit that readers with nasty minds get more enjoyment than others from reading *Lazarillo*. Lázaro's tale is the parable of a youngster whose embarrassment of earthy experience hardened him at a tender age. The narrator aims his story calculatingly at an elite of this-worldly readers whom he counts on to grasp what he has in mind. By virtue (so to speak) of their participation in his business or similar ones, of which implicitly there are many in the world they control, these readers are in the know. Indeed they are in the text. The Prologue's eminent addressee Vuestra Merced ("Your Mercy") is one such, as are also the narrator's influential and obliging "amigos y señores" ("friends and masters") (128), as well as his observant neighbors, the "malas lenguas," whose experience has equipped them to catch many of Lázaro's meanings. These readers and all who are like-minded are invited to derive pleasure from the text, along with a warning: the narrator, who writes with elliptic efficiency, remains capable of casting light on his opacities if need be, to the embarrassment of those who would be exposed standing behind him in the shadows. Lázaro wrote his readers a menacingly attractive and maliciously funny book. The readers he hopes for are certain to accept his invitation to the witty game of hide-and-seek that he constructs for them to play with their common tongue. Some, we imagine, are bound to be amused additionally to discover that, thanks to the narrator's double-dealing, much that amuses them will pass unperceived by ingenuous readers who, let us say, drink in only frothy *deleite* off the surface of the wine-seller's flagon of vintage fermented and distilled *agrado*.[7]

Incorporated in the text to serve the narrator's purpose is much evidence of how a practiced schemer and hardened soul speaks to others of that kind whom he would ingratiate. "Speaks," though metaphorical here, is a better word than "writes," for almost as much as the *Libro de buen amor,* and *La Celestina, La vida de Lazarillo de Tormes,* a crier's tale, asks to be read aloud and to be performed according to instructions embedded in the text. It invites its readers to be raconteurs, to punctuate the text on cue with suggestive winks and glances and wrinkling of brows and the occasional elbow jammed into the ribs of knowing and appreciative companions in orality.[8] That kind of reading, which the innocent cannot perform and the omniverous but lipless mental readers of today seldom slow down enough to experience, teaches readers how the written word works its most routine-disrupting miracles. The written word governed still by the rhythms of orality operates not in the modern manner by propelling eyes, with seldom a pause, ever to the right margin and down the page line-by-soon-forgotten-line. Rather oral prose beguiles the ear, excites the mind's eye, making the reader's tongue its instrument, and induces the reader to slow sometimes almost to a pause, to attend to the narrator as if he were a lively speaker. Processing words at the pace of an artfully insinuating conversation, a pace still habitual for mid-sixteenth-century readers, the ear almost can hear Lázaro and the eye almost can see Lazarillo discourse with his "amigos y señores" in the language they share in their linguistic community of "malas lenguas."[9]

That attentive eye and responsive inner ear, reawakened to the rhythms and thereby to the allusive registers of oral discourse, will be reminded that the Lázaro who writes so engagingly is transferring to the page his own and his *vecino's* ways of talking— talking in the markets where he claims Lazarillo begged bread and scraps of meat, talking in the inns where as a hustling apprentice and apprentice hustler he first ran disreputable errands for his mother and her customers and years later sold water and maybe other utilities; talking at the riverside park where two *rebozadas mujeres* learned, by deconstructing the squire's talk, that neither their hunger nor his would be satisfied at lunch; and talking in the cathedral where Lazarillo engaged in commerce with a busy chaplain.[10] When we perform *Lazarillo* adequately in the theaters of our minds or aloud in the way we hear the words invite, the text says more than it can so long as we regard its pages with either the objectivity or the respectful admiration that the academy favors and at the pace we are pressed to maintain in school. Attending to Lázaro's words at the rate of talk in the market, at the stable, in the back pews, at the river park, in a circle of gamblers, we hear him speak of things and in ways that are usual and intended in those places, less usual and unattended in Literature. Especially we hear the sort of talk talked when talking is free and easy, talk so good that the speakers are moved to wink knowingly at their companions-in-conversation and perhaps to nudge them now and again. In other words, we hear talk of sex.

If the Shoe Fits . . .

Lázaro has achieved remarkable mastery of the rhetorical means for dealing with his adversaries (his betters, his neighbors, and the curious generally). He knows the value of humor as a means of socializing opposition, and he controls diverse techniques for creating and aiming laughter. He appreciates the advantages got by blurring qualitative distinctions among his neighbors and he finds in synecdoche a way to degrade by general contamination. He asserts by these means a base and distinctionless egalitarianism in which he can justify his own conduct as no more and no less defensible than that of others. The stinginess of Maqueda's priest, says Lázaro, came with his clerical habit (47); the squire's posturing is generic too, as the concluding laughter of the policeman and scribe certifies (109); the Prologue's approval-craving soldier, preacher, and gentleman jouster stand for many such, and they also are fundamentally like each other and like Lázaro, "y todo va desta manera" (8) ("and this is the way everything goes").

Leveling distinctions and promoting likeness is what Lázaro is up to from his first words about his parents to his final celebration of his wife as "tan buena mujer como vive dentro de las puertas de Toledo" (134–35) ("as good a woman as lives within the city gates of Toledo"). Pressed down by his birthright and the opprobrium of cuckoldry, and therefore unable to sustain even such vacuous pretensions to goodness as those floated by the squire, Lázaro has recourse to a less assailable alternative strategy: he will set the standards of social and ethical comparability low, and capitalize on his liabilities: he is a *cornudo* (cuckold), but just look at his wife, her lover, and their accusers.

Kenneth Burke has advised readers to begin the search for the principles that underlie the signifying process of texts by asking the deceptively simple question "from what through what to what" does the action proceed.[11] In the case of *Lazarillo de Tormes* the "from what," the starting point of Lazarillo's curriculum vitae, is pretty clear, as is also the terminal "to what" (though another day I will uncover some particulars at each of these extremes that lie masked still from the view of modern speed readers). Plotting the "through what" of Lazarillo's career is less easy. Applying Burke's notion simply for now, we understand that Lazarillo's "from what" is a whore of a mother and a thief of a father, and maybe worse. His "to what" is another, more accomplished, whore and another thief, of a higher order (an archthief, Quevedo would have called him), and a relationship more comfortable, more protected, possibly more durable, and certainly more degraded than the first one. The "to what" is also less productive than the "from what": the first couple engendered a child, and Antona proved her fecundity a second time with Zaide, and cared for her offspring, as did her lover also. The love of the final threesome, in contrast, is sterile. The good padre of San Salvador is neither good nor a father, and Lázaro's spouse is no better a mother than she is a wife; her love produces only abortions, at least three of them (133n32, and Rico's *Problemas* 74n3).

By standards of propriety that governed reading then and do so still, the sex at the beginning of this fiction is depressingly natural—many among the first readers would have called it bestial—and sex at the end is pervertedly unnatural. Measured by his par-

ents' and stepfather's and his current associates' sexual performance, as also by other measures, Lázaro's claim to have risen to
the "cumbre de toda buena fortuna" ("peak of good fortune") is
absurd and risible posturing on his part; and from the perspective
of his author it is ironic double-talk charged with scorn. The beginning and ending of Lazarillo, reduced in this way to their crude
outlines and set end-to-end, the one against the other, produce
sharply profiled meanings that provoke only feelings of repulsion.
It seems a wonder that any reader and any scholar ever developed
sympathy for such a shameless and callous would-be arriviste as
Lázaro. In fact readers seldom react against Lázaro as strongly as
(by the measure I am applying at the moment) he deserves. The
softened reactions of the generality of readers often include un-
critical feelings of compassion for the protagonist. These have led
to scholarly rationalizations dignifying both the protagonist and
the narrator.[12] This confusion is the product of the narrator's
clever manipulation of the "through what" of his story, that is, the
portion of text that reaches from Lazarillo's apprenticeship with a
blind man (midway through chapter 1) through his service as a
petty lawman and resourceful crier (midway through chapter 7).
The attractive effects of his sleight of pen over this considerable
stretch distract us from attending closely to the "from what" and
judging coolly the "to what" of Lázaro's life.[13]

For self-serving reasons Lázaro chooses "no tomalle por el
medio, sino del principio" (10) ("not to begin in the middle but in
the beginning"). Not merely to avoid following a scoundrel's example, I shall start where he chose not to, in medias res, looking at
the middle point that may also be the turning point of Lazarillo's
trajectory, chapter 4. The episode is not usually viewed as central,
partly because it offers so little to view that the significance of the
words is easily passed over. Lázaro himself places his turning
point elsewhere, in chapter 6; attentive readers may put it still further along, outside the narrative altogether in the unrecorded time
and circumstances that follow chapter 7 and precede the writing
of the text and Prologue. Nevertheless, in the series of seven
episodes that constitute Lázaro's pseudo-autobiographical sketch
the fourth is numerically the middle, and if it seems more a mud-
dle and if the narrator contrives to slight its central significance,

this is for reasons that reward study.[14] The reasons have to do with the representation of Lazarillo's own sexual experience, a theme of Lázaro's *Vida* that attains centrality and focuses on the protagonist for the first time at this point in the narrative.[15]

The worst of what Lázaro has to say about his fourth master, the restless Mercedarian, has been sensed and censored many times, but until recently it was acknowledged only in cryptic allusions as elliptic as Lázaro's own. Karl Vossler, Marcel Bataillon, and Maurice Molho, among others, found discreet ways to suggest that Lazarillo was abused by the Mercedarian or feared he would be misused and so left this master behind to seek a better one.[16] Scholars' hints—a brief sentence here, a footnote there— that Lázaro was alluding to *el pecado nefando* ('the abominable sin') diverted little attention away from the paragraph's other titillating matter. This latter, the insatiable heterosexual appetite of a vigorous member of the Order of Our Lady of Mercy, and his indefatigable dedication to celebrating sexual communion, is accepted and explicated more easily and with less embarrassment.

In every period, and especially in the Erasmian first decades of the sixteenth century, it has been tempting, acceptable, and gratifying to call attention to those religious who break the rules, especially the vow of celibacy. Mercedarians, it seems, were commonly accused of worldliness, sensual irregularity, and tepid evangelizing fervor.[17] This means that Lázaro picked a safe target when he nominated as his fourth master a conventional foil of a kind predefined by his community. Lazarillo's experience, whether we regard it as invented by Lázaro or remembered by him, is consistent with his readers', including real readers', perceptions and prejudices in a way that serves the narrator's selfish interests. Mercedarian notoriety corroborates Lázaro's insinuation that corruption and unruliness are widespread among his betters.

Using words playfully to sketch a caricature of sensual excess that contains no critical bite at all and is notably lacking in indignation, Lázaro highlights with puns and an amusing superlative his master's heroic dedication to womanizing: "amicísimo de negocios seglares y visitar: tanto que pienso que rompía él más zapatos que todo el convento" (110–11) ("devoted to secular affairs and to visiting, so much so that I think he wore out more shoes than all the rest of the monastery").[18] Readers take delight in the narrator's measurement of this fellow's sexual prowess in terms of his expenditure of shoe leather. The conjunction of *convento* here and *trote* in the following sentence, just after "perdido por andar fuera" ("crazy about/damned for roaming about town"), calls to mind the convention in literature and folklore, and likely the practice in fact, of the *trotaconventos* ("convent trotter"), of which the Mercedarian represents a virile variant who performs diligently without need of a *celestina* ("procuress").[19]

How many readers, after sipping the *deleite* of this footloose brother's perambulations, drink in the (un)savory *agrado* Lázaro has distilled there for the reader of more educated tongue? Of course *romper zapatos* ("wearing out shoes") is a graphic metaphor for the Mercedarian's efforts to find women; just as certainly, but not often clearly acknowledged in polite discourse and professional prose, *romper zapatos* is also a metonym for what the Mercedarian did with those women once he found them. His is the foot, they are his shoes; the friction he generates is sufficient to wear holes in their soles, one pair after another.[20]

While the friar does not need a *celestina*, he does appreciate the company of a boy. He esteems him so highly that he gives his boy the first shoes he ever wore, "los primeros zapatos que rompí en mi vida" ("the first shoes I wore out in my whole life"). The shoeing of Lazarillo bespeaks his good service.[21] It also represents metonymically the beginning of his material improvement and upward mobility that will accelerate notably in chapter 6, when as a water carrier he acquires proper clothes and a sword—used clothes and a secondhand weapon then as hand-me-down footwear here. But the Mercedarian's gift signifies something more than that symbolic first step, for the narrator has just defined shoe leather erotically in the immediately preceding words. The iteration of the eroticized verb and noun together is an adequate, if minimal, signal indicator from the narrator to his readers: "rompí zapatos," he says, "for the first time in the same way that my master wore them out habitually. That is to say, in giving me shoes, he gave me the means to follow in his footsteps; I mean to say he provided me his hand-me-downs for my sexual initiation." Lazarillo, however, hasn't the Mercedarian's stomach for such work; he labored at it for a week, and then, exhausted, he backed off.

The matter is more complicated; Lázaro's highly sexualized

words carry an additional and heavier charge. The narrator cannot detail, and he does not need to detail, his next confession. It is adequately contained in that same sentence that works with a degree of expressive and suggestive economy we expect to find only in intensely fashioned lyrics. "No me duraron ocho días," "the shoes he gave me didn't last me a week, under the pounding they took." "Ni yo pude con su trote durar más," "nor did I last any longer under his pounding." His secondhand shoes wore out; he wore out; they were comparably exhausted by the Mercedarian's indefatigable shuffle. At week's end Lazarillo was as foot-worn a hand-me-down as any other shoe/sexual object his master wore down, discarded, and sought restlessly to replace. (Lázaro's malicious code depends on readers' awareness of homosexual proclivities, real or alleged, among those of religious vocation. This Mercedarian's consumption stands out in degree but not in kind: among his fellows "rompía él más zapatos que todo el convento." Calling this brother the hottest to trot, what does Lázaro mean to suggest about the brethren who also burn? We must bear in mind that at mid-sixteenth century the distinction between the shod and the discalced in the Church was often moralized and politicized, especially by the discalced and others critical of the shoddy behavior of the scarcely observant unreformed religious, among which at least one of this monastery's Mercedarians must be counted.)

Lázaro tells us that Lazarillo took all he could take of that abuse and then he got up and left. Oddly, not even his retreat, from which one would think the narrator might attempt to derive some moral advantage, is put to the reader in a straightforward way. Instead the narrator says in effect and contortedly: "I could tell you an additional earful about this fellow, if I chose to, but I will not": "Y por esto y por otras cosillas que no digo, salí dél" ("And for this reason and because of other things I am not going to say, I left him"). What does he mean by this odd attention-gathering proclamation of reticence? The "por esto" refers back to more than enough bad business for a single week; one would think a young boy would not require more motive than "esto" to leave a smothering pedophile. What additional experiences or imaginings does "por otras cosillas" point to without naming? What sort of iceberg, the exposed tip of which is dirty, lies below the surface here? Francisco Rico (112n9) and some others who maintain a more charitable view of Lázaro than I think his text permits, hold that "otras cosillas" is nothing more than a common epistolary formula for bringing the episode to an end. We might accept that explanation, were the narrator's way of writing loose and his material at this point ordinarily important. It might have been so also, had the narration of this affair become so distended or tiresome as to leave the narrator needing or his author or reader desiring an easy out.

But chapter 4 is interesting reading. It cannot be thought overlong. Neither is it casually composed. It is layered with inherited erotic signifiers and suggestions of illicit behavior. Scarcely a word of its single paragraph is excluded from the pattern of erotic suggestion, in which *Merced* ("mercy"), *mujercillas* ("[common] women"), *encaminaron* ("put me on the path"), *pariente* ("relative"), *comer* ("eat"), and *visitar* are active and familiar contributors even before the narrator broaches his footware and these other *cosillas*. What is more, the juncture Lazarillo reaches here is the midpoint for the narrator and the turning point for his protagonist in an articulated series of episodes and experiences that together comprise a memorable *Life*. In no way is this moment an improvisation dependent upon tired formulas. Consequently, once we moderate our pace and train our gaze to see this much of what is there to be missed at a glance, we are more resolutely disposed to continue to puzzle out what Lázaro has put before us. Stopped short by the arresting insinuations contained even in an epistolary formula of closure, we are invited and tempted to prowl around rather than to rush on, following Lazarillo, to his next appointment.

Readers must bear in mind that here as at every point in this text the narrator gains advantage from reporting the corruptness of young Lazarillo's master, while admitting to some of his own, and tapping into the secret stores of his readers'.[22] The more the muck, the more the advantage. Cutting short this chapter after awakening the prurient curiosity of the worldly and broadly literate readers, Lázaro suggests disingenuously that there are limits to his shamelessness. In effect he challenges those readers to flesh out from his hints and from their own mental inventories of commensurate erotic experience and imaginings some unspecified degradation that, he pretends, a vestigial sense of seemliness keeps him from recording. If we suppose that in the phrase "por esto y por otras cosillas que no digo" the "otras cosillas que no digo" stands simply for variant forms of the accumulated irregular behavior to which "por esto" refers, we end up with a short paragraph that concludes clumsily and vacuously perhaps but leads to a minimally adequate conclusion: Lazarillo's precipitous departure was overdetermined by his master's habitual nastiness. If we entertain the probability, enhanced by Lázaro's copulative conjunction, that "*y otras* cosillas que no digo" points to other acts unspecified because more unspeakable than the Mercedarian's buggery, we have—aside from Lázaro's syntactical invitation— only our own lasciviously productive minds to blame and to search for just the right perversion to fill in the blank.

I will hazard reading on where the text is enticingly obscure and will point in the direction of an excess that I imagine Lázaro might hope to plant in the minds of his readers. This is the question the narrator provokes: if Lázaro's "por esto" refers to an exhausting week of buggery, what other and worse experiences can he allude to and simultaneously refuse to name from the protective cover of an apparently empty formula, "otras cosillas que no digo"? A tabood complement of sodomy and a form of deviance consistent with our textual evidence and appropriate for Lazarillo would be oral homosexual intercourse. A recurrent preoccupation akin to an oral fixation on foods and food surrogates that Lazarillo stores in his mouth and on his person characterizes him and the narrator through chapters 1–3.[23] In chapters 5 and 7 foods continue to assert considerable symbolic significance, as sensual bribes in the first case, in which the *buldero* ("seller of indulgences") suborns rural priests with gifts of such "cosillas"—yes, that is the narrator's term—as lettuce and choice fruits of the season, including pears of course, because "procuraba tenerlos propicios, porque favoresciesen sus negocios" (113) ("he procured their favor so that they would favor his business"). In the later episode the archpriest's gifts of *trigo* ("wheat"), *carne* ("meat"), and *bodigos* ("buns") are blatant sexual signifiers. The accumulation of coins, which were food surrogates in chapter 1, is central again in chap-

ter 6, in which the measure of Lazarillo's hard-won self-satisfaction is his mouth, "porque mi boca era medida" (126) ("because
my mouth got what it wanted").[24] Chapter 4 then is superficially
anomalous: Lazarillo's hunger, to this point always on his and the
narrator's mind, is quieted here without a word of explanation or
further complaint, without explicit mention of buccal activity or
indication that he paid for the satisfaction of his hunger any other
quid pro quo than those same "otras cosillas que no digo."

In chapter 4 an obsession with sexual appetite (the Mercedarian's) and its gratification has replaced an obsessive craving
(Lazarillo's) for food. The latter is satisfied in the service of the former. The voracious regular satisfies his hunger every way he can,
and Lazarillo satisfies his own any way he must. Following this
episode Lazarillo's versatile oral performance continues to adapt
and evolve and to maintain its significance as a central thematic
pattern in the text, until finally the protagonist comes to earn a
good living as an official mouth-about-town: crier, hawker, merchant, auctioneer, and God knows what else—God, that is, and
the narrator's *vecinos, amigos,* and *señores.* Lazarillo's sexual development, meanwhile, seems to be arrested permanently at the
stage attained in chapter 4. Lázaro reports no genital adventures
following this initiation; he remains to the end an accommodating
middleman who busies himself—ever expanding and consolidat-
ing his hand-to-mouth existence ("que casi todas las cosas al oficio
tocantes pasan por mi mano" [130] ["almost everything touching
the profession passes through my hands"])—profiting from the
satisfaction of others' appetites (130).

Lázaro's verb choice in reporting his departure from the Mercedarian's service—"salí dél"—raises an alternative and complementary image of inversion that also is consistent with his tanta-
lizing invitation to speculate. Opting to say that he withdrew from
the Mercedarian, rather than choosing any of a half dozen available equivalent verbs of leave-taking (such as *dejar* ["leave"],
which he used at the points of closure of chapters 1 and 3, or *irse*
["go away"], in chapter 2, or *huirse* ["flee"], also in chapter 3, or *de-
spedirse* ["take leave of"], at the beginning of chapter 7), the narrator plants and leaves in the text, in a conspicuous place from which
he or the author easily could have removed it, a suggestion that

the intercourse hinted at here is to be construed with Lazarillo filling either of the two roles. The surface meaning of "the first shoes I wore in my life" then would cover not, or not only, Lazarillo's heterosexual initiation (which, I have suggested, seems not to have kindled a lingering interest along that line), but instead or in addition an inverted relation with his master, from whom Lazarillo "withdraws" exhausted after a week of wearing him.

The point finally and certainly is not to choose between these alternative readings, neither of which is so satisfactory as to exclude the other or to dissuade the imaginative reader from pursuing further possibilities. Rather we ought to take note of where and how Lázaro leads his readers (including us outside the fictional world), like birds pecking along a line of seeds arranged craftily to lure us into the hunter's net. "Let me tell you about an overheated monk (ha, ha, . . .), who was a Mercedarian (ha, ha, it figures, . . .), and a tireless womanizer, who wore out shoes/women (ha, ha, . . .), who gave me well-worn shoes/women (ha, ha, . . .), and who wore me out (ha, ha, . . .), and did other little things with me . . . , I'll not say just what (heh, heh, . . .), but will leave that to you to flesh out." Is this not a shameless display of the *arrimarse a los buenos* ("seeking the protection of one's betters") that Lázaro acknowledges is his lifelong master strategy?[25] In his adversaries'—that is to say, in his readers'—own erotic fantasies he finds the refuge, what in his Prologue he calls the "buen puerto" ("safe port"), where he hopes to ride out the storm of "fortunas, peligros y adversidades" in the embrace of the betters whom he has made his "amigos y señores."

In the event we choose any of these ways of filling the narrator's ellipsis, or if we come even to recognize Lázaro's invitation to flesh in his suggestion, the narrator scores big in this smallest of episodes. The reader who evinces an interest in this foreshortened confession of sexual initiation, and who maybe has a knack for reading its enigmatic signals, and perhaps feels satisfaction upon discovering a cogent clue or two, evidences thereby an embarrassing complicity and kinship with the Mercedarian and all who think and do and understand such things. Lazarillo, who (we are led to believe) ran away to tell another day that he *chose* to run away, ends up appearing less blameworthy than the pederast and the conscripted reader. Accomplishing this *tour de force* of double-binding, the anonymous author who created Lázaro damns at one and the same time his narrator and protagonist and the fourth master. No less indicted are those outside the fiction who share the Mercedarian's habit of exploitation, and those readers capable of understanding and enjoying this code, and even the simpler readers who see not and are as fooled by the narrator's words as were "la inocente gente" whom the *industrioso buldero* ("scheming seller of indulgences") of chapter 5 deceived with his talk and legerdemain (123, 125).

Of course this is a risky reading I am proposing. It forces a difficult question about critical reading. When and how far ought we push an intense interpretation where the text is suggestive to the extreme of fascinating its readers but also elliptic and esoteric, and where, what is more, the matter and its investigation are certain to be judged offensive by some? Do we leave possibilities unexplored, or perhaps suppress findings and hypotheses, and quietly withdraw, because the claims are unseemly or some readers may think them so? Do we cap the pen because these matters are (maybe) anomalous in Spanish prose fiction or because the matter is apparently slight, informing but a single paragraph, a single sentence in fact, that has been decorously papered over by a dozen estimable investigators? Or do we persevere, remembering that we are studying a work filled with unprecedented and unpredictable forms of communication, in which inherited formulas are never merely that and nothing more. In *Lazarillo de Tormes* no matter is inert; much is extraordinarily charged with insinuation. Partly in consequence the work exerts an unusual attraction for sophomores and savants alike for a thousand particular reasons, a hundred of them at least still beyond our understanding.[26]

We persevere, I believe, when we judge that the scabrous matters are important to the text and so long as we have hopes of persuading others of their significance. We persevere in careful exploration of a distasteful fragment such as chapter 4 when the findings dredged up can be shown to cohere with other parts of the expressive organization that is *Lazarillo*. That consistency of concern and expressive means is so probable in this instance that, while the risk of misreading seems high (especially as I have here isolated one part from related parts of *Lazarillo*'s expressive system), the undertaking as a critical project is not assailable.[27] It does not matter that the findings will remain subject to revision and adjustment; of what significant matter in *Lazarillo* is that not admitted?

We also persevere in the study of perverse sexuality in chapter 4, pressing the matter to the extreme of scholarly responsibility and then a bit further, for an additional powerful reason: because the narrator dares us to do so. The temptation is irresistible. Not in an isolated fashion, but here as before and afterward, the narrator proceeds with his defense against his neighbors and their authority by admitting some weakness on his part and that of others, implying more, and conscripting his readers' imaginations and memories to complete and generalize his claims.[28] The result for enlisted readers is lively entertainment bought at the cost of complicity in whatever malfeasance we manufacture cooperatively from our and the narrator's raw materials.

It seems that so long as we pay attention to the narrator's claims we are fated to be duped in one way or another. So crafty and seamless is Lázaro's rhetoric that its effects extend beyond the world of his readers into ours. Here—still, after 450 years—the narrator turns innocent readers into sympathizers by moving us occasionally and by entertaining us without cease. Those who on their third or thirtieth reading awaken from this treatment to feel their heads smarting from the *calabazadas* ("blows upside the ears") he administers with his bull, nevertheless submit to more drubbings. "Todo va desta manera," the narrator asserts, and the more effort we spend to resolve his ellipses and fix his allusions, the closer we find ourselves to joining the ranks of the Prologue's soldier, preacher, and gentleman jouster. Leading his readers to concede the typicality of his degraded *amos* ("masters"), *amigos,* and *señores,* and to laugh at them, the narrator induces us—readers in and outside the text—to cooperate in defiling the grounds on which, in a better world than his, he should be made to stand in judgment. Sex is one of the common denominators he uses to reduce us from judges of his behavior to participation in the demeanor he describes and to equivalence with him and his neighbors in Toledo.

Notes

1. I quote from Francisco Rico's edition (Madrid: Cátedra, 1987), at 11 and 6; subsequent page references appear within parentheses in my text. Following recent practice, I call the narrator Lázaro and the narrated life Lazarillo.

2. "Pretext" derives from L. *praetextus*, "outward show, pretense," from *praetexere*, "to weave in front, cloak, disguise, pretend." It seems that the narrator of this text disguises himself in a tissue woven of lies and truths depicting his community. Does the anonymous author invite us to imagine that the narrator is attempting "in good faith" to sketch his life? Or are we to understand instead that the narrator is twisting and turning, fictionalizing his *Vida*, from start to finish to satisfy his own, not Vuestra Merced's, purpose? We have only his twisted and turned testimony on which to form our judgment, and that evidence subverts every claim of *bona fides*.

3. "Perversity" and related terms in this study are understood to denote conduct that by the professed standards of the narrator's time (which is commensurate in many ways with the anonymous author's time) is so wrong and offensive to propriety as to be judged unnatural, grossly degraded, illegal, or ungodly. It is usual in ironic and satiric texts for sexual perversion, so understood, to represent the degradation of the body politic.

4. See Vasvari's persuasive study and bibliography, and Snow's subject index.

5. Rico's first notable contributions were the introduction and notes to *La novela picaresca española* and his Lazarillo de Tormes *y el punto de vista*. Important elaborations are gathered in the introduction and notes to his edition and in *Problemas*. Lázaro Carreter's "La ficción autobiográfica en el *Lazarillo de Tormes*" and "Construcción y sentido del *Lazarillo de Tormes*" are reprinted in his Lazarillo de Tormes *en la picaresca*. Guillén, at 271, affirmed with lucid economy that "Lázaro, más que Lazarillo, es el centro de gravedad de la obra" ("Lázaro, more than Lazarillo, is the work's center of gravity"). Gilman's study of Lázaro's development was titled significantly "The Death of Lazarillo de Tormes." Sieber's ground-breaker in the sexual field and in others is *Language and Society in* La vida de Lazarillo de Tormes.

6. Such experienced readers of *Lazarillo* as Gonzalo Sobejano and Raymond Willis nay say Harry Sieber's revelation of the Mercedarian's deviance. An instance of scholarly miopia might be Francisco Carillo's modern-seeming *Semiolingüística de la novela picaresca*, which cites Sieber from time to time but in summarizing Lazarillo's chapter 4 makes no mention of the ugliness Sieber patiently uncovered there. Carillo instead takes Lazarillo's shoes to be evidence of a "leve mejora" ("slight improvement") in his situation (58).

7. The narrator claims to be leveling with his first reader, to whom he offers the "entera noticia de mi persona" (11) ("complete account of myself"). He has other readers in mind also, and he explicitly recognizes that his layered text admits plural readings and authorizes two kinds, a deep reading yielding *agrado* and another more accessible, superficial, full of *deleite* (3–4). We who write about *Lazarillo* fancy ourselves the deep readers. So long as we read the text in either of these ways prepared by the narrator, the anonymous author stands over us scornful.

8. Valuable instructions for oral performance of *La Celestina* are appended to Fernando de Rojas's *Tragicomedia* in the poem of Alonso de Proaza, the author's friend. When Miguel de Cervantes's Alférez Campuzano nods off to sleep, leaving

his friend Peralta without company (except for us) while he reads the manuscript *El coloquio de los perros (The Dogs' Colloquy)*, we safely conclude that the somnolent soldier is far from cured of syphilis. No matter how much wine he consumed at lunch and during the telling of his own story, *El casamiento engañoso (The Deceitful Marriage)*, Campuzano—self-centered and self-indulgent as he was and remains—would scarcely have foregone the pleasure of observing, sharing, guiding, and correcting his companion's reactions to what is either his own ear-witness testimony of a droll miracle or one of the wittiest stories ever fabricated. Stories of worldly experience, such as Rojas's and Cervantes's and Lázaro's, require experienced, responsive, and demonstrative readers, and such texts surrender only a tithe of their riches to the seemly (readers who, respectful of "masterpieces," accept their authority submissively) and the companionable (readers who in effect nod rather than attend to miracles).

9. Lázaro never achieves Campuzano's rank, but he enjoys a full measure of the beguiling *don de habla* ("verbal facility") that enables both to be sometimes successful confidence men and crafters of twisted tales. Both tellers know that well-spoken claims do not have to be seen to be believed. "Es que yo oí y casi vi con mis ojos a estos dos perros" ("I heard these two dogs and I almost saw them with my own eyes"), says Campuzano, who moments later perjures himself affirming "lo que oí, y lo que vi, y lo que me atreveré a jurar con juramento que obligue . . . " (293–94) ("what I heard and what I saw and what I am ready to swear to on an oath. . . "). Extraordinary claims artfully reported may achieve a semblance of being so nearly palpable that they command belief.

10. On Lazarillo's commerce while in the chaplain's employ see my "Lazarillo and the Cathedral Chaplain. . . " and also "A Case of Functional Obscurity."

11. Burke invites us to "watch, in the structural analysis of the symbolic act, not only the matter of 'what equals what,' but also the matter of 'from what to what'"(3). Later he asks, "Should we not attach particular significance to the situations on which the work opens and closes, and the events by which the peripety, or reversal, is contrived? Hence, along with the distinction between opposing principles we should note the development *from what through what to what*. So we place great stress upon those qualitative points: the 'laying of the cornerstone,' the 'watershed moment,' and the 'valedictory,' or 'funeral wreath'" (70–71) (the italics are Burke's). For present purposes I fix the middle point of the "through what" at chapter 4, which is numerically the central chapter. It remains for us to determine whether it presents the peripety of a life or merely recounts a *faux pas*.

12. Manuel J. Asensio maintained that "el *Lazarillo* nos ofrece un clima artístico y moral, una castidad mental y expresiva, una limpieza, en todo aparte de cuanto es norma en los *fabliaux*; no conocemos sátira medieval ni *fabliau* que presente parecida mansedumbre, moderación y equidad en un mísero hijo del pueblo para juzgar a amos que con tanta crueldad lo trataron" (87) ("*Lazarillo* presents an artistic and moral tone, a mental and expressive purity, a cleanliness, entirely different from what is normal in *fabliaux*; we know of no medieval satire or *fabliau* that endows a lowly child of the people with so much gentleness, moderation, and fairness for judging masters who treated him so cruelly").

13. How many readers pause to ponder the names of Lázaro's parents and can recall them later, or note the narrator's lifelong indifference to the plight of his *hermanico* and the mother he left behind "padeciendo mil importunidades" (20–21)

("suffering a thousand indignities")? As for the end of the story, only recently have most readers accepted the identification of the Prologue's *caso* ("case") with the ménage à trois of chapter 7. The allusive language of that last chapter invites more study, and the significance of the reference to Lázaro's brief employment as an *hombre de justicia* ("officer of the law") remains unclear. Increasingly commentators wonder whether we are to suppose that Lázaro finally—that is, when he writes his account—is at the peak of his good fortune, such as it is, or that he has slipped some significant but indeterminable way down again, perhaps into the clutches of jailers or Inquisitors.

14. Lázaro's narrative is doubly a pseudo-autobiographical sketch: it is a fiction fashioned by the anonymous author; it also is a fiction concocted by his narrator, by shuffling facts, lore, and lies into sufficient order. Rico (130*, 2, 13, 111, and *Problemas* 113–51) argues reasonably that the division of the text into *tratados* ("chapters") was not of Lázaro's doing, nor even of his author's. There are counterarguments for respecting the conventional chapter divisions, but even if we concede the matter for now, the importance of this fourth bit of narrative is but further disguised, not diminished. The text here remains an ellipic, allusive, coherent and decisive part of the whole. Harry Sieber, whose study of this chapter is the most insightful to date, affirms that "the fourth *tratado* plays an integral part from the beginning to the end of [Lázaro's] autobiography; that is, it functions as the central link in the chain of symbols of the implicit: *herraduras-zapatos-calzas*" (55), by which he means a cunningly represented series of exchanges of sexual services for material goods and social comfort.

15. The remarkable brevity of the episode detains for only a few seconds those readers who thirst after a good story. Other readers who have learned the lessons that the text attempts to teach from the first about its intensity, its buried troves of allusion and suggestion, will suspect that the abrupt change of pace, remarked by Manuel Ferrer-Chivite (244), from three crafted stories to a single paragraph lacking anecdote is an invitation to stop and puzzle paradigmatically before ambling on in the amiable company of the *buldero* ("seller of indulgences") and his accomplice.

16. Molho is brief but acute: "El fraile . . . [es] mundano, libertino y vicioso, con tendencia a la pederastia, pues Lázaro corre un púdico velo sobre las razones por las que tuvo que dejarle" (42) ("The friar . . . [is] worldly, a libertine, and vicious, with a tendency to pederasty, though Lázaro pulls a curtain of modest reserve over his reasons for having to leave him"). Francisco Márquez Villanueva agrees: "no cabe duda de que se desea aludir *a lo peor*, a pecados nefandos" (79) ("there can be no doubt that he desires to allude to the worst thing imaginable, abominable sins"). Asensio incorporates Vossler's remarks (from 1941 and 1942) and Bataillon's (1954) into his own 87n29, where his dissent puts a positive spin on Lázaro's "cosillas": "Nosotros creemos que, puestos a imaginar lo peor, avances deshonestos del fraile aceleran su huida; es algo a favor de Lázaro, no en su contra; ni en su carácter ni en toda su vida hay el menor indicio para suponer esa inconfesable relación" ("We believe that the worst we can imagine is that the friar's improper advances accelerated [Lázaro's] flight; this is in Lázaro's favor, not against him; neither in his character nor in all his life is there the slightest indication for supposing an unconfessable relationship"). Fernando Lázaro Carreter, in "Construcción y sentido del *Lazarillo de Tormes*," also concedes the homosexual character of the allusion while sparing

Lazarillo the experience: "La reticencia final . . . parece aludir a asechanzas nefandas. . . . Obviado ese peligro, el muchacho se encamina hacia una varonía que sucumbirá a otra amenaza, pero a esa no" (111–12) ("His reticence at the end . . . seems to allude to an abominable trap. Having escaped this danger, the youngster makes his way toward an adulthood that will succumb to another menace, but not to that one"). Víctor García de la Concha echoes Lázaro Carreter's understanding: "La asechanza de corrupción se perfila . . . ; es el testimonio de una—otra—dificultad vencida . . . ; no cede a ese tipo de corrupción" (103) ("There is a hint of a corrupting entrapment . . . ; it is testimony to another difficulty overcome . . . ; he does not give in to that kind of corruption"); but Gonzalo Sobejano will not allow so much as an allusion to homosexuality: "Puede tratarse de cualquier otra cosa, por ejemplo, de que Lazarillo tuviese que hacer recados de alcahuete"(32) ("It may be any other sort of matter, for example, concerning Lazarillo's having to engage in procuring"); see too his review of Sieber. Recently José Manuel López de Abiada echoes this absolution and dismisses all arguments to the contrary without so much as a bibliographical acknowledgment of their authors (75–76). For Gethin Hughes "the *fraile de la Merced* did not play a vital role in [Lázaro's] development, and their relationship is relegated to a matter of *cosillas*" (4).

17. Bataillon's first, thin evidence of this is repeated by most Lazarillo commentators; see Rico's 110n2, but also Bennassar's chapter 10, esp. 353. Sometimes allusions that Lázaro and his author expected readers to grasp easily are as hard to see today as the nose on one's face; for Víctor García de la Concha, the Mercedarian's features are "perfectamente tópicos" ("perfectly stereotypical"), individualized within a "tradicionalidad generalizada" ("widely generalized tradition"); he adds that "la animadversión contra los mercedarios era general" (177–78) ("the enmity felt against the Mercedarians was general"). No doubt; but his supporting quotation from *La Lozana andaluza*, the sexual charge of which he overlooks, shows that ridicule of the Order could be as phallically pointed as it is sometimes anti-Semitic: the quoted text speaks of "un hermano fraire de la Merced, que tiene una nariz como asa de cántaro y pie como remo de galera" ("a Mercedarian friar who has a nose like the handle on a pitcher and a foot like a galley oar"). It requires no Quevedo to triangulate, identify, and measure the alluded and no doubt comparably oversized concealed member. Our awareness of the allusive potential of the Mercedarian has sharpened in the past decade thanks to several scholars, among whom pride of discovery goes to B. Bussell Thompson and J. K. Walsh; see their "The Mercedarian's Shoes." The present essay is my reply to the reservation they express (445) in the course of a generous and discerning assessment of my previous claims concerning this matter.

18. Joseph Ricapito sees the superlative qualification of the Mercedarian as a sign of the consistency of chapter 4 with the preceding three, each of which introduces a master who is in his way *primus inter pares* (xii).

19. Celestina developed an erotic message and escort service into a full-service community social welfare agency centered on her extraordinary person: she kept a census book; visited her *devotos* in convents, monasteries, and noble houses; provided rooms and girls for repressed clergy; accepted the risks and punishment; tutored the inexperienced; repaired damaged goods; and much more. In contrast the Mercedarian's dalliance is one-dimensional, selfish, and inconsequential. It is easy to understand, easy to attack, and easy to discount as typical, and, consequently,

useful for the narrator's purpose. "Todo va desta manera" ("Everything goes this same way"), Lázaro would have us believe.

20. Much has been written before and since Sieber's revealing pages 50–53 about the sexuality of shoes. William A. Rossi claimed that "the sexual kinship of the foot and the shoe has been inevitable. . . . This male (foot) and female (shoe) relationship is both ancient and universal" (13). Sigmund Freud affirmed that in dream symbolism "shoes and slippers are female genitals" (158), and the foot, male (156). Ferrer-Chivite and Thompson and Walsh adduce corroborating examples from Spanish literature and folklore.

21. The gift of the master's cast-off clothes frequently was part of servants' compensation; recall *La Celestina*, and *Lazarillo*, chapter 7, 131; see Rico 111n8 and especially Sieber 53–55.

22. By "Lázaro's readers" I mean here and throughout the fictional public for whose amusement, distraction, information, and warning the narrative is variously intended and calculated. A marvel of the anonymous author's creation is the thoroughness with which Lázaro's calculations work—in the same various ways—also on several kinds of real readers of this fiction. This prolongation of the narrator's success has made dupes of us all. It remains difficult to resist our identification with Lázaro's readers and to define and sort valid distinctions among readers in and outside the text and their relations to the internal and external authors. For an admirable effort at ordering these author, narrator, reader ratios in *Lazarillo* see Edward H. Friedman's "Chaos Restored: Authorial Control and Ambiguity in *Lazarillo de Tormes.*"

23. Readers will recall the bread Lazarillo stole from the mouth of the blindman's sack (27), the coins he kissed and tongued (29), the wine jug he kissed (30) and sucked from through a straw (31) and then drilled from between his master's knees so as to catch a stream of "dulces tragos" ("sweet gulps") "en la boca" ("in my mouth") without losing a drop (31). He ingests an unfair share of his master's cluster of grapes, and then a sausage, pursued down his throat by the blind man's phallic nose ("luenga y afilada, . . . se había augmentado un palmo," "cumplidísima nariz," "trompa") (38–40) ("long and pointed, . . . it had grown by a hand," "a perfectly huge nose," "a trunk"), which the youngster regrets not having bitten off and swallowed (42). Later Lázaro accounts for his success in begging by calling it a skill "mamado en la leche, quiero decir que con el gran maestro el ciego lo aprendí" (87) ("sucked in my mother's milk, I mean I learned it from my great teacher the blindman"). About his service in Maqueda he recalls bread offerings that he kissed a thousand times and nibbled (58, 60), and cheese rinds (65), and tools for penetrating the priest's bread box: a knife and also a skeleton key that he "metía cada noche . . . en la boca" ("put each night . . . in my mouth") where it whistled with his breath and was identified with a serpent (65–69). In Toledo Lazarillo recommends himself to his new master "entre todos mis iguales, por de mejor garganta" (76) ("the best applicant among many, because of my superior throat"). He mouths down begged bread and sips water from the squire's broken-mouth ("desbocada") jug (77–78), and eats cabbage leaves (86) and gorges additional begged bread (87), calves' feet, and tripe, while the squire stares at his lap, salivating: "que no partía sus ojos de mis faldas, que aquella sazón servían de plato" (89) ("he did not take his eyes off my lap, which at the time was my plate").

Javier Herrero opened critical discussion of chapter 1's phallic sausage and sexualized nose and the blindman's jug, filled with sweet nectar and held on his lap between his legs, through which his boy sucked on a straw to get at the goodness. On the evidence of the sucking and biting in chapter 1, the probing insertions and bashing in chapter 2, and Lázaro's and Lazarillo's gratuitous humiliation of the doglike, bone-sucking, and ultimately uncaring squire in chapter 3, and the protagonist's subsequent career of diverse oral transactions extending beyond chapter 4 to the narrator's present time of oral-conditioned writing, which also is a variant of the bite-the-hand(breast)-that-feeds-me habit, one could describe Lázaro's narrative as an "oral history" in a Freudian sense of the key term. So viewed, the narrator is seen to be arrested in the oral-sadistic stage, in which biting and devouring (remembered and enacted again in the telling of the story) attempt to accomplish the destruction of a life-long series of unsatisfactory objects. The blindman, "que me recibía no por mozo, sino por hijo" (22) ("who took me on as his son, not his servant"), is the first in the sucked and bitten succession of Lazarillo's anaclitic object choices, all of whom are substitutes modeled after the mother (whom he revisits only in memory—if we believe the narrator—and for the purpose of revengeful exposure). In his relations with each surrogate Lazarillo's self-preservative needs remain associated (as they are in the beginning) with sexual satisfaction, but they hold that satisfaction subordinate, perverting it. That is, moved by self-preservative instincts, Lazarillo forever subordinates sexual satisfaction while seeking to punish in one way or another his successive objects, who are reiterations of the prototype who failed to feed and protect him. This way of viewing the text will reward thorough study; J. Laplanche and J.-B. Pontalis provide helpful guidance; s.v. "Anaclisis," "Anaclitic Type," "Oral-Sadistic Stage," "Perversion."

24. I do not recall previous discussion of the sensuality and orality of the *buldero*'s bribes; in Lázaro's efficient prose, so spare on the surface, the specification of several fruits ("limas" ["limes"], "naranjas" ["apples"], "un melocotón" ["a peach"], "duraznos" ["peaches"], "peras" ["pears"]), all but one in pairs, seems to say (at least) that in his recollection or imagination he associates this fruitful episode with the achievement of abundance, and not with the travails ("hartas fatigas") he claims he suffered but does not relate (125). Lazarillo passes from famine (chapter 3) to the bull-seller's feast (chapter 5), from cabbage leavings (chapter 3) to lettuce heads (chapter 5), from exploited factotum (chapter 3) to profiting coconspirator (chapter 5), via the peripety of chapter 4. More remains to be said about the edibles in chapter 7; see André Michalski's "El pan, el vino y la carne en el *Lazarillo de Tormes.*" On the dirt that adheres to the coins of chapter 6 see my "Lazarillo and the Cathedral Chaplain." On chapter 4 as the turning point where sex replaces hunger as principal theme and motivator, see Benito Brancaforte, esp. 566.

25. "Mi viuda madre . . . determinó arrimarse a los buenos, por ser uno dellos" (chapter 1, 15) ("My widowed mother . . . resolved to seek to associate with her betters, to be one of them"); and: "Señor, . . . yo determiné de arrimarme a los buenos" (chapter 7, 133); with variants including: "Hijo, . . . procura de ser bueno" (22) ("My son, . . . procure to be good") and: "Todos mis trabajos y fatigas hasta entonces pasados fueron pagados con alcanzar lo que procuré, que fue un oficio real" (128) ("All of the hardships and frustrations I had suffered up to then were paid for when I procured what I had sought, which was a government position"). We have seen above that Lázaro claims to have learned from the *buldero* of chapter 5 how to profit from satisfying the tastes of the gullible, "procurando tener los propicios" (113).

26. Francisco Rico writes persuasively of the functional efficiency of *Lazarillo* in all its particulars, including its many apparently routine formulas: "Importa insistir en que . . . en el *Lazarillo* no existen materiales *neutros,* y los que pudieran juzgarse tales, si examinados de cerca, acaban por revelarse datos significativos—y más: polisémicos" (*Problemas* 13; the author's emphasis) ("It is important to insist that . . . in *Lazarillo* there are no neutral materials, and those that might be judged so, when they are examined closely, reveal that they are significant data and, what is more, they are polysemic"). The same critic, however, is dismissive of studies that reveal a pattern of sexual innuendo in chapter 4 and in chapter 6 as well. Of the former he laments, echoing Asensio's 1959 assessment: "En años recientes, casi toda la crítica ha querido ver aquí la alusión eufemística a unas relaciones nefandas entre el mozo y el fraile. En la vida de Lázaro, sin embargo, no hay el menor indicio para suponer tal escabrosidad, y del fraile sólo se dice que es amigo de las 'mujercillas'" (112n9) ("In recent years almost all the critics have attempted to see here a euphemistic allusion to some abominable relations between the lad and the friar. There is not, however, in all Lázaro's life, the least reason to imagine anything so scabrous, and concerning the friar it is said only that he is a friend of the 'common women'").

27. This essay has studied the matter of chapter 4 that the narrator screened from easy view, his under-the-counter copy. Elsewhere I will examine the means used to accomplish this screening: the erotic decoration of the surface of the text (mentioned above in passing) and especially the representation of the Mercedarian as a *pariente* and frequent flier to the *mujercillas* who befriend Lazarillo in chapter 3.

28. The blindman is a pious fraud, but the narrator is not critical of him nor does he invite his readers' criticism of the *ciego;* readers are not surprised or offended, because we are led to suppose such fraud is common and accepted. The priest of Maqueda is as empty of charity as his house is bare; the narrator registers no surprise and invites no indignation: the priest inherited his avarice with his clerical habit. Similarly we are induced to think the squire pathetic, laughable, and typical; and so on.

Works Cited

Anonymous. *Lazarillo de Tormes.* Ed. Francisco Rico. Madrid: Cátedra, 1987.

Asensio, Manuel J. "La intención religiosa del *Lazarillo de Tormes* y Juan de Valdés." *HR* 27 (1959): 78–102.

Bennassar, Bartolomé, Catherine Brault-Noble, et al. *L'Inquisition Espagnole, XVᵉ– XIXᵉ Siècle.* Paris: Hachette, 1979.

Brancaforte, Benito. "La abyección en el 'Lazarillo de Tormes.'" *Cuadernos Hispanoamericanos* 387 (1982): 551–66.

Burke, Kenneth. "The Philosophy of Literary Form." *The Philosophy of Literary Form: Studies in Symbolic Action.* 3rd ed. Berkeley: Univ. of California Press, 1973. 1–137.

Carillo, Francisco. *Semiolingüística de la novela picaresca.* Madrid: Cátedra, 1982.

Cervantes, Miguel de. *Novela del casamiento engañoso. Novelas ejemplares.* Ed. Harry Sieber. Vol. 2. Madrid: Ediciones Cátedra, 1981. 2 vols.

Ferrer-Chivite, Manuel. "Lazarillo de Tormes y sus zapatos: Una interpretación del tratado IV a través de la literatura y el folklore." *Literatura y folklore: Problemas de intertextualidad. Actas del Segundo Symposium Internacional del Departamento de Español de la Universidad de Groningen.* Ed. J. L. Alonso-Hernández. Salamanca: Univ. de Salamanca, 1983. 243–69.

Freud, Sigmund. *Introductory Lectures on Psychoanalysis.* Trans. James Strachey. New York: W. W. Norton, 1977.

Friedman, Edward H. "Chaos Restored: Authorial Control and Ambiguity in *Lazarillo de Tormes.*" *Crítica Hispánica* 3 (1981): 59–73.

García de la Concha, Víctor. *Nueva lectura del Lazarillo; El deleite de la perspectiva.* Madrid: Editorial Castalia, 1981.

Gilman, Stephen. "The Death of Lazarillo de Tormes." *PMLA* 81 (1966): 149–66.

Guillén, Claudio. "La disposición temporal del *Lazarillo de Tormes.*" *HR* 25 (1957): 264–79.

Herrero, Javier. "The Great Icons of the *Lazarillo:* The Bull, the Wine, the Sausage and the Turnip." *Ideology & Literature* 1 (1978): 3–18.

Hughes, Gethin. "*Lazarillo de Tormes:* The Fifth 'Tratado.'" *Hispanófila* 21 (1977): 1–9.

Laplanche, J. and J.-B. Pontalis. *The Language of Psycho-Analysis.* Trans. Donald Nicholson-Smith. New York: W. W. Norton, 1973.

Lázaro Carreter, Fernando. "Construcción y sentido del *Lazarillo de Tormes.*" *Abaco* 1 (1969): 45–134.

———. "La ficción autobiográfica en el *Lazarillo de Tormes.*" *Litterae Hispanae et Lusitanae.* Munich: Hueber, 1968. 195–213.

———. Lazarillo de Tormes *en la picaresca.* Barcelona: Ariel, 1972.

López de Abiada, José Manuel. "Alusiones, reticencias y silencios locuaces en el *Lazarillo:* Reflexiones sobre algunos aspectos o pasajes velados y apostillas al léxico erótico del Tratado IV." *Iberoromania* 31 (1990): 65–81.

Márquez Villanueva, Francisco. "La actitud espiritual del *Lazarillo de Tormes.*" *Espiritualidad y literatura en el siglo XVI.* Madrid: Alfaguara, 1968. 67–137.

Michalski, André. "El pan, el vino y la carne en el *Lazarillo de Tormes.*" *La picaresaca: Orígenes, textos y estructuras.* Ed. Manuel Criado de Val. Madrid: Fundación Universitaria Española, 1979. 413–20.

Molho, Maurice. *Introducción al pensamiento picaresco.* Trans. Augusto Gálvez-Cañero y Pidal. Salamanca: Anaya, 1972; first publ. in French, 1968.

Ricapito, Joseph. "Language, Style and Idea in *Lazarillo de Tormes.*" *Tri-linear Edition of Lazarillo de Tormes of 1554; Burgos, Alcalá de Henares, Amberes.* Madison: Univ. of Wisconsin Press, 1987.

Rico, Francisco. Lazarillo de Tormes *y el punto de vista.* Barcelona: Seix Barral, 1970.

———. *La novela picaresca española,* I. Barcelona: Planeta, 1967.

———. *Problemas del* Lazarillo. Madrid: Cátedra, 1988.

Rossi, William A. *The Sex Life of the Foot and Shoe.* Ware: Wordsworth, 1976.

Shipley, George A. "A Case of Functional Obscurity: The Master Tambourine-Painter of *Lazarillo, Tratado VI.*" *MLN* 97 (1982): 225–53.

———. "Lazarillo and the Cathedral Chaplain: A Conspiratorial Reading of *Lazarillo de Tormes, Tratado VI.*" *Symposium* 37 (1983): 216–41.

Sieber, Harry. *Language and Society in* La vida de Lazarillo de Tormes. Baltimore: Johns Hopkins Univ. Press, 1978.

Snow, Joseph T. Celestina *by Fernando de Rojas: An Annotated Bibliography of World Interest, 1930–1985.* Madison: Hispanic Seminary of Medieval Studies, 1985.

Sobejano, Gonzalo. "La picaresca y otros apuntes." *HR* 43 (1975): 25–41.

———. Rev. of Harry Sieber's *Language and Society in* Lazarillo de Tormes. *HR* 50 (1982): 488–91.

Thompson, B. Bussell, and J. K. Walsh. "The Mercedarian's Shoes (Perambulations on the fourth *tratado* of *Lazarillo de Tormes*. *MLN* 103 (1988): 440–48.

Vasvari, Louise. "Vegetal-Genital Onomastics in the *Libro de buen amor*." *RPh* 17 (1988): 1–29.

Willis, Raymond. Rev. of Harry Sieber's *Language and Society in* Lazarillo de Tormes. *Hispania* 63 (1980): 430.

◆ **Chapter 3**

Picturing the Picaresque: *Lazarillo* and Murillo's *Four Figures on a Step*

Janis A. Tomlinson and Marcia L. Welles

In attempting to arrive at a definition of the *pícaro,* Claudio Guillén asks, "Should one attempt a portrait of him, alone and with no background (as in Murillo's paintings of young ragamuffins)?" (75); elsewhere, Paul Julian Smith has challenged what he terms the "pictorialist" readings of the genre. Smith proposes instead "a revised model of literary representation which, unlike pictorialism, does not suppress the contradictions inherent in the picaresque, falsely reducing the works to an aesthetic continuity which may be consumed without effort by the modern reader" (79). Smith identifies the pictorialist with the "unitary" (88), a concept that might be better expressed were he to replace the term "pictorialist" with "perspectival" and in so doing refer specifically to a system that imposes unity on a painted illusion.

Visual metaphors permeate literary criticism of the picaresque: cannot the insights of textual interpretation be applied profitably to an analysis of images? We here explore the interrelationship of the picaresque and the pictorial: as the meaning of *Lazarillo de Tormes* (published in 1554)[1] is in large part determined by visual acts, so is the painting *Four Figures on a Step* by Bartolomé Esteban Murillo (Figure 1) implicitly informed by the literary traditions that preceded it, known and understood by competent viewers. The painting has a textual background—specifically, the *Lazarillo.*

The subject of *Four Figures on a Step,* attributed on stylistic grounds to Murillo's midcareer (ca. 1655–60), is unique not only within the context of Murillo's oeuvre, but also within that of golden age Spanish painting. Its composition contradicts the uni-

Figure 1. Bartolomé Estaban Murillo, *Four Figures on a Step*, ca. 1655–60, oil on canvas, 109.9 x 143.5 cm. Courtesy Kimbell Art Museum, Forth Worth, Texas.

tary aspect attributed by Smith to the pictorial: although encompassed by a frame, these four figures have little relation to one another. Nor are they content to pose in a passive manner, allowing themselves to become the mere objects of the viewer's gaze. Three of them engage us, and in so doing offer a challenge to find out who they are.[2] Staging enhances this appeal as three of the figures lean, lie, or sit on a foreground ledge that appears to be contiguous with the viewer's space. Since it does not offer an explicit narrative, *Four Figures on a Step* forces us to read clues in order to grasp its meaning. Specific details of the *Lazarillo*, upon which literary scholars have focused to recover the repressed and understand the silences of the unsaid, serve to fill in the narrative gaps left by the painter.

The criticism of Murillo's painting to date shows that art historians—like those critics of the picaresque with whom Smith takes issue—have been eager to impose upon the painting a thematic unity that is simply not there. When first exhibited in London at the British Institution in 1838, the scene was described as a group of peasants. When sold at Christie's in 1923, it was described as a Spanish peasant family: "A middle aged woman, wearing horned spectacles, is seated with her hands on the head of a boy who lies in front of her, while another boy is seated, wearing a brown hat, with a girl by his side" (*Catalogue* no. 284). Two years later, the painting was exhibited at the Ehrlich Galleries in New York, where it was identified as "A Family Group—Presumed to be Doña Beatrix, wife of Murillo, and their three children" (*Exhibition*).

Most recently, in an article of 1982, Jonathan Brown discussed *Four Figures on a Step* within the context of a group of erotic paintings by Murillo that includes the better-known *Two Women at a Window* (Figure 2). Brown relates Murillo's work to a *Street Scene* by the Flemish painter Michael Sweerts, part of the Italian group of genre painters known as the Bamboccianti, whose works were collected by Spanish patrons. Comparing the Murillo to the Sweerts, Brown concludes that both portray a theme of prostitution. He also calls attention to the "mirada atrayente e indiscreta de una joven— alluring and indiscreet look of a young woman" (38) who represents sensuality, and suggests that she lifts her veil perhaps to offer herself to the viewer. She places her hand on the shoulder of the young man, identified by Brown as a possible client.

Rosa López Torrijos has discussed *Four Figures on a Step* (entitling it *Familia de mendigos*) in defining the picaresque in seventeenth-century painting. Yet a comparison to other works she mentions serves only to underscore its unique structure. She begins by citing the paintings of tawdrily dressed children by

Figure 2. Bartolomé Estaban Murillo, *Two Women at a Window*, ca. 1655–60, oil on canvas, 125.1 x 104.5 cm. Courtesy Widener Collection, copyright © 1994 Board of Trustees, National Gallery of Art, Washington, D.C.

Murillo and Villavicencio, painted around or after 1670, that attest to a growing market for such themes in late-seventeenth-century Spain. These scenes, however, differ markedly from the *Four Figures*, since they are held together by a unified composition that is reinforced by anecdote; painterly facture and subtle colorism also harmonize the composition. In turning to the *Four Figures*, we discover that its picaresque nature is qualified as much by struc-

Figure 3. Jusepe de Ribera, *Blind Old Beggar*, ca. 1632, oil on canvas, 124.5 x 101.7 cm. Courtesy Allen Memorial Art Museum, Oberlin College, Oberlin, Ohio; R.T. Miller Jr. Fund, 1955.

ture as by subject, and question the application of the term merely on the basis of subject matter.

Perhaps closer in structure to the *Four Figures* is the *Blind Old Beggar* (Figure 3) by Jusepe de Ribera of about 1632. Here the Lazarillo appeals to the viewer as the blindman holds a cup, with a piece of paper that bears the inscription, "Dies Illa / Dies illa" identified by Craig Felton as "a repetition of the second phrase of that segment of the Requiem mass announcing the Last Judgment: "Dies Irae, Dies Illa" (Day of wrath, that day). As in his better-known *Clubfooted Boy*, Ribera uses the cartellino inscription to remind us of the importance of charity in the final accounting of "That Day." Although Ribera's image—like the *Four Figures on a Step*—minimizes narrative, it nevertheless possesses an ulterior rationale as an emblem to inspire Christian charity. The relationship of figure and viewer presented by Ribera anticipates that offered by Murillo, as the figures are placed in the foreground, and Lazarillo, juxtaposed to the blindman, not only sees but confronts the viewer. The meaning of his appeal is elucidated by reference to the *Lazarillo*, where a similar appeal to the reader is made by the fictional character, as narrator of his own life.

At the end of his prologue, the narrator of the *Lazarillo* broadens the horizons of his readership to include others beyond the immediate recipient of the document, identified only as "Vuestra Merced":[3] "and those who have inherited noble estates may see how little is due to their own efforts, since Fortune favored them, but rather how much has been accomplished by those who have rowed hard and skillfully against the tide and reached safe harbor" (xviii).[4] As readers (literate, privileged people), we inevitably find ourselves in a position equivalent to that of the addressed narratee, witness to the prosecution of the ambiguous *caso* at hand—a reference (one can assume) to the illicit *ménage à trois* of Lázaro's protector, the Archpriest of San Salvador, the Archpriest's domestic servant and Lázaro's wife, and Lázaro himself (Rico 5–7; Sieber 46; Shipley, "A Case of Functional Obscurity"). Unwittingly, the reader becomes a member of the jury in a case where wrongdoing is denied.

Even before the sequence of events confronts us, we are implicated from the outset and cannot assume a detached position. The fixed I/you opposition (the narrative "yo—I" vs. "los que heredaron nobles estados—those who have inherited noble estates"), defined objectively along the socioeconomic lines of class and lineage, is established only to be immediately dislodged. Whatever the authorial intention may have been, the result is a forced confrontation between the esteemed state of *being* and *having* and the disparaged state of *doing* and *acquiring* (Molho). Although the narrative persona of the prologuist may be, as Stephen Gilman characterized him, "cynical, ignorant, presumptuous, and adulatory" (153), he imposes upon us the requirement not of sympathy but of empathy: a vicarious identification with a marginalized and disreputable Other, whom we cannot easily cast aside.

Because it is here that the relationship between reader and narrator is established, the prologue acts as a frame beckoning our access to the world represented therein, as the author seeks to charm us in anticipation of the moral transgressions to follow. And, as Paul Julian Smith reminds us in his application of Derrida's discussion of the "parergon" to the picaresque, the frame cannot be relegated to the merely supplemental or marginal (84–88; 119–26). The *Lazarillo* would be a very different work without its prologue: a series of comic incidents involving a protagonist in whose life we are not implicated. Analogously, without a containing frame, *Four Figures* might be seen as four disparate lowlife types. Yet this is not the case. By encompassing four characters—even in the absence of setting or perspective—the frame necessarily implies a beholder and reinforces the gazes of the three figures who solicit our interpretation.

Hereafter it is only "Vuestra Merced" who is addressed directly, in the very first lines of the text ("Pues sepa Vuestra Merced" [99]) and again near the end ("como Vuestra Merced habrá oído" [205]). This figure of authority, therefore, who like us stands outside, is also inscribed within the frame, as is the royal couple in the mirror image in *Las Meninas*. As the characters in the painting are subordinated to the reflected presence of the king and queen, so does Lazarillo defer to the power of Vuestra Merced. Leo Steinberg commented of Velázquez that "he located the picture's dramatic and psychological focus outside itself, displaced from what the picture actually shows to what it beholds. It is as though the depicted scene were a dependency, caught in reaction to its deferred center" (52). The same can be said of the author of the *Lazarillo*, who located the "dramatic and psychological focus" of the narrative outside of the main body of the text, centered on the surveillant addressee. *Four Figures on a Step* similarly implicates the viewer. In painting and text, the frame also serves to delimit, as the looks outward and the scrutiny inward meet at the boundary line between propriety and impropriety.

In *Four Figures on a Step* the characters, like Lazarillo, defy the constraints of their illusionistic world. What in fact unites these figures is the convergence of their outward gaze upon the spectator, whose assumed presence unifies the composition. The work thus presents a radical alternative to what Michael Fried has called absorptive images, which ignore or deny the presence of the beholder; Murillo's figures have no apparent reason for existing other than to address us and to be seen by us. The gaudy costume of the youth on the left, the grimace of the woman behind as well as her conspicuous play with her veil, the stare of the older woman demonstrate a concern with outward display characteristic of a theatrical mode (Alpers 35).

The concept of theatricality might also be applied to the manner in which Lazarillo represents himself to the reader. Conscious of playing a role, Lazarillo offers us a manipulated self-portrait—a narcissistic projection rather than a confessional *mea culpa.* This is accomplished in the *Lazarillo* by means of narrative strategies, which Shipley has identified as "expedient renaming and recontextualization" ("A Case of Functional Obscurity" 226). For example, the emphasis on the early years and the first three masters (80.6 percent of the text, according to Shipley's calculations ["A Case of Functional Obscurity" 226n3]) functions to distract the reader, to displace the focus from the later and older years (when Lazarillo becomes a willing and knowing participant), to the earlier and younger years of innocent victimization. The prologuist's offer to give an "entera noticia de mi persona" (96) by beginning at birth and not *in medias res* is not a technique of greater honesty, but one that enables a more favorable and compelling self-presentation.

We recall that in the end Lazarillo has found satisfaction, married to the concubine of the Archpriest. Again, the conclusion emphasizes the work's dramatic irony, by making the viewer aware of a disparity between Lazarillo's posture and what indeed is going on. There is an abrupt and willed happy ending to the story: "Pues en este tiempo estaba en mi prosperidad y en la cumbre de toda buena fortuna—At long last I was prosperous, and at the zenith of all good fortune" (205, 74). Lazarillo's staged representation is further complicated by the mediation between the self-induced distortions (of the "I") and those necessitated by the demands of the external probing eye of "Vuestra Merced."

These issues of sight and perception are essential to the meaning of *Four Figures on a Step*. The sleeping boy, unseeing, unconscious, and unaware of being seen, might epitomize Lazarillo's state prior to his awakening with his first master, who, though blind, "sees" more than his young guide. Lazarillo is tricked by the blindman into listening to the sound of the stone bull, only to have his head smashed against it. He describes his awakening:

> It seemed to me that at that moment I awoke from the innocence in which, as a child, I had been sleeping until then. I said to myself:
> "This fellow is right. I must open my eyes and be on guard, for I am alone in the world, and must learn to look out for myself." (5–6)[5]

The identification of Lazarillo's awakening, and his entry into picaresque life, with visual perception is a theme implicit in Murillo's painting. The sleeping boy is bracketed by the woman whose sight is sharpened by her glasses (more on these in a moment) and also by the dressed-up, laughing youth.

On a narrative level, the tawdry finery of the youth standing on the left suggests his identification with Lazarillo in the seventh and final *tratado* of the novel. His attitude conveys well the self-satisfaction of the hero at the novel's close. We recall that at the conclusion of the penultimate chapter Lazarillo had saved enough of his earnings to dress himself "honradamente" in secondhand clothing: "a jerkin of old fustian, a worn coat with braided sleeves and collar, a cape that had once been fuzzy, and a sword, one of the early ones made by Cuellar" (70).[6] Although Murillo, painting a century after the novel was first published, does not duplicate this costume, the one worn by the young man might be seen as an updated, exaggerated version that emphasizes the cheap and inappropriate ostentation of Lazarillo's.

The character of the youth is revealed fully only as we turn to the woman standing behind him, who suggests that his good humor and well-being are predicated upon self-deception. She lifts up her veil and grimaces, her distorted face suggesting a wink. That her expression is a conspiratorial one aimed at the viewer (and would have been understood as such by a seventeenth-century audience) is clarified by Covarrubias's definition of the verbs *guiñar* and *guiznar:*

> To make a sign to someone with the eye, closing it and opening it; and beckon, the indication with the eye and some bodily movement . . . And thus he who beckons summons the person, indicating to that person that he should bind himself to the caller's will and intention.[7]

That the woman reveals to us a secret is also suggested by her lifting her *toca* or veil—in so doing, she not only sees, but also unveils before the viewer the ironic nature of the young man's contentment.

The woman's veil also implies something about her character. Because of the anonymity it afforded the wearer, and its consequent adoption by prostitutes, the veil became so highly controversial as to merit a series of legal prohibitions (1586, 1590, 1600, 1639) and eventually, a book-length discussion, León Pinelo's *Velos antiguos i modernos en los rostros de las mugeres, sus conveniencias i daños* (Cruz 139; Perry 150–51). The veil was considered a vehicle of deception:

> Preferred by women because it makes them seem what they are not: she, who judged beautiful when veiled, unveiled is recognized as abominable: because hiding the defects of the face, the veil only displays the best of most women, which are her eyes, and even of these only one, in case the other is lacking, and with this one they incite, beckon, and attract. (León Pinelo 124v)[8]

While the older woman in the *Four Figures* wears her veil far back from her face, the manner in which the younger woman wears hers suggests that, were it not lifted, it would cover one eye, a practice deemed especially disreputable: "El taparse de medio ojo, descubriendo parte de la vista, es uso lascivo, i no necesario, i se deve vedar i prohibir en todas partes—Covering one eye, showing part of one's vision, is a lascivious custom, and not necessary, and should be forbidden and prohibited everywhere" (León Pinelo 127v).

In a decidedly unfeminine way (according to seventeenth-century practices), the woman places her hand firmly on the shoulder of the youth in front of her, implying an intimacy between the two figures. What might be their relationship? As she reveals herself, addresses the viewer, and claims the youth to the left, she becomes a pivotal figure, with more knowledge and power than the male figures who bracket her. By placing her hand on the shoulder of the youth, she establishes both her familiarity and her control; by lifting her veil, she establishes her complicity with us. It is as if Lazarillo's wife (and the Archpriest's concubine) in the final chapter, or the *mujercillas* of chapters three and four, known indirectly in the novel and yet witness to all, now emerge from the shadows to claim a voice.

Lazarillo's self-satisfaction is founded on an illusion upon which he insists: this becomes most evident in the final chapter, as he forces his own happy ending, by ignoring the well-founded gossip about his wife:

> Until this day nobody had heard a word between us about this matter; on the contrary, when I feel that someone is on the point of saying something about her, I cut him short and say:
>   "Look, if you are a friend of mine, do not say anything to vex me, for I do not consider him a friend who causes me trouble, above all, if he tries to sow discord between me and my wife." (73–74)[9]

To fulfill his fantasy he wishes to portray himself as content and successful. Although the town gossips, and his wife, the Archpriest, and the reader of the novel know better, Lazarillo insists that all is well. In so doing, the history (nonfiction) he purports to relate becomes fiction. It is this dichotomy between Lazarillo's self-sustained illusion and reality to which Murillo refers by juxtaposing the youth and winking woman.

Thus far, we have mentioned three figures: the sleeping boy who does not see, the youth who becomes the archetypal theatrical character by presenting himself as he refuses to see, and the woman behind, whose gestures disclose a latent narrative: in so doing, she makes the viewer see, or perhaps better said, see through. The emphasis on sight receives its ultimate confirmation in the figure of the old woman, whose role on a narrative level is problematic. Yet in the painting she is the most clearly highlighted of all the figures and compositionally brings the group together: with the youth on the left she brackets the composition; her veil relates her to the woman behind, and her hands rest on the head of the sleeping boy. We might associate her with a painting by Murillo showing an old woman delousing a child (Munich, Alte Pinakothek): yet in *Four Figures,* her gesture is far more ambiguous, and her concentration is clearly elsewhere.

This old woman wears eyeglasses with black rims that, set against her white face, are one of the first things a viewer of the work will notice. The only literary correspondence is to the *dueña de servicio,* an older, often widowed woman, characterized by her headdress (*tocas*) and eyeglasses (*antojos*) (Doña Rodríguez in the *Quixote* wears "unos muy grandes antojos"—very large spectacles [II.48]). In her survey of the literature of the period, Conchita Herdman Marianella concludes that "typically, the *dueña* is unattractive, middle-aged to old, and may wear eyeglasses" (58). She receives especially negative treatment in the *Guzmán de Alfarache* as an unscrupulous and venal go-between (Marianella 59–62).[10]

Given her inevitable association with the Celestina, the older woman might share the more positive aspect of her literary antecessor. Ruth El Saffar has shown the inherent ambivalence toward a wise old woman, both needed and feared by the society that casts her out. Murillo's conflation of traits traditionally associated with the *dueña/celestina* signals to the viewer the sexual themes underlying the composition. Like the younger woman's gesture of unveiling, the older woman's glasses imply her insight. Her glasses, which sharpen vision, bring into focus what others cannot—or will not—see: they imply the difference between a look that is but a mere glance, and one that pierces beneath surface appearances, forcing recognition and understanding.

If we have suggested parallels between the male characters of the painting and Lazarillo at two stages of his life, it is nevertheless true that the nonnarrative structure of the painting defies imposition of a reductive story line. The disjointed quality of its composition implies a subterfuge comparable to that seen by Shipley and others to account for the elliptical narrative of the *Lazarillo:*

> The narrator's reticence need not signify indifference to his scene; it may evidence a desire to avoid disclosure (as in the instance of the first sentence of the same sixth *tratado*), or it may be an expressive measure (akin to popular, conversation ellipsis, and to the abbreviation in print of certain four letter words) that leaves some of the work of composition to the reader. The latter, presented a familiar but half-sketched scene, may be induced to complete with materials from his own experiences and imagination those aspects of the design that the narrator chose to suggest are "ours" (shared by narrator and reader) rather than "mine" (the narrator's own, his production and hence his own responsibility). (Shipley, "Lazarillo and the Cathedral Chaplain" 225)

Murillo's ellipses imply a similar self-censorship of issues never before identified with this painter, best known for his madonnas and cherubic saints. Studies of the meaning underlying Lazarillo's self-censorship rely upon deciphering details—the shoes in the fourth *tratado* as referring symbolically to sexual initiation and experience (Sieber 45–58), the homosexual connotations of experiences with the Mercedarian (Sieber 57–58; Thompson and Walsh), possibly with the cathedral chaplain (Shipley, "Lazarillo and the Cathedral Chaplain" 238n11) and with the master tambourine painter (Shipley, "A Case of Functional Obscurity" 251–52n45). So must we use a similar method, focusing on the details in order to decipher the painting. Just as the narrator of the *Lazarillo* suggests that one of the values of his text is that it allows us insight into matters that might otherwise remain unknown ("nunca oídas ni vistas"—never seen or heard of before [91]), so as spectators of the *Four Figures* do we see things usually hidden from view.

The aggressive gazes of the three figures challenge us to look, although a counterbalance to all of these insistently outward gazes is the figure of the sleeping boy. On a compositional level, the circle of his revealed flesh balances the faces of the three others. The tear in his pants also picks up the circular form of the old woman's eyeglasses, while the tail of his shirt echoes the lifted veil of the standing woman. But these visual similarities only underscore the essential difference: this revealed flesh is not a face, it does not see, and it is a part of the body usually not to be seen. By revealing it, Murillo heightens consciousness of the act of viewing. Furthermore, because the child remains unaware of our gaze, the viewer is cast in the role of voyeur.

With the figure of the sleeping boy, Murillo offers a knowledge usually hidden from view, confirmed by the boy's shoes, the meaning of which will be apparent to those familiar with the fourth chapter of the *Lazarillo de Tormes*. Foremost in the painting's illusionistic space and contiguous to his bared buttocks, are the boy's shoes—apparently new, unused, and clearly incongruous with his ragged dress. An allusion is clearly being made to that "first pair of shoes" given to Lazarillo by the Mercedarian friar. We recall that those shoes did not last Lazarillo for a week, for "Ni yo pude con su trote durar más"—"Nor would I have lasted longer at the pace he kept" (184, 61). This shortest chapter of *Lazarillo de Tormes* concludes: "Y por esto y por otras cosillas que no digo, salí dél"—"so for this and other reasons which I shall not mention I left him" (184, 61).

Professor Sieber has analyzed the fragmented narrative of the fourth *tratado* that, he convincingly argues, is to be understood as an example of self-censorship. Silence becomes the "practical solution for the suppression of illicit sexual activity," anticipating Lazarillo's desire, in the final chapter, to silence the gossip about his wife's sexual relationship with the Archpriest. Sieber analyzes the simultaneous presentation of two stories—one narrated, the other unspoken. According to Sieber, the shoes stand as the only nonoscillating sign in the narrative, and as such refer to the Mercedarian friar's role as a *trotaconventos*, but also allude to Lazarillo's unspoken homosexual initiation—that is, the "otras cosillas" for which Lazarillo left the friar. A recent article by Thompson and Walsh offers further confirmation of Sieber's thesis by documenting the Mercedarian's reputation, summed up in the proverb "Cuando vieres a un fraile de la Merced, / arrima tu culo a la pared"—"When you see a Mercedarian priest, press your arse against the wall" (444). Although this chapter was expurgated in the 1573 edition of the *Lazarillo de Tormes*, the uncensored version continued to circulate.[11] This painting bears witness—a century later—to knowledge of the original insinuations of sodomy within the generalized portrait of corruption in the novel.

Nor would the painting be without resonance in contemporary society, in which sodomy continued as a practice in spite of the threat of severe punishment: those found guilty were burned alive (Perry, 123–27). That the hole in the child's pants was painted over twice in the twentieth century shows that this detail did not pass unnoticed and was censored accordingly.[12]

Sieber's observations on the Lazarillo's use of language are appropriate also to understanding Murillo's painting:

> The strategy behind nonsaying is in itself a mode of saying. In other words, the speaker arranges his discourse in such a way that it speaks for itself. It is a free-floating discourse, unbound from the speaker by his utterances of denial ("otras cosas que no digo"), whose semantic signification rests solely on the ability of the *destinataire* to interpret properly the function of such a strategy. (48–49)

So too might we say, in addressing Murillo's painting, that the strategy behind nonnarrative representation is in itself a mode of narrative.

Our awareness of the homoerotic connotation of the sleeping boy leads us to reconsider the older youth and his female companion. There is another, admittedly more speculative, level upon which these two figures might be interpreted, a level implied by their comparison to Murillo's well-known painting *Two Women at a Window* (Figure 2). In that painting, a young and pretty girl leans over a ledge now more clearly defined as a window, as a woman behind hides her laughter, and also reveals the nature of the girl's invitation. In *Four Figures,* the young man—adorned like the young girl with a red ribbon in his hat—assumes the position of the pretty girl. Far more attractive than the woman behind, we might ask if he is here being offered. His eyes appear to be rimmed with a dark line, suggesting his identification with the "handsome, painted young gallants" that served as male prostitutes in Seville (Perry, 126–27). This possibility would reinforce the implications of the sleeping boy in the painting, and also recall the ambiguous triangle of Lazarillo, his wife, and the Archpriest, in which the homosexual possibilities cannot be summarily dismissed (El Saffar 263n13).

One is struck by the reversal of gender roles in *Four Figures.* Males are presented as objects of erotic desire, offered by females who comprehend, reveal, and become the seers. The traditionally masculine domination of the gaze is challenged. The older woman, no longer functioning culturally as a coveted sexual object, clearly stands outside the circuit of desire. And the other woman's relationship to the erotic dynamics is at best ambiguous. Though younger, her face is contorted, her posture impudent, her look brazen. If we are correct in reading the homoerotic implications of this work, and the meaning of the two left-hand figures, it appears that it is the younger woman who is offering the youth, who in turn laughingly acquiesces in his role.

He might be compared to the self-satisfied Lazarillo in the final chapter, triumphantly distorting the facts of his situation to preserve a salutary image of himself. He consents to his wife's demands to maintain equilibrium and peaceful coexistence. Although the Archpriest advises Lazarillo to value his *provecho* (202) above all, when Lazarillo actually admits (speaks) what he has heard, it is his wife's fulminating reaction that silences him ("En tal manera que quisiera ser muerto antes que se me hubiera soltado aquella palabra de la boca"—"She was so affected that I wished I had died rather than to have made that remark" [203, 73]). She ceases to bellow only when he promises never to mention the subject again. Her anger is directed not only against her husband but also against the Archpriest ("Y despúes tomóse a llorar y a echar maldiciones sobre quien conmigo la había casado"—"And then she began to weep, and curse the one who had wed her to me" [203, 73]). The joint efforts of both men are required to calm her down. Not willing to risk her wrath again, Lazarillo settles into the passive position of the onlooker—looking on as she comes and goes from the Archpriest's house, night and day. As readers, are we in the presence of a consummate cynic, whose only priority is to live comfortably, although dishonorably, or are we witnessing, once again, yet another henpecked, castrated (figuratively speaking) husband?

Of all the deceits and corruptions disclosed in this story, it is the one centered on the woman (the mother at the beginning, the wife at the end) that is most dangerously problematic. Finally it is her lack of wholeness (the maiden's virginity; the wife's chastity) that threatens to undo the male protagonist's/protagonists'(certainly Lazarillo's; possibly also the Archpriest's) elaborate construction of the spectacle of his life. The boy who has learned his lesson— "avivar el ojo y avisar"—"[to] open [his] eyes and be on guard" (110, 6)—looks away in an act of willed delusion. He can, it seems, look at everything except the female. And at the center of the nest of Chinese boxes—of readers looking at Vuestra Merced looking at Lazarillo looking at the Archpriest—is the female body. Within the broad field of vision available for institutional control, the focus narrows to converge on the private realm of familial sexual relations, and finally on the ownership and control of the female as the key to the general issue of societal regulation. The interest vested in the women of *Four Figures* explicitly underscores the centrality of the female, which in the novel remains implicit.

Like the picaresque novel, Murillo's composition is frankly transgressive as these characters usurp an illusionistic space usually reserved for devotional imagery. The setting of a ledge rarely appears in Murillo's paintings, and then only in early devotional works, where the sleeping Christ child is displayed on a ledge (private collection, England). The use of the ledge in *Four Figures*, then, serves not only to heighten the painting's theatricality; it might also allude to an alternative genre. These lowly types invade a staging usually reserved for the most holy. What is more, the raggedly dressed boy, now turned away from the viewer, presents a profane alternative to the sleeping Christ child. If the picaresque novel offers us the portrait of an "Unholy Family" (Smith 118), so, too, is Murillo's painting an irreverent icon of the Unholy.

The subject matter of both text and painting would not challenge us if we were safely ensconced in our position of private and pleasurable viewing. But our complacency as spectators is disrupted as we are caught in the act of looking, willing witnesses to the display of transgressive sexuality. Dislodged from a position of sole control, we cannot help but experience discomfort as our shameless scrutiny is discovered—both by the figures within the painting and by the prologuist of the *Lazarillo*.

Notes

We are indebted to Professor George A. Shipley for his reading of this essay and insightful suggestions, to Professor David Freedberg, and to those who offered thoughtful responses to this essay when delivered in March 1992.

1. Three editions appeared simultaneously in this year—in Alcalá de Henares (which includes interpolations), Burgos, and Antwerp. For a brief survey of the critical dispute concerning these publications, see pp. 11–15 of Joseph V. Ricapito's Introduction to his edition (Madrid: Cátedra, 1976), which is the one cited throughout this study.

2. Victor I. Stoichita has discussed Murillo's concern with the dialectic between painting and beholder: "Murillo ist also nicht nur ein Künstler, der die Technik der Pinselführung beherrscht, sondern auch einer, der den Rezeptions-Mechanismus kennt, ein Künstler, der es versteht, seine Bilder aus der Sicht des Betrachters zu prüfen" (112). Stoichita makes no mention of the painting discussed here.

3. Parenthetical page citations for the translations of the *Lazarillo* refer to the edition by Harriet de Onis, *The Life of Lazarillo de Tormes: His Fortunes and Adversities* (New York: Barron's, 1959).

4. " . . . y también porque consideren los que heredaron nobles estados cuán poco se les debe, pues fortuna fue con ellos parcial, y cuánto más hicieron los que, siéndoles contraria con fuerza y maña remando salieron a buen puerto" (6).

5. "Parecióme que en aquel instante desperté de la simpleza en que como niño dormido estaba. Dije entre mí:
"Verdad dice éste, que me cumple avivar al ojo y avisar pues solo soy, y pensar cómo me sepa valer" (109–10).

6. " . . . un jubón de fustán viejo, y un sayo raído o manga tranzada y puerta, y una capa que había sido frisada, y una espada de las viejas primeras de Cuéllar" (198).

7. "Hazer señal a uno con el ojo, cerrándole y abriéndole; y guizne, la señal con el ojo y con algün movimiento del cuerpo . . . Y assí el que guizña retrae para sí la persona, advertiéndola se allegue a su voluntad e intención."

8. "Apetecido de las mugeres, porque las haze parecer lo que no son: juzgándose por hermosa tapada, la que descubierta se conociera por abominable: porque ocultandole lo defectuoso del rostro, solo manifiesta lo que las mas tienen mejor, que son los ojos, i aun destos el uno, por si falta el otro, i con este incitan, llaman i atraen" (León Pinelo 124v).

9. "Hasta el día de hoy nunca nadie nos oyó sobre el caso; antes, cuando alguno siento que quiere decir algo della, le atajo y le digo:
—Mira, si sois amigo, no me digáis cosa con que me pese, que no tengo por mi amigo al que me hace pesar. Mayormente, si me quieren meter mal con mi mujer" (203).

10. We thank Professor Gonzalo Sobejano for pointing out the literary occurrences of the *dueña* wearing glasses; we have not found any other portrayals of women wearing glasses in seventeenth-century Spanish painting. That glasses were commonly worn is attested to by a treatise published in 1623 *Uso de los Antojos* by Benito Daza de Valdés, notary of the Seville Inquisition. See Luis S. Granjel, *La medicina española del siglo XVII, Historia general de la medicina española*

(Salamanca: Universidad de Salamanca, 1978) 4: 201–2. Our thanks to Andrew Schulz for bringing this treatise to our attention.

11. The publication history is reviewed by Guillén (137–46). Within the peninsula the *Castigado* prevailed, with the fourth and fifth *tratados* omitted and other emendations. The editions published outside of Spain were based on the original uncensored Antwerp edition. The 1587 edition of Milan (edited by Antonio de Antoni) was published again in Bergamo in 1597, and reproduced in 1615 by Juan Bautista Bidelo. In 1595 the Plantin Press of Antwerp (Leiden?) published the complete *Lazarillo*. Juan de Luna's continuation is published together with the uncensored original in 1620 in Paris. Courtesy of the Hispanic Society of America, we have been able to consult the 1587 Milan edition, as well as the 1595 edition of the Plantin Press and Juan de Luna's publication.

12. According to the files of the Kimbell Museum, the tear in the pants was painted over by 1930, uncovered by 1941, and again painted over before the painting entered the Kimbell in 1984, at which time the overpainting was again removed. Our thanks to Ann Adams, Registrar at the Kimbell, for providing this information.

Works Cited

Alpers, Svetlana. *Rembrandt's Enterprise: The Studio and the Market*. Chicago: Univ. of Chicago Press, 1988.

Angulo Iñiguez, Diego. *Murillo. Su vida, su arte, su obra*. Madrid: Espasa-Calpe, 1981.

Brown, Jonathan. "Murillo, pintor de temas eróticos: Una faceta inadvertida de su obra." Trans. A. Valdés. *Goya* 169–71 (1982): 35–43.

Catalogue of Old Pictures: The Property of Sir Ralph Coote, Bart Christie, Manson and Woods. Monday, May 7, 1923. No. 284.

Covarrubias, Sebastían de. *Tesoro de la lengua castellana o española*. Ed. Martín de Riquer. Barcelona: Horta, 1943.

Cruz, Anne J. "Sexual Enclosure, Textual Escape: The *Pícara* as Prostitute in the Spanish Female Picaresque Novel." *Seeking the Woman in Late Medieval and Renaissance Writings: Essays in Feminist Contextual Criticism*. Eds. Sheila Fisher and Janet E. Halley. Knoxville: Univ. of Tennessee Press, 1989. 135–59.

Derrida, Jacques. "The Parergon." Trans. Craig Owens. *October* 9 (1979): 3–40.

El Saffar, Ruth. "La literatura y la polaridad masculino-femenino. I. Lo que Celestina sabía II. Entre poder y deseo: Lázaro como hombre nuevo." *Teorías literarias en la actualidad*. Ed. Graciela Reyes. Madrid: Arquero, 1989. 229–84.

Exhibition of Paintings by Velázquez and Murillo Never Before Shown in this Country. The Ehrich Galleries. April 4 to 15th, 1925.

Felton, Craig, and William B. Jordan, eds. *Jusepe de Ribera. lo Spagnoletto, 1591–1652*. Fort Worth, Kimball Art Museum; Seattle and London: Washington Univ. Press, 1982.

Fried, Michael. *Absorption and Theatricality: Painting and Beholder in the Age of Diderot*. Berkeley: Univ. of California Press, 1980.

Gilman, Stephen. "The Death of Lazarillo de Tormes." *PMLA* 81 (1966): 149–66.

Guillén, Claudio. *Literature as System: Essays toward the Theory of Literary History*. Princeton: Princeton Univ. Press, 1971.

León Pinelo, Antonio de. *Velos antiguos i modernos en los rostros de las mugeres sus conveniencias i daños.* Madrid: Juan Sánchez, 1641. (Courtesy of the Hispanic Society of America.)

The Life of Lazarillo de Tormes. Trans. Harriet de Onís. Woodbury, N.Y.: Barron's, 1959.

López Torrijos, Rosa. "El tema de la picaresca en la pintura española del siglo de oro." *La picaresca: Orígenes, textos y estructuras.* Actas del I Congreso Internacional sobre la Picaresca. Madrid: Fundación Universitaria Española, 1979. 167–90.

Marianella, Conchita Herdman. *"Dueñas" and "Doncellas": A Study of the "Doña Rodríguez" Episode in "Don Quijote."* North Carolina Studies in the Romance Languages and Literatures 209. Chapel Hill: Univ. of North Carolina Press, 1979.

Molho, Maurice. "El Pícaro de Nuevo." *MLN* 100 (1985): 199–222.

Perry, Mary Elizabeth. *Gender and Disorder in Early Modern Seville.* Princeton: Princeton Univ. Press, 1990.

Shipley, George A. "A Case of Functional Obscurity: The Master Tambourine-Painter of *Lazarillo, tratado* VI. *MLN* 97 (1982): 225–53.

———. "The Critic as Witness for the Prosecution: Making the Case against Lázaro de Tormes." *PMLA* 97 (1982): 179–94.

———. "Lazarillo and the Cathedral Chaplain: A Conspiratorial Reading of *Lazarillo de Tormes, tratado* VI." *Symposium* 38 (1983): 216–41.

Sieber, Harry. *Language and Society in "La vida de Lazarillo de Tormes."* Baltimore: Johns Hopkins Univ. Press, 1978.

Smith, Paul Julian. *Writing in the Margin: Spanish Literature of the Golden Age.* Oxford: Clarendon Press, 1988.

Steinberg, Leo. "Velázquez' *Las Meninas.*" *October* 19 (1981): 45–54.

Stoichita, Victor I. "Der Quijote-Effekt: Bild und Wirklichkeit im 17. Jahrhundert unter besonderer Berücksichtigung von Murillos Oeuvre." *Die Trauben des Zeuxis: Formen künstlerischer Wirklichkeitsaneignung.* Münchner Beiträge zur Geschichte und Theorie der Künste 2. Hildesheim: Georg Olms Verlag, 1990. 106–39.

Thompson, B. Bussell, and John K. Walsh. "The Mercedarian's Shoes (Perambulations on the fourth *tratado* of *Lazarillo de Tormes*). *MLN* 103 (1988): 440–48.

La vida de Lazarillo de Tormes y de sus fortunas y adversidades. Ed. Joseph V. Ricapito. Madrid: Cátedra, 1976.

Chapter 4

The Author's Author, Typography, and Sex: The Fourteenth Mamotreto of *La Lozana andaluza*

Luis Beltrán

The phrase "author's author" needs clarification, since it is susceptible to a perfectly legitimate double reading: it may mean the author in the story, inside the text, the "storic" author, and the one outside it, the historic one. In fact, not only can the phrase mean either one or the other, it unavoidably and simultaneously means both. The general effect is not unlike that produced by the logo of the recent film *Batman* (1989): the mind "chooses" to see or not to see the bat for reasons that seem outside its control, reasons that the mind itself is not aware of at the moment of perception. The phrase "author's author" reflects what I call the primary effect of Francisco Delicado's *La Lozana andaluza* (*Portrait of Lozana, the Lusty Andalusian Woman*):[1] the erosion of the concept of mimesis[2] by creating in the mind of the reader maximum uncertainty as to the distinction between what is imitated and what is imitation, or, to put it in semitheological terms, by the invention of an entity that not only images but also includes its maker. In so doing, *La Lozana andaluza*, as a literary artifact, rejects the Christian model of creation and attempts to become a cosmos at once immanent and transcendent—a notion that was very much present in the Renaissance mind. Consequently, I will often use the phrase "author's author" to designate both (and either) the outside-the-text (historic) and inside-the-text (storic) authors, as I consider how both almost become one, how that "almost-one" takes "flesh" to join the world of his own creatures, and what role the fourteenth *mamotreto* (sketch)[3] plays in the process of its own maker's incarnation. I will also consider *mamotreto* 14 itself together with some aspects of its emotive, referential, and poetic functions. The incarnation process will be considered first. Before I begin, however, it might be helpful recalling here the major components of this complex text.

Its longest and essential one depicts the history of Lozana from her birth in Cordoba to her apparent decision to retire from her professions and leave Rome. This component is preceded and followed by eight short pieces—two before the beginning, six after the end—that appear to frame it, and that provide important information relative to the history of Lozana and, particularly, to one of the characters in it, its author. The two initial pieces are a dedication and a plot summary; the final six are an author's apology, an *explicit*, an epistle by the author, a letter of excommunication addressed to an uncooperative maiden, Lozana's epistle to her woman friends and sisters in love, and an author's digression.

Within the central and major component of the text, we see and hear Lozana practicing her chosen professions. In order to make as honest and pleasurable a living as she can, she meets and dialogues with a considerable number of men and women. One of the former is her own author (the author of her history); others represent different occupations, social strata, ages, minorities, and levels of egoism. The women represent different minorities as well, and come from different parts of the empire of Charles I of Spain. From the point of view of social position, the women are not as varied as the men; for the most part they make a living by either manual or sexual labor, although, among the latter, some have been very successful and enjoy considerable respect and some influence. It is Lozana's incessant activity, her cajoling and arguing, her persuading or failing to persuade many of the other 124 characters in the text (125 is the total number of characters at least according to what the author tells us in the *explicit*) that make the novel, and that make the reading of it such a breathless and absorbing enterprise.

The central part of *La Lozana andaluza* is written in dialogue form with the exception of *mamotretos* 1, 5, and parts of 4 that, as we shall see at the beginning of the next paragraph, are narrative. Its 66 *mamotretos* appear grouped in three major segments. The first one includes *mamotretos* 1 through 23 and covers the initial

years of Lozana's life, her long liaison with Diomedes, Diomedes's father's attempt to have her killed, her arrival in Rome in
1513 (*mamotretos* 1–6), and her first two and a half days in the city
(*mamotretos* 7–23). During those two and a half days she makes the
acquaintance of Rampín, who will guide her in her first long walk
through the streets of Rome and with whom she will spend the
long amorous night described in *mamotreto* 14. The second segment includes *mamotretos* 24 through 40. Lozana is pregnant as a
result of having made love with a priest in the last *mamotreto* of the
preceding segment. She miscarries and, although she continues to
be sexually active, begins to dedicate a considerable amount of her
time to her activities as healer, go-between, and cosmetician. In
the third and final segment—*mamotretos* 41 through 66—the
speeches grow longer and more discursive, and there is more talk
about the past. The reader gets the feeling that the action is slow-
ing down and the protagonist is getting tired. So it doesn't come as
a surprise when in *mamotreto* 66, Lozana announces her intention
to retire. It is 1524. (It was already that year in *mamotreto* 54.) She
has been working hard in Rome since 1513, and as she herself
says, she would rather abandon Rome and her clients than have
Rome and her clients abandon her. The last *mamotreto* ends when,
after Lozana's final speech, her author (and acquaintance) tells us
that it is December 1, 1524, and declares finished his portrait/his-
tory of the lusty Andalusian woman.

It is the author that we find alluded to right at the beginning of
the fourth *mamotreto* when the reader is informed of a change of
voice in the progress of the action. The sentence "prosigue el autor"
("the author continues"; see Figure 6) signals that the dialogue
form, which started at the very end of the first *mamotreto* and has
been maintained throughout the second and third, is about to be interrupted. The text is going to become a narrative again, and we,
the readers, will again be listening to the voice (the inside-the-text
author's) that initiated in our minds their processes of conceiving
Lozana. I am speaking now not only of Lozana but also of her immediate context, that is to say, the text in its entirety, constituted by
the sum total of the transmitters incorporated in it. All its transmitters are valid (although not equally important), for together they
make possible the virtual reality that our minds construct. In-

cluded among them are those transmitters that could be considered as primarily objective—verbal, typographical, pictorial (words, markers, signs, blank spaces, drawings)—and those that could be considered as primarily subjective. The latter are rather complex because they transcend their function as carriers of virtual reality to become components of the reality they carry; they are susceptible as such to being partially disengaged and, for the purposes of analysis, to being considered in relative isolation, whether they be "storic" authors, narrators, narratees, times, places, characters, events, or even the reader, the in-the-text reader. There is the other reader, of course, the one outside the text, the receptor in whose mind every transmitter is ultimately justified and confirmed, and in whom the virtual reality that the mind is processing will be metamorphosed into actual reality, into part of a mind that has been added on to, that now includes a new vision, and that, therefore, has become a different mind from the one it was before it began its conceiving of Lozana and her world.

"Prosigue el autor" not only signals the return of the narrative form, it also projects on the reader's mind the reality of a new transmitter, since the transmitter that the reader is about to hear again (*autor*) cannot be the same as the one informing him or her about it. I am calling this informing transmitter the narrator, and although it is, as all transmitters, part of the context, it seems, at this point, to be contributing to the context only as an activator and intensifier of the reality of another component of the latter, the storic author. The narrator is in fact reminding the reader of this author's existence and performance and, by distancing himself, is confirming the author's presence within a space—the interior of the *mamotretos*—that is soon (*mamotreto* 6) to be occupied exclusively by the characters in the text and by their world and time.[4] The quoted sentence also shows that the new narrator is aware that the voice we heard earlier speaking the *dedicatoria*, the *argumento*, the first *mamotreto*, and the sentences that serve as introductions to *mamotretos* 2 and 3, was the author's and not his own. How the new narrator became aware of this fact and the space in which he existed before the phrase "Prosigue el autor" invented him, can be explained by assuming that up to the instant of the phrase the narrator's role had been subsumed in that of the *autor*.

Between the *dedicatoria* and the first *mamotreto,* under the heading of *argumento,* the author's author offers the readers some information concerning how he intends to proceed, and warns them against falling prey to the temptation of trying to improve his text by adding or eliminating words. Not only does he warn them; he demands that they not do so.[5] The phrase he uses to introduce his wish, "protesta el autor" ("the author demands"; see Figures 3 and 4), is from a syntactic point of view identical to "prosigue el autor," meaning that the third person is again being used to refer to the author and that, again, the possible existence of another voice is forced upon the readers' minds. This possibility is immediately canceled, however, when in the following line the first person singular makes one entity of the author who demands and the prologuist who has just alluded to him. The suggestion of the existence of two transmitters, however short lived, is apparent, and constitutes the first step in the carefully calibrated process that will end with the total insertion of the author's author in the world and time of the characters. The second step is marked by "prosigue el autor." The effects of these two steps consist, then, in briefly suggesting (step 1) and decisively establishing (step 2) the existence of two different voices having to do with the control and the becoming of the text. Until the beginning of the fourth *mamotreto* (step 2) we heard only one voice both inside and outside the *mamotretos:* that of the *autor.* From this point on and until the end of the last one (*mamotreto* 66), exterior space (space between *mamotretos*) will be the narrator's exclusive territory, and the roles of the narrator and the *autor* will remain distinct. Once the *mamotretos* become exclusively dialogued (*mamotreto* 6), we stop hearing the *autor* for a while but by that time we, as readers, already have been made well aware that he can speak to us from within them, that he has done so and therefore can do so again, as indeed he will, unexpectedly, from the center of *mamotreto* 14.

Scholars who have written on *La Lozana andaluza* seem to be in agreement as to the interest and importance of the fourteenth *mamotreto,* as to the joyful intensity of its erotic content, and as to, at least for the vast majority of them, its originality within the literature written in Castilian prior to or around the time of the publication of *La Lozana andaluza* (notwithstanding a shorter passage in *Comedia Thebaida*, which pales by comparison). Nevertheless, no critic seems to have explored this *mamotreto* in depth, in detail, and from beginning to end. I am going to write about it, and about its author's author, using as my basic text the facsimile of the only copy known to exist of the first edition of the *Retrato de la Lozana andaluza*.[6] It is my conviction that Francisco Delicado is experimenting purposefully and significantly with various typographical signs, vignettes, and illustrations (as transmitters operational as both text and context), and consequently I have deemed it appropriate, indeed necessary, to accompany my remarks with the photographic reproduction of the three pages of the facsimile edition that contain the *mamotreto*. Reproductions of other pages that may clarify and support my opinions are also included.

From a typographical point of view, all editions of *La Lozana andaluza* except the first one—which was very likely prepared by Delicado himself[7]—treat the *autor,* when he reappears in the fourteenth *mamotreto,* in exactly the same manner as they treat all the other characters in it. As a consequence, when in reading those editions we reach the moment of his reappearance, we are considerably surprised, because the author who up until then had been providing us with information concerning Lozana and her life (concerning also his own peculiar way of informing us) had at the same time remained transcendent to the literary artifact he was word facturing and the characters that are such an important part of it. Now, all of a sudden, the arrangement of the text on the printed page conveys a message of parity between *auctor*[8] and characters that forces us to understand that they are sharing the same universe. The surprise becomes even more puzzling when, upon reflecting on what the *auctor* has to say, we discover that, although the typographical arrangement is here presenting the *auctor* as if he were a character like all the others, he does not speak as they do, nor does he talk to them, nor can they hear what he is saying; we discover that, in fact, the *auctor* is still only reporting on them.

The original edition does not surprise us in this manner. Its typography is different. Although the speeches are also preceded by the name of the speaker or by some term identifying him or her, these terms always appear immediately after the last word of the preceding speech with no blank spaces at the end of it. A line is never broken to introduce a speaker in the next one. This system is rigorously followed; I have not detected any exceptions. It is obvious that if Delicado had typographically intended to treat *auctor* here in the exact same manner as he treats the other characters— which is what all subsequent editors do—he would have printed the word *auctor* in line 50 right after the word *dormir* (see Figure 9).[9] Instead he left line 50 incomplete, printed the word *auctor* in the center of line 51, and placed right before the word *auctor* the pilcrow or paragraph marker used throughout the book to signal the beginning of a new *mamotreto*. He has also printed on the left side of the page, between lines 51 and 59, an illustration representing a man's face. This illustration appeared earlier at the end of the first page, exactly between the beginning of the *argumento* and the phrase "Protesta el autor" that initiates the second page (A2 verso, according to the edition's numbering; see Figures 3, 4, and 9).[10] The presence of two identical illustrations accompanying the two first appearances of *autor* in the text, and appearing only then, signifies the special and equal importance of both; it also suggests that the face in the illustration could be Delicado's own.

The typographical arrangements surrounding the reappearance of the author's author in the fourteenth *mamotreto* indicate that Delicado was perfectly aware of the unconventionality of what he was in the process of doing, and that he felt somewhat intimidated by his own idea and decided to proceed in a gradual and relatively cautious way. In relation to this, and because it may contribute to justify Delicado's intention to eventually make his author one of his characters' neighbors, I point out that the *autor* stated, when addressing his dedicatee, that it was his intention to tell only what he had actually heard and seen (see Figure 3, line 14). He may or may not be lying when saying so, but there can be little doubt that he is exaggerating, his motivation apparently being his desire to create the impression that he is, to use rather freely a modern phrase, reporting from the field. That he is exaggerating becomes obvious as soon as the first *mamotreto* begins, at least if we take the phrase "heard and seen" as having, as it is generally understood in Castilian, a cumulative meaning (the Castilian "visto y oído" certainly has that meaning, which is even more clear in its negative variant "neither seen nor heard," "ni visto ni oído"). This cumulative meaning implies that the author is not referring here to things that he may have seen and not heard, or vice versa, but to those that he has both heard and seen. For as long as he is still in the narrative mode, Delicado, protected by the umbrella of tradition and conventionality, may not have been totally aware of how much disbelief he was asking his reader to suspend during the relating of Lozana's life from her birth to her arrival in Rome; once he definitively shifts into the dramatic second person, however, into pure dialogue (*mamotreto* 6), the absence of the author-witness becomes more noticeable, and even more so when, in the fourteenth *mamotreto*, he takes Lozana and her new friend, Rampín, to the bedroom so that they might spend the night indulging their sexual urges.

They are literally in the middle of their amorous activities when the author declares himself a presence in their intimacy and begins to report from their bedroom. The reader has not seen the word *autor* since the beginning of the fourth *mamotreto*, and from the beginning of the sixth there has been nothing but dialogue. Why has Delicado chosen this most improbable of occasions to insert his author in the space and time of his protagonists? In my opinion, that very improbability justifies it. His author promised his dedicatee, and through him his intended readers, that he would write exclusively of what he had heard and seen. The extremely private nature of this scene implies a total absence of strangers. The author's author realizing so, and realizing how his predominantly word-factured artifact might be starting to appear too obviously inconsistent, brings himself back to let us know that the promise in the *dedicatoria* was not made lightly, that it is being kept. He will speak four times in this *mamotreto*, and his four interventions will very carefully signal that he is indeed hearing and seeing. He will first inform us about Lozana's snoring (lines 51–52), then about a neighbor, a blacksmith, who does not let the lovers sleep (lines 58–59), and then about how Lozana points to a gourd of wine (lines 73–74).

The abruptness of his intrusion is not as pronounced in the first edition as in all the others I have seen. The appearance of the signifier *auctor* standing alone in the middle of a line (line 50), preceded by the paragraph sign, is setting it—and its signified—apart, outside the action. Typographical arrangements are signaling, then, that the author's insertion in his characters' environment is not total, and that what we have here is a sort of modestly ubiquitous transmitter simultaneously operating at two different levels of truth, diegetic one (level of the main story) and extradiegetic the other (outside and "above" the level of the main story). Another typographical arrangement that contributes to strengthen this impression of a double-natured author is the illustration I mentioned earlier; it equates this *auctor* with the *autor* we found at the beginning of the text in the *dedicatoria*, and *argumento*. Finally, the capital "Q" that initiates line 52 is the same size and configuration as the ones that appear at the beginning of every *mamotreto*.

There can be no doubt that a conscious and considerable effort has been made to differentiate from all his other appearances in the text this first manifestation of the author as witness inserted in the space of his characters. The treatment is indeed unique, and leads me to believe that the mind that planned the typographical layout of the page—and of the entire structure—is the same one that conceived its verbal text and the complicated role of the author in it. The typographic, pictorial, and linguistic components of *La Lozana andaluza*, its objective and subjective transmitters, are all carriers of meaning operating on each other and, in so doing, informing and conforming the singularity of the whole.

The remaining interventions of the author's author in this *mamotreto*, as well as in *mamotretos* 17, 24, 25, 42, and 43, are introduced as those of all other characters. Once the threshold separating the two levels of truth, diegetic and extradiegetic, had been crossed by the author there had been no more need for further differentiation, at least not in typographical terms. The incarnation process, having not yet been completed, will continue progressing, but along two new courses: a linguistic one having to do with the configuration of the signifier, and a dramatic one, with that of the signified, or, to put it somewhat differently, with that of the signified becoming "configured," becoming a physical presence, in the actuality of Lozana's world.

Autor and *auctor* are the two terms that define the linguistic course. They both designate the same transmitter, but different aspects of it. *Autor* is the term used in the *argumento* and right before the start of the fourth *mamotreto;* in both instances the transmitter it is applied to seems to function as narrating author and operates at an extradiegetic level. *Auctor* is the term used in *mamotreto 14,* where the transmitter it is applied to appears inserted in the space and time of the characters in the story and, therefore, operates at a diegetic level. In *mamotreto 17* we find both terms. *Autor* is used three times right at the beginning. The first instance is still in the heading, outside of the action proper, where he is mentioned by the narrator (see Figure 11). Immediately afterward he is introduced—typographically—as a character and as the first one to speak; what he says, however, is not addressed to another character but, as was the case in *mamotreto 14,* to an imagined audience, a public or a reader. His third intervention is very brief and consists of a question provoked by the remarks of one of the characters, Rampín, who, as *autor* tells us, has suddenly walked into the latter's room and whose speech he has just quoted. The *autor*'s brief question, then, is a reaction not to Rampín's speech but to his own quotation of it. The fact that *autor* is putting in his own mouth Rampín's words implies that we are still in a seminar-rative environment in which the physical presence of Rampín has not yet been granted full recognition. This will be granted by the next speech, which, spoken by Rampín in answer to *autor*'s question, signals the beginning of a true dramatic environment. After this third intervention, *autor* will be replaced by *auctor* (see Figure 12, lines 1 and following), the term that will be consistently employed to introduce his remaining fourteen interventions in the *mamotreto.*[11]

On the basis of how up to this point these two terms appear contextualized in the work, it is possible to assert that *autor* is associated with that dimension of the author that suggests the informing narrator, the one who has the knowledge, the authority. *Autor* seems to be stressing *autoridad. Auctor,* however, has been consistently and unequivocally applied to a transmitter who functions as a *dramatis persona,* which is to say one that talks and acts and is not being narrated. The "c" of *auctor* projects action upon *autor* and synthesizes both; it means the play in the storytelling, the perennial now of drama and of the second person alloyed with the unavoidable past of narrative and the third person, the participant author who hears and who sees. That *auctor* includes *autor*, not only at the level of the signifier but also in the way I have just indicated, is confirmed quite convincingly by the meaning given to the term in the heading of the eighteenth *mamotreto*. The narrator says, "Prosigue el auctor tornando al decimosexto mamotreto" ("The author continues by returning to the sixteenth *mamotreto;*" see Figure 13). Except for the "c" "prosigue el auctor" is identical to the phrase "prosigue el autor" found in the heading of the fourth *mamotreto* and considered at the beginning of this essay. "Prosigue el autor" created a narrator that was to be different from the author and to speak the headings of all the remaining *mamotretos;* also, *mamotretos* 4 and 5 are written in the narrative mode, and the *autor* inside them is a narrating author, not an *auctor*. In *mamotreto* 18 we are told that *auctor* is about to continue the story by going back to the sixteenth *mamotreto* and taking it from there, a task that clearly has much more to do with the author as teller than with the author as character, with *autor* more than with *auctor*. Yet the latter has been the term chosen here to signify that the persona we have just heard addressing Rampín fourteen times in the preceding *mamotreto* is the same one that decides what and whom to put next upon the stage, that one and the other are both manifestations of the same transmitter.

We shall never see the term *auctor* again in the text after the heading of the eighteenth *mamotreto*. The word *autor*, however, will appear many times more, fifty-four if I have counted well. Of those, a substantial majority, forty-two, designate the character who under that name is going to speak in *mamotretos* 24, 25, 42, and 43. It seems as if the author's author having made his point as to the functions of the two spellings and shown how *auctor* includes and can function as *autor*, had decided to show *autor* operating as *dramatis persona* to keep us from forgetting that he is indeed telling things he heard and saw.

At this point, I find irresistible the temptation to borrow from the "discoveries" of science fiction, and consider the incarnation process we have been examining as the beaming down (or up) of the author from the interior of one world into the interior of another. Accepting this televisionary transposition, the aspect of the

incarnation process that I am about to discuss next could be compared to the final stages of the beaming, when transparency becomes opacity, and empty space becomes a body starting to act.

As it has already been shown, *auctor* appears for the first time in
the fourteenth *mamotreto*. He does so suddenly and unexpectedly,
and in the bedroom where Lozana and Rampín are becoming
lovers. He begins listening to them, watching them, and verbally
reacting to some of what he sees and hears. But while his attention
and at least two of his senses are within the lovers' space, they are
certainly not in his: Lozana and Rampín are totally unaware of his
presence. Three *mamotretos* later (17), it is *autor* that initiates the action (see Figure 11); we see him alone, in a space that, given the
narrator's introduction and the fact that *autor* is shown working
on his book (the one we are reading), we have to assume to be his.
A moment later, however, Rampín walks right into this space and
tells *autor* about things that are happening in Rampín's world, a
world that obviously has to be that of the *autor* as well. As we listen to what Rampín is saying, we soon become aware that he is
talking about events that took place in a past that when we heard
him last, precisely at the end of the preceding *mamotreto* (16), had
not happened yet. *Autor* and Rampín are at this point inserted in a
not totally convincing reality in which the continuum space-time
appears somewhat dislocated: while its spatial aspect is quite conventional, its temporal one is the future, an impossible time. Thus
Rampín and *autor,* together with the reality in which they are inserted and of which they are part, can be considered an intermediate reality, one not yet properly integrated. Although I am perhaps
forcing the analogy, it could be said that in terms of the science fiction beaming down (or up), the necessary particles constituting
that reality have still not quite coalesced, while other impossible
ones have not yet been filtered out. Enough has taken place, however, to evince that a process is going on. Just as the author's intervention in the fourteenth *mamotreto* makes more acceptable the
sudden irruption of Rampín at the beginning of *mamotreto* 17, so
mamotreto 17 and the long dialogue that constitutes it make acceptable the twenty-fourth *mamotreto,* and the fully unified reality
of characters-author that the readers find in it. Both preparatory
stages have contributed to readjust the readers' expectations and

to get their imaginations ready for the definitive insertion of the author's author in the space-time of his *dramatis personae*.

The fourteenth *mamotreto* is ninety-nine lines long (see Figures 8, 9, and 10) and includes three different scenes. The first is a brief dialogue, eleven lines, between Rampín and his aunt (the action of the *mamotreto* takes place in the aunt's house). The third scene, extending from line seventy-seven to the end, includes the aunt, her old husband, Lozana, and Rampín, who does not speak. The middle scene is the often-mentioned bedroom scene and the one in which *auctor* makes his first appearance. It is sixty-six lines long and is by far the most important of the three.

From its very beginning *mamotreto* 14 is carefully differentiated from all the preceding and following ones. Even before the beginning of its text, typographical signifiers in the narrator's introduction distinguish it from all others and create a particular proximity between what is narrated and what is dialogued. This proximity parallels the one to be found later on between *auctor* and characters, and is already preparing the reader for the contents of a *mamotreto* in which solidly established expectations are going to be put to the test.

The introduction names, besides Rampín, his aunt (the character who initiates the action of this *mamotreto*) and Lozana. What initially caught my attention, and I first disregarded as a meaningless inconsistency, was the surprising way in which two of the three terms naming the characters are printed. They had never been printed that way in any of the previous introductions, and they are never printed that way in any of the subsequent ones. The terms *Tía* (aunt) and Lozana appear followed by a period followed by the closing parenthesis in exactly the same manner as they are printed when used to identify the speakers inside the *mamotretos*. Also, the name of Lozana is abbreviated as it is inside the *mamotretos*, Lo.) (see Figure 8), but never in any of the many other introductions in which it appears. The names of many other characters also appear often in the introductions but are never abbreviated or followed by the point and the parenthesis. The effect of all this is to make the text space associated with the narrator and the narrative mode look more like the one associated with the characters and the dialogic one, and, in consequence, it seems as if even at this typographical level the reader's expectations are being readjusted in preparation for the sudden manifestation of the author on the following page. The fact that this way of printing the names is found only in the introduction to *mamotreto* 14, precisely the *mamotreto* where the crucial step is taken toward making the author fully functional as a character, further confirms my belief that the inconsistency is probably deliberate, and that, deliberate or not, it is possible to understand it as a bearer of meaning, as a typographical nonverbal signifier.

Another marker that contributes to set this fourteenth *mamotreto* apart is the drawing representing the figure of a man that accompanies the first lines of the dialogue. Throughout the book nine different women and six different men exemplify this type of illustration. Most of them (all but two of the men) appear more than once. The one we see here at the beginning of *mamotreto* 14 is the first of any of these illustrations. It will be used only once again, at the beginning of *mamotreto* 58, which is the last one adorned with them (see Figures 8 and 19). That *mamotreto* 14 originates this series, and does so by means of a figure that also closes it, confirms the distinctiveness of the *mamotreto,* particularly if we take into consideration that the illustration adorns the right side of the page, a position where this type of illustration is very infrequently located. This is the only instance in which we find the drawing at the beginning of a *mamotreto,* on the right side of the page, and without a similar figure or figures accompanying it on the opposite side of the page.

The introduction to *mamotreto* 58 states (see Figure 19), "How Lozana goes into Garza Montesina's house and meets two Neapolitan pimps and what they say to her," and right under the introduction, and on the left side of the page, we see a woman, evidently Lozana, looking at and apparently listening to the two pimps. The one next to Lozana is very tall and, I would say, very male and proud of it as the feathers he wears and his moustache seem to indicate. He carries two swords: one, extremely large, hangs from his left forearm; the other, which he holds with both hands, hangs between his legs. The drawing clearly suggests the type of braggart soldier-pimp who pretends to live by his swords and by his women, and who simply lives any way he can. This is the same drawing that appears at the beginning of *mamotreto* 14.

All the illustrations in the book, whether the ones belonging to the series I have just identified, or the ones that occupy a full page or half a page, or a few smaller ones that appear—as many of the larger ones—completely enclosed within a frame (see Figures 7, 14, 16, and 20), are with very few exceptions closely related to the sections of the text they accompany. I should also point out that the author's author is quite conscious of the similarities between his art and the painter's, as he makes clear by calling the sixty-six segments in which he divides the central and most important part of his book sketches (*mamotretos*). It is also evident that some of his actual drawings are meant to be portraits of his characters and show some of the physical peculiarities attributed to them in the verbal text. The drawings of himself, and particularly of Lozana and Rampín are good proof of this (see Figures 1 and 2), but there are also the drawings of what could be called hypodiegetic characters (characters in the tale within the tale) that are only alluded to in the verbal text, but whose story is partially told in the pictorial one. The best and most dramatic example is the elaborate illustration that within the eleventh *mamotreto* and immediately after the mention of Thisbe (see Figure 7) recounts the end of her story and of Pyramus as told by Ovid in the fourth book of the *Metamorphoses*;[12] another example, not so detailed, is the portrayal of five characters from *La Celestina*, found immediately after the beginning of *mamotreto* 37 but introduced by the last two lines of the preceding one (see Figures 15 and 16). It would be possible, in fact, to speak of the illustrations as a sort of pictorial text that, functioning most often as ancillary to the more important verbal one, can at times actually complement and enrich it. The significance, for instance, of the illustrations occupying the recto and verso of the first folio (Figures 1 and 2) and the first page of the first *mamotreto* (Figure 5) is emphasized by the fact that each of them is printed twice, and in places that from a narrative point of view possess considerable strategic value. "The Ship of Fools" (see Figure 1) appears again at the beginning of *mamotreto* 24, which initiates the second section of *mamotretos* (see Figure 14); "Lozana's Kitchen" (see Figure 2) is reprinted at the start of the third and last section in the forty-first *mamotreto* (see Figure 17); finally, the diptych "Peña de Martos-Córdoba" that heads the first *mamotreto* (at the beginning of which we are told that Lozana is from Córdoba; see Figure 5) is printed again at the start of the forty-seventh, where Silvano is going to tell Lozana all he knows—and it is quite a lot—about Peña de Martos and its history (see Figure 18). Any edition of *La Lozana andaluza* that pretends to do justice to the original should include, together with its verbal text, its entire pictorial one with its components printed in exactly the places assigned to them in the first edition. I believe too that the messages the first edition contains that are conveyed by typographical nonverbal means should also be included in any future ones, perhaps by notes or other ways the editors consider most convenient.

Going back now to the beginning of mamotreto 14 and its heavily armed Neapolitan pimp: why has he been placed here obviously to "illustrate" the figure of Rampín, the most active male character in the *mamotreto?* The verbal text has provided the reader with considerable information concerning Rampín's physical aspect. His name, as Claude Allaigre indicates in his edition, is close to *rampino,* which in Italian means "hook" and also to steal or to filch. *Rampinismo,* related to *rampino* (and to Rampín), is the name of a disease that affects the normal development of the hooves of the horse, bending them inward and impairing its balance and its walk. Rampín falls several times, with rather dramatic consequences, and on important occasions. First he falls and breaks two carafes of wine right before the beginning of *mamotreto* 14 and his great night of sex with Lozana. He falls again in the seventeenth, as he is leaving the author to return to Lozana's house. Later, in the long sequence of Lozana's dream and its aftermath (*mamotretos* 30–33), he somewhat fulfills her semiprophetic dream by falling, if not in a river, at least in a pool of excrement. This occurs in *mamotreto* 33, just before the scene when, almost forced to eat ham, he eats it and pays the consequences.[13] Rampín's encounter with the ham is his last major scene in the story; after that he says very little and shows up infrequently. He will not appear any more in the second part, and will speak only six times in the entire third one (*mamotretos* 41, 42, two times in 49, 51, and 66). As a result, Rampín's frequent falls seem even more frequent, and the importance of this trait of his is emphasized. He is also portrayed as a man who has little use for swords—a coward, in fact, whose cowardice Lozana makes considerable and quite successful efforts not to see and, after seeing it, not to recognize (*mamotretos* 31–33). Rampín is in a way Lozana's most important conquest, and she prefers to believe in its value.

"The Ship of Fools" (Figure 1) and "Lozana's Kitchen" (Figure 2) are the two illustrations that provide us with a portrait of Rampín more in accordance with what the verbal text has forced us to visualize. Rampín appears in both as seriously disproportioned, his legs too short, his head too large, his chest too wide and heavy. He looks like what someone born in a brothel, brought up among prostitutes, having too much sex too soon, and surrounded by an unhealthy environment was, according to certain rather conventional notions, almost expected to look like, which is to say, like an unfortunate creature whose normal growth had been doomed at birth and stunted by life. His twisted foot provides the definitive touch to complete the picture. One has to wonder, then, about the reasons for placing such a splendidly sworded individual at the beginning of the *mamotreto*. Perhaps the drawing reflects the aspirations of both protagonists concerning the night they are about to experience. This is, after all, the *mamotreto* where love will occur, where Rampín and Lozana are going to enjoy each other. Rampín is here the great copulator ready to do what he has been doing all his life and must therefore be an expert at. He is still very much the Rampín of Lozana's fantasy, a Rampín she has just met and wants triumphant in her dark bedroom. Lozana desires to be happy, to be served by a good servant who will do well with both his swords. She fancies him attractive now, as she will fancy him courageous later on. Rampín is not attractive, however, and he is not tall, he is misshapen, he does not stand firm on his feet. Lozana's imagination, her erotic urges and hopes, seem to be influencing the text, transforming the appearance that another part of the text attributes to a character; therefore, to a certain degree, she is usurping the function of the author's author. This is so too in the case of Rampín, who tells his aunt, just before arrogantly and confidently he walks into the bedroom where Lozana is in bed, how a cheap cape may cover a splendid drinker (male). One as splendid—the pictorial component of the text suggests—as the Neapolitan pimp drawn in the margin (incidently, Rampín, although not born in Naples, is the son of a woman nicknamed the Neapolitan). *Mamotreto* 14 is where the author is going to start undergoing the process that will make him also one of the characters, and, in it, its two main characters are from the beginning facilitating the rapprochement by taking light steps in the direction of the author, by moving, so to speak, toward convergency.

The illustration, as a component of the pictorial text, is helping the readers of the verbal to enjoy what they are about to experience, and not only because of the obvious ironic contrast between the painted male and the copulating one; the illustration is also inserting in their imagination a more physically acceptable male protagonist. Allowing readers to put aside, at least for the time being, the true appearance of Rampín, might enable them to do the same with that of Lozana. And with Lozana, the readers have a lot to put aside, for Lozana is ugly, not just plain ugly, not ugly by birth or nature; her ugliness, not unlike Rampín's, has been developing, becoming; she is pathologically ugly. Yet many characters in the text, men as well as women, often describe her as attractive, and she certainly finds clients willing to pay her—or to cheat her—for her services. This happens so often that we the readers tend to overlook that, besides minor blemishes (something like a scar in the form of a cross upon her forehead, for instance, or her possible alopecia), she has a hole where her nose used to be before syphilis took it away. Critics tend to overlook this too; the by-now considerable bibliography on *La Lozana andaluza*, while frankly favorable to its protagonist and the way she goes about life and men, shows, for the most part, remarkable discretion concerning her noselessness.

The night she spends with Rampín is only her second one in Rome, but there can be no question that by that time her nose is already missing. That of course poses the problems of when she contracted the disease and who gave it to her. The text is not very precise on these points, but on the basis of the first five *mamotretos* one has to conclude that she acquired syphilis when living and traveling with Diomedes, either from Diomedes or from any one of his clients (in the latter case, with or without Diomedes's permission). This should not lead us to think that Diomedes does not care about Lozana; on the contrary, he is very interested in her, respects her, has two children by her, and even expresses his intentions to marry her. The situation may have been that Diomedes was a merchant eager to succeed, Lozana was willing to help him with whatever means she had at her disposal, and he was willing to let her help him. The decision by Diomedes's father to put Lozana to death might be a little easier to understand if her syphilitic condition was already all over her face by the time she arrived in Marseille. His desire to marry his son to someone else, while possibly strengthening his determination, does not seem enough of a justification for murder. Assuming that this desire was truly there, and we only have Lozana's word for it, other arrangements could have been made or attempted. But having a woman around with such a disease and such a face, and having his friends and neighbors know that she is the mother of his grandchildren, and having to live with the idea that she may one day become his son's wife, was probably too much for the old man to accept. To have her killed was a crime, of course, but the kind of crime toward which his contemporaries of both sexes may have shown considerable understanding. After all, this has much to do with the preservation of a father's honor and the honor of his family. One way or another, this rather formidable woman who has no nose, a cross-shaped scar upon her forehead, and a mighty corpulent body (see Figures 1 and 14, "The Ship of Fools," and 2 and 17, "Lozana's Kitchen") is in the fourteenth *mamotreto* about to spend a night in bed with Rampín, "the hook" with the twisted foot, the uncertain walk, the very large head and trunk, and the short legs; and a man who is, as the conversation between Lozana and his mother already made clear in *mamotreto* 11, much younger than she.

That Lozana has a body that is both big and powerful is clearly stated not only in the pictorial text—the two illustrations I just mentioned—but also in the verbal one. We only have to remember her first morning in Rome, when she became angry and threw down the stairway four Spanish women who apparently did not treat her the way she thought they should have (*mamotreto* 5). At the beginning of *mamotreto* 14, however, both Rampín and his aunt praise her body in no uncertain terms. Her beauty is praised throughout the book, and the possibility exists that Lozana could have possessed a good body for sinning . . . and an even better face for repenting. Be that as it may, there can be no question that observations like those of Rampín and his aunt help us understand both her relative success as a prostitute and the kindness of the critics. Obviously there is also a parallel between this insistence upon the charms of her body and the beautiful male whose drawing appears right above these lines, and this parallel may have a lot to do with the night of love about to get started.

The night begins in line 11 when, immediately after aunt and nephew wish each other a good night, the latter enters the bedroom and Lozana's bed. The long process that leads to the first coitus and its successful conclusion has begun. It will not end until line 34, and thus is about twenty-three lines long. Considering that the whole night lasts only sixty-six lines, and that Lozana and Rampín are going to do the same five other times, the length of this first passage requires some attention. Notice that I have spoken of length and not of duration; I want to stress the difference between the length of the text (number of words, lines used, space they occupy) and the length of the action, between textual time and fictional time. Fictional time extends from bedtime—after dinner and after dark—until noon of the following day. Textual time is sixty-six lines. The hours of the night are used to copulate six times and to sleep; the sixty-six lines are used to let the reader know, through the words of the lovers and of the *auctor*, what they are doing, how they are doing it, their attitude toward it, their degree of concentration, and the way they feel before, during, and after several of their coitus. The degree of concentration brings in another kind of time, one I am going to call subjective: the time in the body-minds of the lovers, a time that although not as easily quantifiable as either the textual or the fictional, is nevertheless locked within the boundaries imposed by both. So we have the time in the written words, the time in the written hours, and the time in the written subjects, the three essentially intertwined, and all of them made possible by a single entity, the text, that invents and transcends them all. It is the relationship between the text, these three aspects of time, and the sexual activity that occupies them that I shall consider next.

The process leading to the first coitus and its completion takes twenty-three lines, but we could add another six if we include the words spoken by Lozana immediately afterward expressing her reaction to what she has just experienced, reaction that will lead from the first to the second amorous bout (lines 35–40). This length is understandable: it is their first time and both have to find a way. Their initial dialogue lasts about twelve lines (11–23) during which the two lovers-to-be use approximately the same number of words; from a strictly linguistic point of view the situation could be described as a fifty/fifty proposition. However, after Rampín utters the definitive words, "Open the door for it and it will do its job as well as any hammer" ("Abridle vos la puerta que él hará su oficio a la machamartillo"), Lozana's voice takes over.[14] Except for a brief statement by Rampín in line 31, "And if I succeed [in bringing Lozana to orgasm], what will I get?" ("Y si la venzo, ¿qué ganaré"),[15] and until line 40, it is she who does all the talking.

As a matter of fact, once the lovemaking really begins much of what Rampín does when he talks is ask for more. That is, of course, not unimportant: it means among other things that he is enjoying what is happening. But his reaction alone would provide rather superficial and not very exciting information concerning the value, duration, and sexual significance of their experience. The true transmitter here is Lozana: she is the one translating flesh into verb and the one who gives us some idea as to the meaning of their true time, which, in sexual affairs, can only be the subjective one, the one that cannot be measured. To put it somewhat differently, if in sex we can measure time, we are not in sex. Lozana is in sex. She herself, Rampín, and the invisible *auctor* hear her say the following words as she is loving toward her first orgasm with Rampín:

> "For once, I am truly happy. And you are just a boy, aren't you? It's not for nothing they say 'Beware of the youth when his beard begins to grow.' If I had only known, I would certainly had let my lust run loose before. Slowly, sweetly, gently, do not press so hard. Move with me. There! That's the way! Oh please, don't go so fast! Don't just think about yourself! You're not alone, you know? And I am not about to be left behind. Wait! I'll show you. Like that, like that! Oh, you'll go far that way. See how good it is? You didn't know it, did you? Don't forget it now. Go on, go on, my master. Keep stirring it. We'll see which of the two

breaks the lance in this joust! Keep in mind that no matter
how early you get up, the sun is not going to rise any
sooner. I have you in the ring, the spear is good, let's see
how you throw it. You've begun well! Keep on—the hare is
on the run. To hell with honor!" (See Figures 8, 9; lines
22–31.)

At this moment Rampín interjects his brief question, "And if I
succeed, what will I get?"[16] Lozana continues:

"Don't you worry that you'll get your reward. But who am I
to teach you; you were born a expert. Hold my hand and
hold tight for the mattress is short. Press harder, dig in, go
in deeper, and all at the same time. Hold on to the mane, my
rider. Now, my life, now. It's here! It's here! Oh, my love! I
am yours in life and death! But take off your shirt; it is drip-
ping wet with your sweat. It's been a long time since I was
last treated to such roast! My luck this man has such a hungry piece! I certainly could use that pestle for I was born
without cheese and garlic[17] and carry enough hunger to
lend some to my neighbors. He's fallen asleep. I never saw a
better looking pestle than his. So fat and straight! It seems
as if it is going to be a bad year for Jerez turnips. It looks like
a new one from Frojolón.[18] It filled me so I couldn't say a
word, it took my breath away. I won't let go of this unicorn!
What's the matter, my love?" (See Figure 9; lines 31–40.)

This intense being in sex of Lozana may well be at least one of
the reasons why we, as well as Rampín, can forget her scarred
forehead and her face scourged by syphilis, her dark hole between
eyes and lips. Maybe that is even what makes us forget the physical appearance of the male she is being in sex with. As for the other
time, how long and far does Lozana's hare run before it gets
caught? How much time does it all take? How much time elapses
between bouts? Does the first coitus last longer than the others?
Obviously it lasts longer for the reader: more words are used. Or
does the diminution of words in the remaining five coitus mean
not shorter time but less anxiety in both partners, an increase in
mutual understanding, a sort of silent eloquence? Is then the
quantity of words a signifier meaning length of time? If so, how
are we to read it? Does less mean more?

One thing is clear: the dialogue between the lovers that precedes the first three coitus keeps getting shorter. Each lover speaks six times before the first coitus; two times before the second; and only once before the third. This progressive shortening can be understood to mean that Lozana and Rampín are becoming more familiar with each other and with what they are doing. During those dialogues, textual and fictional times are running at the same speed and doing so in dramatic contrast to what happens between the coitus. After the first intercourse, he falls asleep, she doesn't. What she does is praise, besides his performance, his penis, which she promotes from pestle to turnip to unicorn. From inanimate object to plant to noble animal, she keeps injecting more and more life into her friend's phallus. In ennobling it so, she loses self-control and her hand reaches for it, with the result that Rampín is awakened (see the words I quoted above, and also Figure 9, lines 35–40): "What's the matter, my love?" she asks him.

How long has Lozana's dithyramb in honor of Rampín's penis lasted? As soon as he wakes up he asks for more, and he immediately gets it. The physiology of sex is a rather complicated matter and little of what concerns it is truly predictable, yet certain things are, at least statistically speaking, true. The textual time employed by Lozana in eulogizing Rampín's glory does not seem sufficient to justify his erotic recovery. But, as it has been said, there are two other times; the fictional time is one of them, during which Lozana has been in her own special time outside of time, ecstatic, and inside which the whole of her has been erotically reawakened. We don't know how long, in terms of fictional time, Lozana's time has lasted; we know that it is from that time and that ecstasy that her hand—herself—leaps out toward the living thing she longs for, and we know that two phrases later, she'll be enjoying it again.

The second coitus lasts three lines, 42 to 44 (see Figure 9), so, as far as textual time and the mechanics of reading are concerned, it is shorter than the first. Lozana (who is again using words as a sexual instrument to increase her lover's ardor as well as her own) makes clear, however, that in terms of her own special time this second coitus has lasted as long as the first:

"Dispose of it ["it" refers here to either her own body or, more specifically, her pudendum] as if it were yours, so long as you keep it to yourself. Oh, the sweetness of this honey! I would never have guessed it! Keep on, keep on, again and again. Don't stop, for they need me home and I am in a hurry. There, there, every bit as good as the first one!"

It is rather obvious that between at least some of her different phrases, an amount of fictional time has been inserted, and that the reading here is much shorter than the lovemaking. The same could be said of the third coitus, but even more so, as it is only a little more than one line long (Figure 9; lines 47–49). Fewer words are coming from Lozana's mouth as the two of them proceed from coitus to coitus, which indicates, along with an increase in mutual carnal knowledge, a certain decrease in enthusiasm and even a suggestion of weariness, as confirmed by Lozana's attitude toward sleep. After the first intercourse has been completed, Rampín falls asleep without any prompting from Lozana, who, being at that point absolutely free from such a need, seems caught by surprise when she realizes her companion is sleeping. After the second coitus, the possibility of such a need is already in her mind: she asks Rampín to go to sleep. She will remain awake, however, to wake him up sometime later by reaching for his virility—at least that is how I read her words in lines 46 and 47. She says: "If I were a great lady, this would never leave my side. Oh, woe is me! Did I wake you up? I didn't mean to." "This" can refer to the whole youth or to his penis. In view of what she says immediately afterward, it is clear that, whatever she meant by the pronoun, she touched some part of his body, for Rampín is suddenly awakened. And where would she touch him but in the same place she had when, after their first coitus, she reached for the unicorn? What has been all along the focus of Lozana's interest? She wakes him up, they copulate a third time, and he falls asleep again, but this time she too decides to take a nap. It is precisely now, after the third of their six coitus, and in that sense right in the center of their amorous get-together, when the voice of the *auctor* lets us know that he is listening and watching.

He tells us that both of them did fall asleep; he also tells us that the reason for informing us of his presence in the bedroom is his inability to write a couple of snores that woke Rampín up. Whose snores those are, he doesn't say, but the couple is in bed together and the snores come from the bed. His discretion here can be understood as a minor realistic touch, intended to reduce somewhat the disbelief provoked in the readers by his sudden manifestation. The moment has also been "realistically" chosen. Both Lozana and Rampín are asleep and no one is there to report what is happening, except, of course, the *auctor,* who will do so while at the same time confirming his initial characterization of self, in the *dedicatoria,* as an author who writes only what he hears and sees. What now appears evident is that, given his characterization, once the text ceases being narrative to become dialogic the presence of the author is assumed. He simply has to be there. And here is the apparent paradox: by his becoming a character, he is becoming a truthful author, a truthful author's author.

Between the first and second of the *auctor*'s interventions Lozana and Rampín copulate for the fourth time. As far as the words are concerned their lovemaking is only one line long (Figure 9; lines 55–56); the fictional time is again in this case longer than the textual and, within both, Lozana moves again into a time of her own. As for sleep, Lozana's need for it is becoming more apparent as Rampín's seems to diminish. After the fourth coitus she does not wait for Rampín to close his eyes but asks him to do so, and for the first time she tells him that she is ready to go to sleep too. Right at the end of the fifth intercourse (Figure 9; lines 69–70) she will do the same and a little later, after a brief exchange, says "Sleep is taking over me. Let us rest" ("El sueño me viene. Reposemos"; Figure 10, line 75). His reply is that he wants to make love again, now with her on top—apparently in the belief that such a position will force her to stay awake. She does not oppose the idea, so the reader has to conclude that they do make love in the manner he has indicated, but this time she does not report on her feelings while doing so. The last coitus is a silent one. There is no textual time, and we don't know how much fictional time is involved either; what we know is that they don't go to sleep between coitus five and six, that the fifth took place not long after midnight, and that we don't hear them again until noontime when, according to the author, Rampín's aunt comes into the bedroom to wake them. The sixth and quietest coitus might well have been the longest, however, and it certainly was the last: the time that could have been used for a seventh was dedicated entirely to rest.

The middle scene of the fourteenth *mamotreto* is a convincing portrayal of the joy and power and beauty of true lust. True because human experience and imagination find everything that happens in that bedroom, every word that is uttered by the lovers, quite believable and totally desirable. Nothing impresses us as ugly, as rooted in vice, as sad. Neither Lozana nor Rampín is making any effort except that of reaching for pleasure; and they both achieve it. What they do can impress no one as too complicated, or "decadent," or less than absolutely natural: all they do is copulate, and they glory in it. Maybe that is why we forget that she has no nose, that he is almost a cripple, that neither could pass as a model of human beauty. But then, beauty is an attribute of the divine and sex is not; wouldn't it be possible to say that the less beautiful the body—fountain and object of lust—the sexier the sex? Pure sex. Unadorned. Undisguised. No aesthetic distractions. What we are witnessing here—together with the *auctor*—is lust's being asserted, insisted upon. The joy of the creative act is repeated six times, as at the beginning of Genesis, and followed by the contented rest that success rarely fails to bring about. That is why it is so important that male and female be so carefully and wisely differentiated. That she be the mortar and he be the pestle, that she be the words that express the meaning of his actions, that she be the one who does not need to sleep at the beginning of their night, that he, having slept earlier, be the one asking at the end for one more, for the last one. Then there is the relation between the textual lengths of the first coitus and the three consecutive ones; the dialogue preceding and following the fifth, when Lozana, tired, is already thinking about the next day and the next meal; and, finally, the last coitus, which blends in wordless time the ending of sex and the beginning of sleep. All these ingredients, aspects of a calibrated process leading from desire to contentment, together with the presence of *auctor,* from whom, as witnesses, we cannot feel too distant—he sees and hears, we read and visualize—contribute to make this erotic scene convincing, and as profoundly serious as it is happy. The author's author has presented himself as suffering from the same disease that afflicts Lozana; he has said that he wrote his book to alleviate his suffering.[19] He knows that what brought it about was an act like the one he is portraying, yet his portrayal shows no bitterness or resentment. He is depicting just what he sees and hears, what he sees and hears is unabashed joy, and he is, apparently, being true to his art. It is true, of course, that Rome was the very emblem of inverted Christian love—Roma/Amor: my pleasure, myself first rather than God; and that, when in Rome, one does as the Romans do, or feels as the Romans feel. But then the Romans must feel good about their way of love, as does the author's author, as do Lozana and Rampín. Perhaps, after the sack of the city, the author's author sensed that he had to insert that epochal event in his book. He certainly included it, probably aware that now that Rome, the whore, had become Rome, the victim, it would not be a bad idea to associate one excess with another, allowing his audience to believe that the second one, the sack, was the proper way of punishing the first, sinful sex, and that the brutal action for which his king and emperor was ultimately responsible had something to do with divine retribution. But that was an afterthought. My contention is that the sack took place after the *mamotretos*—and the first version of the book—were finished, and that while he was "painting" them and Rome, he was not looking at Roman life with the eyes of a severe judge or a resentful loser. My contention is also that Lozana enjoys her Rome, her career, her sex with Rampín; that she is successful, that the years go by, that, at the end, feeling her age, she says she would rather abandon her clients than be abandoned by them. Finally, it is my contention that in the last *mamotreto,* having apparently saved enough money to be able to do so, she decides to retire and live as happily as possible ever after in the company of Rampín, her true friend and lover.

What I have just said in no way implies that the author's author in the *mamotretos* thinks differently from the one in the pieces—particularly the *Apología* and the *Digresión*—at the end of the book. Rather, he is a pragmatist and as such is trying to adjust and make compatible old and new realities: his reality before the sack of the city to his reality after it, his Roman weltanschauung to his Venetian one. Both Venice and Rome—his Venice and his Rome—are in the book, of course, as are many of his activities in both places.

At the beginning of this essay I presented the phrase author's author and talked about how in *La Lozana andaluza* historic and storic authors become *almost* one. It is obvious that there must be a historical author, someone who actually thought the words and, by whatever means, had them penned down. His existence is to be recognized. But how can we separate him from the storic one? Where does one begin and the other end?

La Lozana andaluza was published anonymously in Venice sometime between 1528 and 1530. That meant that the author inside the text was the only one the readers knew, and that the author was exactly and exclusively what the text made him to be. Then, in February 1534, in Venice, the editor of a Castilian narrative, the *Primaleón,* stated in the introduction to his edition that his name was Francisco Delicado and that he had written *La Lozana andaluza.* Just by doing so he created himself as a historic author, one who had certain characteristics that were not apparent in his storic counterpart: he wanted, for instance, to be recognized as a writer of *mamotretos,* wanted to be remembered, and believed in the importance of his name. Yet by being in Venice and having his *La Lozana andaluza* published there, he was putting in the mind of his readers the idea that he was not just the author of that text, but the author in it.[20] This idea was strengthened by the discovery that, besides editing other Spanish books, he had written *Modo de adoperare el legno de India occidentale* (On the use of the West Indies wood), something the author inside the text of *La Lozana andaluza* said he had done himself.[21] As a result the readers to this day have been inclined to identify the historic Francisco Delicado with the storic author of *La Lozana andaluza* and, because so little is known about the former, to project upon him all that the text attributes to the latter. The storic Francisco Delicado is, however, a character within a text, limited by it. Even if everything the text tells us about the author was actually part of the historic reality named Francisco Delicado, still the Delicado in the text would be the invention of the one outside it, of what the one outside it perceived himself to be as he was writing under the influence of whatever he conceived his text should be. Thus the Francisco Delicado in the story would have to be and is the result of the other Delicado's selective process, the process by which he eliminates from his created alter ego everything that was part of himself, of his biographic reality, but did not suit his artistic purposes. Therefore there are two Delicados, but two—and here is where the phrase author's author comes in—who have much in common. The desire to express this commonness is, perhaps, the main reason why the historic Delicado tells us his name four or five years after the storic one wrote that he could not identify himself because of the nobility of his *oficio*. Delicado, who had been taught that the Creation mirrors its Creator, seems to have tried to put something more than just his reflection upon his work. Carried by his desire to translate reality into text, he developed his concept of *mamotreto* and invented a written author that can hardly be distinguished from the writing one, and who can appear as the author who makes or as the author who is made or as both, depending on how the mind of the reader acts upon him. Delicado then brings this author's author, who can be one and/or the other, deeper and deeper into the reality of his invention, changing him from omniscient narrator, to witness from another time-space, to present and invisible witness, to participant in nonsequential time, to full participant. He does so by combining verbal, typographical, and pictorial elements in such a way that his readers hardly notice how they are being carried, together with the author's author, from level to level closer to the world of Lozana and Francisco Delicado.

Notes

1. Bruno Damiani, *Portrait of Lozana, the Lusty Andalusian Woman.* Potomac, Md.: Scripta Humanistica, 1987.

2. *La Lozana andaluza* was probably published in 1528 (certainly no later than 1530) when mimesis ruled the arts. Concerning date of publication, see Giovanni Allegra, "Sobre una nueva hipótesis en la biografía de F. Delicado," *Boletín de la Real Academia Española* 56 (1976): 522–33.

3. Besides sketch, *mamotreto* may mean memorandum, notebook, a bulky folder or a book containing data or presenting not always relevant information in a disorderly and excessive way. Delicado uses the word to designate each of the sixty-six sequences in which the central and longest part of his book is divided. In *mamotreto* 63 Lozana uses the term to signify either copulation or orgasm. Because the semantic field of *mamotreto* is obviously quite different from that of sketch, I will use *mamotreto* throughout.

4. Only the first line of *mamotreto* 6 is not part of the dialogue. As if to signify that this line is in the same mode as the one spoken by the narrator to introduce the *mamotreto*, there is no blank line between the two and there is no indentation.

5. I am speaking here of the inside-the-text reader, the one that exists only in the imagination of the author's author. The latter is inventing a reader who becomes sufficiently involved with his text to desire to improve it. This invented reader might be expected to influence the reaction to the text of the other reader, the outside-the-text one.

6. The facsimile edition was prepared by Antonio Pérez Gómez and published in Valencia in 1950.

7. Much has been written about the activities of Delicado in Venice where he was to publish, after some minor changes and additions, *La Lozana andaluza* that he had written in Rome. See Tatiana Bubnova, *F. Delicado puesto en diálogo: Las claves bajtinianas de "La Lozana andaluza"* (Mexico City: Universidad Nacional Autónoma de México, 1987): 81–85; and Francesco Ugolini, "Nuovi dati intorno alla biografia di Francisco Delicado desunti da una sua sconosciuta operetta," *Annali della facoltà di Lettere e filosofia della Universita degli Studi di Perugia* 12 (1972–75): 445–615.

8. The first edition uses both *autor* and *auctor*. Later on in this essay I will show a possible reason for this.

9. I have numbered the lines of the fourteenth *mamotreto* to facilitate communication. They are not numbered in the original.

10. The numbering system is as follows. Beginning with A and proceeding in alphabetical order, each group of four folios—eight pages—is assigned a letter. Except for group A, whose first folio contains the title page (recto) and two large illustrations (verso), the first folios of all groupings (rectos) are marked on the lower righthand corner with the corresponding letter without a number; all second folios (rectos)—including A—are marked by the corresponding letter followed by two i's. Versos are never marked, nor are folios 3 and 4. The series ends with the N group that, unlike all others, contains six folios and carries markings N iii on the recto of the third one. The letter I is not included in the alphabetical series because it is used—lowercase—as a number.

11. According to Bruno Damiani there are thirteen rather than fourteen subsequent interventions. He believes that the intervention of *auctor* in line 13 (Figure 12) is a mistake and eliminates it. Claude Allaigre disagrees with Damiani and keeps it, but reduces it to the phrase "¡Mirá qué le aconteció!" which I would translate as "Wasn't that something what happened to her!"

12. In his edition of *La Lozana andaluza* (Madrid: Cátedra, 1985), Claude Allaigre, after pointing out what in his opinion is Damiani's mistake concerning this illustration, writes a two-page analysis of it without mentioning Pyramus and Thisbe. Damiani calls the same illustration "Alegoría de la pronosticada destrucción de Roma" (*La Lozana andaluza* [Madrid: Castalia, 1969], 65). It is not easy to figure out the reasons why he gave it such a title. He doesn't mention Pyramus and Thisbe either.

13. About the *converso* condition of Rampín and of other characters in *La Lozana*, see F. Márquez Villanueva, "El mundo converso de *La Lozana andaluza*" (Sevilla: Archivo Hispalense, 1973). See also Claude Allaigre's edition.

14. I quote from Damiani's edition (Madrid: Castalia, 1969). The translations are mine and as close to the original as I have been able to make them.

15. The feminine form of the pronoun refers here to a hare, *liebre*, mentioned by Lozana as emblematic of her arousal. We should remember that a little earlier she has called Rampín's penis a ferret, and that ferrets for a long time were used to

hunt rabbits (they can enter their warrens). Hares and rabbits were never very far from each other in popular tradition, and both are equally emblematic of strong sexual urges and fecundity.

16. Rampín's question could be read as an example of masculine teasing, and it makes "masculine" sense. Because he is sure of his own orgasm no matter what, he is asking what would he gain by helping her get her own. Her answer is in the joy she expresses immediately after experiencing it, in the very enthusiastic comments she dedicates to his penis, and in her behavior during the rest of the night.

17. I agree with Claude Allaigre and understand garlic and cheese to mean here the male genitalia.

18. I do not understand the last two sentences. Why Jerez? Which Jerez—de la Frontera or de los Caballeros? What are the characteristics of turnips from Jerez? Damiani states that *frojolón* may be the name of an Italian town. My guess is that Lozana is thinking of two different types of turnips. In Castilian, *nabo* (turnip) is used to refer to penis. The "turnip" from Jerez may be a less attractive variety, perhaps more mature, less smooth, not so straight, and associated with masturbation; the other (from Frosolone?) may be picked earlier, "younger," and be as appealing as Rampín's "nabo."

19. See the author's *apología*, which initiates the series of six pieces that close the text.

20. See the author's digression at the end of *La Lozana andaluza* where we are told that he published it in Venice and why.

21. He says so in his *apología* right after the end of the last *mamotreto*.

Works Cited

Allegra, Giovanni. "Sobre una nueva hipótesis en la biografía de F. Delicado." *Boletín de la Real Academia Española* 56 (1976): 522–33.

Bubnova, Tatiana. *F. Delicado Puesto en diálogo: Las claves bajtinianas de "La Lozana andaluza."* Mexico City: Universidad Nacional Autónoma de México, 1985.

Delicado, Francisco. *La Lozana andaluza.* ca. 1528.

———. *La Lozana andaluza.* Facsimile edition. Ed. Antonio Pérez Gómez. Valencia, 1950.

———. *La Lozana andaluza.* Ed. Bruno Damiani. Madrid: Castalia, 1969.

———. *La Lozana andaluza.* Ed. Claude Allaigre. Madrid: Castalia, 1985.

———. *Portrait of Lozana, the Lusty Andalusian Woman.* Trans. and introduction by Bruno Damiani. Potomac, Md.: Scripta Humanistica, 1987.

Márquez Villanueva, F. "El mundo converso de *La Lozana andaluza.*" Sevilla: Archivo Hispalense, 1973.

Ugolini, Francesco. "Nuovi dati intorno alla biografia di Francisco Delicado desunti da una sua sconosciuta operetta." *Annali della facolta di Lettere e filosofia della Universita degli Studi di Perugia* 12 (1972–75): 445–615.

RETRATO DE

la Loçana:andaluza:en lengua española:
muy clarissima. Cópuesto en Roma.

Al qual Retrato demuestra loque en Roma passaua y contiene munchas mas
cosas que la Celestina.

Figure 1. *La Lozana andaluza*, Ai recto.

Figure 2. *La Lozana andaluza*, Ai verso.

Lluftre Señoz. Sabiédo yo q̃ v̈ia Señozia toma
plazer:quando oye hablar en coffas de amoz:q̃ de
leytan a todo ombze. y maxime quando Siente de
zir de perſonas q̃ mejoz Se ſupieron dar la manera para adminiſtrar las coſas ael pertenecyentes.
y poz q̃ en v̈ios tienpos podeis gozar de perſona:q̃
para ſi y para ſus cótépozaneas q̃ en ſu tiépo flozido ſueró:en eſta
alma cibdad/có igenio mirable y Alte muy ſagaz/ diligēcia grá
de:verguéça y cóciécia:poz el çerro ó vbeda: Hoa adminiſtrado
ella.y vnſupzeterito criado(como abaxo diremos) El arte de a-
q̃lla muger q̃ fue en Salamáca:en tienpo de çeleſtino ſegundo:
poz táto hederigido eſte retrato a v̈ia ſeñozia para q̃ ſu muy vir-
tuoſo ſenbláte/me de favoz para publicar el retrato de la ſeñoza
Loçana.y mire v̈ia Señoza:q̃ ſolaméte dire lo q̃ oy/ y vi/ con
menos culpa q̃ Juuenal:pues eſcriuio lo q̃ en ſu tienpo paſaua.
Y ſi poz tiépo alguno ſe marauillare q̃ me puſe aeſcriuir ſemejan
te materia. Reſpódo poz en tóçes q̃ (epiſtola enim nó erubeſcit)
y aſſi miſino q̃ es paſſado el tiénpo/ q̃ eſtimauan los q̃ trabajauā/
en coſas meritozias. y como dize el coroniſta Fernando del pul
gar/aſſi dare 'oluido al doloz. y tanbien:poz traer a la memozia
múchas coſas: q̃ en nros tiépos paſſan/q̃ no ſon laude a los pze-
ſentes/ni eſpejo a loſa venir/y aſſi vi/q̃ mi yntenció fue mezclar
Natura conbemol/ Pues los ſantos ombzes poz mas ſaber. y o
tras vezes poz des enojarſe:leyan libros fabuloſos. y coglian en
tre las flozes las mejozes. y pues todo Retrato tiene neçeſſidad
debarniz. ſuplico a v̈ia Señozia ſe lo mande dar: favozeſciendo
mi voluntad. Encomédádo a los diſcretos lectozes el plazer y ga
ſajo/q̃ del certa la Señoza Loçana les podra ſuçeder.

Argumento en el qual ſe contienen todas las
particularidades:q̃ a de auer en la púte obza.

Dezirſe a primero la cibdad / patria / y li-
naje/vétura/deſgracia/y fortuna/ſumo
do/manera/y cóuerſacion/ſu trato/platica/y fin/
poz q̃ ſolamente gozara deſte Retrato / quien
todo lo leyere.

A ij

Protesta el autor / que ninguno quite:ni añada / palabra / ni Razon/ni lenguaje/porq̃ a qui no conpuse modo de hermoso dezir:ni saque de otros libros ni hurte eloquençia por que para dezir la verdad poca eloquencia basta:como dize Seneca.ni quise nonbre/Saluo que quise Retraer munchas cosas: Retraiendo vna/y Retraxe lo que vi:que se deuia Retraer:y por esta conparaçion que se sigue/veran q̃ tengo Razon.

Todos los artifices: que eneste mundo trabajan. dessean que sus obras sean mas perfectas que ningunas otras que jamas fuessen. y vee se mejor esto en los pintores / que no en otros artifices.por que quando hazen vn Retrato.procuran sacallo del natural / e a esto se esfuerçan. y no solamente se contentan de mirarlo / e cotejarlo / mas quieren que sea mirado por los transeuntes/e çircunstantes / y cada vno dize su parescer/mas ninguno toma el punzel y emienda/saluo el pintor:q̃ oye / y vee la Razon de cadauno.y assi emieda/cotejado tame:lo q̃ vee/mas q̃ lo que oye Lo q̃ munchos artifices/no puede hazer/por q̃ despues de auer cortado la materia/y va dole forma/no puede sinperdida emedar.y por q̃ este Retrato es tan natural q̃ no ay psona. q̃ aya conoscido la Señora Loçana en Roma/o fuera d̃ Roma/ q̃ no vea claro ser sacado desus actos/y meneos/y palabras/y assi mismo por q̃ yo he trabajado d̃ no escreuir cosa/q̃ primero no se casse en mi dechado la lauor/mirado en ella o a ella. Y viendo vn mucho mejor q̃ yo ni otro podra escreuir/y dire lo q̃ dixo eschies po leyedo vna/oracio/o.pcesso q̃ demostenes auia hecho/cõtra el/no pudiedo expremir la mucha mas eloquecia/q̃ auia enel dicho Demostenes/dixo/q̃ haria si oyerades ael(qd si ipsa audissetis bestiã)y por esso verna en fabula. mucho mas sabia la Loçana q̃ no mostraua/y viedo yo en ella munchas vezes manera/ y saber q̃ bastaua para caçar Sin Red.y en frenar a quien mucho pesaua saber.Sacaua lo q̃ podia: para Reduzir a memoria:que en/ otra parte mas alta(q̃ vna picota)fuera mejor Retrayda/q̃ en la presente obra/y por q̃ no le pude dar mejor matiz.no quiero que ninguno añada ni quite. q̃ si miran en ello lo q̃ al principio falta se hallara al fin:de modo q̃ por lo poco entiendan lo muncho mas/ ser como deducion de canto llano. Y quien el contrario bizieri sea siempre/enamorado y no querido.Amen.

Figure 4. *La Lozana andaluza*, Aii verso.

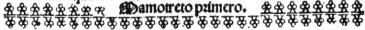

¶ Comiença la hiſtoria/o Retrato Sacado del Jure çeuil natural. De la Señora Loçana: cõpueſto el año mill y quinie
tos y veynte e quatro. a treynta dias del mes de Junio:
en Roma alma cibdad/ y como auia de ſer parti-
do en capitulos va por/ mamotretos / por
que en ſemejante/ obra mejor conuiene
Mamotreto primero.

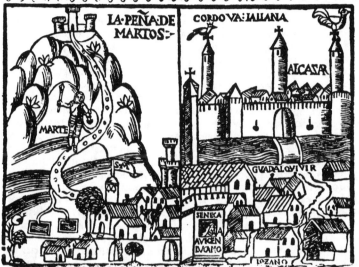

LA·PEÑA·DE
MARTOS:-

CORDOVA: IALIANA

ALCAÇAR

MARTE

GVADALQVIVIR

SENECA
IA
AVICEN
JUANO

LOZANO

A Señora Loçana fue natural conpatriota de Seneca/ y no me
nos en ſu intelligencia: y Reſaber. laqual-deſde ſu niñez tuuo Ingenio, y memoria, y biuez grãde: y fue muy querida de ſus padres
por ſer aguda en ſeruillos, e cõtentallos, e muerto ſu padre fue ne
ceſſario que a cõpañaſſe a ſu madre: fuera de ſu natural. Y eſta fue
la cauſa que ſupo/ y vido mũchas cibdades villas/ y lugares/ deſpaña', q̃ agora ſe,
le Recuerdan de caſſi el todo, y tiñe tanto intellecto : q̃ caſſi eſcuſaua aſu madre
procurador para ſus negocios/ ſienpre q̃ ſu madre la mãdaua yr o ve
nir hera preſta: y como pleyteaua ſu Madre/ ella fue en Granada mirada: y tenida por ſoliçitadora perfecta: e prenoſticada futura: acaba
do el pleyto e no queriendo tornar a ſu propria cibdad: acordaron
demorar en Xerez/ y paſar por Carmona/ aqui la madre qſo moſtrar

Figure 5. *La Lozana andaluza*, Aiii recto.

fablos/dubdo lafaní:lad.y pues ya voy acallз fuplicò a vĩa merçed fe venga co/
nugo.L O.yo Señor verne a la fiũ del mũdo.mas dexe fubir anũtia a Rĩba/y pues
quiſo mi ventura fere fienpre vĩa mas que mia. Tia.Aldonça.̃ Sobrina.̃ que ha/
зeys donde eſtays.̃ o pecadora de mi / el ombre dexa el padre y la mudre por la
muger/y la muger oluida por el ombre funido.Ay Sobrina:y fi mirara bĩ en vos
viera que me a vie des de burlar/mas no teneys vos la calpa fi no yo . ḡ teniendo
la yeſca,bus ḡ el eſlauon,mira ḡ pago.̃ ḡ fi miro en ello ella miſma me hizo alca
gueta.va va que en tal pararas.
    ❡Mamotreto.IIII.   Proffigue el Autor

Vntos a caliз , y fabido por Diomedes / a que fabia fu Señora:fi era con/,
cho ò veramente afado/començo a ynponella fegun ḡ para luengos tien/
pos durafen Iuntos:y viendo fus lindas carnes,y lindeзa de perſona: y no
tando en ella el agudeзa/que la patria y parentado le auian preſtado,de cada dia
le creſcia el amor/en fu coraçon y an fi determino deno dexalla/ y paſſando el en
leuante/ con mercadançia/ que fu padre era vno de los primos mercaderes de
Italia . lleuocòfigo a fu muy amada Aldõça/y de todo quãto tenia la hazia par/
ticipe/y ella muy cõtenta/viendo en fu caro amador Diomedes todos los gene/
ros y partes de gẽtil ombre/y de hermofura en todos fus miẽbros / ḡ le pareſçia
a ella/que la natura no fe auia Referuado nada/ que en fucaro amante no huuieſe
pueſto . e por eſta cauſa/ miraua defer ella pſta/a toda fu voluntad, y como el era
vnico en tre los otros mercadantes,fienpre en fu caſa auia concurfo de perſonas
gentiles/y bien criadas/y como veyan ḡ ala Señora aldonça / no le faltaua nada
ḡ fin maeſtro tenia Ingenio y faber/y no taua las coſſas minimas por faber y ẽ tẽ
der laſgrãdes/y arduas.holgauan de ver fu eloquẽcia. y a todos fobre pujaua de
modo/ḡ yano auia otra en a ḡ llas partes ḡ en mas fueſſe tenida / y era dicho en
tre todos de fu loçania/an fi en la cara como en todos fus miẽbros . y viendo ḡ
eſta Loçania era de fu natural , quedoles en fabula que ya no entendian por fu
nonbre Aldõça faluo la Loçana/ y no folamẽte entre ellos mas entre las gẽtes de
a ḡ llas tierras deзian la Loçana por coſa muy nõbrada/y fi mũcho Sabia eneſtas
partes/mũcho mas fu po en a ḡ llas prouincias.y procuraua de ver y faber quãto
a fu facultad perteneſçia. Siẽdo en Rodas fucaro Diomedes/la pgunto/mi feño
ra.̃ no ḡrria Seos hiзieſe de mal venir aleuante.por ḡ yo me tengo de diſponer/a
feruir y obedeçer ami padre elqual manda ḡ vaya en leuãte:y andare toda la ber
beria, y principalmente donde tenemos trato, que me fera fuerзa de demorar, y
no tornar tan preſto/como yo querria / por que folamente en eſtas cibdades que
agora/ oires tẽgo de eſtar años/ y no meſes como fera en Alexãdria/en Damaſco
en Damiata/en Barut en pte dela Soria,en Chiple,en el Cayre y en el Xio en Cõ
ſtãtinopoli/en Corinthio en Teſalia.en boecia.en Cádia a Venecia y Flãdes.y en
otras partes ḡ vos mi Señora vereys/Si quereys tenerme copañia.Loçana.y quã
do quiere vĩa merçed ḡ partamos/ por que yo no delibro deboluer a caſa por el
mantillo. Viſta por Diomedes la Refpueſta y voluntad/tan fuſcinta ḡ le dio cõ
palabras anti penfadas/mũcho fe alegro, y Suplicola ḡ fe eſforçaſſe ano dexarlo

Figure 6. *La Lozana andaluza*, Aiiii verso.

para vna perfona bafta para dos.Loçana.Señora yo lo do poz Refçebido dadaca
fi quereys q os ayude/a effo q hazeys,Napolitana. quitaos primero el paño y mi
ra fi traes ninguna cofa q dar aguardar,Loçana.Señora no:fi no vn efpejo para
mirarme y agora veo que tengo mi pago/q folia tener diez efpejos en mi camara
para mirarme q de mi mifma eftaua como Narciffo y agora/como Tifbe ala fon,

tana/y fino memiraua çien vezes nome miraua vna/y he auido el pago de mi pro
pia merçed/Quienfon eftos q vienen a qui.napolitana anfi goze de vos q fon mis
hijos,Loçana.bien pareçen a fu padre/y fi fon eftos los pinos de oro/a fus ojos.Na
politana.que dezis.Loçana.Señora q pareçen hijos de Rei (naçidos enbadajos)
que veays nientos dellos,Napolitana,anfi veays vos de lo q pariftes,Loçana.nia
çebo debien llegaos aca y moftrame la mano,Mira q feñal tenes en el monte de
Mercurio y huñas de rapina,guardaos de tomar le ageno q peligrares,Napolita
na,a efto trobizarro me mira.Loçana.effe barbitaheño/como fe llama. veni/veni
efte mote de Venus efta muy alto vro peligroefta feñalado en faturno de vna pri
fion/y enel mote dela Luna peligro poz mar.Rapin.caminar pordoua el buey.Lo
çana moftra efotra mano.Ranpin.que quereys ver. que mi ventura ya lafe: dezi
me vos donde dormire efta noche,Loçana.donde. donde no foñaftes.Ranpin.
no fea en la prifion y venga lo q veniere.Loçana.Señora efte vro hijo mas es ven
turofo q no penfays/q hedad tiene. Napolitana/de diez años le facamos los bra
çicos/y tomo fuerça en los lomos.Loçana.fuplicos q le deys liçençia q vaya co
migo/y me mueftre efta çibdad.Napolitana.fi hara q es muy feruidor dequien lo
mereçe/anda meteos effa camifa/y ferui a effa Señora honrrada.

            Mamotreto

Figure 7. *La Lozana andaluza*, Biiii recto.

alça el bꝛaço mira que de Ramareys/ quien melo dixo ami ſ ĝlo auia deſ de haƶerſ
Tia.) aſſi/ anſi veys caydo el vanco. Y la Señoꝛa ſe aura hecĥo mal. Lo.) no he ſi
no que todo el vino me cayo eꞃcima buen feñal. Tia.) Yd poꝛ mas y veys lo eeĥo.
paſſaos aqui que ſiempꝛe haƶeys vꝛas coſas peſadas, no cortes ſ que vꝛo ſobꝛino cõ
tara ſ veys ay çape/çape, alla ua Lo mejoꝛ ſelleua elgato/poꝛ ĝ no eſperays ſ que pa
reſçe ĝ no aucys comido ſ Viejo,) dixame haƶer. Y terne mejoꝛ aliento para beuer.
Tia.) Venis ſobꝛino. Rá.) vẽgo poꝛ alguna coſa en ĝlo trayga. Tia.) y las dos gar
rafas. Rá.) cay Y quebꝛclas. Tia.) pues toma eſtejarro. Rá.) eſte es bueno y ſi me
diƶe algo el tauernero dalle cconel. Tia.) anſi lo haƶe/ Señoꝛa mia yo me querria
meter en vn agupero yno ver eſto quando ay gente foꝛaſtera encaſa/mas vos Se
ñoꝛa aueys de mirar ĝ eſta caſa es vꝛa, Lo.) mas gana tẽgo de doꝛmir ĝ de otra co
ſa. Tia.) ſobꝛino çena voſſotros entãto ĝ uo/e/la ayudo adeſnudar. Rá.) ſeñoꝛa ſi.

¶ Mamotreto, XIIII.　Como toꝛna ſu Tia,) y demáda dõde a dedoꝛmir Rápio
y lo que paſſaron la Lo.) y ſu futuro criado en la cama.

Dꝛme ſobꝛino as de doꝛmir alli cõ ella que nꝍ me a dicĥo na
da/ Y poꝛ mi vida que tiene lindo cuerpo. Rá.) pues que ſi
la vierades vos deſnuda en la eſtuſa, Tia.) Yo ĝſiera ſer om
bre tábien me ha pareſçido/ o que pierna de muger / y el neçio de ſu
5　marido que la dexo venir ſola a la tierra de cornualla : de ve deſer
qual ĝ babió/o veramẽte ĝ ella deue deſer buena de ſu cuerpo. Rá.)
yo lo vere eſta nocĥe: ĝ ſi puedo tẽgo de pegar cõ ſus bienes. Tia.)
a otro ĝ tu auria ella de meneſter ĝ le hallaſe mejoꝛ la beƶmellerica
y le hincĥeſe lamedida. Rá.) anda nocures ĝ debaxo yaƶe buen be/
10　uedor como diƶen ſ Tia.) pue allas dexe el candil va paſico ĝ duerme/y cierra la
puerta. Rá.) ſi hare buenaꞧ nocĥes. Tia.) Va en buen oꝛa. Lo.) ay hijo/ y aqui os
hecĥaſtes ſ pues doꝛmi y cobijaos ĝ harta Ropa ay ſ ĝ haƶeys ſ mira ĝ tẽgo matido.
Rá.) ĝes no eſta agoꝛa aq para ĝ nos vea. Lo.) ſi mas ſabello ha. Rá.) no hara eſte
ĝ da vn poquito. Lo.) ay ĝ bonito y deſos ſoys ſ poꝛ mi vida ĝ me leuáte. R.) noſea
15　deſa manera ſi no poꝛ ver ſi ſoy capon me dixeys deƶiros dos palabꝛas con el din
guilindon. Lo.) no hare la verdad te ĝero deƶir ĝ eſtoy virgin. Rá) anda Señoꝛa
ĝ no teneys vos ojo de eſtar virgen/dexame agoꝛa haƶer ĝ no pareſçera ĝ os toco
Lo.) ay/ ay ſoys muy mucĥacĥo y no ĝrria haƶeros mal. Rá.) no hareys que yaſe
me coꝛto el frenillo. Lo.) no os baſta beſarme y goƶar demi anſi ĝ quereis tanbien
20　copoy cõdedura/cata ĝ me apretays/vos peſays ĝ lo hallareys ſ pues hagos ſaber
que eſſe huron no ſabe caçar eneſta floꝛeſta. Rá.) abꝛil de vos la puerta ĝ ʾl hara ſu
ofiçio ala macĥa martillo. Lo.) poꝛ vna buelta ſoy cõtéta mochacho heres tu ſ poꝛ
eſto diƶen/guardate del moço quádo lenaçe el boço: ſi lo ſupiera mas pꝛeſto ſolta
ua las Riendas ami ĝrer. paſico/bonico/ĝ dico/ nome a hinqueys/ anda comigo/
25　poꝛ ay van alla/ay ĝ pꝛieſa os days/y no mirays que eſta otrie enpaſamiento: ſi no
vos: cata ĝ no ſoy de a ĝllas ĝ ſequedan atras: eſpera veƶaros he/ anſi/anſi / poꝛ av
ſereys maeſtro/veys como va bien ſ eſto no ſabie des vos pues uo ſe os ol vide: ſus

Figure 8. *La Lozana andaluza*, Ciii recto.

dal de maeſtro es loda q̃ aqui ſeuera el correz deſta lança:quien la q̃ulebza. Y mira
q̃ poz nuicho madrugaz no amaneſçe mas ayna/enel coſſo te tengo la garrocha es
30 bucna/no q̃ero ſino veros latiraz:buē pzicipio Heuays/camina q̃ la liebze eſta cha/
cada/aq̃ va la hoorra.Rã.)y ſi la veço q̃ ganareſ Lo.)no cureys:q̃ cada coſa tiene
ſuprenuo/a vos veço yo q̃ naçiſtes veçado:da ca la mano y tēte ami/q̃ el al madra
q̃/es coſto/apaieta/y caua/y a hoya/y todo a vn tiẽpo. Alzs clines coredoz agora
poz mi vida q̃ ſeua el Recuero.Ay amores q̃ ſoy vrã muerta y biua/ qtaos la camiſ
35 la q̃ ſudays/quāto auia q̃ no comia cocho vētura fue en cõtar el ombze tābuē paz
tiçipio/a vn paſto/eſte tal majadero no me falte q̃ yo apetito tengo dende q̃ naſci
ſin apo/y q̃to/q̃ podria pſtar amisviçinas/Dormido ſea/en mi vida vi mão de moz
tero tãbiē hecha/q̃ gordo q̃ es: y todo parejo mal año para nábo dexerez:pareçe
billoño de frojolõ:la habla me quito/ no tenia pozdo Reſollar/nó es de dexar eſte
40 tal vnicoznio,q̃ aueys amoreſ Rã.)no nada ſino de mãdaros de merçed q̃ toda
eſta noche ſeays mia.Lo.)no mas aſi goçeys.Rã.)Señoza poz q̃ noſ falte algo en la
paladaſe mēdallo hemos q̃ la noche es luēga.Lo.)diſpone como de vrõ/cõtáto q̃
ure lo tēgays ſecreto:Ay q̃ miel tã ſabroſa: no lo pēſeſ aguça/aguça dale ſiledas q̃
me llamã en caſa /aq/aq̃ buena como la primera / q̃ no le falta vn pelo/ dozmi poz
45 mi vida q̃ yo os cõbijare,q̃ te dios de mis dias/y põga en los tuyos:q̃ quáto en ojo
traya incas qtardo/ſi fuera yo grã Señoza no me qtara jamas eſte de mi lado/o pe/
cadoza de mi y deſperteos no q̃ſiera.Rã.)anda q̃ no ſe pierde nada.Lo.)ay/ay aſi
ua poz mi vida q̃ tã bien camine yo/alli/alli/mehozmiguea/que/q̃/paſareys poz mi
puerta. Amoz mio toda via ay tiẽpo Repoſa alça la cabeça/toma eſta almohadaſ
50 mira que Sueño tieneq̃ no puede ſer mejoz quiero meyo dozmiz.

¶Auctoz.
Vi fiera ſaber eſcriuiz vn paz de Rõgdos alos q̃les
deſperto el/y q̃riẽdo la beſar deſpto ella/ y dixo ay
Señoz es de dia.Rap.)no ſe:q̃ agoza deſperté q̃ a q̃l
55 cardo me a hecho dozmiz.Lo.)q̃ hazeys:y qtroſ ala qura cãtu
el gáto/no eſtare q̃ da/no eſtare q̃ da haſta que muera: dozmi
que ya es de dia/y yo tã biẽ/ mata a q̃l cãdil que me dã en los
ojos/echaos y tira la Ropa a vos.Auctoz)alli jūto moraua vn
herrezo el q̃l ſe leuáto a media noche/ y no leſdexaua dozmiz
60 y el ſeleuáto auer ſi era de dia y tomãdoſe ala cama la deſperto/y dixo ella/ de do,
venis.q̃ nos ſenti leuátaz. Rã.) fui alli fuera q̃ eſtos veçinos haçē de la noche dia
eſtan las cabrillas ſobze eſte hozno q̃ es la pūta de la media noche / y no nos dexan
dozmiz.Lo.)y en cueros ſaliſteſ frio venis.Rã.)vos me eſcalẽtareys. Lo.)ſi ha
re mas no deſſa manera/no mas q̃ eſtoy harta y me gaſtareys laçena . Rã)tarde a
65 cozdaſtes/q̃ dẽtro yaz q̃ no Rabea/harta me deçis q̃ eſtays y pareçe que comẽçays
agoza/canſada creeria yo mas pſto q̃ ns harta. Lo.)pues q̃n ſe harta q̃ no dexe vn
Rincõ para lo q̃ viniere/poz mi vida q̃ tãbiẽ batis vos el hierro como a q̃l herrezo
a tiempo y fuerte q̃ es açero/mi vida/ ya nonas q̃ baſta haſta otro dia/q̃ yo no puẽ
do mãtener la tela y lo demas ſeria gaſtar lo bueno/ dozmi q̃ al mozçar q̃ero en le
70 uantádome.R.)no cureys q̃. mi tia tiene gallinas y nos dara de los hueuos y mũ/

Figure 9. *La Lozana andaluza*, Ciii verso.

eha máteca y la calabaça llena. Lo.)Señoz fi dire yo como desta la buena muger
de pues de bié harta. Rá.)y como dezia. Lo.)dixo harta de duelos cõ múcha ma/
zilla como lo fabe a qlla que no me dexara métir. Auctoz.) Y feñalo a la Calaba/
ça. Rá.)puta vieja hera eſta ala máteca llamaua mazilla lobos. Lo.)luéga vala jura
75 lo moço y ſer de cordoua me falua, el Sueño me viene Repofemos, Rá.)Soy cõté
to A eſtelado y me tamos la y leſia ſobze el câpanario. Auctoz pſigue.)hera medio
dia quádo vino la tla a defpertallos y dize ſobzino abzi / cata el ſol q̃ entra poz to/
do.buenos dias como aueys dozmido. Lo.)Señoza muy biẽ y vño ſobzino como
lechõ debiuda/q̃ no ha meneado pie ni pierna haſta agoza:q̃ yo yame feria leuáta
80 da fino poz no defpertallo/q̃ no he hecho ſi no lloza: pélando en mi marido/q̃ ha
ſe/odo eſta/q̃ no viene. Tia.)no tomeys fatiga andad aca q̃ qero q̃ veays mi caſa,
agora q̃ no eſta aq̃ mi maridoveys aq̃ en q̃ paſo tiempo/q̃reys q̃ os las qui te a vos?
Lo.)Señora fi y defpues yo/os pelare a vos/poz q̃ veays q̃ mano tégo. Tia)efpera
traere a q̃l pelados oeſcoriadoz/y vereys q̃ no dexa vello ninguno / q̃ las jodias lo
85 huſá múcho. Lo.)y de q̃ ſe haze eſte pegote o pellejadoz. Tia.)de q̃, de tremétina
y de pez greca/y decalçina virgen/y çera. Lo.)aq̃ donzelo poſiftes ſe nze a hincha
do y es coſa ſuzia/mejoz ſe haze cõuidrio fotil y muy delgado/q̃ lleua el vello y ha
ſe mejoz cara/y luego vn poco de olio de pepitas de calabaça y agua de floz de ha
uas ala veneciana q̃ haze vna cara muy linda. Tia.)eſſo qero q̃ me vezeys Lo.)bu
90 ſca vna Redomilla q̃ bzada mira q̃ ſu aue q̃ es/yes coſa linpia. Tia.)no cureys q̃ ſi
os caen enel Raſtro las corteſanas todas q̃ Ran puar/y cõ eſſo q̃ vos le fabeys dar
vna ligereza/ganareys quáto quiſieredes: dios de lante/veys aq̃ do viene mi ma/
rido. viejo.)eſteys enbuẽ ora. Lo.)feays biẽvenido. Viejo)Señora q̃ os ha pareſcí
do de mi ſobzino. Lo.)Señor ni amarga/ni ſabe a ſumo. Tio.)Por mi vida q̃ te/
95 neys Razon/mas yo fuera mas al ppofito q̃ noel. Tia.)mira q̃ ſedexara dezir ſepa
ſan los dos meſes q̃ nome dize q̃ tienes ay/y ſe quiere agora hazer gallo / paza gen
nos conofce teneys vos palabra? Lo.)Señora no os altereys(q̃ mi bõdad es táta)
q̃ ni ſus palabzas/ni ſu ſobzino/no me enpreñará/vamos hijo. Rápin q̃ es tarde/pa
ra lo q̃ tenemos de hazer. Tia.)Señoza yd ſana y ſalua y tozname auer cõſanidad.

¶Mamotreto. XV. Como fueron mirando poz Roma: haſta que vinieron
ala juderia y como hozdeno deponer caſa.

L Oçana. Poz do hemos deyr? Rá.) poz aq̃ poz plaça Redõda y veres el téplo
de pâteon/y laſe pulturade Lucrecia Rõaña/y el aguja de piedra q̃ tiene la
ceniza de Romulo y Remulo/y la colõna labrada coſa marauilloſa/y vereys
(feté zoneis)y Repoſares en caſa de vn cõpaño mio q̃ me conoſce. Lo.) vamos q̃
a q̃l vño Tio finpecado podria traer aluarda/ella pareſce de buena cõdició yo la
tengo de vezar múchas coſas q̃ſe. Ran.) deſo os guarda no vezeys a ninguna
lo que ſabeys guardadlo para quando lo aureys meneſter y fino viene vño ma/
rido podreys vos ganar la vida / que yo dire a todas q̃ ſabeys mas que mi ma/
dre/y ſi quereys que eſte con vos/os yre a vender lo que hizieredes / y os pre/
gonare que traes ſecretos de leuante. Loça.)pues veni aca : que eſſo miſmo quie/
ro yo que vos eſteys comigo / Mira q̃ yo no tengo marido ni pena me el amez/
y de aqui os digo que os terne veſtido / y harto como barua de Rey/y no quiero

Figure 10. *La Lozana andaluza*, Ciiii recto.

PRIMA.

do yo feruir. Lo.) Efte mançebito: medize que os conofçe y qué foys muy bueno/ y muy honrrado. Iodio.) honrrados dias biuays vos y el. Lo.) Yo no tengo cafa vos me aueys de remediar/de vueftra mano. Iodio.) Si bien/y aque partela que/ reys de Roma? Lo.)do veays vos que eftare mejor. Iodio.) Dexa hazer ami/vení voz comigo que foys ombre Tina? apareja vn almofrex o matalaçe y vn xergon linpo y effa filla/pintada/y aquel forçel. Tina.)que forçel? nos entiendo? Iodio.) aquel que me dauá diez y ocho carlines/por el la portuguefa/que vino aqui ayer. Tina.)yaya? Iodio.) quereys mudar veftidos? Lo.)fi rábien, Iodio.)dexame ha/ zer que efto os efta mejor: bolueos: fi para vos fe hiziera no eftuuiera mas a propo/ fito efpera Tina? daca aquel paño liftado que compre dela Ymperia? que yo tela hare/a/efta Señora vnica en Roma? Lo.) no cureys que todo fepagara. Iodio.) todo os dize bien fi no fueffe por effa picadura de moyca. graçia teneys vos que va le mas que todo. Lo.)Yo hare de modo que çegara quienbié me quifiete/ que los duelos con panfon buenas/nunca me matare por nadie. Iodio.) procura vos de no hauer menefter aninguno/ que como dize el judio no me veas mal pafar que no me veras pelear. Lo.)Son locuras dezir effo. Iodio.) Mira por q lo digo/por que yo querria fi pudieffe fer: que oy eneftedia fueffe des Rica. Loçana.)es el culantro heruir/ heruir. Iodio.)por vida defa cara honrrada que mas valeys que penfays/ vamos atraer vn ganapan/ qlleue todo efto. Rá.) veys alli vno llamaldo vos q̃ la cafa yofe do efta/ tres tanto pareçeys mejor defamanera/yd vos delante buen ju/ dio : que nos otros nos yremos tras vos. Iodio.) y donde es effa cafa que dezis? Rá.) ala Aduana. Iodio.) bueno anfi gozen de vos/pues no tardeys q̃ yo la paga/ re. Y efta efcoba para linpialla Con buena manderecha.

❡ Mamotreto. XVII. Informaçion que interpone el Autor para que fe en/ tienda loque adelante hadefeguir.

A Vtor. el que fiebra alguna virtud coie fama Quiédizela verda/cobra odio por effo notad. Eftado efcriuiendo el pafado capitulo. del dolor del pie de xe efte quaderno fobre la tabla/y entro Rápin y dixo que teftamero es efte? Pufolo aenxugar y dixo: Yo venia aq̃ fueffedes acafa/ y vereys mas de diez putas y qulé fequita las çejas/ y quiéfepela lo fuyo. Y como la Loçana no es efta da bue na ja mas defumal el pelador no tenia harta atanquia que todo hera calçina / affe quemado vna Bolonefa todo el peguijar/ y poffimos le buturo y dimos le aenten/ der qué heran blanduras / alli dexo dos julios a vn quele pefo/ veni que Reyreys con la hornera que efta alli/ y dize que traxo afuhija virgen a Roma: faluo que cõ el palo/ocabo/dela pala la defuirgo/y miente que el facriftan cõ el cirio pafcualfe lo abrio. Autor.)como y fu madre la traxo a Roma? Rá.)Señor fi para ganar que era pobre. Tanbien la otra vueftra muy querida/dize che ella os fanara/mira que quieren hazer verengenas enconferua / que aqui lleuo clauos degelofe / mas no amis efpenfas que tanbien feyo azer del neçio/ y defpues todo fe que da en

Figure 11. *La Lozana andaluza*, Dii recto.

cafa/quereys venir que todo el mal feos quitara / fi las voys. Auctor.) no quiero
yr que el tiépo medapena pero deji ala Loçana / que vn tienpo fue que nome hi
ziera ella ellos harrumacos / queya veo que os enbia ella y no quiero yr / por
que dizen defpues que nohago fi no mirar / y notar lo que paffa / para fcreuir de
fpues / y que faco dechados / pienfan que fi quifieffe dezir todas las coffas que
he vifto que no fe mejor Replicallas que vos/que ha tantos años que eftays enfu
cópañia/ mas foyle yo feruidor como ella fabe/y es de mi tierra o çerca della. y no
la quiero en ojar/y a vos nos conofçi yo. En tienpo de Julio fegundo/en plaça na
gona quando firuiedes al Señor canonigo Rá.) Verdad dezis/mas eftuue poco.
Auctor.)Effo poco alli os vi/ moliendo no fe que. Ran.)Si. fi. verdad dezis/o bue/
na cafa / y venturofa mas ganaua ella en tonçes alli que agora la meitad / por que
paffauan ellas defimuladas/y fe entrauan alli/calla/callando. Mal año para lade/
los Rios a vn q̃ fue muyfamofa. Auctor.) Mira q̃ le a conteçio no ha quatro dias
vino alli vna muger lonbarda/que fon bouas/y era ya de tienpo/y dixo que la Re
mediafe:que ella lo pagaria. Y dixo Señora vn palafrenero que tiene mi amiftad/
no viene a mi cafa/mas hade vn mes/queria faber fi fea enbuelto có otra/quando
ella oyo efto/me llamo y dixo/dante aca aquel efpejo dealinde/ Y miro/ y Refpon
dio le / Señora aquies menefter otra cofa que palabra : / Si metraes las cofas que
fueren menefter feres feruida. La Lonbarda dixo. Señora ved aqui çinco Julios
. La Loçana dixo. Pues andauos Ranpin. Yo tome mis dineros y traygo vn mara
uedi de plomo/y végo y digo q̃ no ay leña/ fi no caruon/y que coftomas/y ella di
xo que no fe curaua. Yo hize buen fuego que teniamos de affar vn anfaron para
çenar que venia alli vna putilla confu amigo a çena / y anfi la hizo defnudar que
erael mejor de porte del mundo/y le echo el plomo por debaxo en tierra/y ella en
cueros / y mirando enel plomo / le dixo que no tenia otro mal fi no que eftaua de
tenido/pero que no fe podia faber fi hera de muger o de otrie / que tornaffe otro
dia y verialo de mas efpacio.dixo ella que mandays que trayga? Loçana) vna
gallina negra y vn gallo que fea de vn año. Y fiete hueuos / que fean todos nafçi/
dos a quel dia/v traeme vna cofa fuya/dixo ella traere? vna agujeta? e vna efcofia
La Loçana/ Si. fi. y forraba mi perrica. Ranpin.)Hera el mayor deporte del múdo
vella como eftaua hecha vna eftatua/y mas cótéta viene otro dia cargada/e/traxo
otros dos Julios/y me Tio ella la clara de vn hueuo en vn orinal/ y alli le demo/
ftro como el eftaua abraçado có otra/que tenia vna veftidura/azul. Y hezimos le
mater la gallina/y lingar el gallo con fu eftringa / y afi le dimos a entender que la
otra prefto moriria/y que el q̃ daua liga do con ella/y no có la otra/ y q̃ prefto ver
nia/ y anfi fe fue/y nofotros comimos vna capirotada có múcho q̃fo. Auctor.) A
effa me quifiera yo hallar. Rá.) Veni a cafa que tábien a vra parauos. Auctor.) An
da puerco, Ran.) Tanto es pedrodedios. Auctor.) que no temiedre dios? Rá.) Ve
ni vos y vereys el gallo/qu: para otro] dia lo tenemos. Auctor.) Pues fea anfi que
me llameys/y yo pagare el vino. Rá.) fi hare fanaprefto. No quereys vos hazerlo q̃
hizo ella para fumal:q̃ no cueftafino dos ducaros/que fu fatiga no queria ella na/
da/que todo feria vn par de calças / para efta inuernada / mira ya ha fanado en
belitre a vn Efpañol/ de lo fuyo/y acabo de ocho dias fe lo quifo hazer/y era per/

Figure 12. *La Lozana andaluza*, Dii verso.

fona que no per dieta nada/y por que andauan entonçes por defpofar nos : anfi y
a ella (por ḡ ceffaffe la pefte) nolo hizo. Auctor.)Anda.ˀ ḡ eres bouo / ḡ ya fequien
es y felo hizo/y ledio vn tauardo o caparela/para que fe defpofaffe ella mifma nos
le conto.Ran.)Pues veys ay:por que lo fano.Auctor.)Effo pudo fer por graçia de
dios.Rá.)Señor no:fino confu vnguento , fon mas de quatro ḡ la Ruegan/ y por
que no fea lo de fauftina/que la tomo por muerta/ y lafano / y defpues no la quifo
pagar/dixo ḡ vn voto que hizo laffano/y dio le el paga/nunca mas/en pacharfe có
Romanefcas.Auctor.)Ora andad enbuen ora y en comendamela / y a la otra des
yirga viejos/ḡ foy todo fuyo/valaos dios.ˀRan.)No que no cay.Auctor.)Teneos
bien que efta peligrofa effa efcalera/cayfte valate el diablo. Ran.) Agora fi ḡ cay.
Auctor.)Heziftes os mal poneos efte paño decabeça.Ran.)afi meyre hafta cafa ḡ
me en falme. Auctor.) Que en falmetedira.ˀ Ran.)El de mal fracorum.Auctor.)
Como dixe.Ran.)Erantres cortefanas y tenian tres amigos pajes de fráquilano.
La vna lo tiene publico/y la otra muy callado/ala otra lebuelta có el lunario quié
efta oration dixere tres vezes a rimano quádo nace fea fano Amen.

❡Mamotreto.XVIII.   Proffigue el Auctor tornando al decimo fexto mamo
treto.Que veniendo de la iudaica dixe Ranpin.

Si aquel Jodio no fea delantara:efta gelofia fe vende/y fuera bue/
na/para vna ventana/y es grã reputaçion tener gelofia. Lo,)Y en
que veys que fe véde.ˀRá.)por ḡ tiene a ḡl Ramico verde puefto/
que aqui alos cauallos o alo ḡ quiere véder le poné vna hoja verde fo/
bre las orejas.Lo,)Para effo mejor fera poner el Ramo fin la gelofia / y
véderemos mejor.Rá.)Mas Ramoˀḡreys ḡ trigo ˀ ḡ lodira por quátas
cafas de feñores ay en Roma.ˀ Lo,)Pues veys ay Auos ḡero yo ḡ feays
mi gelofia/que yo no tengo de ponerme ala ventana: fino quando mũ
cho a fomare las manos, O que lindas fon a quellas dos mugeres.ˀ por
mi vida que fon como matronas no e vifto en mi vida cofa mas honrrada/ni mas
honefta.Ran.)Son Romanas prinçipales.Lo.)Pues como van tan folas.Ranpin)
Por que anfi lo hufan : quando van ellas fuera / vnas a otras fe aconpañan : faluo
quádo va vna fola ḡ lleua vna fierua mas no ombres/ni mas mugeres/a vn que fea
la mejor de Roma/y mira que van fefgas/y a vn que vean a vno que conozcan no
le hablan/en la calle/fi no que fe apartan ellos y callan / y ellas no abaxan cabeças
ni hazen mudança a vn que fea fu padre/ni fu marido.Lo.) O que lindas que fon
paffan aquantas naçiones yo he vifto / y a vn a violante la hermofa en Cordoua.
Rá.) Por effo dizen.ˀ Vulto Romano/y cuerpo fenes/andar florentin/. y parlar bo
lofies.Lo,)Por mi vida que enefto tienen Razon:effotro/mirare defpues verdad
es quelas Senefas fon gentiles de cuerpo/por que las he vifto que fus cuerpos pa/
reçen torres yguales Mira alla qual viene a quella vieja cargada de cuétas/ y mas
baruas que efçid Ruy diaz.Vieja.)Ay mi alma pareçe que os he vifto yno fe dõ/
de.ˀ por que aues mudado veftidos.ˀ nome Recordaua . Ya / ya/ dezime yau eys os
hecho puta.ˀ a marga deuos que no lo podres çufrir: que es grã trabajo. Lo.)Mira

Figure 13. *La Lozana andaluza*, Diii recto.

PARTE.

⟨Mamotreto.XXIIII. Como començo ha cõuerſar con todos/y como el Autor la conoſçio por ynterçeſion de vn ſu cõpañero, que era criado de vn'enbaxador milañs / al qual ella ſiruio la primera vez, Con vna moça/no virgen: ſino apretada, Aqui comiéça la/ Parte ſegunda,

Siluio quien me tu viera agora que a quella muger que va muy cubierta no le dixera qual que Remoquete/por ver que me Reſpondiera/y ſupiera quien es Voto a mi q̃ es andaluza/enel andar y meneo ſe conoſçe/o q̃ pierna en velela ſe me deſperezo la cõpliſſion/por vida del Rei que no eſta virgen/ay q̃ meneos que tiene/q̃ boltar aca: ſiẽpre que me vienen eſtos lances vẽgo ſolo/ella ſe para alli cõ a quella paſtelera/quiero yr Auer como habla/y que cõpra, Autor.) Ola! aca! aca! que hazeys! doys! Siluio.) Quiero yr alli auer quien es a quella que entro alli que tiene buen ayre de muger, Autor.) O que Reñegar: tandoſo / por vida de tu amo di la verdad! Cõpañero,) Hi/hi, direyo como dela otra q̃las piedras la coñoſçien, Autor,) Donde eſta! que trato tiene! eſcaſada o ſoltera! pues A vos quiero yo para que melo digays, Conpañero.) Peſe al mundo coneſtos ſantos ſin auiſo paſa cada dia por caſa de ſu amo/y mira que Regatear que tiene / y porfia que no la conoſçe Miralda bien/que a todos da Remedio/de qual quier enfermedad q̃ ſea, Autor.) Eſſo es bueno / Dezi me quienes! Y no me hableys por circunloquios! ſi no dezi me vna palabra Redonda: como Razon de miel cochero/di melo por vida de la corzeta, Conpañero.) So contento/eſta es la Loçana que eſta preñada de a quel canonigo que ella ſano de lo ſuyo, Autor.) Sanolo para que la enpreſiaſſe, Tuvo Razon/Dezi me es corteſana! Conpañero No: ſino que tiene eſta la mejor vida de muger que ſea en Roma/Eſta Loçana es ſagaz/y bien mirado todo lo que paſſan las mugeres eneſta tierra / q̃ ſon ſujetas a tres coſas/ala pinſion de la caſa

Figure 14. *La Lozana andaluza*, Eiii verso.

una en que es hermofa:que tiene el mejo? ver y judicar / q̃ jamas feuido / po? que
beuio y paffo el Rio denilo/y conoçe fin efpejo:po? qne ella lo es/y como las tiene
en platica/ fabe cada vna en quepoede fer loada / yes muy vniuerfal / en todas las
otras cofas que para efto de amo?es fe re quiere/y mirela ental ojo que para la có¿
diçion de vueftra Señozia es vna perla/defta fe puede muy bię dezir:(Mulier que
fuit in vrbe : habens feptem mecanicas artes:) Pues alas liberales Jamas le falto
Reto?ica /ni Logica/para refpondet / aquien las eftudio / el mirable ingenio que
tiene/da que haze? alos que la oyen/Mófeño? vamos defta parte/efperemos auer
fi me conofçé. Enba.) Al cuerpo de mi efta dona yo la vi enbancos que parlaua
muy dulçe/y có audaçia/que pareçia vn Seneca. Cauallero.) Es parienta del Ro¿
pero/conterrana de Seneca/Lucano/Marçial/ y Auicena:la tierra lo lleua/ efta in
agibilibus/no ay fupar/y tienc otra exçeléçia (que luftrauit p?ouinçias. Enba.),Es
pofible como reguarda yn qua. Lo.) Ya/ya conoçido es vuefra merçed /;po? mi
vida/que aun que fe cub?a/que no ap?ouecha/que yafe que es mi Señoz/po? mi vi
da tantico/lacara que yafe que es deuer/y degoza? / effe Seño? nolo conozco mas
bien veo que deue fer gran Seño?/A feguridad lefuplico que me perdone que yo
lo quiero fo?ça?:po? mi vida que fon matado?es,effos ojos/quié es efte feño? / que
lo firua yo/po? vida devueftra merçed/y defutio/y mi feño?,Caualle.)Seño?a Lo
çana efte Seño? os fuplica , que le metays debaxo de vueftra caparela / y entrara
auer la Señoza Angelica/po?que vea fi tengo Razon/en dezir que es la mas acaba
da dama que ay enefta tierra. Loçana.) A vueftra Señozia metelle heyo encima/
no debaxo / mas yo lo trauajare efperen aqui / quefi fu merçed efta fola yola ha¿
re poner ala Ventana/y fi mas mandaré/yo verne abaxo/ bien eftare media ho?a,
pafeenfe vn poco / po?que le tengo de rogar p?imero que haga vn poco po? mi,
que eftoy engran neçefidad:que me echan dela cafa/yno tengo de q̃ paga?,que el
borracho del patron,no quiere menos defeys meffes pagados antes.Cauallero.)
Pues no os detengays/ en nada defo/que la cafa fe pagara : enbiame vos a vueftro
criado ami pofada, que yo le dare con que pague la cafa/po? que fu Señozia no es
perfona que deue efpera?¡!Loçana.) Quien es po? mi vida? Cauallero.)Anda fe
ño?a Loçana/que perfona es que no perde?eys nada/con fu feñozia. Lo.)Sin effo
y con effo/firuo yo alos buenos efperen. Cauallero.) Mófeño? que le pareçe? dela
Señora Loçana ? fus inxertos fiempe toman. Enba.) Me pareçe que es aftu?a/que
çierto ha dela fierpe/e dela paloma/Efta muger fin lagrimas, parara mas ynfidias
que todas las mugeres con lagrimas/po? vida del vifo Rei,que mañana coma co
migo/q̃ yo le quiero dar vnb?ial. Cauallero.) Mirela vueftra feñozia ala ventana
no ay tal Loçana enel mundo/ ya ab?e veamos que dize / cabeça que entremos,
dondeni fierro / ni fuego ala virtud enpeçe. Enbaxado?.) Qua piu bella la matre
que la filla,Cauallero.)Monfeño? Efta es Carçel de Amo?: aqui ydolat?o Califto
aqui no fe eftima Melibea,aqui poco vale Celeftina.

¶Mamotreto.XXXVII. Como de alli fe defpidio la Loçana/y fe fue en cafa
de vn hidalgo q̃ labufcaua/v eftado folos fe lo hizo/
po? que diefe fe a otra que lo fabia haze?.

H

Figure 15. *La Lozana andaluza*, Hi recto.

Señores aq̃ no ay mas que hazer la priſſion es ſeguriſſima: la priſſionera piadoſa la libertad no ſe conpra: la ſujeçion aqui ſe eſtima por q̃ ay merecimiento para todo/vueſtra Señoria ſea muy bien venido / y vueſtra merçed me tenga la promeſſa : que eſta tarde/ yra mi criado a ſu poſada / y ſi. V.M manda q̃le lleue vna prenda de oro o vna toca toniçi:la lleuara , por que yo no ſalte de mi palabra/q̃ pmeti por todo oy / A eſte Señor / yo lo viſſitare.Cauallero.)Señora Loçana no enbieys prēda: que entre vos y mi no ſe pueden pder ſino los barriles/enbia como os dixe y no cureys de mas / y.

mira que quiere ſu Señoria que mañana vengays auerlo. Lo.) Beſo ſus manos,y vueſtros pies/ mas mañana no podraſer por que tengo mi guarnelo lauado / y no tēgo que me veſtir.Cauallero.) No cureys que ſu Señoria os quiere veſtir a ſu modo/y al vueſtro/ veni anſi como eſtavs/que os cōbida a comer y no/a/eſperar que ſu Señoria come de mañana,Lo.)Por la luz de dios/ no es tu vieſe ſin beſar tal cara como eſſa/aun que ſu pieſſe enojar a quien lo vee.Angelica/anſi Loçana no cureys/anda dexaldo que me enojare/aun q̃ ſu merçed no me quiere ver. Cauelle.) Señora deſeoſa yo ſeruir por tanto le ſuplico / que a Monſeñor mio:le mueſtre ſu caſa.Y ſus Joyas:por q̃ ſu ſeñoria tiene muchas, y buenas:que puede ſeruir a vueſtra merçed:Señora Loçana mañana no ſeos oluide deuenir.Loça.)No ſe ſi ſe me oluidara / que ſoy deſmemorada deſpues que moui,que ſi tengo de hazer vna coſa es meneſter ponerme vn ſeñal enel dedo. Cauallero.) Pues veni aca toma eſte anillo/y mira que es vn eſmeralda/no ſe os cayga. Lo.) Sus manos beſo que mas la eſtimo/q̃ ſi mela diera la ſeñora Angelina dada . Angelina.) Anda que os lado, y traelda,por mi amor. Lo.)No ſe eſperaua menos deſa cara de luna llena / ay Señora Angelina , mirenme que pareſco obiſpo / por vida de vueſtra merçed , y mia que no eſtoy mas aqui/ven/açerra: Matehuelo / q̃ me eſperan alli aquellos moços del deſpoſado de hornachuelos,que no ay quien lo quiera/y el porfiar , y contodas ſe caſſa/ya ninguna ſirue/de buena tinta.Matheuelo . Cerrar y abriros todo a vn tiēpo.Moços.)venis ſeñora Loçana:camina cuerpo de mi q̃ mi amo:ſedes itra

ſe firman de mi pobleza / pnes ſaben q̃ ſoy toda ſuya. Por vida del Rei / que no me la
vayã apenar al otro mũdo los puercos / q̃ les e hecho mill honrras q̃ dõ eſtauamos
en Damiata / y en Tunez de berueria / y agora cõ palabras pĩtadas me an pagado /
dios les de el mal año / quiſiera yo peſſe al diablo / que metieran la mano ala bolſa
por qual que dozena de ducados / como hazia yo en aquel tiempo / y ſi no los tenia
ſelos hazia dar a mi Señor Diomedes / y aſus criados los hazia veſtir / y agora
amala pena me conoçen / por que ſenbre en porcuna / bien me dezia Diomedes
guardate / que eſtos a quien tu hazes bien / te an dehazer mal / Mira que canes Reñe
gados / villanos ſecretos / capotes de terçiopelo Por eſtos tales ſe deuia dezir / ſirrui
no me acuerdo quien ſirue a munchos no ſirue a ninguno.

❡ Aqui comiença la Tercera parte del Retrato / y ſeran mas glacioſas coſas que
lo paſado. Como torno a caſa y aſeito / co lo que traya: las ſobre dichas / y
como ſe fueron / y ſu criado conellas / y que do ſola y contaua todo
lo que auia meneſter para ſu trato / q̃ queria començar / y de
aqui a delante le daremos fin.   Mamotreto, XLI.

❡ Loçana.

A Gora que me Aremangé / aponer trato en mi caſa: vale todo caro / andar
paſe por agora por contentar eſtas putas / que deſpues yo ſabre lo que tẽgo
de hazer. Griega.) Miramela qual viene q̃ le nazcan baruas / narizes de me
dalla. Lo) Pareçe mi caſa atalaya deputas: Mas puſe del mio q̃ no me diſtes. Tulia)
Sus

Figure 17. *La Lozana andaluza*, Hiiii verso.

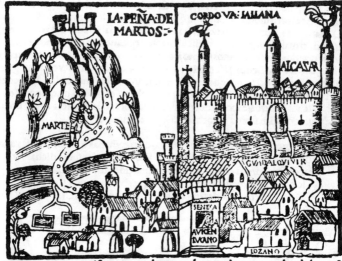

Señora Loçana quisiera que acabaramos la materia començada,: de la meri
trosia/mas como notuuo Replica/manda vra merçed que digamos Reliqua
para que se sienten y vayan Reposadas/donde la Rueda de la carreta las a es
bara/y tornado a Respôdetos de aquel señor que de vras cosas haze vn Retrato
quiero que sepais/que so estado en su tierra/y dareos Señas della, Es vna villa çer
cada/y cabeça de maestradgo decalatraua/y antiguamête fue muy gran cibdad/
dedicada al dios o planeta Marte. Como dize Apuleyo/ quando el planeta Meri
curio andaua en el cielo al dios Marte ā a quella peña era su trono y ara/de dôs
de tomo nonbre: la peña de Marte / y al presente de los martos por que cadauno
delos que alli morâ son vn Marte en batalla/que son ombres inclinados al'arte de
la milicia/y ala Agricultura por que Remedan alos Romanos que Rehedificarô
dôde agora se Abita/alpie dela dicha peña. Porque alli era sacrificado el dios de
las batallas/y ansi son los ombres de aquella tierra muy actos para armas / como si
oystes dezir lo que hizieron los couos de Martos/enel Reyno de granada/por tan
to'que dezian los moros ā el couo viejo/y sus çinco hijos: eran de hierro y aun de
azero, bien ā no sa bien la causa del planeta Marte/ā en a quella tierra Reynaua
de nonbre y de hecho/por ā alli puso hercules: la terçera piedra o colona ā al pre
sente es puesta en el tēplo hallose el año. M.D.IIII. Y la peña de Martos nûcala pu
do tomar Alexandro magno nisugête por ā es ynexpuñabile / A quien la quisiesse
por fuerça, Ha sido siépre hôrra/y defensiô de toda Castilla. En a quella tierra ay
las Señales de su antigua grâdeza/en abûdança. Esta fortissima peña es tan alta ā
se vee Cordona que esta catorze leguas de alli/esta fue Sacristia/y conserua ſ quâ
k

Figure 18. *La Lozana andaluza*, Ki recto.

Monſeñor/que ya eſta veſtida de regaço/y ua apie. Altobelo)Señora Loçana ſobꝛ
que ſu merçed os demanda/que os quiere hablar:antes que ſe parta,Lo.)Donde
eſta la Señora꞉ enla anticamara꞉ o enla Recamara꞉ Altobelo)Entra alla alaloſa/q̃
alla eſta ſola.Lo,)Señora que quiere dezir que vueſtra merçed haze eſtas noueda
des꞉ como꞉ he yo ſeruido a vueſtra merçed des de que veniſtes a Roma / y a vꝛa
madre꞉ haſta que murio꞉ que hera aſi linda Corteſana como enſus tiépos ſeuido꞉
y por vna buelta que me tardo꞉ llamays aquien mas pꝛeſto os gaſten la cara/q̃ no
adornen꞉ como hago yo꞉ mas no me curo/que no ſon coſas que turan / que ſu fin
ſe traen como cada coſa꞉ eſta/me pornaſal en la mollera/y ala Jodia/yo le dare ſu
mereçer,Xereзana)Veni aca Loçana꞉ nos vays que eſſos vellacos os deué hauer
dicho qualque coſa por enojaros/quié me ſuele ami aſaitar꞉ ſi no vos꞉ dexa'dezir
q̃ como aueys tardado vn poco os dixeron eſſo/nos cureys que yo me contento꞉
quereys quenos ſalgamos/ alla ala ſala꞉ Loça.)Señora ſi / que traygo eſte paño liꝛ
ſtado mojado / y lo metere ala fineſtra/ Xereзana)Pues ſea anſi / que es eſto꞉ que
traes aqui꞉ en eſta garrafeta꞉ Lo,)Señora es vn agua para luſtrar la cara / q̃ me la
mádo hazer la Señora Môteſina/q̃ cueſta mas de tres ducados / y yo no la queria
hazer/y ella la pago/y me pꝛometio vna carretada de leña/ y dos barriles de vino
dulçe:para eſta ynuernada.Xereзana.)Tenes mas q̃ eſta꞉ Lo.)Señora no.꞉ ere.)
Pues eſta quiero yo/y pagalda veys aqui los dineros / y enbia por vna bota de viꝛ
no/y haze dezir a los mulateros de Moſeñor que toda eſta ſemana vayan a deſcar
gar a vueſtra caſa.Lo.)Av Señora que ſoy perdida que me pꝛometio꞉ que ſi hera
perfetta/que me daria vn ſayo para mi criado,Xereзana)Mira Loçana ſayo no té
go:a quella capa de Môſeñor/es buena para vueſtro criado/tomalda/y anda noꝛ
ra buena/y veni mas pꝛeſto otrodia. Lo.)Señora no ſe quien llama / miren quien
es꞉ porq̃ quádo yo ſalga no entre alguno,Xereзana)Va mira quien es.Montoya)
Señora los dos Señores janiçeros,Xereзana)Di que no ſo en caſa.Lo.)Haga Seꝛ
ñora que entren y contaran a vueſtra merçed como les fue en el côbite q̃ hizo la
Flaminia a quantos fueron con ella que es coſa de oyr.Xereзana)Que podia ſeꝛ
poco mas omenos/que bien ſabemos ſus coſas della.Lo.)Mande vꝛa merçed que
entren/y oyra marauillas.Xereзana)Oraſus por côtentar ala Loçana va abꝛelos.

❡Mamotreto.LVIII.　　Como va la Loçana en caſa dela Garça Monteꞏ
　　　　　　　　　　　　ſina/y encuentra côdos Rufianes Napolitanos/
　　　　　　　　　　　　y loquele dizen.

Eſe al diablo con tanta Juſtiçia como ſe
hazedelos que poco pueden,que vos mi꞉
auiades deſer꞉ para ganarme de comer:
mas como va el múdo al Reues no ſe oſa el om
bꝛe alargar/ſino quitaros el bonete/ y con gran
reuerençia poneros ſobꝛe mi cabeça.Lo.)Quiꞏ
taos alla hermanos/que coſas ſon eſſas꞉ y a ſoy
maſada/nes ca'ebuꝛlar/que caſtigan alos locos꞉ Rufian)Señora per dona que Raꝛ

Figure 19. *La Lozana andaluza*, Mi verso.

mallorquinos/y dos Parmefanos/y puefto vofotras llenafelo afu cafa.Lo,)Señora
quien ofara yr ami cafa q̃ luego me matara mi criado que le prometio ella mifma
vna capa.Montefina.)Capa no la ay en cafa q̃ fele puedadar/ mas mira fileuerna
bueno efte fayo/q̃ fue del protonotario. Lo.) Señora lleuemela el moço / por que
no vaya yo cargada no feme enfuelua el Sueño/en todo/q̃ efta noche foñaua que
caya en manos de'ladrones.Montefina.)Anda no mireys en Sueños q̃ quãdo ve
niades aca/os viyo hablar cõ quatro.Lo.) Buen parayfo aya quien aca os dexo q̃
verdad es/efclaua foy a vr̃a merçed/por q̃ no bafta fer hermofa y linda/mas quãto
diʒe hermofea/y adorna cõfu faber . Quuien fupiera oy haʒerme callar y amanfar
mi defeo q̃ tenia de ver:q̃ me hauia de dar/madona Clarina la fauorida por mi tra
bajo y fatiga.Laqual vr̃a merçed ha fatiffecho en parte/y'como diʒen la'buena vo
lũtad conq̃ vr̃a merçed me lo ha dado vale mas/q̃ lo mũcho mas q̃ ella mediera/y
fobre todo feyo q̃ vra merçed/ no me fera ingrata/y befole las manos q̃ es tarde/
Mirefe vr̃a merçed al efpejo y vera q̃ no fo pagada fegun lo que merefco.

¶Mamotreto.LIX,   Como la Loçana fue a cafa de madona Clarina fauorida
y encontro cõ dos medicos y el vno hera çirugico/y to
dos dos diʒen.

S Eñora Loçana adonde fe va ! q̃
efpeçieria es effa ! q̃ de baxo lle
uays? ay curas? ay curas? danos
parte.Lo.)Señores mios la parte por
el todo/ y el todo por la parte/ y yo q̃
foy prefta para fus feruiçios. Fifico,)
Señora Loçana aueys de faber que fi
todos los medicos / q̃ al prefente nos
hallamos en Roma / nos juntafemos
de acuerdo:q̃ deuiamos haʒer lo que
antiguamente hiʒieron nr̃os anteçe
fores/ En la via de fã Sebaftiã/eftauã
vnas tres fofas llenas de agua:laqual
agua hera/natural / y tenia efta vir
tud /q̃ quantas perfonas tenian 'mal
dela çintura abaxo/yvan alli tres ve

ʒes vna femana/y entrauan en aquellas fofas depies/ y eftauan alli dos horas: por
buelta/y anfi fanauan:de qual quier mal que tuuieffen/en las partes inferiores/ de
modo que los medicos de aquel tiẽpo/no podien medicar fino dela çintura a Ri
ba / vifto efto / fueron todos /'y çegaron eftos fofos omanantios/ y hiʒieron que
vn Arroyo que y va por otra parte que pafaffe por ençima/ por q̃ no 'fe hallaffen/
y agora aquel Arroyo tiene la mifma virtud / para los cauallos /'y mulas repre
fas / y finalmente a todas las beftias Reprefas que alli meten fanan / como aueys
vifto fi aueys pafado por alli: Efto digo que deuiamos haʒer ! pues que ni dela çin
tura aRiba/ni dela çintura abaxo nonos days parte, Cirugico,) Señora Loçana

Figure 20. *La Lozana andaluza*, Mii verso.

◆ Chapter 5

Breaking the Barriers: The Birth of López de Ubeda's *Pícara Justina*

Nina Cox Davis

The cluster of fictive autobiographies that initiate the Spanish picaresque genre—the *Lazarillo*, *Guzmán*, and *Buscón*—bear the imprint of an artistic genesis that assumes peculiarly masculine terms. They constitute the "lives" of *pícaros* who scheme to escape the powerlessness of the marginality into which they were born—of parents marked by undesirable blood, religious practices, or lack of socioeconomic status—by fabricating linguistic identities to replace their pasts. While they pay parodic lip service to their less than honorable family trees, these male narrators strive quickly to bury their progenitors under ellipses, and in a series of displacements that take the form of narrative odysseys through time and space as well as discursive journeys through the figures of their language. After being thrust forth from or escaping the nest and the malforming influence in particular of their mothers, these connivers plot to succeed by becoming the authors of themselves in a world ordered by male economies: the university, ecclesiastical offices, trades and *oficios*, the court, military service, and the nobiliary hierarchy. From early on, they thus appear to flee the environs of women—homes, inns, and the streets—and the lack of position associated with them, hoping to find their "historical" place, paradoxically, in transit. The nameless maternal world from whence they depart accompanies them, transformed into women who serve them not as origins but currency, wives to be pandered or prostitutes to be pimped, along a circuit of social mobility. For most of the narrative in the *Lazarillo*, the *Guzmán*, and the *Buscón*, however, women are not even present or mentioned. When they do figure as characters, the narrators rarely cite their words. In these works, clearly, the powers that be (and that may be overcome) are engendered masculine.

López de Ubeda's *La pícara Justina* (1605) ruptures the homosocial economy of this initial tercet of picaresque novels with its startling construction. It is an upstart account that intends to better its rivals both in the complexity of its discursive articulation and in the entertainment of its narrative. This anomalous autobiography strives to accomplish its goals with a disconcerting flair, by making them serve the autoinventive purposes of a brilliantly iconoclastic *pícara*—a femininely engendered counterpart to the scheming trio, who is presented as being both better at artifice and a worse denigrator of her society's norms. While she is made to appropriate their discourses in the literary composition of her life, López de Ubeda's Justina does not in the narrative of that life ape the political behavior and values of her social betters in the male power hierarchy, as do her *pícaro* counterparts; she gleefully besoils her betters and rubs their noses in it, figuratively castrating and usurping male authority as she sows deception with her words.

Besides its sexual difference, this first example of a female narrative within the Spanish picaresque genre does not fit among the "old favorites" of the genre in other obvious ways. Its language is so extravagantly difficult that it is—as it apparently was—hard for Ubeda's readers to follow the story of Justina's life.[1] After Ubeda's two prologues ("Prólogo al lector" [41–45], "Prólogo sumario" [47–49]) and the narrator's "Introducción general" as "La melindrosa escribana" (The affected scribe [51–80]), which warns readers by its title to question the veracity of the life recorded by her highly rhetorical discourse, the plot is organized into four books that depict major formative periods in her life: "La pícara montañesa" (The highland rogue [81–150]); "La pícara romera" (The pilgrim rogue [151–383]); "La pícara pleitista" (The litigious rogue [385–466]); and "La pícara novia" (The betrothed rogue [427–66]).[2] Within these books, we find it hard to trace the human side of the protagonist: the wily *pícara* decomposes into self-referential words more often than she takes shape, as her alleged attempts to portray her individuality are subsumed in extensive word plays that parody a wide array of literary sources while linking discourses on class, race, religion, and other indicators of status for her society. In Book One, the *pícara* satirizes by reviewing her own heritage the preoccupation with legitimacy and privilege of old Christians such as is demonstrated by her dogged commentator, "Perlícaro," the fictive autobiography's parody of Quevedo (Bataillon 30), whose insistence to have the pedantic if not irrelevant last word is mirrored in the "Aprovechamiento" that ends every subsection.[3] The first book takes shape through a long series of vignettes that represent her heritage of marginalization by "grounding" in metaphors of sexual deviation the many immaterial, ideological transgressions attributed to her progenitors. In this first segment, where she audaciously usurps the identity of a "montañesa," or old Christian from the north, the narrator's discourse of entertainment—the stated purpose of her "libro de entretenimiento"—articulates corrosive commentaries on blood purity, monied versus feudal economies, religious affiliation, and the other preoccupations of the ruling hierarchy in Ubeda's Spain, while it advances our knowledge of her own life relatively little. The plot serves primarily to verify that she is indeed her parents' daughter, an admitted transgressor from her infancy onward. After her pilgrimages among and deceptions of victims from all walks of life in Book Two, Book Three approaches the end of this marginal character's account with her again speaking—paradoxically—from within the ranks of those who have cast her out. Here she communicates as a manipulator of judicial language and a wheeler-dealer—a courtly "pleitista"—who delivers the inside scoop on the court circles that she as writer has infiltrated, while she gives few clues about the end of her life. We learn in the brief final book that she has run through various suitors, married a gambler, and is likely to marry at least twice again, in a forthcoming volume. The closing pages promise a continuation that will incorporate, as one of the objects of her affection and a character in her own narrative, Guzmán de Alfarache, that famous rival among *pícaros* who is her literary predecessor on the market. The virtuoso narrator taunts readers at the end of her first tome by hinting thus that the difficult volume they have finally mastered is barely the beginning of her account.[4]

Because the details of her own "life" may be extracted only with difficulty from the work's chaotic and often obscure language, Justina is a picaresque subject whose construction costs readers considerably more than that of her male counterparts in the Spanish genre. We must assume, however, that for some of Ubeda's immediate contemporaries—if not Cervantes—this translated into greater pleasure in reading, the titillation of her narrated social transgressions, in effect, being intensified by the density and charged multivalence of the words promising to reveal their outcome. The *pícara's* discourse, we quickly find, is the real locus of the text's seduction of readers, for the language of her self-portraiture not only discloses prurient details about her person that readers may hope to find, it wages a campaign of playful aggression against their very expectations in so signifying. To heighten the readers' vexed desire, working toward a fuller definition of her deviancy through complicated descriptions of her material being, the usual episodic wanderings of the *pícaro*—most fully developed in Book Two, "La pícara romera" (The pilgrim rogue [151–383])—are combined in Justina's case not only with a standard complement of *burlas pesadas* (injurious practical jokes) in the form of thefts, swindles, and the humiliation of her social betters, but also with the particular *burla*—not made explicit in the male picaresque, though certainly a dominant subtext—of marketing her body. The narrative never delivers the full pornographic effect of its consumption, however; what readers find in the body's displacement is simply more verbiage. As she claims to have done with suitors in the narrative, the narrating *pícara* lures with the language of her authorial discourse only to heighten their desire by proffering vexation, in the form of lexical gymnastics and a discontinuous plot that leave them hung up repeatedly on the vertical rather than the horizontal axis of their reading. We must wonder why López de Ubeda chose to weave together such an elaborate, unstable context for the delivery of the elitist witticisms that ultimately signal his own aggressive presence in the text. Why ground "word plays, symbolic interpretations, historical and mythological allusions, fables, rhetorical analogues, refrains, and hieroglyphic or emblematic representation" in "hair" (Friedman 87), not to mention an extensive series of references, in descending order, to the rest of the female body?[5] His decision to write for voracious consumers of wit precisely through the disseminated images of a female body in its engagement with society is a strategic move that appears to be designed with considerable acumen to disarm their assumptions. For although the narrator of this work is a female at whom they will certainly snicker, and one cast in most ways as an archoutsider, with respect to the dominant hierarchy of her male readers, in the offering of both story and body she proves to be neither an object they can domesticate nor a force they may dismiss.

In the following pages I will focus upon the complex discourse of the body that structures the narrative of Ubeda's *pícara,* by examining its opening lines—her birth (Chapter One, Number One, 83–84). In so doing, I will refer to a not readily available but very useful semantic study of segments from *La pícara Justina* done by the French scholars Allaigre and Cotrait ("Estratos de significación"), whose analysis of "off-color" word plays in the text has confirmed and enriched my own understanding of the lexical problems of this key opening section.[6] At the same time, I feel compelled to take issue with their assumption, as complicit as they argue was Ubeda's (28), that the use of "las segundas intenciones eróticas y pornográficas, cuya inteligencia requiere un desciframiento semántico" (secondary erotic and pornographic intentions whose wit requires semantic deciphering) in the text, in effect, sought only to guarantee López de Ubeda's renown as author of "literatura de clase" (literature of a certain class), champion of "el público social e intelectualmente aristocrático" (the socially and intellectually aristocratic public, 47). The protagonist's raunchy inception, which launches the work's iconoclastic verbal reordering of relationships and values in the world represented, derives its ideological impetus precisely from the material experience of her body and the reaction of that body to aggression from without, upon its first attempted incorporation into society. From this moment of her "life" onward, like her male counterparts the *pícara* will define herself through acts of marginalization and usurpation that render a commentary upon that society into which she is not successfully born. However, I will stress—again differing in my interpretation from the French semanticists—that rather than voicing claims to position and possession by one male faction before others, in the parody of gender that she places before us Ubeda's Justina explodes pretense to privilege attributed to the dominant, male social order itself. This female picaresque narrative indeed demands the readers' admiration of Ubeda for having authored its conceptual and linguistic artifice. But the language that constructs the work's competitive bid for respect works its wit by deconstructing in the figure of Perlícaro the position of male readers—from their places in society to their very bodies. In effect, the aristocratic savorers of its wit are dealt an unanticipated blow to their private parts in multiple figurative senses by this female-engendered narrative. The representational contradictions woven by the discourse of the *pícara*'s life, in effect, to borrow Gossy's words, tell readers the "untold story" of her/ Ubeda's narrative—the chronicle of themselves as Justina's Other, as objects of her own transgressive discursive operations. In the troubled linguistic portrait of Justina's person, we encounter a series of references to her would-be possessors—images rendered to match Ubeda's readers—that, as the following discussion will demonstrate, through parody of their language, replace elitist pretension with ridiculous, even subhuman qualities.

The *pícara*'s narrative of her life opens with the challenge presented to readers by the relationship of body, or material position, to discourse, in the very description of her birth. The dense series of lines that announce her biological birth simultaneously proclaim her discursive birth as narrator of the book we read, thus preparing readers for a network of textual operations that link both levels. Chapter One, Number One of the first book is preceded by *octavas* whose first lines predict the combative relationship to follow between the *pícara* who will narrate for Ubeda and the figure of a male critic, Perlícaro, the previously mentioned caricature of Ubeda's literary rival at court, Quevedo: "Al comenzar Justina, entró Perlícaro" ([At the moment of Justina's beginning, Perlícaro entered] 83).[7] The rest of the preliminary verses (83–84) depict the conflictive relationship they are to have by projecting a prolonged struggle for discursive authority, specifically. In spite of the opening lines' characterization of this masculine opponent as also a *pícaro* ("Miró a medio mogate, al uso pícaro" [He looked about carelessly, in the manner of a rogue] 83), Perlícaro, whose first-person voice is quoted, jumps at the opportunity to judge Justina authoritatively. As "theólogo," he lambastes her untitled literary beginning as "nefando": "Yo, el theólogo, / Condeno por nefando ese capítulo, / Pues va sin nombres, prólogo ni título" (I, the theologian, / Condemn as abominable that chapter, / For it goes without names, prologue, or title). The still silent Justina is ridiculed by this gadfly in following verses (83) as a loud-mouthed chronicler who acts like God ("chronicona" and "deífica"), and she is warned not to meddle with men's work: "Métase a bruja, que es arte más pacífica" (Learn witchcraft, it's a more peaceable art). The final two verses of the *octavas* (84), which close with the third-person description of Justina's brazen rejection of her male counterpart's command, launch her into an economy that is typically male: "Corrióse Justina, bravea como un Hércules, / Aquel que dio famoso nombre al miércoles" (Justina was ashamed / came, she retorts arrogantly, bellowing her merits like Hercules).[8]

Immediately following is the first paragraph of prose narrative, also in the third person, which signals the other coordinate of importance in the book of Justina's life: her material being, or sex, which serves as the backdrop for a complex and volatile engendering of bodily experience. As Allaigre and Cotrait demonstrate (32), the obsessive repetition of terms etymologically rooted in *sex* (the number six) suggests, in fact, that her role in commerce of the body will enjoy higher visibility than will Justina's bid for discursive authority.

Justina's own voice erupts with authority in the second paragraph, which switches to first-person narrative in the present tense, to lead readers to the site and moment of her biological birth itself. Placing readers in the lower material stratum of the picaresque world, the narrator focuses their attention upon her own naked female body and upon the genitals that serve to mark her mother. The birthing of López de Ubeda's dubious heroine is, we are startled to find, not simply a maternal, female act, but rather one that is graphically sexual. It sets the stage for the tension between appropriation and evasion that will develop Justina's narrative contention with her dismissive male critic, Perlícaro, throughout the text of her life:

Am I already being born? Augh, it's cold! Cover quick, or
they will see me be born naked! I am returning to the womb
of my lady mother, for I don't want my birth to be in one
thrust, like a dead bolt. It's better to come [out] in two
thrusts, like the curse of a Manchegan wagon driver. (84)[9]

Justina's primal words announce a precarious sense of selfhood
marked not by separation from the mother—for she quickly reen-
ters the womb—but by violation of this integrity from without,
"de golpe," an obscene molestation, we find in subsequent lines,
committed by none other than the self-important Perlícarlo. The
semantic clusters that depict her fleeing the violent impact of a
birth "de golpe" link her own forceful exit from private space to
potential invasion of that same space: "cerradura de loba," the
lock that may be shot home with one swift turn, is a feature cus-
tomarily found in the *mancebía* (Allaigre and Cotrait 33), where the
uneuphemized business of the day, the "golpes" (thrusts, beating)
of coupling, is semantically reinforced through implicit bodily
reference, in the following words, to the rapid "salir" (coming) of
the "carretero manchego," in two "golpes."[10] The reference to "dos
golpes" at the same time suggests the female narrator's desire, in
this retreat to the womb, to be born twice. Allaigre and Cotrait (33)
trace this nexus of words further, to support suggestion that the
novel self-consciously points readers to a two-level reading. While
the French critics argue that Ubeda's work is formed by a principal
set of references to witty authorship backed by a secondary, joking
obscenity, I would instead argue that the obsessively sexualized
language of the narrative establishes a primary verbal economy of
the narrator's marketed body, which is cleverly subverted by the
authority of the discourse with which Justina parodies—or misap-
propriates—the language of her so-called betters. Convincing evidence lies in Allaigre and Cotrait's own allusion (33–34) to variant
meanings of the words employed in the previous passage and in
plays upon them: the "golpe" that Justina attempts to double, bettering the male teamster's efforts, they argue also means "'en las
obras de ingenio, parte que tiene más gracia y oportunidad'" (in
works of intellectual wit, the part that has the most grace/attrac-
tiveness and impact) and the inversion of the *cerradura loba* (the
whorehouse deadbolt that she rejects as too plebeian an index of

golpes), *loba cerrada* (s.v. *loba*), is reference to the garb worn outside of teaching by scholars and others so authorized as indicator of their position ("'el traje que fuera del colegio usaban las colegiales y otras personas autorizadas por su estado o ejercicio para el uso de esta vestidura'").[11] Because I have not been able to trace all of their references in *Dic. aut.* myself, I am not certain that we should accept some of their more speculative assessments of certain semantic unities, but Allaigre and Cotrait's detailed study confirms that we must read the *Pícara Justina* simultaneously as the history of both a "literary"—or discursive—and a "biological" —or bodily—subject. We must not overlook the conceptual and ideological impact of the representation of that body.

The infant Justina's second birth clearly will not take the pathway of her first, for exit through the female vagina will submit her to a grotesquely disproportionate penetration by the adult male member of the pedantic "theólogo," Perlícaro, who appears through subsequent references to be "golpeando" her mother, in dogged pursuit of the narrator herself:

> I want to return to the belly of my mother, although it is empty, and I will be groaning up against that barrier, for I need everything possible to respond to the challenge to combat of a prying joker, who, yesterday walking around with a bare neck, today has come [out] with a ruff of linen as filthy as it is sticky, as stiff and spiky as if he had break-fasted on six whole skewers-full.[12] And for those who don't know him, I'll paint his appearance, bearing, and form. . . .
> His name is Perlícaro. . . . (84)[13]

These lines recall the strangely worded description of Justina's inception in the *octavas* preceding the opening of her narrative (83), where we learn that "Al comenzar Justina, entró Perlícaro" (At the moment of Justina's beginning, Perlícaro *entered*), the latter a reference to an enclosed space whose location is not initially clarified. In her own words that follow, the sounds that she will make as she struggles against the physical barriers of her containment within another body and Perlícaro's entry into the same, "uchoando de talanquera," fortify the staging of Justina's biological birth as entry into a sexual economy of violent penetration, by adding to previous bodily references ("golpes" and the teamster's calling) further semes for bestiality and physical combat. Allaigre and Cotrait (35) trace "de talanquera," generally a term for covering, to barriers erected for the running of bulls, and to a synonymous expression utilizing *pared* in *La Lozana andaluza* ("'Las paredes me metió aden-tro'" [He was up against the walls in me]) to refer to excessive force in sexual penetration. "Uchoando," etymologically related to *ox*, a sound associated with animals, particularly dogs (Allaigre and Cotrait 33), transfers from Justina, attempting to ward off this ag-gression, two paragraphs down to her assailant, who moves and breathes in coitus like a "perro perdiguero" (bird dog):

> The big rogue entered sniffing me out with his nose like a bird dog, wielding pointer and claw, as if he were walking on eggs, his shoulders disappearing as he strained his head forward to see what I was doing. (85)[14]

The violent sexual context of the opening two pages (84–85) is fur-ther defined by the seme for weaponry underlying use of the term "fisgón" (malicious joker) early in the first page (84): *fisga* or fish-ing spear (*Dic. aut.*, s.v. *fisga*). Ubeda's female narrator erupts as author of her life into this hostile physical environment in the staging of her birth as a discursive act. She takes over the first-per-son voice of her story, and in usurping the authority of language from her assailant Perlícaro, she erects a protective barricade from which to view him as object in the world she will create. Justina's launching of both her story and her life at the same time repre-sents a breaking of those literary and social barriers that militate against representation of the female sex and gender in positive re-lation to power.

If the threat to Justina's hopes for biological autonomy is ini-tially expressed by dense clusters of sexual references such as the ones just cited, a concurrent series of indumentary and culinary semes stages both her nonbiological birth, as incipient narrator describing the event, and her own aggressive response to male bodily domination. As is to be expected, the latter takes the form not of invasion, but instead of a deft evasion, both of the mascu-line body and of metaphors that might typically serve to glorify its engendered activities in martial terms. Justina's description of the rape attempted by Perlícaro is obscure for modern readers precisely because it does not work through denotative or even clear figurative description of the phallus and its function. It is established instead by a complex network of metaphors from different cultural registers, whose meaning tends to transfer among lexical series and multiply—or contaminate—the sense attributed to the narrative's referents. In this system, the role of each organ or body part is subject to different interpretations and the engendering of its function changes with context. Hence, Justina's opening references to Perlícaro's physical aggression, or definition in martial terms valued by the male nobiliary hierarchy to which his historical referent, Quevedo, belonged, quickly give way to evocations of his fornicating bodily status as subhuman: bestial, vegetable, even inanimate. The potency of Justina's own act of "salir" in this scenario lies in her discursive ability to disseminate what comprises the maleness of Perlícaro's body as it attempts to inseminate her incipient self-expression.

The narrator moves from reference to Perlícaro as challenging "fisgón," malicious courtly jester (*Dic. aut.*, s.v. *fisgón*) whose figural power is derived metonymically from the part most resembling a *fisga* or long fishing harpoon, the phallus, to reference to that same member, paradoxically, as symbol for a social declassification or powerlessness that material markers such as clothing attempt to belie. In what Allaigre and Cotrait (34) take as obscene reference to previously attempted penetration, Justina refers to Perlícaro jocosely (84) as the formerly bare-necked scholar (*Dic. aut.*, s.v. *cuellidegollado*) who has made a new debut with the starched ruff of higher social circles: "andando ayer cuellidegollado, ha salido hoy con una escarola de lienzo tan aporcada como engomada, más tieso y carrancudo que si hubiera desayunádose con seis tazones de asador" ([a prying joker, who] yesterday walking around with a bare neck, today has come [out] with a ruff of linen as filthy as it is sticky, as stiff and spiky as if he had breakfasted on six whole skewers-full). Her foe is ridiculed not simply by the allusion to his preoccupation with clothing and cutting a well-turned figure (presumably analogous to other literary references to male hairdos and makeup as effeminate).[15] The figure evoked by this and subsequent descriptions of body parts appears to be that of a phallus, decked out pejoratively through etymological jibes with the soil of its own operations. The ruff, on the one hand commonly a symbol of social elevation, and on the other, here metaphorizing nothing more than a common head of curly escarole (*Dic. aut.*, s.v. *escarola*, "valona alechugada," a lettuce-like or pleated ruff), bears a shiny crust of dried starch or other sticky substance (*Dic. aut.*, s.v. *engomado*). The process by which it has grown to its fullest physical state, problematically, has been through concealment under a mound of mud or soil (*Dic. aut.*, s.v., *aporcar:* "cubrir con tierra la hortaliza, para que madúre y se ponga mas en sazón" [to cover a vegetable with soil, so that it will mature and ripen to size]). Readers may or may not accept the suggestion of Allaigre and Cotrait that these lines form obscene reference to the appearance and condition of male genitalia embodied in Perlícaro (36–37). It seems clear to me that in this opening figurative attack upon the likes of Quevedo, the shift of narrative register to the subhuman, in the plays upon the bird dog, as well as to the vegetable, in the ruff sequence, by deforming and subverting the authority of the martial semes previously associated with this character, intensifies the ridicule already inherent in treatment not of his intellect—or discourse—but an obvious vulnerability, his body.

Justina's pedantic challenger is not allowed to define the terms of their interaction by aggressive insemination; instead, he is defined in context, through the parodic description of his phallus, as the object of other operations (*aporcar, engomar*). Indeed, his very name is attributed to the assessment made by a previous recipient, "una su doña Almirez," of his physical parts:

> He is named Perlícaro, as a result of careful perusal by one his lady Almirez, who because of the great impression that she conceived of his physical attributes, called him Perlícaro, giving him the name of pearl for his beauty, and that of Icarus for the height of his round-tipped affectation of knowledge. (84)[16]

This vision of Perlícaro is structured by references that oscillate between traces of his animate function and a larger world of inanimate things and ideas that threatens to destroy his presumptive bid for importance. The first segment of the rogue's name, "perla," allegedly alludes to his "hermosura" (beauty). It connotes a limpid milkiness that in love poetry is often a metaphor for higher body attributes such as the teeth of a woman's face. Given the parodic, lower body focus of the narrative context in which it occurs, however, we must consider that "perla" may well be a reference to the liquid by-product of sex whose color is milky. The second half of his name, "Icaro," plays upon the mythological figure, Icarus, who dared to fly too close to the sun and fell to his death. The "height" of the intellectual presumption attributed to Perlícaro is expressed not in the elevating spatial context of solar metaphors that the mythological derivation of his name leads readers to expect. It comes, discordantly, through the modification of an already deprecatory term for mental superiority—"sabiondez" (*Dic. aut.*, s.v. *sabiondez,* a malicious, or harmfully aggressive intelligence)—with a lower body metaphor, in an adjective taken from the noun for a receptacle for liquids—a flask—whose shape impedes their pouring out: "redomada," not simply "wily" (*Dic. aut.*, s.v. *redomado*) but semantically from *redoma* (*Dic. aut.*, s.v. *redoma*), "vasija gruessa de vidrio, de varios tamaños, la qual es ancha de abaxo, y vá estrechandose y angostandose hácia la boca" (a vial of thick glass, of various sizes, which is wider at the base and grows thinner approaching its opening). In this reference the semantic register moves to the realm of the inanimate, to depersonalize Justina's enemy by rendering him through the graphic evocation of an inhuman, potentially fragile phallic object.

The "theólogo" who pursues her, Perlícaro, is defined sexually at the outset of Justina's narrative by the fragmenting of his body, just as will be the narrator herself in many sections to follow. The movement executed by Justina discursively in narrating her own life in these terms, however, will enable her to escape the fate of being merely the object of male desire, and to become a radically self-questioning subject. Indeed, the narrator's discourse of her body (and hence, the body of others) becomes the major political text of Ubeda's book, for she critiques identity through a description of the body whose terms defy its material limits, converting its social presence into a dangerously theatrical ideological discourse. The fate of her masculine-gendered male critic, who would ridicule her lack of compliance with hierarchical literary protocol, is his displacement from the expected status of subject to that of object—or receptacle—a feminized definition imposed from without by the semantic context of López de Ubeda's work.

In this fictive autobiography, Justina—a wildly improbable, street-wise Ms. Malaprop—goes on to relate verbal wiles and physical forays that define her existence in a hierarchical society whose economies are—in her account—obsessively differentiated by sexual metaphors. The book lures readers (in Ubeda's context, I think we must assume, principally male) to savor in pornographic detail successive narrative encounters in which the power or degradation of Justina with respect to other characters is defined in terms of bodily possession, of material domination.[17] Justina's figural body is everywhere in López de Ubeda's densely layered work; it is the locus and the object upon which the economy and semiotic arrangement of the "libro de entretenimiento" depend. Yet what we in fact find is that the narrator negotiates as a prostitute while never quite delivering the goods—at least not in the represented context of her story. In functioning as the discursive voice that organizes her story, the apparent prostitute—whose body is described as suffering the aftereffects of syphilis—is quite deliberately made to suppress reference to her own subjugation in the very economy she operates.[18] In the words of Friedman (87), "López de Ubeda transforms the sexual reprobate of *La Lozana andaluza* into a virgin sinner. Justina's body is a selling point, but not for sale; she takes men's money and escapes before they can abuse her." Whether we are to believe the latter system of references, or the former—detailed in graphic word plays such as those of the *pelo* or the *flauta* ("parece nací con la flauta inserta en el cuerpo, según gusto della" [it seems that I was born with the flute inserted in my body, such was my pleasure in it], 113)—is, I think, irrelevant; both are operative in in López de Ubeda/Justina's story. What commands the attention of the frustrated reader—in addition to the recognition that repetition of promises for substance, in this case her body, seems intended to carry the often truncated reading forward by mobilizing a desire that is never fulfilled—is the fact that the *pícara's* "objectivity" as desired body is rendered just as "tenuous" as is her discursive "subjectivity"; the power of her account lies precisely in what is left unsaid about what she embodies in the material economy of López de Ubeda's titillating narrative. Although she is positioned as the object of male desire, the body that Justina sells is never delivered in apprehensible terms; suitors and readers in the end face only the terms of their own desire, in a narrative whose underlying homoerotic tension belies López de Ubeda's intent to confront them with a disturbing specularity of their own unfulfilled ambitions and the lacks that these reveal.

Readers of the female *pícara's* unexpected verbal aggression are, of course, aware from the start that *La pícara Justina* is not composed solely, or even primarily, by the discursive emulation of a relatively unschooled, female self-expression. The fictive autobiography is revealingly fraught with the echoes of its other subject, López de Ubeda, the man whose voice takes the form of artistic drag. Speaking for many readers who doubt the success of this projection in rendering the work's protagonist, Friedman asserts that the *pícara's* subjectivity appears to derive from a "tenuous interiority" (73), for the fabric of the story that seeks to justify her bawdy disregard for (male) social authority is warped by echoes of the same pedantic, rhetoricized discourse that defines that dominance. The narrator Justina's words, in fact, sound a lot like the intrusion of the male López de Ubeda into her discourse of self-definition, with a resulting diminution in the verisimilitude that gives her character coherence.

I suggest, however, that the *pícara's* true impact as subject of the fictive "autobiography" lies precisely in the deconstruction of her primacy by means of this dissonant discourse, for the dissolution of her own image in the novel impels readers to examine the social economy that unsuccessfully defines it. By speaking through his protagonist, Ubeda appears to challenge readers with the question posed in different terms today by Butler (*Gender Trouble*), who asks first (x): "Is drag the imitation of gender, or does it dramatize the signifying gestures through which gender itself is established? Does being female constitute a 'natural fact' or a cultural performance?" and then (xxi): "What political possibilities are the consequence of a radical critique of the categories of identity?" The effect of Ubeda's narrative cross-dressing is to study what is revealed to be the entirely fictive production of cultural meanings for Justina's sexual body, in a panorama of shifting circumstances. Neither other characters in the narrative nor readers are allowed the facile response of being able to identify and label the example posed in Justina; she is not simply or even only, in terms of her power relationship to others, a woman. In the construction of López de Ubeda's narrator, Butler's proviso regarding the production of the "gendered subject along a differentiated axis of domination" is amply illustrated: Justina's function in social relationships, or gender, appears to be at variance with her actual sex, for in discursive contexts within the narrative she clearly has the upper hand. This dominance is evident beginning with the opening lines in which she moves to defend herself from incursion by Perlícaro, in spite of her apparently helpless physical status as infant/victim of an attempted rape, by rewriting the terms of her birth. This literary surprise forces readers to define the protagonist's subjectivity primarily in terms of the relative power enabled by language rather than by the material accidents of nature. Furthermore, we find that the mobility of this most problematic aspect of identity in Justina's life is reinforced through its confusion with other indicators of who she is. To quote Butler's more general formulation, which is well demonstrated in Ubeda's text, this subject's "gender is not always constituted coherently or consistently in different historical contexts" and "intersects with racial, class, ethnic, sexual and regional modalities of discursively constituted identities" (2–3). Clearly, the forefronting of a sexual identity in terms that are self-consciously selected, and the highly theatrical—continually evolving—rendering of gender function in this narrative force readers to conclude that the relationship of the protagonist's bodily, or material, status to her power over others is unpredictable, unbound to social codes that Ubeda's original readers, at least, quite likely took for granted. Although in its obsessive sexual typing his representation of Justina parodies a host of denigrating precursors, López de Ubeda's riotous romp through Justina's person cannot be dismissed as simply derivative of a long misogynistic literary tradition, precisely because the *Pícara Justina* is structured by the creative or generative repositioning of its female character, the liberation of Justina's gender as social behavior from her sexual body. Her words, in effect, serve to redefine her body.[19] In the narrative that composes her life, Justina finds expression not only as the embodiment, or object, of many male anxieties and desires. She is made to monopolize the center of the novel as a writing subject whose engendered discursive function coincides with the masculine, if we consider the authorial function of this gender within the rest of the genre. Much like her counterparts, Lázaro, Guzmán, and Pablos, she is made capable of self-reflection both to exonerate and to expose sardonically the terms of her own existence.

Her terms, betraying Ubeda's, dictate that readers attracted to the lure of her language confront their own worst reflections as they attempt to assemble her image. The story that Justina tells "untells" itself at each breath, as dizzying word plays, hieroglyphics, and literary allusions pile up around hair, face, legs, and belly, and readers are forced to shift their attention from the fragments of her person to the troubled world distilled in the language with which she describes herself.[20] The female body, Justina's *figura,* thus serves merely as the point of departure for the relations figurally represented through it. The often ornamental language of this highly artificial jest book in this respect gives form to a number of "serious," apparently real, issues in the material world from which it arises. The deplorable conditions particularly of lower-class women's lives are artistically parodied while they provide the scenario through which López de Ubeda, according to Bataillon and Damiani (*López de Ubeda* and "Introducción," *La pícara Justina*), represented his criticism of other marginalizing and penalizing drives by Spain's official cultural institutions—principally the stigmatory investigation of *limpieza de sangre,* which forced many important courtiers with *converso* ancestry to falsify genealogies in attempts to attain or retain positions of rank, either nobiliary or in the state and church bureaucracies. The parody of this political struggle over the terms of social position, already an issue central to the picaresque, assumes particular historical significance in Ubeda's *La pícara Justina.* As Bataillon clarifies (29–30), the book ridicules the many obstacles to the controversial ennoblement of its *converso* patron, Rodrigo Calderón, the second most powerful figure in the court of Felipe III. We therefore find in this picaresque "life" the coincidence of three focuses seen by Smith as important in considering literary representation of gender and sexuality: "the problematic status of woman in a male culture; the possibility of resistance to an authority always already in place" and "the dual role of the body as material and theoretical protagonist in that resistance" (1–2). *La pícara Justina* opens upon López de Ubeda's decision to cross-dress as Justina, and the conscious artistry through which he accomplishes this parody of material—sexual—position as well as of gender function forces readers to examine the ways in which he is thus able to restructure the relationships of all those represented. The author appears indeed to compose from within the instability of his narrator's voice and the indeterminacy of her physical attributes a derisive resistance to authority without—a posture that rejects the terms of the legitimacy sought mistakenly by the likes of Lázaro and Guzmán.

There is no evidence in this aggressive "libro de entretenimiento" that the male author of *pícara* Justina's life was interested in bettering the material conditions that oppressed women in the early seventeenth century. In this respect, I think we all would agree that his intentions are far from "feminist." Nevertheless, the writing that conveys his protagonist's narrative is distinctly "feminized," in its engendered response to the elitist masculine literary and cultural models that it ridicules. Ubeda seems to have anticipated in his creation of Justina, as the vehicle for his own response to a society shaped by such models, the true metaphoric potential of a feminine discourse, whose relationships are not normative or restricted by bodies whose authority it must serve. By freeing his *pícara*'s words from a tradition of referentiality that privileges discourse over the body and material existence, Ubeda in effect enhances the political potential of the picaresque. The birth of Justina —a discursive act that insists on manifesting itself through her body—is in multiple senses a breaking of age-old barriers, for it results in the figurative decomposition of Perlícaro and the feudal values that he is shown to embody. As *La pícara Justina* unfolds, from the first pages of Chapter One onward, this male voice that initially prefaces her story in verses from the position of first person, Perlícaro, is transformed in the opening subsection to a third-person obsession who haunts Justina, and then in ensuing chapters into a minor character whose occasional verbal attributions have little to do with her or anyone else's existence. Justina's first-person development, on the other hand, is allowed to explode in verbal configurations so numerous and geometrically multiple in senses that we cannot logically restrain the functions of the body with which her narrative overwhelms us. Ubeda's *pícara* is all that her male counterparts are, but in her representation of gender and the power of its creative function, she is also a lot more.

Notes

1. While the early picaresque narratives all reveal a preoccupation with language and the deceptiveness of its signifying potential, none match the lexical and rhetorical density of Ubeda's text. The effect of "defamiliarization" produced by the difficulty of his *pícara*'s discourse clearly did not intensify the pleasure of all members of his original public; Cervantes went so far as to deny Ubeda's legitimacy as a poet, satirizing him not as an artistic rival but as a "pseudopoeta" in verses from Chapter 7 of *El viaje del Parnaso* and in those of Urganda la Desconocida preceding the *Quijote*. See the discussions of Bataillon (50–53; 67–75) and Damiani (*Pícara Justina* 4–5); also the latter's overview in *López de Ubeda* of negative versus positive literary criticism of the *Pícara Justina* from the eighteenth to the twentieth century (22–27).

2. All English translations of Ubeda's text are mine. The only extant English translation of the work, John Stevens's rare 1707 London edition of *The Spanish Libertines; or, The Lives of Justina, The Country Jilt, Celestina, The Bawd of Madrid, and Estevanillo González,* includes merely a loose adaptation of some of seventy-some pages of Ubeda's work.

3. Quevedo was one of those writers who most violently supported the primacy of the old Christian nobility against incursions, both literary and social, by the likes of Ubeda and his patron. Emond Cros's work, *L'Aristocrate et le Carnaval des Gueux: Etude sur le "Buscón" de Quevedo* (Montpellier: Etudes Sociocritiques, 1975), analyzes the representation of this conflictive relationship in Quevedo's own picaresque work, using a Marxist framework that "demystifies" the nature of many social tensions expressed by the work's systems of metaphors.

4. Damiani (*López de Ubeda* 22) cites Puyol's 1912 edition for specific lines to this effect.

5. For excellent analyses specifically of the self-conscious literariness of this picaresque work, see López de Tamargo ("Cuadros y recuadros") and Joseph Jones ("Hieroglyphics").

6. Had they been able to finish a comprehensive analysis of the book before Cotrait's death, a project that would presumably have entailed years of research, the French semanticists would have provided picaresque scholars and historians alike with an indispensable companion reader to Ubeda's difficult text.

7. See Francisco López de Ubeda, *La pícara Justina,* ed. Bruno M. Damiani (Potomac, Md.: Studia Humanitatis, 1982). All references to the novel are taken from this edition.

8. Semantic juxtapositions in these verses deftly confront readers' expectations of the woman's modest retreat with the surprisingly ejaculatory nature of her verbal response, preparing them for the gender oscillations that will follow when she becomes the voice of the narrative.

9. "¿Ya soy nacida? ¡Ox, que hace frío! ¡Tapagija, que me verán nacer desnuda! Tórnome al vientre de mi señora madre, que no quiero que mi nacimiento sea de golpe, como cerradura de loba. Más vale salir de dos golpes, como voto a Dios de carretero manchego" (84).

10. *Diccionario de autoridades* (hereafter *Dic. aut.*), s.v. *golpe,* renders the primary definition as "la colision de dos cuerpos duros al movimiento de algun impulso, de que resulta algun sonido."

11. The French critics claim to quote *Dic. aut.* for the figurative use of *golpe* to refer to wit, but I have not been able to trace this passage in the dictionary. The closest I find, s.v. *golpe en bola,* is "metaphoricamente vale el acierto y seguridad, con que se executa ò logra algun dicho, ù acción, especialmente contra otro."

12. I have not been able to find an adequate explanation of the term *tarazones,* though it is clearly related to a culinary register in the context of Ubeda's narrative. Allaigre and Cotrait (37) trace the reference "asador" to a definition of "andar muy tieso" in *Dic. aut.* that seems to reinforce the phallic sense of "de asador": "parecer que come asadores."

These and other semantic clusters that I have not discussed in this essay lead the French critics to support the reading of Justina's birth as a context of sexual aggression also (cf. 36, 39).

13. "Quiero marchar de retorno a la panza de mi madre, aunque vaya de vacío, y estaréme uchoando de talanquera, que todo lo he bien menester para responder al reto de un fisgón, que, andando ayer cuellidegollado, ha salido hoy con una escarola de lienzo tan aporcada como engomada, más tieso y carrancudo que si hubiera desayunádose con seis tazones de asador. Y, para los que no le conocen, yo les pintaré su traza, postura y talle. Llámase Perlícaro" (84).

14. "Entró el muy pícaro husmeando como perro perdiguero, jugando de punta y talón, como si pisara sobre huevos, deshombreciéndose por mirar lo que yo hacía, . . . " (85).

Dic. aut. lists several definitions under *jugar* (for example, *jugar el lance* and *jugar las armas*) that refer to the dexterous use of weaponry; I assume that "jugando de punta y talón" should be translated similarly. Damiani, n. 152, 85, states that "*deshombreciéndose:* quiere decir que Perlícaro se *quedaba sin hombros* a fuerza de bajarlos y elevar sobre ellos la cabeza para ver lo que escribía Justina." The play also appears to involve the sense of "des-*hombre*cerse"—hints of latent unmanliness— intensified by his fear of "breaking eggs" in this encounter with Justina.

15. See, for another picaresque example, the description of Guzmán's father in Mateo Alemán's *Guzmán de Alfarache,* ed. Benito Brancaforte (Madrid: Cátedra, 1984) I: 118.

16. "Llámase Perlícaro, a contemplación de una su doña Almirez, que por el gran concepto que concibió de sus buenas partes, le llamó Perlícaro, dándole nombre de perla por su hermosura, y el de Icaro por la alteza de su redomada sabiondez" (84).

17. Cruz ("Sexual Enclosure" 141) argues that the protagonist's presentation of herself as female merchandise at both temporal levels reveals the work's inherent sexism: "the licentiousness of the *pícara* does not give her license to break away from authorial control: the protagonist remains at the service of the author, a seductive figure of speech ready to lure the reader into a male-dominated and male-oriented discourse." Rodríguez ("Aspectos de la primera variante feminina" 180),

on the other hand, defends a sort of protofeminism in the novel. While Rey Hazas, Dunn, Hanrahan, and Ronquillo discuss the literary phenomenon of the female rogue, they do not consider in either feminist or antifeminist terms the broader implications of engendered writing in this work.

I agree with Cruz that through the appropriation of the loose woman figure, Ubeda's work reflects the subjugation suffered by most real women in seventeenth-century Spain. However, I do not think that we should overlook the function of the *pícara*'s voice as literary artifice intended to parody and hence question the constitution of such identity and position within the power hierarchy.

18. The book opens with Justina's reference in a dense series of word plays to the "amargas memorias de mi pelona francesa" or "enfermedad venérea" ("Introducción general," "Número uno," 56 and n. 42a).

19. Bloch's complex article examines "the extent to which the practices of medieval hermeneutics and the discourse of misogyny are bound up in each other" (8), revealing that the female gender has long been a central trope in debates over discursive authority.

20. Although I do not cite any specific portion of her argument, the conceptual framework of Gossy's *The Untold Story* proved extremely valuable in my early formulations of this paper; she was one of the first critics whom I encountered to address directly the importance of the female body to literary discourse during the Golden Age, a literary period in which the presence of the female has by criticism traditionally been trivialized and overlooked. Other recent critics whose innovative work focuses specifically on discursive representation of the female body and who shaped my interests generally in this paper are: Smith (*Body Hispanic*), Ann Jones ("Surprising Fame: Renaissance Gender"), Michie (*The Flesh Made Word*), and Vickers ("Diana Described: Scattered Woman"). And both of Cruz's excellent articles, which deal directly with the woman's body in the Spanish picaresque and in seventeenth-century Spain, were key readings for my consideration of the prostitute figure in *La pícara Justina,* as I have indicated elsewhere. Her focus is more properly historicist than is mine in this paper, in which I have limited myself primarily to the linguistic problems of Ubeda's text.

Works Cited

Allaigre, Claude, and Cotrait, René. "La escribana fisgada: Estratos de significación en un pasaje de *La pícara Justina." Hommage des hispanistes françaises à Noel Salomon.* Intro. Henry Bonneville. Barcelona: LAIA, 1979. 27–47.

Bataillon, Marcel. *Pícaros y picaresca.* Madrid: Taurus, 1969.

Bloch, Howard R. "Medieval Misogyny." *Representations* 20 (Fall 1987): 1–24.

Butler, Judith. *Gender Trouble: Feminism and the Subversion of Identity.* New York: Routledge, 1990.

Cruz, Anne J. "Sexual Enclosure, Textual Escape: The *Pícara* as Prostitute in the Spanish Female Picaresque Novel." *Seeking the Woman in Late Medieval and Renaissance Writings.* Eds. Sheila Fisher and Janet Halley. Knoxville: Univ. of Tennessee Press, 1989. 135–59.

———. "Studying Gender in the Spanish Golden Age." *Cultural and Historical Grounding for Hispanic and Luso-Brazilian Feminist Literary Criticism.* Ed. Hernán Vidal. Minneapolis: Univ. of Minnesota Press, 1989. 193–222.

Damiani, Bruno. *Francisco López de Ubeda*. New York: Twayne 1977.

———, ed. *La pícara Justina*. By Francisco López de Ubeda. Potomac, Md.: Studia Humanitatis, 1982.

Dunn, Peter N. *The Spanish Picaresque Novel*. Boston: Twayne, 1957. 113–33.

Friedman, Edward H. *The Antiheroine's Voice: Narrative Discourse and Transformations of the Picaresque*. Columbia: Univ. of Missouri Press, 1987.

Gossy, Mary S. *The Untold Story: Women and Theory in Golden Age Texts*. Ann Arbor: Univ. of Michigan Press, 1989.

Hanrahan, Thomas. *La mujer en la novela picaresca española*. Vol. 2. Madrid: Porrúa Turanzas, 1967. 2 vols. 195–261.

Jones, Ann Rosalind. "Surprising Fame: Renaissance Gender Ideologies and Women's Lyric." *The Poetics of Gender*. Ed. Nancy K. Miller. New York: Columbia Univ. Press, 1986. 74–95.

Jones, Joseph. "Hieroglyphics in *La pícara Justina*." *Estudios literarios de hispanistas norteamericanos dedicados a Helmut Hatzfeld con motivo de su 80 aniversario*. Ed. Josep M. Sola-Solé, Alessandro Crisafulli, and Bruno Damiani. Barcelona: Hispam, 1974. 415–29.

López de Tamargo, Paloma. "Cuadros y recuadros del discurso picaresco: El caso de *La pícara Justina*." *Actas del 8 Congreso de la Asociación Internacional de Hispanistas*. Vol. II. Eds. Kossoff, Amor y Vázquez, Kossoff, and Ribbans. 2 vols. Madrid: Istmo, 1986. 193–99.

Michie, Helena. *The Flesh Made Word*. Oxford: Oxford Univ. Press, 1987.

Rey Hazas, Antonio. "La compleja faz de una pícara: Hacia una interpretación de *La pícara Justina*." *Revista de Literatura* 45 (1983): 87–109.

Rodríguez, Luz. "Aspectos de la primera variante feminina de la picaresca española." *Explicación de textos literarios* 8 (1979–80): 175–81.

Ronquillo, Pablo J. *Retrato de la pícara: La protagonista de la picaresca española del XVII*. Madrid: Playor, 1980.

Smith, Paul Julian. *The Body Hispanic: Gender and Sexuality in Spanish and Spanish American Literature*. Oxford: Clarendon Press, 1989.

Vickers, Nancy J. "Diana Described: Scattered Woman and Scattered Rhyme." *Writing and Sexual Difference*. Ed. Elizabeth Abel. Chicago: Univ. of Chicago Press, 1982. 95–109.

Chapter 6
Defining the Picaresque: Authority and the Subject in *Guzmán de Alfarache*

Carroll B. Johnson

I want to begin by observing that the subject of this essay, Mateo Alemán's *Guzmán de Alfarache* (1599 and 1604), perfectly enacts the proposition contained in the subtitle of this volume: "tradition and displacement." Having decided it was important that something be said here about *Guzmán,* and preferably about its central role in the formation of the picaresque canon, such as it is, I thought I might examine the paradoxical relation between masculine figures of authority (the cook, the captain, the cardinal, Guzmán's uncle, etc.) and the speaking subject, Guzmán, who presents himself as the author of the text. My original idea was that this relation of author to authority, latent in *Lazarillo de Tormes* and full-blown in *Guzmán,* established Alemán's novel as the canonical paradigm.

Here are Michel Cavillac's thoughts on exactly the same matter: "In following the path opened up by *Lazarillo de Tormes,* Alemán offers us in the person of the rogue/merchant of Sevilla one of the very first examples of the 'problematic hero', the bearer of modern bourgeois values. If, as Michel Butor has written, 'the modern Western novel really begins with the great picaresque narratives of the Golden Age,' the time has come to allow *Guzmán de Alfarache* to assume its rightful place at the head of that patrilineal succession."[1] It is still possible, however, to consider the questions of authorship and authority in the *Guzmán* from slightly different perspectives.

I have to confess (an archipicaresque discursive practice) that I am an unreconstructed and, it now appears, an unreconstructible humanist. But not in the sense bandied about on the high-priced visiting lecturer circuit; i.e., a humanist is someone who believes in the existence of an irreducible essence called "man," and that this "man" is everywhere and forever identical to himself, a being whose characteristics are generically determined and consist chiefly in inner consistency and a sense of wholeness, and whose existence is furthermore independent of his historical moment and social context. For Paul Julian Smith, for example, a humanist is someone who believes in "the myth of 'Man' as founding father of the text and as integrated, active subject within that society which the text is thought to reflect" ("The Rhetoric of Representation" 88). In my opinion, the myth of Man defined by Smith is what used to be called in Latin class an "objective genitive." That is, it is not the myth that belongs to man; rather it is a myth about man. I'm not sure anyone believes it, or that anyone has ever believed it (I certainly don't), but you can't pick up any piece of trendy litcrit these days without having to witness yet another flaying of that poor dead horse. Or one might say, in the ludic spirit that has also, with more fortunate results, come to pervade our profession, that with respect to the myth of Man, the myth is a myth because the Man is a straw.

On the other hand, there really is such a thing as Man, or mankind, or humankind. Like it or not, we all belong, just like all the other animals, to a species, and our species, just like all the others, has some characteristics that set it apart from the rest. We walk upright, we see in three dimensions, we don't have tails, we smile, we make tools, we make language, and we are ready to copulate at just about any time. The feature that we in our line of work are especially proud of is our language-making ability. Language causes us to enter into a different relation with reality than do our mammalian cousins. Celestina had that figured out in 1499 when she told Pármeno that the really great thing is talking, because "lo al, mejor lo fazen los asnos en el prado"—"that other, the asses in the fields do it better." Language is what enables the symbolic order, which in turn is the environment in which we humans live out our lives. Language is what enables us to invent natural law and other moral and ethical constructs. So that when in 1978 I quoted Jean-Paul Sartre to the effect that man is that being through whom value comes to exist in the world, or to the effect that man is that being who is always in search of his being because it resides not in himself but in the Other, I was merely remarking some of the characteristics of our species.

I am also puzzled by the current orthodoxy that locates the origin of "humanism" not in antiquity or in the Renaissance but in the nineteenth century and in particular in the Balzacian novel. I associate humanism with the historical rise of the concept of the individual, in the sense of an individual human consciousness placed in a dialectical relation to its circumstances, and changing and evolving through time, since the notion of dialectic assumes a sequence of events, which can only occur in time. Thus not monolithic, not essential, and not integrated. Who can read *Lazarillo de Tormes* or *Guzmán de Alfarache,* not to mention *Don Quijote,* and come away believing that they rest on the myth of Man? It seems apparent that what these texts have in common is precisely the assumption that man, a man, a human subjectivity, is not an essence genetically determined and given at birth, but is rather a process of becoming, not becoming something or someone foreordained or even the person one had in mind, but participating willy nilly in an ongoing and unpredictable dialectic terminable only by death. Ginés de Pasamonte had that figured out in 1605, when he asked Don Quijote how could his life be finished when it wasn't finished. And it was his own experience with the *Quijote,* after all, that led Ortega to conclude that man does not have an essence, only a history.

The notion of self-fashioning made fashionable by Stephen Greenblatt is what Lázaro de Tormes is engaged in when he offers what he calls the "entera noticia de mi *persona*"—"a complete account of my *persona*." He is simultaneously who he thinks he is, who he wants us to think he is, and who we decide he is. And that might range from a sympathetic victim to a callous and morally bankrupt image maker, the first Madison Avenue huckster in Western literature. I think Oliver Wendell Holmes and Unamuno were close to the truth when they observed around the turn of our century that the individual is not one but several, depending on who is watching and bothering to think about it. Sartre subsequently spun this out into a system with parts like "Being-for-the-Self" and "Being-for-the-Other." And Fernando de

Rojas had already figured that out and written a book about it in 1499. For a long time now the notion of the integrated self has been in disrepute.

Now some thoughts on the author. A lot of current debate focuses on and seeks to define this slippery critical concept. One usually begins by remarking that not so very long ago the existence and status of the author were taken for granted and totally unproblematic. I must confess that I really can't remember a time in my professional life when the notion of "the author" was not problematic. My generation of students grew up on Percy Lubbock (1935), Meyer Abrams (1953), Norman Friedman (1955), and Wayne Booth (1960). I can even recall my dear old hopelessly-behind-the-times Raimundo Lida speaking in class of "la personalidad poetica del autor, claro, no la emprica"—"the author's poetic personality, naturally, not the empirical one." But we are much more sophisticated now; we ask the hard questions. Is the author a biological, empirical entity, or is he/she/it rather a textual presence or construct? Is the author the originator or creator, the "founding father" of the text, or is he merely a scriptor or *bricoleur?* Is the author the giver or the repository of meaning; that is, is he the authority who determines the validity of interpretation (meaning being identical to the author's intention), or is the author merely another presence in the text with no greater claim to authority than any other textual presence? The obligatory references, or, dare I say, authorities, are Roland Barthes, "The Death of the Author," a piece so widely anthologized as to render citation otiose, and Michel Foucault, "What Is an Author?" of similar repute. One of the more intelligent treatises in this general line is Pierre Machery's *Pour une théorie de la production literaire,* which isn't as frequently cited, probably because in the land of Reagan and Bush we like our French food for thought a little less pink, thank you, even if that moves some of us to wonder where's the beef.

The notion of author inevitably involves that of authority. Indeed, the word "author" has its origin in the Latin *auctor,* which my dictionary defines as "an originator, a progenitor," as "Lucius Brutus, praeclarus auctor nobilitatis tuae" (Cicero); or "a founder," as "Troiae Cynthius auctor" (Virgil); or "author of a work of art, especially a writer," as "rerum Romanarum auctores" (Cicero). An *auctor* is also a "cause," as "auctores belli esse nolebant" (Caesar). My dictionary goes on to observe that an *auctor* is therefore "an authority or person responsible for a statement or a doctrine," as "in antiquissima philosophia Cratippo auctore versaris" (Cicero). By the Middle Ages the term was considered to contain its own abstraction, *auctoritas,* and had come to mean someone who was at once a writer and an authority, someone not merely to be read but also to be respected and believed. In the eighteenth century Giambattista Vico derives *auctor,* whence *auctoritas,* from Greek *autos,* which in Latin gives *proprius* or *suus ipsius. Proprius* also means property, proprietary. Hence, authority has to do with property. Vico's performance repeats an important aspect of Huarte de San Juan's some 150 years earlier: a dubious etymology becomes the basis for a profound meditation, and for a powerful pragmatic effect as well. The original correlation of voting rights with property ownership in our country as well as others is the application of Vico's concept of authority to democracy.

For Edward Said, the notion of authority "suggests a constellation of linked meanings." Some of these derive from *auctoritas* and include things like the power to enforce obedience, the power to influence action, and a person whose opinion is accepted. Others derive from *auctor* and include the concepts of a person who originates or gives existence to something, a begetter, beginner, father, or ancestor. Still other associations derive from the relation of *auctor* to the past participle (*auctus*) of the verb *augere,* and include the notion of augmentation or increase, leading again to those of procreation and generation (83). Said's concern to relate authority in general to what he calls a process of filiation is well known, although he goes on to affirm, with a nod to Bakhtin, that one of the defining features of the novel is "the strong sense of doubt that the authority of any single voice, or group of voices, is sufficient unto itself."

It is interesting to note the contrast between Said's acceptance, not to say embrace of the notion of founding fathers and filiation, and the headlong flight from the same by such thinkers as Barthes, and among ourselves, Paul Julian Smith. I would like to return to this fascinating question later. For now I would like to offer a reduction in the terms of the debate concerning authority, to define the problem of authorship and authority rather narrowly but in a way that seems to me useful to the analysis of picaresque narrative.

It seems to me that what is at stake in deciding where, if anywhere, the authority resides in a given text, is the question of who has the power to control the production of discourse. I think this is a variant of Foucault's affirmation that authority is a property of discourse. In any case, the question as I see it is not necessarily who speaks, but who has the power to call speech or discourse into existence, and who has the power to shut it off.

In light of Vico's conflation of authority and property, we might rephrase the question as: who owns the discourse? This particular rephrasing locates the question of textual authority within a kind of entry-level Marxism and defines it first as an economic question, and then as a theory of production. The ownership of the discourse would be analogous to the ownership of the means of production, or capital. The actual production of discourse would correspond to labor. This formulation allows us to retain the currently fashionable notion of the author as a textual presence of very limited authority, a scriptor whose labor is exploited for the benefit of some higher authority who calls the discourse into existence and decides when it's finished. In some texts the class struggle thus potentialized is explicitly enacted; in others it remains latent.

The notion of ownership also suggests the relations of power defined by the oedipal situation, in an entry-level psychoanalysis. Authority is vested in the father by virtue of his ownership of the mother. The unequal struggle for possession of this property, the son's desire to take the place of the father, to become himself the father, motivates the production of the discourse. This formulation also recoups the notion of *auctor* as "a person who originates or gives existence to something, a begetter, beginner, father or ancestor," already realized in the father/*auctor*, a potential in the son/scriptor.

The picaresque narratives present a special instance of the problems we have been surveying, because there is an author overt in the text, who addresses the reader as "I," who tells the reader his name and who raises the questions of authorship and authority explicitly in his discourse. At least in *Lazarillo de Tormes* and *Guzmán de Alfarache*, the question of the origination of the discourse is discussed at some length by the fictional author. The same question appears *passim* in the works of Cervantes and is especially central to the *Casamiento engañoso y Coloquio de los perros*.[2] Real authority, in the sense I have attempted to define, resides outside, anterior to and above the fictional author, who is thus reduced to an exploited scrivener, a symbolically castrated son, or a textual representation of Sysiphus. Foucault has observed that confessional discourse, of which picaresque narrative is a subcategory, "unfolds within a power relationship, for one does not confess without the presence (or virtual presence) of a partner who is not simply the interlocutor but the authority who requires the confession," and that "the agency of domination does not reside in the one who speaks, but in the one who listens and says nothing" (I: 63). In *Lazarillo de Tormes* authority is vested in Vuestra Merced, who calls the discourse into existence and forces Lázaro to grovel before him (in the same way, we might observe in passing, that Lázaro forces the *escudero* to grovel before him within the narrative). We might also observe in passing the same relation of authority to author in the autobiography of Santa Teresa, or in the criminal confessions studied by Antonio Gómez Moriana (69–94). In the case of Cervantes's *Casamiento/Coloquio*, which I have read as the story of a writer trying to become one, Campuzano is forced to relinquish at least a part of his authority to his friend Peralta, and he himself is of course called into existence and finished off by an invisible higher authority. In every case, however, the author/scriptor enters into some kind of a dialectical relationship with the authority, and in the process becomes something more. The exercise of authority over him seeks to force him to cough up what he has inside, to make his private self public. But it happens that the scriptor becomes an auctor by generating, or as we now say *constituting*, a "self" through the discourse he produces, in the very act of knuckling under to the authority.

In the case that concerns us, Guzmán de Alfarache's writing hand responds to something beyond its control. His discourse is called into existence by something over which he clearly exercises very limited mastery or none at all. But there is no Vuestra Merced as in the case of Lázaro de Tormes, no confessors as in the case of Teresa de Jesús, and no inquisitors who compel the production of discourse by the exercise of their institutionalized authority. There is nothing or no one outside the scriptor, which is why it is so frustratingly rewarding to analyze the problems of authorship and authority in the canonical text of the picaresque tradition.

I want to examine Guzmán's struggle with authority in two contexts and on two levels. First, within the narrative, the narrating I experiences himself as locked in an unending and unequal context with forces and persons who exercise authority over him: institutions and *amos*. Second, there is a similar contest between the I and those forces beyond his control, the real authority as I have defined it, that determine the shape of the discourse he produces.

The world as experienced by Guzmán de Alfarache is divided into the powerful and the powerless, the *ricos y poderosos* and the *pobres y desvalidos,* or in another formulation the *desechados* and the *admitidos.* As a *pícaro*, with the social cards stacked hopelessly against him by the facts of his lineage, his mother's descent into poverty, his own pervasive experience of servitude, he clearly belongs to the group deprived of power. He experiences life in society as a series of rejections. He is rejected by the Church on his first night away from home. He is rejected by the wealthy who refuse to take him on even as a servant because he looks so disreputable, an event that validates Fr. Diego de Guadix's sixteenth-century definition of the term *pícaro:* "In Spain, a *pícaro* is a vile, low-class man who goes around poorly dressed and looking like he has no honor."[3] Fr. Diego defines the picaro in terms of a relationship with social norms and structures of power, in other words, in terms of an Other. In the second part of the novel Guzmán brings a lawsuit against a member of the local power structure in Bologna, and although he is clearly in the right, he loses the case. His opponent countersues for defamation of character, and Guzmán winds up in jail, observing ruefully: "Yo escup al cielo; volviéronse las flechas contra mí, pagando justos por pecadores"—"I spit at Heaven; the arrows came back at me, and the righteous paid the penalty for the sinners" (II, *ii*, 2). He establishes a series of linking hierarchies of power, revealing the similarities between the judicial hierarchy, the wealthy in general, including wealthy thieves and criminals, other figures of authority such as innkeepers, and finally God himself, all arrayed against him, thwarting his efforts, mocking his attempts at social mobility, knocking him back down to the bottom of the pile. Benito Brancaforte's metaphor of Guzmán as Sysiphus is particularly apt.[4]

Within the narration Guzmán's ability to produce discourse is constrained by the authority of the powerful. He serves a series of masters who are all experienced as displaced versions of the father, that is, of authority. There is first the cook and his wife in Madrid, with whom Guzmán plays out a real oedipal drama which I discussed at some length in 1978 (184–87). This father finally exercises his authority by throwing Guzmán out of the house after discovering the boy had seen his wife's naked body. The ostensible reason for Guzmán's banishment, however, is that the cook catches him with stolen property, a displaced version of the theft of the wife's intimacy. In fact, the cook steals food himself, and on a grand scale. He hypocritically unmasks Guzmán's theft in order to ingratiate himself with his own superiors (another, not incidental, demonstration of where authority resides). Guzmán would like to speak up, to denounce the cook to his face, but the master's authority renders him speechless. "In my anger I wanted to tell him: 'The walls of your house are covered with what you stole and I carried there for you, and you make a big deal of a half-dozen little eggs you find on me? Don't you see that you offend yourself by offending me?' But it seemed better to remain silent, for the best remedy for insults is to overlook them."[5] The same pattern is repeated two pages later, when the cook catches Guzmán selling stolen pieces of meat and fires him on the spot. "I was so ashamed I didn't know how to answer him, although I could have, and I certainly had plenty to say. But because he had been my master and it wasn't permitted to me, I lowered my head and without saying anything slipped shamefacedly away."[6] At the moment of action, *le temps de l'énoncé*, when Guzmán could theoretically have spoken up, he is reduced to silence. At the moment of action, the cook is the master of Guzmán's discourse. It is he, not Guzmán, who determines what, if anything, will be said. The discourse that constitutes the text we are reading is generated much later, at the moment of narration (*le temps de l'énonciation*), when the cook's authority has been superseded by that of other figures I shall discuss shortly.

When a short time later Guzmán arrives in Italy in the service of the captain, this master too summarily dismisses him. Once again, although the master's act is arbitrary and capricious, a negative reward for loyal service Guzmán has performed, Guzmán is unable to tell him so. "I walked along the street with my head down, pondering the force of virtue. . . . I would have liked to have told my master the risks I had taken for him, the debts and tight spots I'd rescued him from, and all at my own expense; but then it occurred to me that he was accusing me of precisely those things, and cutting me away from him like a cancerous member."[7] Once again, it is the master who controls the production of discourse. Instead of speaking up to him, Guzmán assumes (again) a physical posture of subservience, "la cabeza baja," remains silent, and finds a way to assume himself the blame that properly belongs to the master.

Sometimes Guzmán is silenced by the simple fear of retaliation by others, frequently his own peers, should he say something. He describes the pranks other servants played on him, the jokes of which he was the butt, and his own exemplary docility in the face of them: "Y a todo esto paciencia, sin desplegar la boca, corrigiéndome para conservarme"—"And to all this, patience, mouth closed, checking myself to preserve myself" (I, *ii*, 5). He elaborates this into a rationalization that allows him to participate in the authorship/authority of God himself. "I always tried to keep peace with all of them, because peace is the daughter of humility, and the humble man who loves peace loves and is loved by the maker of peace, who is God."[8] To be silenced at the moment of action is discovered in retrospect, at the moment of narration, to have been not a victim of external authority, but a part of it.

Public opinion, the famous *qué dirán* that by its very linguistic form reveals who controls the production of discourse, also exerts a powerful effect on Guzmán. Here is an example derived from his experience as the servant of the French ambassador in Rome, a time during which his repeated attempts to procure women for his master kept ending in failure and in the exposure of his own role in the affair. On one occasion he is forced to spend the night on a garbage heap. In the morning he sneaks home, goes to bed, and ponders how he might translate his experience into discourse.

"I stayed this way until almost ten in the morning, without being able to sleep, from shame, thinking and worrying about what I could say to my master. Because if I told him the truth it would be a terrible affront to my reputation, and the kids would beat me with sticks and laugh in my face."[9] This episode combines the authority of the master, which determines the kind of discourse Guzmán might produce, with the authority of "los niños," whose own discourse has the power to inflict physical wounds. Contemplation of these double external authorities determines the shape of Guzmán's discourse, mendacious instead of truthful, to the ambassador.

In all the foregoing examples Guzmán as protagonist is silenced altogether, or severe constraints are placed on the kind of discourse he can produce, by forces and persons external to himself: the *qué dirán*, the *niños*, the other servants, the cook, the captain, the ambassador. It might be argued, however, that although those agents do in fact exist outside the protagonist, his behavior is not the result of anything they do to him, but is rather a function of the way he perceives them and the qualities he attributes to them. Some years ago I suggested that Guzmán suffers from an unreasoning fear of persecution by some authority (93). This fear is what leads him to remain silent or to lie, as we have just seen. In the case of the cook who dismisses him, for example, Guzmán has already been victimized by the man's very real exercise of authority. He has done to Guzmán all that he can do to him. He no longer has any real power over Guzmán, yet Guzmán still regards him as an authority, the owner of the discourse, who must be kowtowed to, literally, with head down, "la cabeza baja." In other words, Guzmán's discourse as protagonist, his speech to his fellow characters, is called into being, or not, and its shape is really determined by something within himself, but something of which he is not the master and over which he has no control, which he in turn projects onto and then attributes to those forces and persons outside him.

Having reached this point in our analysis of the production of discourse at the moment of action, I would like to turn to the more interesting question of the production of discourse at the moment of narration. Guzmán's text is of the type Emile Benveniste would call "discursive," that is, one that comments on its own production and reception, that invokes insistently the presence of the inscribed audience, and correlatively of the narrator (237–50).

Everyone talks about Guzmán's personal ambiguities, both moral and ethical, as well as about the division of his text into the two apparently irreconcilable modes of narrative and commentary. The debate has traditionally been joined in the arena of morality, ethics, theology. Its formal dimension surfaces in the consideration of the relation of narrative to commentary and how the one either complements and supports or subverts and invalidates the other, all in the service of discovering the "real" ethical and theological posture of the book and its author.

The preoccupation of much modern critical discourse with the fact and the act of writing allows us to consider the traditional dualities in a new theoretical and thematic context. It allows us to observe, for example, that this is a book filled with writing about its own writing, "discursive," in Benveniste's sense. The text offers a dramatization of the writer struggling with his own impulses, making choices, defining himself through the text he produces. We are accustomed to thinking of Cervantes as the poet of the creative process, the self-conscious writer who dramatizes in his text his own experience of writing it, but Mateo Alemán's created alter ego Guzmán is immersed in the same process. In fact, it might be posited that Guzmán's engagement with himself as writer is more humanly gripping than is Cervantes's, because Guzmán is not in the habit of intellectualizing, of assimilating his personal conflicts to readily identifiable theoretical issues, as Cervantes is.

Guzmán struggles in public with his own divergent tendencies, which would also define his character through the discourse he produces. Should I recount my adventures? That is, am I a narrator? Or should I sermonize, expose institutionalized social disorders, which exposure might culminate in the exposure of the shaky underpinnings of divine as well as human authority? That is, am I a commentator and critic of society, of human and perhaps divine nature as well? These two poles also imply two different situations of the speaker vis-à-vis his fellow man. As narrator, he is immersed in the mass of humanity and the flow of history. As narrator, he is subservient to his audience, which by granting or withholding its approbation exercises authority over him. As commentator, he is outside and above the rest of humanity. He is superior to his fellow man because he possesses privileged knowledge of the real, hidden workings of human nature and of the corrupt social systems that human nature devises. And he is fearsome, because he makes his private knowledge public. He is a writer, an *auctor*, an authority. He possesses the power of the pen (already acknowledged by conventional wisdom to be mightier than the sword), which actualizes, realizes, makes the privileged knowledge something to be feared, by making it public. Deprived of the power of the pen, the privileged knowledge has no effective existence.

To narrate and to critique imply two distinct identities. The choice of which one to assume is not made in a vacuum, however. The fact of a writer posits the existence of a reader, or many readers. Some of these readers are real individuals the writer knows and whose opinion he either values or despises, or anything in between. Value may be attached to these peoples' opinions for reasons that range from true intellectual equality to a toadying compulsion to ingratiate himself with the powerful. The reasons for ignoring, or professing to ignore these opinions are similarly varied. But no writer, at least not since the advent of print, writes only for the reduced circle of his own friends and acquaintances, as Lázaro de Tormes observed in 1554. There is the vast, anonymous reading public out there to be addressed, and every writer conceptualizes this public in some way. The title of Walter Ong's classic study, "The Writer's Audience Is Always a Fiction," neatly encapsulates the fundamental principle.[10] The larger public may exist independently, as the writer's own circle multiplied to infinity. Or the reader may be the "ideal reader" of so much recent critical speculation, or the construction of the "implied reader" from the text, by other readers. Or the writer may project his own ambivalences and insecurities onto an imaginary Other who raises the kind of questions and objections that only the writer really knows enough to raise, a reader he creates ultimately in order to discuss himself with himself. This I suppose brings up the distinction between reader, narratee, and inscribed reader. The reader can only exist outside the text. Any receptor dramatized within the text, overtly or implicitly, is really a narratee. The narratee is always a creation of the writer, either from his real experience of other people, or from his own insecurities, or (as is most likely) from some uneasy combination.

So the question of choosing one discursive mode over another, narrative or commentary, implies the choice of an identity within an intrapsychic and a social context. The question is more complex than it first appeared. Not only: who am I (which is also: who do I want to be?), but: for whom am I (for whom do I want to be?)? My parentheses imply another duality, between inner and outer, between being for the self and being for the Other. The fact that the Other intervenes, and in such a decisive way, in the constitution of the self, may in turn be rephrased as another question or questions: Who does the Other want me to be? Who will the Other allow me to be? In this context, the discourse generated, narrative or sermon, and consequently the identity so constituted, is thus the product of the authority of the Other over the writing I. We are back to the situation of Lázaro de Tormes and Santa Teresa, except that the real authority, the real owner of the discourse, is now located in that fiction which is always the writer's audience.

A feature noted by virtually all the critics is the presence in Guzmán's text of an inscribed reader, a reader the narrator every now and then describes and whom he every so often interpellates directly. One of the more recent of these critics is Antonio Rey Hazas, who in 1983 characterized the *Guzmán* as the "autobiographical half of a dialogue," and remarks Guzmán's "frequent interpollations of the reader as *tú,* inviting him on occasion to understand his attitude and to have patience with his extensive and impertinent digressions."[11] One of the shrewdest observations concerning the relation of the *tú* to the writing *yo* was made in 1971 by Edmond Cros: "Sin primera persona no existe, en efecto, el *tú;* éste sólo existe con arreglo al *yo*"—"Without the first person, the *tú* cannot exist. The second person only comes into being as a function of the first" (162). Which is what I have been trying to imply: the *tú* is a function of the *yo.* I want at this point to offer a few examples of the struggle for authority, for ownership of the discourse, between the writing I and the inscribed reader.

There is an inscribed reader we might describe as anonymous and unthreatening. This reader is in need of instruction and is presumed to be receptive to the sermon or commentary addressed to him. This reader appears, for example, in I, *i*, 5: "-Por qué piensas que uno raja, mata, hiende y hace fieros? Yo te lo diré"—"Why do you think somebody slashes, kills, cleaves, and rages? I'll tell you" (174). In I, *i*, 7: "—Quiéreslo ver? Pues oye"—"Do you want to see it? Well, just listen" (186); "—Quiéreslo ver? Advierte"—"Do you want to see it? Pay attention" (189). In I, *ii*, 5: "—Quieres conocer quién es? Mírale el nombre, que es el mismo del demonio, nuestro enemigo. Siembra buenas obras, cogerás el fruto dellas"—"Do you want to know who it is? Look at his name; it's the same as our enemy, the devil. If you sow good works you'll reap the fruit from them" (295). Sometimes the *tú* is simply the receptor of the ongoing narrative, as in I, *ii*, 8: " . . . como verás adelante"—" . . . as you'll see further on" (329); I, *iii*, 1: " . . . como verás en la segunda parte"—" . . . as you will see in the second part" (373); I, *iii*, 10: "Oye lo que con él nos pasó"—"Listen to what happened to us with him" (457).

Sometimes the inscribed reader is identified by age, sex, or profession: "cualquier terminista"—"some freshman student of logic" (I, *i*, 1); "alguno del arte mercante"—"someone of the mercantile art" (I, *i*, 1); "el murmurador"—"the slanderer" (I, *i*, 1); "y tú, cuadrillero de bien"—"and you, my good trooper" (I, *i*, 7); "—oh epicúreo!"—"O epicurean!" (I, *ii*, 1); "algún bachiller"—"some Bachelor of Arts" (I, *ii*, 3); "Rico amigo, —no estás harto?"—"Rich friend, aren't you satisfied yet?" (I, *iii*, 6); "Algunos ignorantes dicen . . . Hermano mio, . . . "—"Some ignorant fools say . . . My brother, . . . " (I, *iii*, 10); "La señora doña Calabaza"—"Mrs. Calabash" (II, *i* 1); "Dice la señora doña—como es su gracia—'Yo, señor, . . . ' "—"Mrs.—what is your name?—says, 'I, sir, . . . ' " (II, *ii*, 2); "Señores letrados, notarios, y jueces, abran el ojo"—"You lawyers, notaries, and judges, open your eyes" (II, *iii*, 3); "Señora hermosa"—"Beautiful lady" (II, *iii*, 3); "Entiéndame, señor vecino"—"Understand me, neighbor" (II, *iii*, 3); "No lo digo por la señora Hernández que me oye"—"I'm not saying so because of Mrs. Hernández, who is listening" (II, *iii*, 4).

The text begins with a statement of the struggle for control of the discourse, and from the very first the relations established between the writing I and the other textual presences are complex and conflicted. "The desire I had—curious reader—to tell you my life, made me in such a hurry to get you swamped in it without preparing a few things which, as a first principle, it's a good idea to get straight—because they are essential to this discourse and they'll also be entertaining—that I forgot to close a gate where some freshman student of logic could sneak in accusing me of bad Latin and even of sin, because I didn't proceed from the definition to the thing defined and before starting on my life I didn't tell you who my parents were and the confused facts of my birth."[12] The narrator's desire to write about himself to a first inscribed reader who is evoked as "curioso," that is, interested in reading about Guzmán, is immediately challenged by the demands of a second inscribed reader, identified as a freshman student of logic who might find fault with Guzmán's presentation. The discourse that results from this encounter is in fact not the story of Guzmán's life, but a description of his parents and the narration of their courtship. Guzmán's desire succumbs to the authority of the freshman, who determines the form of the discourse.

Guzmán wanted to be a narrator, but he finds himself instead in the role of apologist for his father, a role he finds supremely uncomfortable. He feels constrained to pass in review a series of unpleasant facts and innuendos, to constitute his father as morally repugnant, in response to the probing and (Lacan would love this) to the presumed knowledge of a series of inscribed readers who appear in his discourse and make demands on him. The first of these is a *tú* who stands ready to criticize Guzmán as *tonto* or *necio* because he exposes his father's shortcomings (101). He would rather remain silent, he says, but devotion to a higher authority, in this case Aristotle, compels denunciation: "Por no ser contra mi padre, quisiera callar lo que siento, aunque si he de seguir al filó-sofo . . . "—"In order not to go against my father I would rather not say what I feel, although if I am to follow the Philosopher . . . " (110).

Guzmán's father, that is, the implied father who emerges from his discourse, was a businessman who engaged in questionable or downright illegal practices, which the authority of the freshman has caused to appear in the discourse. The exposure of these practices elicits a criticism from a new inscribed reader, a merchant, who attacks Guzmán for a presumed ignorance of the facts, and consequently no claim to authority to write about them. This reader is powerful; he actually seizes control of the discourse himself, as Guzmán's voice gives way to his. "Someone of the mercantile art will say to me: 'Look at the cardinals and pope who are voting on this one. Who gives this idiot, galley slave, this picaro the authority to establish laws or criticize dealings he doesn't understand?' "[13] Guzmán's response is to knuckle under to this reader's authority by refraining from speaking with the authority, that is, the insider's knowledge of shady business practices, we discover later that he in fact possesses. "I can see already I'm making a mistake in telling you something that isn't going to do any good, because I would gladly suffer your criticism as long as this honorable means of thievery were punished and brought under control, even if my own father swung for it. But let it go, because the reformation of these and similar things and others that are even more important is blocked, and it's not my responsibility anyway. It's like shouting at the wolf, holding back the sun, and preaching in the wilderness."[14] Here Guzmán would like to be a sermonizer, to situate himself outside and above society and denounce its structural flaws, but the reader's presumed authority, here figured as indifference, forces him to be something else. The discourse here is the record of the struggle for control of the discourse.

The implied father was also a suborner of justice, and the inscribed reader is presumed to be familiar with the case. Guzmán is therefore constrained to offer a defense. Because the defense recapitulates the inscribed reader's prior knowledge, it becomes the means by which a real reader can infer the father's guilt.

A new inscribed reader, a *murmurador,* enters the discourse to insinuate the father's homo- or bisexuality, forcing another defense that in turn allows a real reader to add another dimension to the creation of the implied father. This episode offers another one-sided dialogue: "I can already hear the slanderer talking about his bad reputation: curling his hair, using makeup and other things I won't repeat, money that moved, presents exchanged, women who solicited, it all leaves me with a thorn in my finger. Accursed man! You're crowding me, and I'm tired of it. I'm going to satisfy you once and for all and not respond any more to your comebacks, because you could go on forever with your sophistries."[15] This time Guzmán concedes the possible truth of the allegation, hastening to line up on the side of society's official homophobia. If the father's effeminate appearance was natural, well and good. "But if it's true, as you say, that he used creams and lotions . . . I'll concede everything you say about him and I'll be his fiercest enemy. . . . You won't be able to say about me that I've been bribed by my love for my father or for my homeland, and you won't find me acting unreasonably or without regard for the truth."[16]

What is important throughout this first chapter is that the damning presentation of the father is called into existence by the presumed authority of that freshman student of logic who appears at the beginning and demands that the author, Guzmán, proceed from the definition to the defined. He is followed by a series of other inscribed readers presumed to know, who demand explanations of particular aspects of the father. The situation is analogous to what we find in *Lazarillo de Tormes*, where Vuestra Merced already knows about the *caso* and forces Lázaro to make his private shame public. But the analogy is only superficial, for as we have already observed, Vuestra Merced really does exist outside and above Lázaro, and really does exercise authority over him, while the whole parade of readers that engage Guzmán and demand that he expose his father are all hypothetical, figments of his imagination.

Sometimes the power struggle is clearly the result of Guzmán's own insecurity. How can a *pícaro* dare to come forward as a preacher? He attempts to cover his insecurity by an aggressive bluster that unfortunately serves only to make it more apparent. "Oh what a masterpiece of nonsense! What a sage simpleton I am to be spouting this doctrine! . . . Don't worry about who is saying it, but about what is being said. I'm telling you now, either arm yourself with patience or quit reading. I'm well aware it's impossible to be well received by everyone."[17]

Especially in Part II the text enacts a struggle for authority between the writing I, whose wealth of business experience qualifies him as a real authority on such subjects as *mohatras* and *contraescrituras*, and the reader, who simply wants to be entertained. "Is anything I've said going to be of any use? I think I'm breaking my head and wasting my labor without getting either profit or honor in return. I can hear my reader telling me to go lie down in the corner because he's tired of listening to me. He's completely right, because since I'm telling truths, they're not for entertainment, but to be studied and pondered." "Oh what a beautiful and well-aimed shot that was! How I'm tempted to break every bone in their bodies! Because I'm the thief from within the house, I know their every thought. Do I have your permission to give them a good thrashing? I already know I don't. . . . But because I don't want it said that my whole book is about reforms, I'll let them go." "Shall I say something here? I can already hear you saying no."[18]

The situation at the beginning of Part II is similarly conflicted. The entire first chapter is devoted to an elaborate justification for the continuation of the text, where no such justification is in fact required. This chapter dramatizes the power struggle between the writing I and the inscribed reader. Curiously, Guzmán begins by establishing an identification between himself and all men: "A mí me parece que son todos los hombres como yo, flacos, fáciles, con pasiones naturales y aun extrañas"—"It seems to me that all men are like I am, weak, willess and full of natural and unnatural passions" (II, i, 1). After this uncharacteristic lapse, to which we shall return, the adversarial relationship that dominates the discourse reasserts itself. Guzmán wants to *proseguir*, but the reader insists on *perseguir*.

"O te digo verdades o mentiras," writes Guzmán. I'm either writing sermons or fictions. I'm either a pundit and therefore superior to you, or an entertainer and therefore your servant. Or in the language of the text, I'm either a *pícaro* or an *atalaya*.[19] As he observes later: "Esto propio le sucedió a este mi libro, que habéndole intitulado *Atalaya de la vida humana*, dieron en llamarle *Pícaro* y no se conoce ya por otro nombre"—"The very same thing happened to my book. I had given it the title of *Watchtower of Human Life*, but people began to call it *The Pícaro*, and now nobody calls it anything else" (II, i, 6). Guzmán insists on his identity as pundit: "No, not lies, and would to God that they were, because I know your inclination and how you're chomping at the bit to hear them. I'm feeding you truths and you don't like the way they taste. You're annoyed with them because they sting."[20] The reader and Guzmán are locked in a struggle for control of the discourse. The reader's inclination is to be entertained, which in turn forces a certain identity upon Guzmán. Guzmán wants desperately to instruct, and correlatively to assume a different identity. The reader keeps slipping out of his control like an eel. Guzmán proposes to figuratively line his hands with fig leaves to prevent the reader-eel from escaping: "I'll line my hands with sticky fig leaves against your slippery sophistries. You won't slip through my fingers this time."[21] It is worth observing in passing that twice in this passage Guzmán demotes the reader from human to animal status, first into a horse by suggesting that he is "champing at the bit" to be entertained, and second in his more elaborate metamorphosis into the slippery eel.

Guzmán proceeds to establish a series of complementary relationships between himself and the reader. The reader is *enfermo*, Guzmán the *pharmakon*. What might cure one patient might poison another. The reader is the diner at a banquet, Guzmán the cook. It is impossible to satisfy every taste. "I see around me so many different tastes, all pulling me in different directions, each one trying to take me to his own tent. This one wants sweet, that one sour, one says to fry the olives, and the other won't have salt even on the eggs."[22] This cliché turns into an overt power struggle, exemplified in the anecdote about the man who forced his wife to eat some withered radishes she had attempted to throw out.

Each different reader wants to make Guzmán over in his or her own image, while Guzmán fights to construct his own identity through his discourse, which in turn, he says, is the product of the life he has lived. "The melancholic, the sanguine, the choleric, the phlegmatic, the composed, the carouser, the sophist, the philosopher, the religious, the damned, the courtier, the rustic, the uncouth, the discreet and even Mrs. Calabash, they all want me to write especially for them and to accommodate my style to theirs. It's not possible. Besides having to write a separate book for each one, I would have to have lived as many different lives as there are readers' opinions. I have only lived one, and those others they attribute to me are lies."[23]

At this point something new enters. It now appears that there is an authentic Guzmán, defined not by the discourse, but by the life that preceded it. And this true Guzmán turns out to be Christ himself. The reader is figured finally as an innkeeper, and Guzmán the traveler who arrives at his door. The reader can choose to take him in or turn him away. "I am determined to follow the path that I think leads to the haven of my desire and the place I'm heading for. And you, discreet host who awaits me, since you have such a clear account of the misery someone like me suffers on his peregrination through life, don't turn away from me when you see me in your land and when I come hungry to your door, but treat me the way you deserve to be treated yourself. For it is you that I seek and for you alone that I make this voyage."[24] But this identification, the supreme self-validation and self-vindication, is itself only a discursive product. It is by no means self-evident that Guzmán and Christ are identical or even analogous. It is Guzmán's discourse, the interpretation he gives to the facts of his experience, that allows him to grasp at the one identity that will put him safely out of reach of his reader-critics. And this is what explains his uncharacteristic willingness to identify himself with the common humanity of his readers. Just as Christ became man and walked among us, so does Guzmán. Or so he says. What is at stake is not the facts of Guzmán's life but their meaning. This is what he means when he says, "Una sola he vivido y la que me achacan es testimonio que me levantan"—"I have only lived one, and those others they attribute to me are lies." The question of meaning always involves the question of who interprets the data.

Guzmán's discourse posits a struggle for authority, for control of the discourse, between the writing I and an inscribed reader. This struggle for discursive hegemony is in turn a struggle for an identity: *pícaro* or *atalaya*, narrator or sermonizer, entertainer or teacher, servant or master. This struggle in turn determines the form of the discourse itself, which is devoted in part to dramatizing the conflict and in part is the result of the inscribed reader's exercise of authority over the writing I. But as we have had ample opportunity to witness, the demand to which the writing I responds, and which determines the shape of the discourse, comes from within itself. The inscribed reader-critic has no objective existence. He/she/it is a projection of Guzmán's own insecurities, of his own inability to be the person he thinks he wants to be, what he wants his life to mean, because he thinks he knows who he really is, what his life really means. This revelation demonstrates better than many pages of abstract theorizing the fact that this book, this *Guzmán de Alfarache*, which is the only universally accepted exemplar of the picaresque genre, springs from and depends on an assumption Paul Julian Smith would call antihumanist and I consider profoundly human, namely, that the writing I is anything but an integrated whole.

Notes

1. "En prolongeant la voie ouverte par le *Lazarillo*, Alemán nous offre bel et bien en la personne du Gueux/Marchand de Séville l'une des toutes premières figures du 'héros problematique,' porteur de valeurs bourgeoises. Si, comme l'écrit Michel Butor, 'le roman moderne occidental commence veritablement avec les grandes oeuvres picaresques du Siècle d'Or,' il serait temps d'accorder au *Guzmán de Alfarache* la place qui lui revient dans cette paternité" ("La question du 'père'" 205).

2. James A. Parr has recently offered a reading of *Don Quijote* as a massive exercise in the subversion of all textual authority. *Don Quixote: An Anatomy of Subversive Discourse* (Newark, Del.: Juan de la Cuesta, 1988).

3. "Pícaro llaman en España a un hombre vil y de baja suerte, que anda mal vestido y en semblante de hombre de poco honor." (Cited by Agustín González de Amezúa, *Cervantes creador de la novela corta española* [Madrid: CSIC, 1958] 73.)

4. See "El mito de Sísifo y la estructura de *Guzmán de Alfarache*," in Brancaforte's edition of the *Guzmán* (Madrid: Cátedra, 1979) I: 17–36.

5. "Quisiera decirle con la cólera: '—Pues, como, ladrón, tienes la casa entapizada de lo que hurtaste y yo llevé, y haces alharacas por seis tristes huevos que me hallaste? —No ves que te ofendes con lo que me ofendes?' Parecióme más acertado el callar, que el mejor remedio en las injurias es despreciarlas" (I, *ii*, 6).

6. "Quedé tan corrido, que no supe responderle, aunque pudiera y tuve harto pao. Mas no siéndome lícito por haber sido mi amo, bajé la cabeza y sin decir palabra me fui avergonzado" (I, *ii*, 6).

7. "Iba la cabeza baja, considerando por la calle la fuerza de la virtud.... Quisiera entonces decirle a mi amo lo en que por él me había puesto, las necesidades que le había socorrido, de los trabajos que le había sacado, y tan a mi costa todo; mas consideré que de lo mismo me hacía cargo, apartándome por ello como a miembro cancerado" (I, *ii*, 10).

8. "Siempre procuré con todos tener paz, por ser hija de la humildad; y el humilde que ama la paz, ama y es amado del autor de ella, que es Dios" (I, *ii*, 5).

9. "Desta manera pasé hasta casi las diez del día sin poder tomar sueño, de corrido, pensando y vacilando en lo que podría responder a mi amo. Porque si decía la verdad, fuera con afrenta notable mía y me habían de garrochear por momentos, dándome con aquella burla en las barbas, riéndose de mí los niños" (II, *i*, 5).

10. *PMLA* 90 (1975): 9–21.

11. "autobiográfica mitad de un diálogo, ... frecuentes llamadas al 'tú' del lector, invitándole, en ocasiones, a comprender su actitud, a que tuviera paciencia con sus extensas e impertinentes digresiones" (132).

12. "El deseo que tenía—curioso lector—de contarte mi vida, me daba tanta

priesa para engolfarte en ella sin prevenir algunas cosas que, como primer principio, es bien dejarlas entendidas—porque siendo esenciales a este discurso también te serán de no pequeño gusto—que me olvidaba de cerrar un portillo por donde me entrara cualquier terminista acusando de mal latín, redarguyéndome de pecado, porque no procedí de la definición a lo definido y antes de contarla no dejé dicho quiénes y cuáles fueron mis padres y confuso nacimiento" (I, *i*, 1).

13. "Alguno del arte mercante me dirá: 'Mirad por qué claustro de pontífice y cardenales va votado. —¿Quién mete al idiota, galeote, pícaro, en establecer leyes ni calificar los tratos que no entiende?'"

14. "Ya veo que yerro en decir lo que no ha de aprovechar, que de buena gana sufriera tus oprobios, con tal que se castigara y tuviera remedio esta honrosa manera de robar, aunque mi padre estrenara la horca. Corra como corre, que la reformación de semejantes cosas importantes y otras que lo son más, van de capa caída y a mí no me toca: es dar voces al lobo, tener el sol y predicar en desierto" (110).

15. "Ya oigo al murmurador diciendo la mala voz que tuvo; rizarse, afeitarse y otras cosas que callo, dineros que bullían, presentes que cruzaban, mujeres que solicitaban, me dejan la espina en el dedo. —Hombre de la maldición! Mucho me aprietas y cansado me tienes: pienso desta vez dejarte satisfecho y no responder más a tus replicatos, que sería proceder en infinito aguardar a tus sofisterías" (117).

16. "Pero si es verdad, como dices, que se valía de untos y artificios de sebillos, . . . confesaréte cuánto de él dijeres y seré su capital enemigo. . . . No me podrás decir que amor paterno ni el natural de la patria me cohecha, ni me hallarás fuera de razón y verdad" (118–19).

17. "—Oh qué gentil disparate! —Qué vida de Juan de Dios la mía para dar esta doctrina! . . . No mires a quién lo dice, sino a lo que se te dice. . . . Ya te prevengo, para que me dejes o te armes de paciencia. Bien sé que es imposible ser de todos bien recibido" (I, *ii*, 2).

18. "—Ha de ser de algún fruto lo dicho? Antes creo que me quiebro la cabeza y es gastar en balde la costa y el trabajo, sin sacar dello provecho ni honra. Ya le oigo decir a quien está leyendo que me arroje a un rincón, porque le cansa oírme. Tiene mil razones. Que, como verdadermente son verdades las que trato, no son para entretenimiento, sino para con mucho estudio ser miradas y muy remiradas" (II, *iii*, 3). "—Oh qué gallardo y qué cierto tiro aquéste! —Qué tentación me da de tirarles y no dejarles hueso sano! Que como soy ladrón de casa, conózcoles los pensamientos. —Queriésme dar licencia que les dé una gentil barajadura? Ya sé que no queréis. . . . Mas porque no digan que todo se me va en reformaciones, les doy lado" (II, *iii*, 3). "—Diré aquí algo? Ya oigo deciros que no" (II, *iii*, 4).

19. The dialectic of these two possibilities is what Michel Cavillac's brilliant application of the figure of the *atalaya* to late-sixteenth-century economic theories overlooks with respect to *Guzmán* ("Le regard de l'utopiste" 141–56).

20. "Mentiras no; y a Dios pluguiera que lo fueran, que yo conozco de tu inclinación que holgaras de oírlas y aun hicieras espumas de freno. Digo verdades y hácensete amargas. Pícaste de ellas, porque te pican" (37).

21. "Yo buscaré hojas de higuera contra tus bachillerías. No te me saldrás por esta vez de entre las manos" (38).

22. "Veo presentes tantos y tan variados gustos, estirando de mí todos, queriéndome llevar a su tienda cada uno. Pide aquéste dulce, aquél acedo, uno hace freír las aceitunas, otro no quiere sal ni aun en el huevo" (41).

23. "Querrían el melancólico, el sanguino, el colérico, el flemático, el compuesto, el desgarrado, el retórico, el filósofo, el religioso, el perdido, el cortesano, el rústico, el bárbaro, el discreto y aun la señora doña Calabaza que para sola ella escribiese a lo fruncido y con solo su pensamiento y a su estilo me acomodase. No es posible; y seráme necesario, demás de hacer para cada uno su diferente libro, haber vivido tantas vidas cuantas hay diferentes pareceres. Una sola he vivido y la que me achacan es testimonio que me levantan" (42).

24. "Determinado estoy de seguir la senda que me pareciere atinar mejor al puerto de mi deseo y lugar donde voy caminando. Y tú, discreto huésped que me aguardas, pues tienes tan clara noticia de las miserias que padece quien como yo va peregrinando, no te desdees cuando en tu patria me vieres y a tu puerta llegare desfavorecido, en hacerme aquel tratamiento que a tu propio valor debes. Pues a ti sólo busco y por ti hago este viaje" (44).

Works Cited

Alemán, Mateo. *Guzmán de Alfarache.* 2 vols. Ed. Benito Brancaforte. Madrid: Cátedra, 1979.

Benveniste, Emile. "Les relations de temps dans le verbe français." *Problèmes de linguistique générale.* Paris: Flammarion, 1966.

Cavillac, Michel. "La question du 'père' dans le roman picaresque." *Les parentés fictives en Espagne (XVIe-XVIIe siècles).* Ed. Augustín Redondo. Paris: Sorbonne, 1988.

———. "Le regard de l'utopiste: Les métamorphoses de l'*atalaya* dans l'imaginaire du Siècle d'Or." *Las utopías.* Madrid: Casa de Velázquez, 1990. 141–56.

Cros, Edmondd. *Mateo Alemán: Introducción a su vida y a su obra.* Salamanca: Anaya, 1971.

Foucault, Michel. *The History of Sexuality: An Introduction.* New York: Vintage, 1990.

Gómez Moriana, Antonio. "Autobiografía y discurso ritual. Problemática de la confesión autobiográfica destinada al tribunal inquisitorial." *L'Autobiographie en Espagne.* Aix-en-Provence: Université de Provence, 1982. 69–94.

Hazas, Antonio Ray. "Género y estructura de 'El coloquio de los perros,' o cómo se hace una novela." *Lenguaje, ideología y organización textual en las "Novelas ejemplares."* Ed. José Jesús de Bustos Tovar. Madrid: Universidad Complutense, 1983.

Johnson, Carroll B. *Inside Guzmán de Alfarache.* Berkeley and Los Angeles: Univ. of California Press, 1978.

Machery, Pierre. *Pour une théorie de la production littéraire.* Paris: Maspero, 1980.

Said, Edward. *Beginnings: Intention and Method.* New York: Columbia Univ. Press, 1985.

Smith, Paul Julian. "The Rhetoric of Representation in Writers and Critics of Picaresque Narrative: *Lazarillo de Tormes, Guzmán de Alfarache, El Buscón.*" *MLR* 82 (1987): 88–108.

——— . *Writing in the Margin: Spanish Literature of the Golden Age.* Oxford: Clarendon Press, 1988.

Chapter 7

Trials of Discourse: Narrative Space in Quevedo's *Buscón*

Edward H. Friedman

*Milicia es la vida del hombre contra la malicia del hombre. Pelea la
sagacidad con estratagemas de intención.*

Baltasar Gracián, *Oráculo manual y arte de prudencia*

One of the legacies of structuralism is a focus on the inseparability
of story and discourse. Emphasis on the deep structure of literary
texts leads to the thesis that, to a great extent, the discourse *is* the
story. Texts ultimately are about their own textuality, about their
internal nature and about the ways in which the artistic enterprise
endeavors to represent and to relate to the so-called real world.
Autobiography is a key mode in this regard. One may note that, in
autobiography, the subject and the object are the same. That this
statement may be both true and untrue underscores not only the
rhetorical intrusions of poststructuralism but also the difference
between observation and expression, even in self-representation
(or, as it perhaps more accurately has been called, self-fashioning).
The act of writing introduces a graft onto the story; in the telling,
the subject expands his or her life, so that the created self includes
the creating self. Writing adds to the curriculum vitae of the subject, whose wholeness nonetheless cannot be captured. With respect to the autobiographer, it is possible to speak of the need for
selection, of the impossibility of knowing oneself completely,
and—to the degree that self-knowledge is attainable—of the dis-
tortion, or deferral, implicit in the mediating ground between
observer and observed, world and word. In the case of fictional au-

tobiography, the controlling element may be the distance between life and art. Rather than hidden or scorned, the creative impetus may be elevated as autobiography cedes to the imagination and the self-portrait to a decentering of point of view. This essay will examine the narrating space in Francisco de Quevedo's *La vida del buscón*, in an attempt to retell the story of *El buscón*'s discourse.

The anonymity of *Lazarillo de Tormes* enhances the autobiographical framework of the narrative. The "I" of the prologue shifts, without a marked transition, from the artist who contemplates public and commercial response to his book, on the one hand, to the mature Lázaro who justifies the form of his reply to Vuestra Merced's request, on the other. There is no known author and hence no biography to impose upon Lázaro's "life." In contrast, the autobiographical illusion in *Guzmán de Alfarache* is affected by the vested interests of Mateo Alemán in his protagonist's story. It is difficult, at times, to separate the grievances of the New Christian protagonist from the author, and the ingenious means by which the novel takes vengeance on the writer of a spurious continuation points to Alemán rather than to Guzmán. The events that culminate in Guzmán's conversion become less important in the narrative scheme, it would seem, than the competition between Guzmán and his alter ego Sayavedra. As Alemán exposes Juan Martí as the man behind the pseudonymous Mateo Luján de Sayavedra, he inscribes himself into Guzmán's story and, inescapably, into the first-person discourse. There is, then, a double shaping of the data of Guzmán de Alfarache's life, by a narrator who recognizes the poetic license of self-portraiture and by an author with an agenda of his own. The *Buscón* reflects a similar pattern, in that the reader may be inclined to insert Quevedo into the space that nominally would belong to Pablos as autobiographer. By analyzing the narrative as if it were exclusively Pablos's domain, one can point to pressure on the reader to look beyond the *pícaro* in determining the structure of the novel. Let us begin by resisting the urge to bring Quevedo into the picture.

Pablos's story begins with little in the way of a conventional pretext and with only a cursory nod to a narratee identified as "señor." When Pablos presents his father and mother, a barber/ thief and a witch/prostitute, he shows that they aim to glorify their status through euphemism. The "shearer of beards" and the "daughter of the Litany" use words—names—to place themselves into mainstream society, to give themselves an air of respectability. Language becomes the agent of their intended transformation, as a barrier to truth and exposure, yet in a rigidly hierarchical society renaming is hardly the answer to ostracism. Pablos's parents seem to have no interest in altering their lifestyles but, instead, wish to be perceived as guiltless. Thus, they are condemned to suffer the recriminations of a dogmatic and vengeful ruling class. In descriptions that recreate the deceptive lexicon of his parents, Pablos repeats this flaw in his own writing. His jocular tone may be interpreted as a means of combating the misfortunes of lineage, but he proves that he has inherited linguistic habits along with undesirable genes. In an effort at detachment from his family, he shows that history is inclined to repeat itself. The closing of the first chapter, in which Pablos recalls having thanked God for giving him parents "so zealous of his well-being," sets the reader at a distance from the narrator/protagonist by aligning him with his progenitors. Like them, he wants to integrate himself into society, and, like them, his wish to move upward—to be a gentleman—is far removed from noble thoughts or actions. Striving to turn away from his bloodlines, Pablos ends by arguing the case for social determinism.

Using as his point of departure Freud's *Jokes and Their Relation to the Unconscious,* James Iffland views the humorous treatment of the domestic situation as a type of release mechanism, whereby Pablos is able to shield his shame through language. Pablos's suppressed emotions find an outlet in verbal plays that allow him to attack his enemies throughout the text. Iffland seeks internal consistency in Pablos's narrative. He suggests that the reader need not go beyond the voice of Pablos (to the voice-over of Quevedo) unless markers within the text would justify doing so. Restricted and inhibited in society, Pablos the narrator is relatively free to vent his rage. And, according to Iffland, he is willing to play the buffoon—to make himself the object of the laughter inspired by his jokes. Because Pablos mocks himself, his social criticism becomes more palatable: "In fact, by not striving to place himself in a patently untenable role as a judge of humanity, by allowing us to laugh at him as well, it may make us more willing to join him in the campaign of aggression which is in large part the *raison d'être* of the narrative" (241).

Iffland's superb essay leaves several issues unresolved. If Pablos undertakes a conscious strategy to win reader sympathy by presenting himself as a victim of social evils, is the Freudian unconscious the proper locus for discussion of the linguistic humor of the *Buscón?* Can buffoonery and social critique go hand in hand? Is Pablos's "campaign of aggression" aimed at a target audience amenable to radical social change, and is this campaign what the narrative is about? Are what Pablos accomplishes as narrator and the message of the text one and the same? What is the advantage of basing a reading on Pablos's designs rather than on Quevedo's? And, finally, how does the *Buscón* define its goals, and how successfully does it achieve these goals?

While we cannot transform ourselves into seventeenth-century Spanish readers of *La vida del buscón,* we might suppose that the general reaction to Pablos (and to his narrative voice) would have been less than fully sympathetic. The social codes implicit in the text probably reflect the status quo; Pablos seeks upward mobility in a textual analogue of the real world. Although Pablos may be able to convey the failure of his social ventures and, at the same time, to promote laughter, it is hard to imagine him winning over his early readership. Iffland notes that "jokes and witticisms are social phenomena; they *must* be told. This is particularly true of the tendentious kind which strive to win converts to the aggression of which they are vehicles" (226). The argument would seem to presuppose, first, that Pablos believes that there is a chance that he could convince others that his cause is legitimate and, second, that his readers would revere him more if he played the jester. It may be easier, however, to demonstrate that Pablos's rhetoric would tend to alienate rather than to ingratiate him before his public. The more he entertains his readers with his travails, the less persuasive his social cause. In contrast, reception of the *Buscón* in the late twentieth century may give greater credence to the underdog and may consider the factors that position the *pícaro* in the margins of society. The institutions of the State, in turn, may become decentered images and the marginalized individual a new center. Poststructuralism teaches us how to operate in the subtextual realm, how to produce counterreadings. We may hypothesize that Quevedo exploits Pablos just as society exploits Pablos, and, as a result, we may choose to deconstruct the notion of the rogue's autonomy over his "life."

Anthony Close has shown that readings of *Don Quijote* often are influenced by the symbolic vision of the knight errant that is the legacy of German Romanticism. By the same token, the outsider of picaresque fiction may stir our feelings for the underclass, for social equality, and, as critics in search of difference (or *différance*), for the undercurrents of the text. We may find a protagonist entrapped by the machinations of the author, and we may relish those occasions in which, as Edwin Williamson phrases it, "Pablos occasionally wriggles out of Quevedo's coercive grasp and seizes a fragile fictional life which follows the logical direction of his own ambition rather than the vicious circularity of his creator's manipulations" (59). Even as we concur with Williamson's analysis, need we wonder if the disposition to root for Pablos derives from a form of institutionalized thought that merely would reverse the priorities of baroque Spain? By what criteria should we establish Pablos's role in the text that claims to be his own?

Quevedo's *pícaro* sets forth his life from childhood to his projected voyage to the New World. At the time in which he writes, he has made that journey, and he notifies the reader that the move has been a failure, as are all geographical shifts when they are unaccompanied by changes in habit. This could be considered the antithesis of Guzmán de Alfarache's professed conversion, which can serve as a focus for discourse analysis of Alemán's novel. Readers have to weigh the strength of the conversion not from the events that follow—for the story ends at this point—but rather from the manner in which the repentant Guzmán depicts his life. The mature and supposedly contrite narrator, as distinguished from the sinful protagonist, must relate through language a metamorphosed self, a new and redeemed man, an alter ego in every sense of the term. *El buscón* is not about change but about the absence of change. The pretensions of the protagonist threaten the very heart of baroque culture: its deterministic view of social status. For Pablos to succeed, society would have to modify its operating premises. The presentation of the chain of misfortunes that beset the *pícaro* is realistic, that is to say, a reflection of the real world and of the reality principle of the time. Pablos's account is by no means a success story but, arguably, precisely the opposite, not just the story of a failure but an undermining of the narrator's discursive space. Pablos engages the reader in his dream of being a gentleman. He has a definite flair for words and proven rhetorical skills. And yet, recalling Iffland's effort to show consistency in the narrative voice, we may question whether Pablos has authority over the mechanisms through which he communicates his story.

Paradoxically, any examination of perspective will reveal its own perspective, its own selection or strategy, and therefore it would seem important to consider multiple aspects of the narrative structure as one stands in judgment of the story and its teller(s). Among the features of Pablos's discourse that warrant attention are the sophistication of the language, the force of the descriptions, the representation of failure, and the impact of moralizing statements. A unifying element—and a ma(r)ker of difficulty —is irony, given that it is likely that readers will not relate to Pablos as much as weigh his words and actions against their own standards, social and literary. Those readers disposed to commiserate with him perhaps will be moved by the marginality dictated by his blood rather than by his personality or ambition. We may ask ourselves whether Quevedo's achievement is greater if Pablos's voice within the text belongs to the narrator alone, free of the imposing presence of the author. Iffland, among others, finds what might be termed a balance between story and discourse; what Pablos says seems plausible and consistent with the decisions he makes and with what the reader learns of his character. Not only does the reader have to discern the narrator's particular pattern of representation but also the organizing principles of his writing. In the final analysis, the answer may lie in the distinction—a crucial but highly problematical distinction—between irony contained from within or conspicuously encoded from beyond the text.

When Lázaro de Tormes complies with a request to explain "the case," he decides to start from the beginning, from early childhood. He seems to understand, precociously, that heredity and environment are fundamental to human development. From the vantage point of rhetoric, he appears to want to lessen the burden of his sins by opting for shared responsibility. Lázaro is, he would seem to contend, as others have made him. A narrative analogue of the redistribution of guilt is the act of writing as evasion, as screen. Lázaro's life story fills the explanatory space, and the real readers, without the preknowledge enjoyed by the narratee, end with only conjectures as to the meaning of "el caso." The narrator equates the explanation of the case with the account of his ignoble origins and of his travails on life's journey. In the Prologue, he extends praise to those who, disadvantaged by blood and circumstance, manage to survive in society, and this may be the crucial lesson of his life. In exchange for a story about the case, Lázaro the writer argues for his own point of view. He defers to the narratee by honoring the request, which he treats not so much with deference as with deferral. The reader outside the text must deal with the absence of the background information as a sign of what the narrative is about, namely, the need to differentiate between events and their emplotment. Every history is necessarily a revisionist history, and, aware of the power of words to recast a life, Lázaro arranges the raw material at his command. The fact that Vuestra Merced and others may not interpret the story in exactly the way desired by Lázaro is a function of the variability of reader response and a function of irony.

As in the exaggerated version of the theme in *Don Quijote*, *Lazarillo de Tormes* illustrates the interdependence of process and product. The reader is privy to Lázaro creating himself, *haciéndose*, both on the page and in conformance with the image he would like to convey. By exposing its seams, so to speak, the text elevates the writer's task, while at the same time it underscores the peculiar rhetoric of the narrator. Lázaro's defensive strategy is less than persuasive because the evidence he puts forward is often more incriminating than convincing. He breaks the silence that has protected him. Testing the waters between mimesis and diegesis, he fails to prove that the scenario that he describes at the end of his story would be, even for the beleaguered orphan, "the height of all good fortune." It is ironic that Lázaro's upward movement in society brings him into the realm of honor, which he could avoid during his years of abject poverty, and that middle-class morality may be his undoing. It is ironic that Lázaro's apparent authority over story and discourse is not sufficient to remake the life. And it is ironic that, for all its satirical effects and social critique, the narrative keeps the *pícaro* in his place. The butt of the humor—and the victim of the irony—is, when all is said and done, the man whom the reader could presume to be in control. The very rhetoric that should be the ally of the narrator betrays him. That is ironic, but not, I would submit, a miscalculation. Despite poststructuralism's distrust of origins, one can make a case for sources of the irony in *Lazarillo de Tormes.*

Picaresque narrative offers an ironic alternative to idealistic fiction, to confessional literature, and to Renaissance humanism. The picaresque rewriting of the intertext shows what happens when exaltation of the individual comes into conflict with the social ideology of Habsburg Spain. Among the consequences are an overdetermined discourse, which accentuates the incongruities of Lázaro's stance as he judges those around him, and·a self-defense ripe for deconstruction. The dialectical tone of the narrative may suggest a competing voice, a voice-over that could help to explain Lázaro's rational oversights and rhetorical excesses. Prosperity in society and honor among literati become linked through the negative connotations of the upstart as citizen and as writer. Because Lázaro lacks credentials, he lacks credibility. His dubious status in the world and in the text affects the faith associated with narrative reliability. It is a commonplace in discussions of *Lazarillo de Tormes* and its progeny to note that the picaresque narrator views life from below. Society and the middle-class reader stand above him as arbiters, mediators, of his behavior and of his discourse. Class consciousness enables the text to render a verdict against Lázaro, the purported inventor of the discourse, by keeping him at an ironic distance from the center of authority. He has neither creative freedom nor creative license. Subservient to the Archpriest of San Salvador, he is at the mercy of Toledo's gossipmongers, and his story articulates what he admonishes them to keep hidden. Critics have argued that Lázaro is happy at the end of his account because he is immune to the norms of society, because he has no social conscience. I would submit that, ironically, the opposite is true. Fed, clothed, and gainfully employed, he remains in the margins, with only the headaches of those in the center. And despite the discursive recourses that should work to empower him, he cannot convince us otherwise.

Guzmán de Alfarache bears a different kind of rhetorical burden. His story ends at the moment in which he claims to see the light, so that as narrator he must move away from his former self, from the protagonist. For the text to recount a spiritual evolution, the bitterness and anguish must belong to the disposed other, as opposed to the convert. Not only is this distinction almost imperceptible, but Mateo Alemán introduces his personal suffering into story and discourse. Through various means, Guzmán's story is redirected, deflected. The first part of the narrative puts bloodlines and alterity in the foreground, to stress, at least in part, the need to break away from ignoble roots. Guzmán's pretensions stem from society's mistreatment of the outsider. His attempt to create distance from his family—through flight and through words —only leads to the conclusion that escape is impossible; all events remind Guzmán of his family history, and the narrative immortalizes his marginality. His large array of grievances notwithstanding, Guzmán takes a certain amount of pride in his delinquency, and the author's intrusion into the plot line, as prompted by the spurious sequel, veers the reader away from the postpenitential sensibility that should inflect the narrator's voice. The "real" author accuses the usurper of his literary art of misreading the character of the protagonist, but Alemán, intent upon proving himself and his *pícaro* superior to their rivals, changes direction through an awkward emphasis on Guzmán's criminal prowess. If the futile attempt at social mobility casts the narration in an ironic light—by making story and discourse work at cross-purposes—the inscription of the author's frustration into the text is equally ironic. Alemán's New Christian status unites him with a man who seeks to shed his identity through the written word. This is, of course, an example of high irony, and it is fascinating, and equally ironic, to see the distancing devices recede as a new player enters the battle for authority.

Juxtaposed with *Lazarillo de Tormes* and *Guzmán de Alfarache*, *La vida del buscón* provides a dialectical middle ground between historical underdetermination and historical overdetermination. The anonymity of the *Lazarillo* forces the reader to project an author on a text whose messages do not seem fully clear to the narrator. Mateo Alemán, in contrast, superimposes himself, or his social and creative tribulations, onto the plot structure. The reader may find it hard to resist the temptation to view Guzmán as the watchtower from which to consider the rhetorical ploys of Alemán. The *Guzmán* adds a dimension to the metaliterary thrust of the picaresque. Autobiography is about life as process and about self-representation. Fictional autobiography explores broader parameters of representation, through which we may sense the complexities of narrative performance. The author controls a narrator who operates selectively upon his self and circumstance. What is implicit in the *Lazarillo* becomes explicit in the *Guzmán:* fictional autobiography shows the making of a life and the making of a text. As the narrator confronts his life, the author seeks his own signature, through confrontation with the intertext and with a world that cannot remain beyond the frame. (This is one of the major points of contact, I believe, between the picaresque and *Don Quijote,* but that is another story.) I would submit that the *Buscón* brings together the generic potential of the earlier texts through a unique and mystifying engagement of narrator and author.

Quevedo follows his predecessors by foregrounding the opposition of mimesis and diegesis. Lázaro de Tormes pretends to tell his narratee about a case in which he is involved, but he strays from the initial premise—vaguely defined in itself—to show the nature of his survival skills. Lázaro the town crier breaks an implied code of silence in order to honor Vuestra Merced's request. His life exposed, he takes refuge in a rhetoric built around his rise in society and his progression from near-starvation to enjoyment of the creature comforts. By suggesting in the seventh chapter of the account that he is no worse than his neighbors, he makes evident that the reversal of fortune removes him from the position of satirist to the object of satire. Lázaro inscribes himself into a society obsessed with appearances and with honor, a society bound by inquisitorial judgments. The ambiguities of the text make it difficult to point with assurance to Lázaro's motives or to justify the contradictions in his response. Disparity becomes a sign, a symbol, of the difference between character and storyteller, child and adult, narrator and author.

Guzmán de Alfarache converts the absent author into a presence, thus emphasizing not only the dialogism of the text but also the confused and confusing direction of the narrative. Whether the models include the sermon, confessional literature, or the figure of the sinner turned saint, Guzmán becomes a commentator on (his) life without the benefit of a fixed plan. Whatever master narratives guide Guzmán and Alemán, the movement toward repentance is disrupted by the resentful attitude of the narrator and by the personal struggle of the author. In the climactic debate in Chapter 31 of *Niebla*, Miguel de Unamuno stands in the middle between the fictional Augusto Pérez and the Unamuno *de fuera* who writes himself into the dialogue. Bridging the gap between the real and the imaginary, Unamuno demystifies the notion of authorial control while redefining the concept of control from within. If the debate is a draw, or perhaps an ironic victory for Augusto, the indisputable winner is Unamuno, who would have the most to gain from a literary analogue of immortality. Mateo Alemán enters *Guzmán de Alfarache* in a somewhat different fashion. The allegory of the literary theft, the invention of a picaresque rival, and the unmasking of the pseudonymous author of the sequel attest to creative brilliance, but this strategy diverts the reader from the penitential stance that could serve to unite event and commentary. Although Guzmán's voice is inflected by the authorial voice-over well before the counterattack occurs, the retaliation signals a disjunction in the narrative structure. Alemán praises the *pícaro*'s delinquency as proof of Guzmán's superiority over his rival, and he steers the text (and Guzmán) away from the road to redemption. Much of the critical debate on the *Guzmán* has centered on the question of whether the narrative is a moral work or a book of entertainment, a series of sermons enlivened by picaresque adventures or picaresque adventures legitimized by a series of sermons. Alemán's intervention takes the narration out of Guzmán's control, in the sense that the synthesis of story and discourse seems to lie in the life and in the art of the author. Ironically, however, Guzmán de Alfarache and Mateo Alemán lead parallel lives. As they aspire to distance themselves from what society views as negative identities, the force of blood seems ever stronger. As a result, their ulterior motives supersede the announced aims of the narration. Guzmán stands in the margins of story and discourse, while Alemán, whose goal may be to discredit the life he has invented, shows that he is intimately linked to that life.

Alemán has greater ties with his narrator/protagonist than he apparently would want to admit. The reader may be made uncomfortable by Guzmán's unflattering portrait of his father in the first chapter of the novel, to cite but one example, because the distancing devices simply do not work. By articulating his heritage, he becomes a part of the picture. The same is true of Alemán, who shares a similar heritage. When readers note only negligible connection between the autobiographical episodes and the commentaries that precede and follow the action, they may choose to write Alemán into the account. This is not unlike the case of *Lazarillo de Tormes,* in which one may decide to look beyond Lázaro in order to describe the comprehensive design of the text. If reading includes our attempts to resolve what Michael Riffaterre, in *Semiotics of Poetry,* labels *ungrammaticalities,* it may be that readers will be inclined to turn to the agent who allows them to acknowledge an ironic edge to story and discourse. In the *Lazarillo,* the obscurities of the narrative stem not only from what is left unsaid but, most emphatically, from the difference between text and pretext (and, one may add, from the difference between Lázaro and his narratee/audience). The anonymity of the author, as the engineer of irony, gives the counterdiscourse an abstract quality. Mateo Alemán inverts the premise through a concrete, almost audible presence in the *Guzmán.* The motifs of escape, of victimization, of rivalry, and of revenge are as applicable to Alemán as they are to Guzmán. The grafting of the author's identity—his biography— onto the narrative seems to be borne out by the doubly marginalized status of Guzmán and by the ironic alliance of Alemán with his fictional creation. When we examine the text as process, we may observe the composition of a life from a number of perspectives. Alemán embraces metafiction, and, probably unwittingly, he posits himself within the frame. Seeming to favor distance, he holds a mirror to his own life.

It is a paradox in the development of the novel that perhaps the most striking example of dialogic discourse in early modern narrative comes in an anonymous text, a text whose prologue alludes to the Ciceronian adage that the art object brings honor to its creator. The achievement of *Lazarillo de Tormes* rests to a smaller degree on Lázaro's success story than on the satiric balance of the narrative. The reader can note the criticism directed toward society and toward the critic himself. This is, in part, the story of Lázaro's discourse, which elaborates the inequities of the social hierarchy while seeming to prefer the exclusion of marginal elements to a rewriting of the social code. There is manipulation on both sides, for, as the institutions of the State perpetuate themselves by treating social law as if it were divine law, Lázaro the narrator overstates his case. The argument for advancement in a relative sense offsets the appeal for absolute justice. More important, the combination of Lázaro's lowly position in society and his intrusion into a literary realm traditionally reserved for superior beings hardly aids his defense. Distanced from the narrator/protagonist, readers may be more inclined to scrutinize his calculated effort at persuasion. Authority in the text shifts from the designs of the narrative persona to the ironic structural design of the text, which, in turn, calls attention to a power behind the scenes. *Guzmán de Alfarache* begins in a similar way, with emphasis on the pronounced incompatibility of the young Guzmán's lofty goals with the social norms of his time. Because the author of the *Guzmán* has a name and a biography, however, the reader may notice similarities as well as differences between the artist and his subject, most particularly with respect to a dual system of distancing devices. When the author of the false *Guzmán* invades his literary territory, Alemán begins to identify—willfully, as opposed to unconsciously—with his protagonist. They now have a shared stake in the validity, or authenticity, of the account. Consequently, of the two sets of rhetorical strategies, Alemán's may be the more easily discernible, due less to the subtleties of irony (as in the *Lazarillo*) than to the obvious personal motives of the author.

It would be reasonable, I believe, to suggest that picaresque narrative features an interplay of posturing and emotion. The narrators approach their lives from a rhetorical, often defensive, perspective while putting their psyches on display. The *pícaros* are damaged human beings, and their accounts reflect the harm that has been done to them. They show that survival in itself is an achievement, but they also show that their expectations are higher than mere survival, and clearly too high. The declamatory character of their rhetoric is matched by a layer of sensitivity projected, knowingly or unknowingly, onto the narration. Needless to say, appeal to emotion may be yet another rhetorical strategy, but the texts take us (to borrow from the title of Carroll B. Johnson's study of *Guzmán de Alfarache*) "inside" the protagonists. Alongside the errant deeds are psychological profiles that lead to what may be termed a dialectical tension between action and motivation, appearance and reality, story and discourse. Readers operate at a distance from the events portrayed and, of course, from the one who portrays them, but they may find themselves involved in the lives and, possibly, sympathetic to the plight of the *pícaros*. This is something more than a Romantic misreading of—or intrusion into— the text. Whatever the primary impetus behind the narrative act, the process includes a bearing of souls. The discursive situation represents a radically different, even ludicrous, treatment of literary and nonliterary models. By his presence alone, the professed creator of the discourse defies all rules of social and artistic decorum. His illusions of grandeur are as preposterous as they are antisocial, threatening, subversive. His data is often contradictory, and his arguments are more likely to incriminate him than to boost his prestige. In spite of the obstacles that surround him, the *pícaro* manages to survive in the text as he survives in the world, through his wit and through the forum provided both by Renaissance humanism and the marketplace. The reader may deplore his background, his ambition, and his behavior—and this, certainly, is no longer a given—but the simple humanity of the *pícaro* is hard to overlook. Lázaro de Tormes knows the Bible and folkloric tradition, and he alludes in his prologue to Pliny and Cicero. He is versed in general principles of rhetoric, and, if anything, he uses too many persuasive tacks. He seems to want the reader simultaneously to applaud his accomplishments and to blame society for his shortcomings. He cannot reconcile the discrepancy between events that punctuate the need for silence and the words that break the silence. His rhetorical zeal is impressive but counterproductive. Guzmán de Alfarache, for his part, is highly educated. His language is often elegant, and his discourse at times has the flavor of an oration. As a writer, he has little trouble in maintaining linguistic control, but his emotional fervor tends to lead him to raise tangential issues and to air grievances that have little bearing on the matters at hand. This is not a question of speech versus silence, as in the *Lazarillo*, but rather of Guzmán versus Alemán. It is their shared destiny that gives unity to the narrative.

Pablos has more formal education than Lázaro and less than Guzmán. His training will have prepared him to write, but it is doubtful that he could rise to the conceptist heights of Quevedo, for few, if any, writers have done so. Quevedo and his fellow baroque stylists seek to exclude the general public from their audience. Art becomes elitist, exclusionary. Pablos is hardly the ideal reader, the narratee, the *destinataire,* of this type of literature, and certainly not the logical candidate for writer. How can one fit Pablos into the discourse as well as into the story of his life? Iffland proposes a view of the autobiographer as jester, which may explain the self-mockery and some of the ironies of the text but does not account for the intricate word play identified with *conceptismo.* When critics debate the aim of the novel—most commonly, as a verbal artifice or as a moral exemplum—Quevedo plays a prominent role in the analysis, whether as agent of ingenuity or encoder of messages. Quevedo does not concentrate, as do the author of *Lazarillo de Tormes* and Cervantes in *Don Quijote*, for example, on delineating a narrative pretext (or context) for the narrative. Pablos begins at the beginning and indicates where the untold sequel will lead, but in his discourse he makes no attempt to meditate upon or to prepare the reader for the lesson of the concluding paragraph. Baroque literature in Spain—both the difficult "new poetry" and the exaggerated battles of wit—is built around the motif of competition. Quevedo competes with a textual past that includes a variety of narrative forms, some markedly idealistic, others part of the emerging picaresque mode. His literary enemy Góngora and the proponents of *gongorismo* seem to be constantly on his mind, and *conceptismo* offers a form of alterity, and of individuality, within the baroque sensibility. To what extent does an implied competition between Quevedo and Pablos affect the direction of the *Buscón*? Stated in another way, how far can the internal narrative premises take us, and how much of the discourse should we attribute to Pablos?

It may be worthwhile to consider points in the text at which the reader may differentiate between Pablos's voice (and authority) and Quevedo's. In my opinion, the most obvious shift occurs in the fourth chapter, which marks a significant change in the linguistic direction of the *Buscón*. Quevedo opens the narrative with an array of puns, witticisms, and piercing humor. The term *double entendre* is especially appropriate here, because behind the word play we may see revealed not only the characters described (notably, Pablos's parents, companions, and teachers) but also the calculated effort of the protagonist himself. Quevedo exhibits his conceptist wares—his artistic signature—while undermining, through language, the narrator's ability to establish the direction of the text. Particularly in Chapter 1, Quevedo vies with other masters of the conceit and with Pablos. The language of the early chapters seems to serve two purposes: it emphasizes the verbal and comic ingenuity of the (real) author, and it underscores Pablos's unavoidable ties to his family. Quevedo manipulates the narrative scheme in such a manner as to resolve the question of authority from the first chapter. The elevated discourse and the wry, sardonic humor would seem to place the creation of wit over content, that is, to draw the reader's attention from Pablos and the illusion of control to Quevedo as metaphorical puppeteer. The event that should produce the greatest empathy on the part of the reader—Pablos's near-starvation at the hands of Cabra—replaces the empty stomach with an abundance of words. Admiration of the descriptive powers of Quevedo may supersede the reader's pity for the young Pablos. The author seems to sense that it would be difficult to laugh at the conceits (and to applaud the creative mind behind them) and to cry for the victim at the same time. In addition, the initial chapters demonstrate the futility of Pablos's yearning for life as a gentleman and, with respect to rhetorical strategies, of his plan to separate himself, as son and as writer, from his parents.

Bearing in mind the competitive spirit and the arguably uneven struggle of the early chapters, one may wish to examine the impact of Pablos's character and discourse in these chapters, as well as the possibility that his status in the text may grow as the force and the frequency of Quevedo's conceits—his overt display of wit and rivalry—diminish (although by no means do they disappear) in the chapters that follow. Throughout the narrative, Pablos articulates the anguish that he suffers by virtue of his lineage and the social position prescribed to him by and from birth. Ironically, the revelation of his innermost thoughts comes from passages in which he speaks of suppressing emotions and of hiding his true feelings. We see how his friends, his teachers, and, most important, his parents hurt him, despite his fervent need to please and despite his will to succeed. Perhaps no trauma is greater than his mother's admission, with no tinge of guilt, that she is upset that people would call her a witch and a prostitute, not because what they say is untrue, but because her privacy has been invaded (Chapter 2). The breaking of a protective silence is crucial here, for it operates at two levels. The reader may empathize with the protagonist, since the event marks a type of spiritual death, but, when viewed in light of the ill-fated adventures that culminate in Pablos's disgrace as boy-king, the confession only accentuates the absurdity of the search for respectability.

In the introductory chapters, there is a distinction between Pablos as form and substance, outer and inner self, posturer and sensitive being. If language separates him from Quevedo as verbal stylist and representative of the aristocracy, Pablos's acknowledgment of the effect of repeated humiliation on his psyche makes him more human, more worthy of sympathy. Admission of suppressed feelings helps to explain his recourse to delinquency, for which he has been chided by a number of critics, who perhaps choose to ignore the factors that move him in this direction. Picaresque narrative emphasizes the formation of character, the definition of the subject, in social and textual terms. Pablos's self-fashioning, that is, his invention of an identity, shows us a process that may cause the reader to differentiate between society's perception of Pablos (and, it may be assumed, the author's image of his protagonist) and the complex character uncovered in the text. Edwin Williamson writes of Pablos's somewhat assertive break from Quevedo, but I would suggest that, ironically, the *pícaro's* strength is his weakness. Dominated by his creator, he is humbled by the text as he is humbled by his fellow man. The glory of his language is borrowed glory. His thoughts, long suppressed, are most genuinely his own. They would seem to compromise his position, but they may give him a psychological, and affective, advantage. There is no question that Quevedo seizes upon the satiric aspects of *Lazarillo de Tormes* and *Guzmán de Alfarache*. The presumption that informs Pablos's aspirations lies at the center of the *Buscón*, which builds, as well, on the incongruity of his role as writer. I believe that James Iffland is right to point, with hindsight, to Freud, but I would focus less on the objects of Pablos's discourse than on what the discourse tells us about the subject.

From earliest childhood, Pablos overcompensates for his lowly station in life, without even moderate success. His failed attempts to disavow his heritage ("I am not my mother," "I am not *ecce homo*") remind him that he is forever his parents' son and that mortification lurks behind every door of opportunity. The first-person narration, especially the asides that communicate the hurt that he has kept hidden from others, allows readers to understand Pablos's delinquency as something more than antisocial behavior for its own sake. The suppression of emotion offers a means by which to gauge the value of the discourse. *La vida del buscón* deals with conflicting attitudes toward identity. Pablos engages in a program to transform himself into a gentleman, to erase his past, to revise his family history. Society, bent on conformity and rigidly protective of the hierarchy, is his nemesis. Not without irony, Don Diego Coronel, scion of a New Christian family, serves as a symbol of this society in the text. Within the geography of the *Buscón*, Pablos tries repeatedly to move away from his parents, but distance is illusory. His birthright is a sign that remains in his heart and in the minds of others. Pablos is a marked man. Other characters can see through him, and, on the rare occasions in which he seems poised for success, fate intervenes to maintain the status quo. After a series of traumatic experiences in Alcalá de Henares, where Don Diego enjoys the privileges of rank, Pablos opts for delinquency as a cover for his insecurity. Dismissed from Don Diego's service, he refuses to enter the employ of another master. Just as he rejects his family, he rejects the notion of being defined as an extension of his social superiors. The laws, people, and signs around him indicate the advisability of resignation to his predetermined role in life, but Pablos chooses another course and other identities.

On the road to Alcalá, Pablos and Don Diego are relative equals. Both are inexperienced, and both fall victim to pranks. There is no social etiquette to shield Don Diego until they reach the university town, where the master is received by associates of his father and the servant is left defenseless. The discourse belies, to a degree, the lesson Pablos must have learned about human worth. In Chapter 6, he describes Don Diego as "quiet and religious" and himself as "mischievous" and "cunning"; they become standard bearers, respectively, for virtue and vice. If one bears in mind that Don Diego dismisses Pablos's ill-treatment by admonishing him to look out for himself, the ending of the chapter—in which Pablos speaks of the esteem in which he held his master and the devotion that Don Diego showed to him—may seem to echo the paean to the thief and the witch at the conclusion of the first chapter. It must be remembered that the narrator knows the story that is to follow. In that story, Pablos's greatest scam—his proposed marriage to the wealthy and socially prominent Doña Ana—is thwarted by her cousin, Don Diego. One explanation for the generous description of Don Diego is the weighty presence of Quevedo as ironic refurbisher of Pablos's discourse. Another is the suppression of emotions, which affects not only the protagonist but also the narrator. Pablos holds back, as if restrained by forces beyond his power. He cannot condemn Don Diego without casting aspersions on the system for which his master stands. He can neither comprehend the nature of his delinquency nor expect society to view his behavior with compassion.

The theme of suppression in the *Buscón* has points of contact with the liar paradox. By recalling moments in his past in which he has concealed his feelings, Pablos invites the reader to look for markers that would expose the inner being. The inclusion of what has been suppressed gives us the chance to delve into the character's psyche, yet, of course, the act of writing removes the material from the realm of the unarticulated. There is irony in the situation, but I do not see the imposing figure of Quevedo as the producer of

a counterdiscourse. Pablos's admissions of hidden pain come almost in passing, without fanfare, without critique, and without
humor, even when the events leading to the statements are rendered in burlesque fashion. Pablos seeks distance from his roots,
but he resists solitude in favor of notoriety. Never free of his fore-
bears, even as an orphan, he joins other figurative families, including a gang of juvenile delinquents, a band of makeshift gentlemen,
and a New Christian jailer with a grotesque wife and daughters.
The new life is no better than the old, and the familial settings are
clear (and ironic) reminders of an inescapable past and, perhaps,
reminders of Quevedo as Pablos's ultimate nemesis. Despite his
protean bent and (meta)theatrical skills, Pablos cannot settle into a
stable identity. The final passage of the text is about change, and
the message is far from hopeful. Pablos warns us that a person
must adopt different, and presumably positive, customs in order
to improve his lot, but what sort of transformation would he, his
author, or his readers envision? Golden Age poetry often presents
variations on the theme of the inevitability of change, while emplotment in narrative, with a stronger foundation in social reality,
may prove more resistant to those who, like Pablos, advocate a reordering of hierarchies.

In *Coming to Terms*, Seymour Chatman separates discourse into
the three categories of narrative, description, and argument.
Distinguishable within a given text, each category may become a
function of the others. In the case of the *Buscón*, the distinction is
useful as a means of identifying passages seemingly beyond the
narrator's control and those in which Pablos seems to speak as
himself. The early descriptions of the parents and of the pious Don
Diego (viewed against the portrait of a wayward Pablos), for example, would seem to direct the reader to a perspective imposed
by Quevedo onto the text. Chatman notes the force—the weight—
of certain descriptions in a chapter entitled "Description Is No
Textual Handmaiden" (22–37), and Pablos is a master in this regard, but to his detriment. The *pícaro* encourages us to laugh at
him, not with him, for the textual message appears to be at odds
with his social and literary ambitions. This is detachment in the
broadest sense. In a similar vein, Pablos as narrator, in the relatively few commentaries on his actions, argues against himself,

most notably in the concluding lines of his account. It is in the narrative proper, through almost fleeting asides, that the text allows the reader to get a glimpse of Pablos as interior being, neither actor on the stage of life nor rhetorical poseur. Here Pablos finds a forum, a personal space, an ironic voice of his own.

Building on Wayne Booth's construct of the "implied author" in *The Rhetoric of Fiction* and adding to his own commentary in *Story and Discourse,* Chatman contends that "it makes sense to attribute to every narrative fiction an agency that does not personally tell or show but puts into the narrator's mouth the language that tells or shows. The implied author has no 'voice.' The implied author only empowers others to 'speak.' . . . Insofar as the implied author (the text itself) communicates something different from what the narrator says, that meaning must occur between the lines" (*Coming to Terms* 85). Picaresque fiction would seem to presuppose the double agency to which Booth and Chatman refer. The protagonist's decision to become a writer—that is, to be his own subject, to present himself as worthy of the status of subject— defies literary protocol, just as the *pícaro* defies social protocol as he conspires to erase his heritage and to move upward. A text such as the *Buscón* demands detachment from its subject, or from its subject turned object. What Pablos reveals is the underside of Renaissance humanism and a lack of propriety on all levels. Like his predecessors, it may be assumed, Quevedo offers a life to be ridiculed rather than admired, a deconstruction of traditional autobiography. The very premise of the *Buscón* indicates a type of entrapment or blind alley. Were Pablos to respect his place in the great scheme of things, he would remain subservient to Don Diego Coronel and to others deemed his superiors. Were he to surrender to what others call his assigned role on the stage of life, he would have no story to tell. In general, the autobiographer relies on fame, on some form of exemplarity. The *pícaro* has the option of notoriety or of obscurity. When he attempts to construct a confessional or apologetic frame for his story, the results are suspect, at best, because one notes difference, as opposed to correspondence, between text and intertext.

If Pablos's vision stresses vertical movement (social ascendancy), Quevedo reverts time and again to circularity as the reigning motif of the *Buscón*. Lázaro de Tormes, despite his many trials, makes a name for himself, even though his victory may be pyrrhic. Guzmán de Alfarache adopts a penitential stance, if not a complementary voice. In contrast, Pablos, in a desperate struggle to renounce his family, aligns himself with degenerate "families" and ultimately with a band of hardened criminals. He battles for legitimacy through illegitimate, ill-advised means. The nadir and apex of his life occur early in the text, in Alcalá, where he is most alone and then most triumphant, at the height of his youthful delinquency. The letter from home, which informs him of his father's death and his mother's imprisonment, breaks the spell of his notoriety and leads to his break with Don Diego. Out on his own—and physically free of his parents—he can only court success, for now his crimes bring punishment. In the process, he loses his name, without gaining comfort from his invented identities: Don Alvaro de Córdoba, Don Ramiro de Guzmán, Don Felipe Tristán, Alonsete, and so forth. (One may note the assonantal link with Lázaro de Tormes in the first of these names and the obvious "parentage" with Guzmán de Alfarache in the second.) When Pablos undertakes to give up his past, he discovers that fate would deny him a future. A missing sign of that future is a stable name. Don Diego resurfaces in order to expose Pablos, to name him, and thus to reassert the influence of his heritage.

It would be fair to say that an author, as creator and director of words and events, controls the destiny of his characters. In the *Buscón*, Quevedo creates a pattern of failure marked by humiliation, by physical and figurative falls, and by radical coincidence. This is nowhere more apparent than in the return of Don Diego Coronel as spoiler and as avenger. Authorial power is evident in *Lazarillo de Tormes* and in *Guzmán de Alfarache*, as well, but the effect is different. Not only is Lázaro's most important master absent through anonymity, but the writer gives his narrator a pretext and a rhetorical mission. Lázaro can claim independence, even if some readers (who exist outside the narrator-narratee design of the text) wish to view his discourse as a rhetoric of irony. Guzmán, for his part, uses the spiritual confession as a model, seemingly in order to back up his rhetoric with theology. The incompatibility of form and content—for Guzmán's life is nothing if not secular—

joins with Alemán's special agenda to challenge the sincerity of the confession. Nevertheless, the combination of the professed repentance with what some have referred to as Guzmán's sermonizing establishes a focal point or unifying principle from which to judge the narrative, even though the judgment may be harsh. Quevedo employs neither an external device (such as Vuestra Merced's request for an explanation of the case) nor an internal motive (such as the progression from sin to reformation) as pretext. He alludes to the entertainment value of the book in the prologue and Pablos moralizes in the most perfunctory of manners in the closing, but the author entrusts to his narrator no persuasive task that would parallel those of his predecessors.

As if to underscore the misguided direction of the *pícaro*, Quevedo furnishes, at best, a minimalist pretext. As narrator, Pablos does not position himself to acknowledge a correct path, to show remorse, or to acknowledge the benefits of a moral conscience. *Lazarillo de Tormes* pretends to allow us into a closed circuit, so to speak, in the private communication between narrator and narratee. *Guzmán de Alfarache* alternates event and commentary (though not necessarily in that order) in a movement toward the enlightenment of the protagonist. Neither text is fashioned as pure autobiography; one is, among other things, an exercise in self-defense, and the other claims to illustrate a sinner's conversion. Each narrator attempts to persuade his audience, be it large or small, of his own worth and of the significance of his efforts to survive in a hostile world. In other words, the discourse of the two texts has a rhetorical goal, which, of course, may feed into the counterdiscursive strategies of the authors. Quevedo, in effect, deprives Pablos of the persuasive frame that helps to balance the hardships and the ironies of the earlier narratives. The opening words of Lázaro's first *tratado* exaggerate the difference between this "life" and autobiographical tradition, idealistic narrative, and spiritual confession. Guzmán's futile endeavor to distance himself from his father (and from his bloodlines) in the first chapter of his account likewise may orient the reader toward irony that certainly is sustained. There remains, however, a dialectical relation between what the narrators tell and what they show, due in large part to the tension between the narrative premise and the institutions of the

State, which include the literary domain. Without a structural frame, the *Buscón* seems constantly to bring its own existence into question. Why does this particular man write his autobiography? To whom does he address his story? Does the narrator give us sufficient grounds to examine Pablos's commentary on its own terms? Can the reader devise a pretext that would serve as motivation and frame?

It seems far easier to imagine the life "inventing" Pablos than to justify Pablos's independence in the authorial role. Autobiography is seldom the source of negative exemplarity, with the notable exception of the spiritual confession, in which the sinner has seen the light. The baroque discourse of the early chapters of the *Buscón* places the reader at a distance from Pablos, who cannot assert himself by way of an overriding plan. By failing to include a reason for Pablos's writerly enterprise, Quevedo intensifies the dialogic nature of picaresque narrative. He inverts priorities by giving the voice-over the first word, the privileged position in the text. The term *implied author* may be too subtle in this context. The discourse seems closer to the elitist man of letters than to the déclassé narrator. The plot design seems more the product of a conservative mindset than of a subversive scheme. Seeking to enumerate the lessons or messages of the *Buscón,* and guided by the inescapable distance between teller and tale, the reader quite likely will read "into" Pablos, that is, read "against the grain" of the narrative. The *Buscón* may be about the need to respect the forces that supersede the individual, that stabilize society, and that perpetuate the status quo. Pablos is subjected to a brand of determinism that seems to be inspired by faith in retributive justice, here equated with morality.

Pablos's project is antisocial, disrespectful of class and custom. Pablos is no literary Spartacus, surrounded by sympathizers, and his addressees may have little cause to rally around him. If his actions bring detachment on one level, his language will do so on another. He defies social practice and the tenets of literary decorum. His illusions of grandeur condemn him in the eyes of the State, and his way with words hints at another source of authority. In story and discourse, Pablos represents alterity, otherness. He is a character in search of the happy ending that seems destined to elude him and, it would appear, in search of a voice of his own. Perhaps the major base of irony of *La vida del buscón* is the interplay of Pablos's dream and the reality principle that only he seems to ignore. This obliviousness to—or disregard of—the ways of the world separates the protagonist from readers privy to the power of society. Quevedo compounds the detachment by elevating Pablos's speech, to the extent that the maker of wit seems to be other than the storyteller. Pablos's place in the text relates, I would suggest, to issues in feminist theory. Note, for example, the following commentary by Paul Smith on the critique of Luce Irigaray: "Irigaray's view of the female 'subject,' then, is that there is not and has not been such a thing permitted in the purview of masculinist discourse: that discourse, because of its own constitution, is unable to *specify* femininity. A woman can thus only speak there *as if* a man (miming the discourse of patriarchy), or as a 'subject' without specificity, without her own language" (144). Quevedo reshapes first-person narration and the autobiographical format, both of which would tend to underscore the authority of the speaker, in order metaphorically to dislodge Pablos from the center of story and discourse. There is never an unmediated "I" in fiction, and Quevedo confirms this point in a manner befitting the intensity of the baroque age.

A number of literary forms, such as Juan del Encina's pastoral eclogues, to cite but one example, strive to recreate the language of lowborn characters. In Lope de Vega's model for drama, servants and lackeys may speak in verse, but their voices are easily differentiated from those of their masters. Lázaro may cite Pliny and Cicero, but much of his discourse comes from folkloric tradition. While the text of *Lazarillo de Tormes* hardly could be classified as crudely written, its wordplays are not overly sophisticated, and the anonymity of the author strengthens the illusion of direct discourse. *Guzmán de Alfarache* details the education of the main character, so that it is not the incompatibility of voice to situation but the overt intrusion of Mateo Alemán into the text that may result in a sense of narrative doubling. The content of the discourse rather than the tenor of the narrator's voice bespeaks an authorial presence in the *Guzmán*. The *Buscón* builds upon patterns of irony in the preceding texts, but Quevedo is able to marginalize his narrator/protagonist to the maximum degree. The self-portrait—the self-identification—is devastating in its mockery, which extends most profoundly to the narrating subject.

Rejecting his heritage and finding himself without legitimate means to alter his fate, Pablos can neither shed his hereditary baggage nor gain comfort in assumed identities. His link with the past and his masquerades become an ironic lifeline. With them, he exists as a severed being, a trace of his former self or a travesty of real social types. Without them, he is a nonentity. Don Toribio and his brotherhood of rogues personify the paradoxical intermediate space between the authentic and the artificial, between reality and appearance. Life with this group is, at the same time, a burlesque of home and family and the closest thing to acceptance that Pablos will encounter. Wishing to redefine his social role, he falls victim to the hierarchy of the State. Attempting to articulate the stages of his journey through life, he falls victim to a rhetoric of wit and ingenuity bearing the implied signature of another. *La vida del buscón* is baroque picaresque. High discourse and low action would seem to comply beautifully with the extremist vision associated with baroque art. Story and discourse operate dialectically in Quevedo's rewriting of the intertext. Viewed from within, however, Quevedo's *conceptismo* threatens to leave the socially disconnected Pablos without a voice, or at least without a voice that would match his position and background. Pablos's linguistic alienation is, of course, an analogue of his social alienation. Margination of the undesirable lies at the core of the *Buscón,* at the very heart of its deep structure. Quevedo, as a defender of the ideologies of the State, usurps control of the first-person narrative. This glowing achievement on the literary level—the transference of discursive authority—demonstrates how Pablos is silenced in circumstances that would seem to empower him.

The *pícaro* chooses civil disobedience over resignation to a subordinate role on the great stage of the world. Delinquency ensures him a story, but he is the pawn of an unkind destiny. His minor victories consistently lead to major defeats. He is sharp and he is resourceful, and his failures are not due to inferior intelligence or to lapses of logic as much as to chance, to confrontation with forces beyond his control. Pablos is punished, as female characters in fiction are often punished, for not knowing his place. It is important to emphasize, once again, that this knowledge could only obliterate him from the text, for few dutiful servants are called upon to write their lives. Survival comes at a cost, however. The baroque conceits of the opening chapters probably will oblige readers to focus their attention on Quevedo's wit rather than on Pablos's trials. Pablos is a function, a means to an end, less a figure who arouses sympathy than the butt of satire. Quevedo, who is bound to condemn Pablos's social aspirations, refuses to allow him to vacate his space in the margins. Not only does the discursive situation fail to empower Pablos, but he is compelled to verbalize his excruciating experiences through an idiolect that, in general, tends to disengage him from his own life story. Like Don Quijote, Pablos endeavors to remake the world around him according to an alternate model. While Cervantes seems to favor a blurring of distinctions between the real and the imagined, Quevedo's message about society and about language—in essence, the same message, which stresses the need for differentiation—is evident and clearly expounded.

Khachig Tölölyan notes that "in *The Discourse of Modernism,* which is perhaps the most satisfactory extended application of Foucauldian theory we have, Timothy Reiss implies that the novel's rise need not be viewed as always initiated by the intersection of pre-existing discourses" (246). For Reiss, as read by Tölölyan, "it can also be seen as part and parcel of European culture's larger, evolving response, in the period 1590 to 1650, to the imperatives which simultaneously resulted in the development of science, (utopian) narrative and other instantiations of an 'analytical referential' master-discourse. In Reiss's account, the dialogue between prose fictions (not yet quite the novel) and culture is enacted within each text by the simultaneous representation and critique of this discourse, which promises power, knowledge and progress" (Tölölyan 246–47). As a response to this commentary, one can view the *Buscón* within several dialectical frames, each of which will show, I believe, the special authority of Quevedo. The anonymous writer of *Lazarillo de Tormes* offers a critique of the intertext (the spiritual confession, idealistic literature, Renaissance humanism) and of the society of the time. The objects of the satirical vision include Lázaro and his various masters, the first for his presumption as autobiographer and as citizen, and the others, among them several clerics, for not living up to the ideals implicit in the roles that life has assigned to them. The *Lazarillo* establishes a balance between story and discourse, a balance generated by the presence of irony in both areas. *Guzmán de Alfarache* also critiques the narrator/protagonist and those around him. Alemán repeats the ironic complementarity of story and discourse through a structure that, consciously and unconsciously, it would seem, denies the individual the option of forsaking his roots. The author is like and unlike his creation; he occupies a different point on the social scale, but he is equally unsuccessful in maintaining a distance from his heritage. The Martí continuation exacerbates the dilemma of a writer whose personal circumstances bring him ever closer to the marginated character. The *Buscón* posits a variation on the relation between the author and the *pícaro.*

The question of the emerging novel as critique is affected by Quevedo's rigid conservatism. Quevedo works aggressively to stifle Pablos's implied critique of the social order, by serving as minister of his destiny and by invading the discursive domain. *Conceptismo* is indeed a reaction—a critique—of literary precedent, but that is the author's campaign, not the narrator's, and it is an elitist recourse. Quevedo may challenge the form but certainly not the content of the master discourse, the doctrines and politics of the State. If *La vida del buscón* tells other stories, it may be because the author cannot take away authority without granting verbal (and social) recognition, albeit begrudgingly, to the outsider. The motif of suppression, in the multiple senses of the term, becomes Pablos's ironic saving grace. Pablos's blind alley is the subtext of Quevedo's treatise on deviant behavior. The subdued voice offers an additional—and, by virtue of the resistance to it, symbolic—version of the ironically dislocated life.

Lazarillo de Tormes is built around the breaking of a protective silence. Lázaro's defense may serve to incriminate him because the act of enunciation, no matter how well crafted the rhetoric, cannot have the value of the unarticulated word. Lázaro finds himself in a double bind: he must respond to Vuestra Merced's request when he prefers to remain silent, and he must write in order to attain artistic laurels. His artistry is, at the same time, an advertisement of his problematic domestic situation and his last best chance at upward mobility. The (implied) author creates a distance between the narrator and the reader in order to underscore the irony of story and discourse. In one sense, at least, *La vida del buscón* represents an inversion of the narrative circumstances of the *Lazarillo*. Pablos as social type resides in the margins until the book into which he is inscribed gives him a nominal centrality. His discourse is elevated and, on occasion, cultured. The fact that Quevedo obstructs Pablos at every step of his trajectory does not negate the undeniable presence of the outcast in the text. The image of the author erasing or effacing his character becomes ironic in light of the operating premises of the *Buscón*. The humiliating vita and the borrowed discourse notwithstanding, Pablos is the protagonist of autobiography, thus the principal character and the writing subject. Quevedo effects a decentering of Pablos, who nonetheless remains the filter through which all messages pass. Pablos is to Quevedo what the broken silence is to Lázaro de Tormes, namely, the acknowledgment of an unwanted other. Lázaro is trapped by the narrative situation in which Vuestra Merced has placed him. Correspondingly, Pablos is forced to utter the words that a baroque artist and militant reactionary puts in his mouth, and he must declare, before his readership, the indignities that he has endured.

The anonymity of the author of the *Lazarillo* makes it difficult to explore the full implications of the ironic structure of the narrative, which, it must be remembered, is directed internally to a single narratee. Quevedo the public persona stands at such a far remove from Pablos that the counterdiscursive strategies (and their objective) seem obvious. This works to the advantage of Pablos, who becomes a victim of literary machinations and, perhaps, despite his follies, worthy of our sympathy. Even more emphatically, Quevedo cannot "decenter" Pablos until he has positioned him in the center, that is, delivered him from the margins, accorded him a space that society and literary precedent have denied him. If Cervantes had completed Part II of *Don Quijote* without alluding to the Avellaneda sequel or without modifying his own text accordingly, the spurious continuation and its author would have faded into oblivion. Cervantes is enraged by the turn of events, but, in his zeal to prove the superiority of the "true history," he immortalizes the illegitimate. Quevedo, for his part, highlights the offender, the offenses, and the narrating "I" as he does battle against them. He provides the opening that, in general, the culture of the baroque does not provide.

In "Popular Culture and Spanish Literary History," Wlad Godzich and Nicholas Spadaccini note the influence of printing on the reception of literary works. An example is the dialogue on the romances of chivalry at Juan Palomeque's inn in *Don Quijote* I, 32: "What emerges from the discussion . . . is that a largely illiterate, lower-class audience has at least partial access to books that a century earlier had been the pastime of aristocratic readers. For the occasional, lower-class consumers, listening to stories of knights errant had a practical function: to find solace from the trials of daily life. For them, listening to stories that expressed aristocratic values was not a way of consecrating idleness; it was merely a respite from labor and toil" (55–56). The commentaries at the inn demonstrate that each reader or listener, with different horizons of expectation and different "discursive circuits," responds individually to a text and, as a corollary, that no one grasps the totality. Godzich and Spadaccini pose the key question of their essay: "A hundred years after the publication of the original, Cervantes shows that the Amadís is no longer read as a totality. But one can turn the question to Cervantes's text as well: who can read it? In other words, who can read the fragmentation in such a way that it will be perceived in its fragmentary reception and yet somehow be added up, totalized?" (58). In early modern times, urbanization brings together people from diverse linguistic areas for settlement and commerce, and the various professional groups increasingly are regulated by "the state apparatus and thus become answerable to it. The emergent state bureaucracy, having abandoned Latin, favors one sociolect, and, within it, one discourse (or style, as it is known at the time), and makes all others answerable to it" (59). As a result, "all dealings that involve interdiscursive crossing must be mediated by the dominant discourse. . . . The individual discourses lose their autonomy and . . . their self-sufficiency as well. . . . Their speakers also lose autonomy and self-sufficiency, and must recognize that they are speakers of fragmentary discourses which can never be totalized. Only the state can achieve this totalization" (59–60). Yet if the State is the ideal reader, the novel ultimately, and ironically, is at the service of difference, for "whereas the state can assert its hegemony over the realm of culture through gestures of exclusion from that realm of those elements it wishes to proscribe, the novel by including all the elements of official culture (both the elite and the mass) as well as the excluded elements of unofficial culture, almost by definition engages in the practices we have called popular" (61). Quevedo, loyalist and exclusionist par excellence, enters into the realm of the popular by writing a picaresque novel.

Godzich and Spadaccini describe the novel in paradoxical terms. The State is designator and guardian of the dominant discourse, but it is also the most competent reader of the collective discourses. (*Competition,* like *competence,* derives from the Latin *competere,* to be suitable.) Reading fiction is, to a great degree, an open enterprise. Cervantes devotes a number of passages in the second part of *Don Quijote* to reception of the published volume. He emphasizes the range of reactions and of affective priorities. The conspicuous absence of firm directions for reading the text— given the playful context in which its purpose is elaborated in the prologue to Part I and given the rivalry of texts, authors, and narrators within the novel, or history—would seem to encourage an approach based on the endorsement of fragmented discourse as the product of an eclectic and constantly revised intertext. While a totalizing or selective vision could be imposed on Cervantes's novel, the spirit of the text seems to lie elsewhere (in the glorification of diversity, some might say). The *Buscón,* in contrast, does seem to adhere to the power of the dominant discourse.

Quevedo's venture into the popular may be seen as a cautious and qualified descent, and one that he himself will later regret (see Mariscal 101). Pablos of Segovia is no Everyman but rather a sign (or personification) of alterity. Nor is this alterity an inevitable or complementary otherness but an unacceptable alternative. As agent of story and discourse, Quevedo gives only to take away, to chastise, to bear witness to the social (and, by extension, divine) order. Baroque poets and prose stylists in Spain more commonly practice exclusion from the outset of their production. They devise linguistic and conceptual conundrums that only a select few can master; that is, they define and determine their readership according to class and education. Incomprehensibility thus has a social function, as gauge and limit of propriety. The autobiography of a *pícaro*, when cast by Quevedo, never becomes a concession to a changing society or to a changing world, or even a questioning of traditional values. Pablos's "pretensions," introduced in the first chapter amid a barrage of data that illustrate the absurdity of the endeavor, bear little gravity. The reigning sentiment in the *Buscón* is probably not hope, which would stem from reader identification with the narrator/protagonist, but disdain for the misguided quest. There would seem to be less focus on the creation of suspense, which would imply possible success, than on irony, which would stress the futility and certain failure of the undertaking. If *La vida del buscón* manifests the competition among discourses within fictional narrative less fully and less forcefully than *Don Quijote*, Quevedo's novel is an especially strong example of the victory of the discourse of the State, around which Godzich and Spadaccini build their argument. The oxymoron of the picaresque purveyor of baroque art is hardly a proposal for contemplation but, instead, a marker of disdain, a confirmation of society's—and the author's—attitude toward equal opportunity.

Reflecting a tendency of Spanish baroque art, the *Buscón* presents the clash of a stabilized social and political agenda with a semiotics of difference. In many texts, including *comedia* scripts, a movement toward rebellion is undermined by a conservative dénouement, which at times seems less motivated by the causal structure of the literary object than by external pressures (see Casa, for example). The multiperspectivism associated with baroque literature would lead away from permanently inscribed meanings and, of course, would bring the consumer of art (and, accordingly, the progression of time) into the equation. In the *Buscón*, Quevedo employs the recourses of baroque composition without compromising, or jeopardizing, the institutions that he and the reigning powers cherish. Pablos, not he, is the social dissident, the one who is out of place as writer and as advocate of reform. In many ways, the *Buscón* flouts the operative codes only to indicate the danger inherent in all types of insurgence and to show the incongruity—and the potential danger, as well—in lapses of protocol. The distancing devices in the narrative are too numerous and too glaring to be ignored. In spite of the irony that frames their lives, Lázaro de Tormes and Guzmán de Alfarache seem to make earnest attempts to win over their readers. There is a tension between a rhetoric built around victimage and the need for sympathy, on the one side, and the hierarchical policies of society, on the other. The "absence" of the author of the *Lazarillo* helps to forge a balance between the individual and societal points of view. Mateo Alemán achieves a similar effect by vacillating between his distaste for Guzmán and his awareness of their shared grievances. The *Buscón* is notable in this respect precisely for the imbalance between individual aspirations and what is perceived as the collective good. If early picaresque narrative suggests the possibility of an inversion of privilege within the dualistic structure of society, Quevedo seems to want to profess his faith in the status quo.

Quevedo encodes Pablos's transgression of decorum into the text. Low style and oral tradition should be the *pícaro*'s domain. Ingenuity, in this case, is a departure from the norm. The third person—the position of object—is more appropriate to the outsider than the role of narrating subject. The moral of the story is that Pablos has chosen the wrong path, but he must do so for there to be a story. The irony is replicated on the authorial level, since Quevedo violates the elitist design of *conceptismo* and the segregationist practices of society by writing in the picaresque mode. He must deviate from convention in order to preserve convention, but to realize this aim he must release Pablos from the margins. Aurora Egido argues that the *Buscón* is not about narrative unity, about the interplay of author and protagonist, or about the inner life of literary characters, but about rhetorical games, concepts, and masks (197). Steven Cohan reminds us, however, of the illusionary nature of fiction, in pointing out that "character is . . . readable, not as representation, but as a coherently perceived figure existing, during the reading act, in the imaginative space produced in the reader's mind by the transmission of that figure (the text's coded instructions for perceiving it as a figure) and its reception (the reader's acting upon those instructions to imagine it as a figure)" (113). Quevedo's obvious intervention and his positing of a counterdiscourse notwithstanding, the format of the

Buscón qualifies Pablos, warts and all, as a readable character, the construction of which "depends, not on psychological delineation as the primary impetus, but on our absorbing the figure into that space beyond the text, where it can be transformed from a series of linguistic signals and semantic referents into a virtual existent" (Cohan 136). The reader can despise Pablos (or pity him, for that matter) only by knowing him, by relating to him, by likening him to real people.

La vida del buscón invites us to judge the words and actions of the *pícaro*. The ending of the novel focuses on behavior modification, to wit, on Pablos's recognition that personal change comes about from mental resolve as opposed to geographical distance. Pablos has failed in life, he informs us, because he has refused to correct his bad habits. Recalling the narrator's assertion at the close of the first chapter that "yo quería aprender virtud resueltamente, y ir con mis buenos pensamientos adelante" (48), Henry Ettinghausen comments that Pablos "is motivated by the desire to better himself, at first, it seems, morally as well as socially" (127). By the time he chooses the course of delinquency in Alcalá, Pablos "has surrendered whole-heartedly to the values of the *vulgus*. . . . Having once abandoned any idea of virtue, [his] exclusive preoccupation with honour and wealth is made to lead him from one disaster to another. Misfortune pursues him from the moment he decides to 'mejorar su estado' not in a moral but in a purely material and social sense" (Ettinghausen 127–28). Pablos is condemned for giving up admirable goals for selfish ambitions. He is seen as initiating the journey away from his parents with success within his reach, as a function of proper conduct. One may be tempted to question the premises of this argument.

Pablos refers to "learning virtue" and to "lofty thoughts" at the same time that he gives thanks to God for honoring him with such solicitous parents. If this is the basis of his moral imperative, it is rather brief and deflated by context. More important, perhaps, if the reader were to take Pablos at his word, then, is the question of to what or to whom should the moral decline be attributed? Can behavior be separated from experience? Is Pablos's treatment in Segovia, at Cabra's school, on the road to the university, or in Alcalá determined by what he does or by who he is? Is there not a degree of logic in his adoption of a negative identity? The narrative shows how fate conspires against Pablos, yet blame is placed on him. One need not applaud Pablos's delinquency, but the text documents its causes. The *pícaro* is placed in a moral bind: he must recognize his lowly status and resign himself to abuse, or he must seek an identity that will not predispose his neighbors to hate him. The first is the moral path. The second is the road to adversity. The first would mitigate the impact of his story, while the second makes him the subject-turned-object of the lesson. Misfortune pursues Pablos not from the moment of his decision in Alcalá but from the moment of his birth. His seizure of control is only a means by which he can be controlled. As Ettinghausen points out, Pablos's obsession with honor and wealth "*is made to lead him* from one disaster to another." Respectability, for Pablos, is the unattainable other, a prize for which he would have to give up his own alterity. That, of course, is his goal, but deference is arguably the last thing his creator would concede.

In *Telling Stories*, Steven Cohan and Linda M. Shires note that "codes are so much a part of our cultural knowledge that we may often forget that what we are reading *is* a code. Signification occurs through all sorts of 'invisible' codes, some of which define various social divisions, some of which cross them" (115). In a section entitled "Decoding Cultural Meanings," Cohan and Shires suggest that "the origin of a text's many voices, as Barthes says, is 'lost' because, in transmitting cultural meanings, codes locate signification in *ideology*. Ideology is a somewhat difficult term to define because it is primarily evident through its effects. . . . [I]deology is not a system of true or false beliefs and values, a doctrine, so much as it is the means by which culture represents beliefs and values" (133). Analytical readings, in one manner or another, attempt to uncover the codes that inform and energize texts. For a number of reasons, including the acknowledgment of a separate reality constructed of verbal signs, reading is a symbolic activity. Reading is a rhetorical activity, as well, and both symbolism and rhetoric operate dialectically on writer, text, and reader. By posing as autobiography, picaresque narrative brings to the fore the process by which a life is converted into a document, a system of words. Autobiographers are divided selves, and their lives grow as they write. As imaginative literature, the picaresque expands the process to incorporate an author, as other, onto the already fragmented scheme. The rivalry for control of the narrative is affected by the status of the *pícaro* and by the relation of his text with rival fictions.

How do the linguistic codes of *El buscón* relate to ideology, to a shared deep structure? Pablos's idiolect is an intrusion into baroque art. His discourse thus becomes an analogue of his efforts to integrate himself into respectable society. The elegance of the style and the incongruity of this style with both the subject matter and the writing subject serve to alienate the narrator from what is narrated. Pablos is eloquent and ingenious in descriptions that provide humor at his expense and in statements that would verify his suppressed anger (praise of his zealously concerned parents and of the "pious" Don Diego, for example). The disengagement of teller and tale allows us to see rhetoric at work, allows us to see Quevedo at work. The object—the lesson, or moral—of each episode is the return of the overreaching *pícaro* to the margins. In one sense, Quevedo breaches the elitist ideology of the baroque, but only to displace the interloper, who ends by blaming himself for his tribulations. In another sense, he remains faithful to the hierarchy by refusing to cede to Pablos the authority due him as autobiographer. The conceptist slant of the opening chapters announces Quevedo's presence. The mixed messages of the first chapter and the audacity of Pablos's gentlemanly aspirations seem to prompt readers to dissociate themselves from the narrator/protagonist. Irony, not empathy, is the dominant rhetorical tool. Quevedo is less assertive a discursive presence after Pablos succumbs to delinquency, but it is evident who is not only directing but inventing the actions that bring the narrator down.

Picaresque narrative in general departs (doubly so) from a noble intertext. The *pícaro* defies the protocols of idealistic literature, the spiritual confession, and Renaissance humanism, among other models, much as fictional autobiography inverts the premises of its legitimate other. The novels in question do not redefine literary or social decorum but underscore the indecorous, the inappropriate, the ludicrous, and the even the dangerous aspects of change. The narrative situation, like the goal of upward mobility, is inconsistent with established norms. The picaresque exceeds the parameters of change wrought by time. Whereas secular humanism presents man in a new light, for example, the *pícaro* is clearly not the type of individual to be honored by the shift to exemplary souls in this life. True to baroque form, the *Buscón* offers the most extreme case. Pablos seduces and abandons a nun, adding robbery to sacrilege. He joins a band of criminals in Sevilla, and he and his colleagues seek refuge in a church following a street fight with casualties. The man who would be a gentleman challenges the laws of society, as well as divine law. Redemption in the world seems unlikely for Pablos, nor does he appear close to salvation. In the early chapters, when the reader may be inclined to view the *pícaro* with sympathy, Quevedo overpowers the narrator through explosively intricate language and self-deprecatory humor, just as he overpowers the youthful protagonist with beatings, falls, maledictions, and other accoutrements of rejection. Readers may be moved by the account of the first day in Alcalá and perhaps by Pablos's lack of options, but the *pícaro* becomes hardened at a tender age, and his judgment, especially with regard to the selection of alternate "families," is deplorable. The outsider poses a threat to society, and the *Buscón* addresses that threat. The author is not out to reproach Pablos but to excoriate him and those like him who oppose the status quo. Quevedo finds in the picaresque a paradigm of negative exemplarity through which to confront the enemies of the State.

Pablos is most articulate when he alludes to the suppression of his true feelings. The silence of his agony is his strongest defense, for it is the marker of a hidden strain of humanity and of a tortured soul. Pablos's act of rebellion stems from his wish, early in life, to divorce himself from his parents. Quite wisely, he does not want to be like them, but escape is by no means easy. Pablos seems to carry his identity with him, and, when he relinquishes himself of his parents' control, he cannot find a fit master. Don Diego Coronel is a spoiled rich boy who at no point seems to care for Pablos. He does nothing, either in the first part of the novel or in his reappearance near the end, that would corroborate the garland of piety that Pablos confers on him. Friendship and mutual suffering at the hands of Cabra mean little when class consciousness and the master-servant dichotomy intervene. Delinquency in Alcalá takes Pablos from the depths of despair to notoriety, broken by the news of his father's death, the rejection of Don Diego's offer to help him locate a new master, and the return to Segovia. The resounding break from his uncle and the freedom of the road give Pablos a release from the binds of the past—victory in an abstract sense, so to speak—but he is never able to profit from the opportunity. The reason for this failure is obvious. There is no acceptable identity for Pablos other than the one he has refused to consider before leaving Alcalá: that of the dutiful servant, who can only avoid abuse through a figurative disappearance. The mishaps that befall him, from his time with Don Toribio to the experience in the New World, confirm the futility of his dream and the need for society (and for the authorial persona) to preserve deeply rooted ideals.

La vida del buscón is the product of a period, and of an author, that would tend to unite the laws that govern this world and the next. Following Frank Warnke, Malcolm K. Read refers to "the insistence [by baroque writers] on reducing the two worlds to one, by capturing the absolute reality that embraces all phenomena" (*Birth* 162). Whatever the deeper implications of the union, the connection is exceptionally astute from a rhetorical perspective. By equating social law with natural or divine law, the State can justify its hierarchical and exclusionary structure. If it is not the quality of one's role but the quality of the performance that matters—and if roles are God-given—the mechanisms are in place both for social stability and a resistance to change. The *Buscón* illustrates, among other things, the risk of tampering with the premises that determine the order—*en toda la extensión de la palabra*—of the universe. Quevedo and his contemporaries often view the world synecdochically, that is, with the part representing the whole, but it could be argued, I believe, that they insist that the macrocosm conform to the microcosm, not vice versa. Once the secular is linked with the divine, there is less need to rationalize social practice or political ideology, and points of origin may become blurred. Significantly, baroque thought seems to allow morality to emanate from the microcosm as it finds itself empowered by the macrocosm.

The issue, once again, is the moral judgment against Pablos. Is the narrative about a flight from morality or about a moral dilemma? The *Buscón* associates morality with control: the greater Pablos's control over his destiny, the greater his moral responsibility. Throughout the text, we see that people respond to Pablos on the basis of his inherited identity. He is his mother's son, a member of the rabble, a New Christian, an ironic *ecce homo*. His falls are physically and metaphorically intense. Excrement and mucus are reminders of the past and omens of the future. Malcolm Read states that "ontogenetically, Quevedo saw life as an ascent from the body to the soul," such that the individual's progression through life is a gradual rejection of material being in favor of spirituality. "Only with adulthood, however, when rationality blossoms forth, does man assume his true position of eminence in the Creation" (*Visions* 60). One could perhaps make a case, from a spiritual perspective, for Pablos's arrested development. Quevedo's *pícaro* is never able to shed the trappings of his lowly birth. Figuratively, it might be said that the author never allows him to remove himself from the dirt. To do so—or to give Pablos the opportunity to do so—would be to redistribute power. Forward movement comes with maturity and discretion. Pablos's adulthood is spent not in refining his legitimate identity but in fabricating false identities. Quevedo gives him—or he gives himself—no room for reformation, for contemplation, for choosing the spiritual over the mundane. What, then, are his moral options?

No matter how rigorous the ordeals presented by life, each person has the moral responsibility to treat others in as just a manner as possible; abuse should not be answered by abuse. Few readers of the *Buscón* would praise Pablos for his deceptions and misdeeds. Nevertheless, having suffered the slings and arrows of an undeniably outrageous fortune, Pablos makes a somewhat weak moral center. Because all factors—heredity, environment, chance, (Quevedo's) authorial license—conspire against him, he is too easy a target. His actions are too negatively determined, or predetermined, to create a moral balance or even the semblance of suspense. Deprived of space in which to develop, Pablos errs, and the magnitude of his crimes increases with time. Depending on the particular focus of the analysis, the primary topic may be transgression, or it may be the imbalance of elements. The first possibility is metasocial, offering, it would seem, the message that all organs of the State should join to combat threats to the established order. The second is metaliterary, with an eye on the manipulation of narrative recourses. The first directs us toward the author, the second toward the reader. Pablos, mired in the middle, is audible, in great part, by virtue of his ironic silencing. Within this framework, Pablos's topic, or theme, may be suppression, which relates both to the moral (sociopolitical?) admonition and to the usurpation of narrative authority. The *pícaro's* limited space includes, paradoxically, the enunciation of his suppressed feelings.

In a chapter of *Fictional Truth* entitled "Symbolic Systems in Narrative," Michael Riffaterre shows how sustained metaphor and subtext in narrative create a type of poetic truth, as opposed to "truth by verisimilitude" (54). He argues that "significance cannot be produced without first voiding, displacing, or repressing an established meaning, whether this meaning originates in the sociolect or in the context" (83). While Riffaterre's discussion moves toward an unconscious process of encoding, the examples demonstrate calculated efforts to set forth patterns of images or wordplays, as well. *La vida del buscón* fits into the scheme as a double allegory. Quevedo surrounds Pablos's life with falls and scatological excess in order to drive him into—and to associate him with—inescapable materiality. While describing the reversals of fortune that mark his life, Pablos, in turn, presents evidence of his entrapment by the social hierarchy and by Quevedo as defender of the hierarchy. Disgrace characterizes one set of images, obstruction the other. One subtext helps to determine the direction of the narrative, the other its displacement from within. Quevedo's overriding presence and the *Buscón's* rhetoric of irony may turn the text into a manual of its own demystification.

The autobiographer is not a single self but a connecting agent, one who appends, recreates, and grows in the process. In fictional autobiography, we see the making of character, story, and discourse, and, quite probably, we sense the presence of another agent standing above the arrangement of events and of words. The illusion of authority is precisely that: an illusion. Pablos's status and motives may encourage us to read against the grain and, at the same time, may lead us to question the foundations of a counterdiscourse. Quevedo, standard-bearer for social stability, points to the instability of the verbal sign. He may count on the reader to stabilize meanings—to detect the ironic discourse and to recode it appropriately—but he has disturbed the analogy of word and world. One could contend that because Pablos wishes to disrupt the literary order just as he wishes to disrupt the social order, Quevedo's intervention, like society's, is necessary to uphold operative laws. This may be a false parallel, however, given that Pablos has borrowed his discourse and the moral of his story from the author. The *Buscón* becomes a mimetic give-and-take, an object lesson in which the narrator has little claim to freedom, despite the autobiographical format. Mediation is so prominent a feature of the text that the relation between the narrative circumstances and the social circumstances is a function of Quevedo's "heroic" role in Pablos's life. The autobiographer is an outsider with impertinent and potentially harmful goals. Quevedo does not choose to write, on the character's behalf, a treatise in which he makes a case for advancement and which would self-destruct on the basis of its inflammatory premises. He produces, instead, an entertainment, in which the baroque *pícaro* becomes object as well as subject. Pablos ends not only with a number of identities—of selves—but also with a number of voices, the most ironic of which is, perhaps, most truly his own.

Time and human history mediate the criteria by which we assess literature and its diverse components. Societies, in general, have come to modify their views of marginality and of upward mobility. Some now treat difference with greater sensitivity. Culture criticism, which unites literature and society, allows us to see how phenomena, ideas, and words intersect and react against each other. Rhetoric becomes a common denominator and, it could be argued, the ultimate mediator in conflicts of philosophy and ideology. Authority if not lost, is redefined, contextualized. Authors, for their part, if not dead, are decentralized, decentered. As narrator of *La vida del buscón*, Pablos actualizes poststructuralist views of the author, as elaborated, and debated, by Roland Barthes, Michel Foucault, and others. Pablos has ties, for example, with Foucault's "author-function," who, rather than inventing discourses, makes choices from existing systems, and, finally, who becomes one of a series of discourses that comprise the text (see Foucault and, for an overview, Pease). There is a reversal of power at work here, and the new power base is the reader or critic, armed with a neorhetorical curiosity that is rarely distant from skepticism. Pablos's strength lies in his modernity, as manifested in his projection of a different society and in his abject lack of authority. Quevedo represents the old order, whose faith in absolute values—or misreading of relative values—has fallen victim to time and to change, its most notable enemy. Pablos remains in the margins, but these are margins with a difference. Our own distancing devices let us examine the text and the period through multiple angles of vision. The motif of the elusive identity is a mainstay of Pablos's story and of his discourse. The *pícaro*'s vulnerability becomes his strength. In the Unamunian spirit, the creation seems to transcend the creator. This probably would not have displeased Cervantes. It would most assuredly have displeased Quevedo.

Works Cited

Alemán, Mateo. *Guzmán de Alfarache*. Ed. Benito Brancaforte. 2 vols. Madrid: Cátedra, 1979.

Booth, Wayne C. *The Rhetoric of Fiction*. Chicago: Univ. of Chicago Press, 1961.

Casa, Frank P. "Affirmation and Retraction in Golden Age Drama." *Neophilologus* 61 (1977): 551–64.

Cervantes Saavedra, Miguel de. *El ingenioso hidalgo Don Quijote de la Mancha*. Ed. Vicente Gaos. 3 vols. Madrid: Gredos, 1987.

Chatman, Seymour. *Coming to Terms: The Rhetoric of Narrative in Fiction and Film*. Ithaca and London: Cornell Univ. Press, 1990.

———. *Story and Discourse: Narrative Structure in Fiction and Film*. Ithaca and London: Cornell Univ. Press, 1978.

Close, Anthony. *The Romantic Approach to "Don Quixote."* Cambridge: Cambridge Univ. Press, 1978.

Cohan, Steven. "Figures beyond the Text: A Theory of Readable Character in the Novel." *Why the Novel Matters: A Postmodern Perplex*. Ed. Mark Spilka and Caroline McCracken-Flesher. Bloomington and Indianapolis: Indiana Univ. Press, 1990. 113–36.

———, and Linda M. Shires. *Telling Stories: A Theoretical Analysis of Narrative Fiction*. New York and London: Routledge, 1988.

Egido, Aurora. "Retablo carnavalesco del buscón don Pablos (Artículo-reseña)." *Hispanic Review* 46 (1978): 173–97.

Encina [Enzina], Juan del. *Eglogas completas de Juan del Enzina*. Ed. Humberto López-Morales. Madrid: Escelicer, 1968.

Ettinghausen, Henry. *Francisco de Quevedo and the Neostoic Movement.* Oxford: Oxford Univ. Press, 1972.

Foucault, Michel. "What Is an Author?" *Textual Strategies.* Ed. Josué V. Harari. Ithaca: Cornell Univ. Press, 1979. 141–60.

Godzich, Wlad, and Nicholas Spadaccini. "Popular Culture and Spanish Literary History." *Literature among Discourses.* Ed. Wlad Godzich and Nicholas Spadaccini. Minneapolis: Univ. of Minnesota Press, 1986. 41–61.

Iffland, James. "Pablos' Voice: His Master's? A Freudian Approach to Wit in *El Buscón.*" *Romanisches Forschungen* 91 (1979): 215–43.

Johnson, Carroll B. *Inside Guzmán de Alfarache.* Berkeley: Univ. of California Press, 1978.

Lazarillo de Tormes. Ed. Francisco Rico. Madrid: Gredos, 1987.

Mariscal, George. *Contradictory Subjects: Quevedo, Cervantes, and Seventeenth-Century Spanish Culture.* Ithaca and New York: Cornell Univ. Press, 1991.

Pease, Donald E. "Author." *Critical Terms for Literary Study.* Ed. Frank Lentricchia and Thomas McLaughlin. Chicago and London: Univ. of Chicago Press, 1990.

Quevedo, Francisco de. *La vida del buscón llamado don Pablos.* Ed. Fernando Lázaro Carreter. Prologue and notes by Juan Alcina Franch. Barcelona: Juventud, 1968.

Read, Malcolm K. *The Birth and Death of Language: Spanish Literature and Linguistics, 1300–1700.* Potomac, Md.: Studia Humanitatis, 1983.

———. *Visions in Exile: The Body in Spanish Literature and Linguistics, 1500–1800.* Purdue University Monographs in Romance Languages 30. Amsterdam and Philadelphia: John Benjamins, 1990.

Reiss, Timothy J. *The Discourse of Modernism.* Ithaca and London: Cornell Univ. Press, 1982.

Riffaterre, Michael. *Fictional Truth.* Baltimore and London: Johns Hopkins Univ. Press, 1990.

———. *Semiotics of Poetry.* Bloomington: Indiana Univ. Press, 1978.

Smith, Paul. *Discerning the Subject.* Minneapolis: Univ. of Minnesota Press, 1988.

Tölölyan, Khachig. "Discoursing with Culture: The Novel as Interlocutor." In *Why the Novel Matters* 246–56.

Unamuno, Miguel de. *Niebla.* Ed. Mario J. Valdés. Englewood Cliffs, N.J.: Prentice-Hall, 1969.

Vega Carpio, Lope Félix de. *El arte nuevo de hacer comedias en este tiempo.* Ed. Juana de José Prades. Madrid: Consejo Superior de Investigaciones Científicas, 1971.

Warnke, Frank J. *Versions of Baroque.* New Haven: Yale Univ. Press, 1972.

Williamson, Edwin. "The Conflict between Author and Protagonist in Quevedo's *Buscón.*" *Journal of Hispanic Philology* 2 (1977): 45–60.

Chapter 8
Picaresque Elements in Cervantes's Works

Manuel Durán

As I write this essay I am aware that I do so five hundred years after Columbus's first voyage toward the New World. It was virtually impossible to resist an analogy between the invention of the picaresque, a new kind of novel destined to explore social and psychological spaces hitherto unknown, and the travels of exploration and conquest starting in 1492.

In both cases the initial discovery was followed by a period of uncertainty and doubt. Columbus looked in vain for Oriental landmarks and landscapes as described by Marco Polo that he could not possibly find because they were not there. What had he really discovered, and how could his discovery become useful to all? The problem was not solved right away. Similarly, after the initial discovery of new literary lands with *Lazarillo de Tormes* in 1554, a period of confusion follows. Neither the readers, however enthusiastic, nor the critics, and even less the possible imitators of the intriguing, amusing, and disquieting novel knew exactly what to do with it. Hence the long hiatus between the first picaresque novel and its sequel, the full-blown, overlong, fully self-conscious second picaresque novel, *Guzmán de Alfarache*, published in 1598. Forty-four years of silence and infertility (at least in the field of the picaresque novel, since *Lazarillo* did not have a progeny until almost the end of the century) constitute a negative record by any standard, especially given the infectious and enduring vitality the new literary trend was about to acquire.

An explosion of new knowledge, of new facts and new possibilities, is bound to create anguish, chaos, vertigo. After a while an attempt is made to put the pieces together in a rational way and understand what has happened. Exploration is followed by description of the new lands, the drawing of maps, conquest and settlement.

The settlement of the immense lands in the realm of literature opened up by the discovery of the picaresque mode in the novel has lasted until the very present and will probably continue for a long time to come. Opening at random novels by Camilo José Cela, by Günter Grass, by selected American authors (*Fanny,* by Erica Jong, comes to mind) will show us that picaresque attitudes are still very much with us.

Conquest and settlement assume a victory, announcing the creation of an empire. Fortunately for the writer and his or her readers the expansion of literary empires does not entail bloodshed, victims, or slaves. It does frequently upset the system of values that most people had taken for granted, therefore accelerating social change in the short run, political change in the long run. Our modern world owes much to those who, like the creators of the picaresque novel, and like Cervantes, introduced a new sensitivity and changed forever in subtle or obvious ways our way of seeing man and society—a new vision is also a new way of judging and creates often an urge to change things in order to correct the crooked, distorted view that the new sensitivity has surpassed.

After the initial period of confusion and chaos that the increase in information entails seems to abate, another need comes to the fore. It is imperative to consolidate and beautify the land that had been previously discovered and partially explored. Out of the ruins of Tenochtitlán, Mexico City, with its baroque cathedral and its Main Square, is about to emerge.

While this great activity of consolidation and reconstruction goes forward in the Spanish Empire that Columbus and Cortés helped to create, another effort aimed at transforming and beautifying existing structures takes place in an invisible empire, one that we could perhaps call by its eighteenth-century name, the "Republic of Letters." Cervantes is about to rework and rearrange, rethink and transcend, the materials that have been handed to him, and of course to any thoughtful reader and author, by the picaresque Revolution.

It was indeed a revolution: it broke down old taboos related to idealization that had been a part of Western culture since the ancient Greeks, since Phidias and Plato—even before that, since the first systematic idealizations of the human body by Egyptian carvers and relief sculptors. Anything ugly, humble, despised, debased, misshapen, could now be treated seriously and become a source of knowledge and wisdom. Everyday life in its triviality and imperfection was worthy of attention and could become a springboard to wisdom. Thus an omelette made with rotten eggs, eggs in which the chickens are already visible, a shocking, nauseating experience for young Guzmán at the very beginning of his adventures, becomes an image, a paradigm, a summing up of a rotten society in which no one scruples to cheat, to deceive, to rob, to poison, for the sake of a few coins or a feeling of self-esteem, vanity, pride, arrogance. Small, humble, debased objects and people are all around us: we must see them, really see and understand them, if we want to understand the world and our role in it, since the ugly, debased, humble objects and people make up perhaps nine-tenths of what exists and condition the rest.

Cervantes, however, would not agree. Not, at least, wholeheartedly, not without reservations. Perhaps Cervantes remembered that it was not the first time a gloomy vision of the world around us had been offered in a literary work. There was a text considerably older than the *Lazarillo*, a text much admired by Cervantes, who calls it "divine," if only human failings and errors had been more carefully disguised in it. This text is, of course, *La Celestina*, and more specifically its end, the final speech by Pleberio.

A case can be made that the whole of picaresque literature came out of Pleberio's speech. Life, Pleberio claims, is a trap, a bait we swallow without realizing we have also swallowed the hook. Life is a vale of tears. Every moment of hope has to be paid for by many moments of despair. Pleberio's daughter has just committed suicide, and neither Pleberio nor his wife realized until it was too late that Melibea had a secret life her parents knew nothing about. Life is indeed a dark passage, full of ugliness and suffering. Can there be a clearer blueprint for the picaresque novels that are to follow?

Obviously, we may object that *La Celestina* is not a true novel, and moreover that Pleberio's despair has a metaphysical, philosophical, existential quality that bears little resemblance to the urgent problems poverty and low birth introduce in the picaresque novels. Yet many of the gloomy musings of Guzmán parallel Pleberio's statements.

Is it perhaps due to the fact that both Rojas and Alemán are *conversos* who have abandoned the traditional security of their original religion and yet are not quite at ease within the framework of their brand-new Christianity? If this is so, if only *conversos* possess the magic touch that allows them to write true picaresque literature, how are we to explain Quevedo's success, whose *Buscón* exhibits all of the classic characteristics of the genre, and moreover offers wit and cold bitterness beyond all expectation? (We know, of course, that Quevedo is not only a true "Old Christian," but also the most rabid anti-Semite, possibly, that the Spanish Golden Age produced.)

La Celestina, it is true, was not a novel—yet it offered a reader such as Cervantes a literary model that in many respects could be more useful than the example of the picaresque novels. The situations outlined in *La Celestina* are psychologically richer, more varied, than the monotonous misadventures and setbacks that can be found in most picaresque novels. Basically a picaresque text offers us one single viewpoint; it shows us the world through the eyes of its hero, whose personality, problems, and predicament change slowly or not at all. The opposite is true in *La Celestina*. Dialogue is at its very core, and through dialogue we can witness the deep changes that take place in each main character. Duplicity is, for Celestina, the name of the game, and she shows us many facets of her complex personality, many colors, as a chameleon would, before being overtaken by death. Calixto, seen at first as a young lover intoxicated by the lofty feelings and conceits of *cancionero* poetry, will later become a young man totally dominated by his sexual urge, who will almost rape Melibea, tearing off her clothes and justifying his actions with the coarse comparison that one has to pluck a bird in order to eat it. Both Pármeno and Sempronio change in the course of the play. Briefly, the message is one of dynamic interaction and deep change in the behavior and personality of the characters, a secondary message being that of misunderstanding. Neither Calixto nor Melibea nor even clever Celestina fully hears what the other characters say; they hear only or mostly what they want to hear.

Obviously *La Celestina* offers also many instances of what we might call *ur*-picaresque characters and situations. The banquet at Celestina's house is not only a possible parody of Plato's *Symposium* but also a clear vision of the world as seen from below, by characters such as Areusa who are full of resentment at the advantages that a young lady, Melibea, has been granted by society or destiny.

Briefly, Cervantes could find in *La Celestina* a text so rich and complex that practically all the elements needed for a novel as sophisticated and innovative as *Don Quixote* can be found in it: idealization, parody, misunderstandings, slow changes of mind, evolution of characters, interaction among characters, dialogue, a sad yet illuminating ending, and, of course, a profusion of "lowly" details, characters, and situations. These are building blocks that the picaresque novels would later appropriate and standardize. The only drawback, yet a considerable one, was that *La Celestina* was not a true novel.

Let us now try to identify ourselves with Cervantes as he must have felt in 1598. *Guzmán de Alfarache* had just appeared, Cervantes had read it and enjoyed it, and he was also aware of the instant success of that novel. It had become almost from the very beginning what we would call today a "best-seller," just what Cervantes needed to write, what he must have prayed for, the only possible solution to his anguishing economic situation. Cervantes was in need of a clear literary success. It would have been easy for him, given his talent, to write a novel very much like the *Guzmán,* not necessarily a sequel to it, simply a good picaresque novel patterned after it.

No writer works in a vacuum. Literary tradition always stands behind the writer, providing him or her with models and building blocks, with materials to be recycled and used once more. This is still true today but was especially true during the Middle Ages and the Renaissance: imitation was not only not frowned upon, it was encouraged. Literature was seen as a continuum, and the good writer could insert himself into it only by acknowledging the existence of literary traditions and attaching his own works to the wave of time that continued and preserved such literary traditions. It is only after the Romantic experience that writers search deliberately for the new, the original, the pristine word, the dream never before dreamed, the character absent from every previous novel, and plunge "au fond de l'Inconnu pour trouver du nouveau," according to the Baudelairian prescription. Cervantes was not averse to come to terms with literary tradition, but he also had found certain artistic principles that he was not about to forsake. The use of picaresque materials, situations, and characters could give his works a most necessary fashionable look, yet such materials had to be handled in such a way that they could be integrated into a more complex literary structure. Perhaps an example taken from the discipline of art history will show more clearly what, according to my interpretation, Cervantes had in mind when, after reading *Guzmán de Alfarache,* he was getting ready to start *Don Quixote.*

All along the sixteenth century tension grows between two approaches to the plastic arts, and especially painting. On the one hand, the Italian style, with its refined, idealized figures set in a framework dominated by symmetry, true perspective, and allusions to classical antiquity. Leonardo, Raphael, Michelangelo, and Titian are among the high priests of this style, which becomes more and more fashionable and slowly invades the rest of Europe. On the other hand, in Northern Europe, especially in Germany and Flanders, a realism still rooted in the Gothic world gives birth to robust, down-to-earth pictures of everyday life, often without any attempt at idealization. A good example of this style can be found in the paintings of Pieter Bruegel. In sixteenth-century Flanders the legacy of the Middle Ages was strong. The primary aim of art was still to preach Christian morality or instill pious feelings. Man was seen as clumsy and small, his habitual follies ruthlessly exposed. Everything in his paintings is to be judged and enjoyed both as a symbol and as an accurate portrayal of real life. Bruegel's canvases stir with life, everyday life devoid of glamour, with man working at worldly enterprise—but doomed to final failure. There is scarcely a hint of personal feeling in any of his paintings and never any appeal for the viewer's sympathy. Bruegel's cripples, his beggars, his blindmen tumbling into a ditch are just there, part of the world as it is. This, Bruegel seems to say, is the world. This is man. Take him or leave him if you can. There is a feeling of malaise and pessimism in many of his canvases that relates them to the Spanish picaresque novels. A close friend of Bruegel's, the scientist and mapmaker Abraham Ortelius, makes his pessimistic views clear enough in letters kept secret at the time: "We live in a very disordered time, which we have little hope of seeing soon improved. The patient [Flanders, or probably all of Western Europe] will soon be entirely prostrate, being threatened with so many and various illnesses, as the Catholic evil, the *Gueux* fever [that is, the rebellious Protestant Dutch] and the Huguenot dysentery."[1] Or, to put it in other words, a pox on both your houses. Pieter Bruegel probably agreed with him. It is quite probable that Bruegel took no sides at all, and that, like the philosopher Erasmus, he disapproved of all violence committed in the name of Christianity, by Calvinists and Catholics alike.[2] Erasmus, whose influence upon Spanish thought and letters was thoroughly researched by Marcel Bataillon many years ago, seems to have influenced Bruegel, the anonymous author of *Lazarillo de Tormes*, and also Cervantes.

Grotesque elements, as well as the acceptance of ugliness as part of everyday life, came to characterize many Flemish and German painters, although their attitude in turn was sternly criticized by Italian artists:

> Flemish use of perspective, it was pointed out, was determined more by rule of thumb than anything else and fell far short of Italian geometric exactitude. Flemish handling of the human figure too, far from being noble and stately, was sometimes downright grotesque. Flemish Virgins, notably those by the Master of Flémalle and Memling, were often dumpy-looking and pale as a poached fish. Hugh van der Goes's Eve, naked in the Garden of Eden, was plainly pot-bellied and stringy. Such things were entirely against Italian Renaissance principles. It was not long before the greatest artist and most powerful personality of the South, Michaelangelo himself, was denigrating the Flemish fondness for chatty detail and for painting everyday things as

they are. "Their paintings," he observed in conversations collected by the Portuguese artist Francesco da Hollanda, "are of stuffs, bricks, mortar, the grass of the fields, the shadows of trees . . . and little figures here and there. And all this, though it may appear good in some eyes, is in truth done without . . . symmetry or proportion."[3]

The struggle between Platonic idealization and realistic caricature took place in the mind of Cervantes not once but throughout his career as a writer. We must not forget his Italian experiences, his love for Renaissance Italian literature, and the fact that his first novel, *La Galatea,* published in 1585, is a pastoral novel, with all the idealization and rhetoric that the pastoral genre entails. Four days before his death, while writing the preface to his *Persiles,* he still remembers fondly his first novel and hopes to write an addition or second part to it if God allows him a few months of life. We can find pastoral subjects and descriptions in several of his works, especially in *Don Quixote,* where pastoral themes in a literary framework appear in the episode of Marcela and Grisóstomo, and a rustic pastoral scene is described in the chapters dealing with Camacho's wedding. A great Spanish critic, Américo Castro, has pointed out that "the pastoral subjects are ideologically and aesthetically essential to Cervantes" (190).

Yet the same Cervantes who praises the nobility and harmony of pastoral life is capable of approaching this same world with mocking irony. In *El coloquio de los perros* one of the dogs, Berganza, who has lived among shepherds, comes to the conclusion that pastoral novels lie, for shepherds in real life do not sing beautiful songs accompanied by bagpipes, violins, and other musical instruments, but rather scream or grunt, and pass the time killing the fleas that infest them and mending their muddy rustic sandals.

Cervantes's mind is, we have to assume, extremely complex. The opposition between lofty ideals and everyday life with all its imperfections and even its ugliness is a problem that cannot be totally solved by Cervantes and will become a part of his worldview during all his career. There are problems that cannot be made to disappear, yet they stimulate the creative mind, helping us to create a new, more subtle, more complex image of the world around us. Cervantes did believe in an ideal reality, one that could be as real as everyday reality. In it one could find a myriad of perfect values, all worthy of his admiration and his attention, even if they were reflected only in part, only imperfectly, in the everyday world in which we all must live. But this ideal world was to be found only in the mind of the artist, the philosopher, the lover, all exceptional beings, and to enter this ideal world was both an exhilarating experience and a discouraging limitation, since it meant giving up on the world of everyday events, the world that for most of Cervantes's contemporaries was the only real world.

Cervantes could not be entirely satisfied by being inside the world of idealization and high moral values, yet being outside it was felt by him as a loss, almost a fall into a private hell. Hence the need to ironize and criticize both worlds. We have seen how the pastoral is mocked in *El coloquio de los perros*. Yet, we may conclude, perhaps a dog is not the best judge of the world of shepherds and shepherdesses: perhaps there is more to the pastoral world than meets the eye of a dog.

All along his literary career, from his first novel to his last, Cervantes will experiment with two opposing forces, the idealizing attitude with roots in the Italian Renaissance and courtly love, and the world of caricature, want, cruelty, and petty crime with medieval roots. We must emphasize, of course, the continued presence of the second force, the picaresque elements, in the author's life, in his total experience, from boyhood to old age.

Yet there was for him, Cervantes the avid reader, another world. Cervantes was an admiring reader of Garcilaso, and no doubt had also read Petrarch, Sannazaro, Ariosto, in their original Italian text, as well as Jorge de Montemayor and Gaspar Gil Polo, the creators of the Spanish pastoral novel, in Spanish, together with hundreds of texts permeated with courtly love, Platonic idealization, fantasy, a quest for beauty and truth. Cervantes had written love poetry and a pastoral novel. On the other hand, he had known thieves and pimps while in jail, or perhaps out of jail while in Seville, and his descriptions of the Seville underworld in *Rinconete y Cortadillo* ring true.

Two worlds in opposition that somehow seem to coexist in Cervantes's mind and experience: one might be tempted to compare them to matter and antimatter, which are supposed to destroy each other on contact.

Cervantes will avoid such a dangerous contact by conducting a series of experiments in which idealization and the picaresque are brought close to each other in limited quantities and different proportions.

His main experiment, one that turned out to be totally successful, consists in placing idealization and the picaresque face to face, making them confront each other, but in a privileged space where whatever happens cannot affect us directly since we are far removed from such a space, protected from it by an invisible barrier. This privileged secluded space is of course the mind, and the vital experiences, of a madman. We can examine the clashing principles inside the mind and the adventures of Don Quixote without being involved in the painful surprises and constant readjustments this clash entails: after all, we are mere spectators of a unique event, one that cannot be repeated in our own mind and our own experience. Similarly, another great Spaniard, Velásquez, will allow idealized, exquisite beauty and misshapen, grotesque ugliness to confront each other in his most famous painting, *Las Meninas*, where the young Spanish princess is shown very close to a dwarf: this happens also in a privileged space, the royal court of the Spanish Hapsburgs, a place where the whim of kings and princes overrules all principles of aesthetics and harmony.

There is another characteristic of picaresque novels that must have intrigued Cervantes: the fact that they are "open works," without a clear conclusion, lacking a definite end. Their characters remain restless, ready to depart for a new adventure like Quevedo's Pablos, who announces a voyage to the New World in the last page of the novel, and lets us know that the results of his American adventures were not happy, as it was to be feared, since he had changed his surroundings without getting rid of his roguish behavior.

Neither *Lazarillo* nor *Guzmán* ends in ways that could be considered satisfactory to a reader or a writer examining them under the guidance of Aristotle's *Poetics*. For Aristotle a literary work reaches perfection only if the fable turns around one single action, whole and complete, having a beginning, a middle, and an end. Picaresque novels, with their truncated endings, would be shapeless and monstrous when judged by an Aristotelian. Was Cervantes an Aristotelian in his own writings, as we have been told so many times during the past thirty years? The problem is much more complex than it appears at first.

Among the galley slaves that Don Quixote frees in Chapter 22 of Part I is a famous rogue, Ginés de Pasamonte, also known as Ginesillo de Parapilla. He has written the story of his life, and a fine book it is: "It is so good . . . that Lazarillo de Tormes will have to look out, and so will everything in that style that has ever been written or ever will be." Don Quixote then asks Ginés if his book is finished. "How can it be finished," replies Ginés, "if my life isn't?"

It is fitting that the picaresque novel being written by Ginés de Pasamonte should remain unfinished, just as unfinished as the other canonic picaresque novels of the Golden Age, and should be described by its author as such, in a manner that recalls Umberto Eco's definition of an "opera aperta." Yet what can we say about the end of *Don Quixote, Part I?*

It is obvious today, and was equally obvious to Cervantes's contemporary readers, that the end of Part I remains open. We do not know exactly what happened to Don Quixote and Sancho. Don Quixote's death has been reported, yet in an uncertain way. His epitaph has been written, but this fact in itself proves nothing. Moreover, Cervantes himself invites other writers to continue Don Quixote's adventures in his quotation of Ariosto: "For's altri canterà . . . con miglior plettro. Perhaps somebody else will sing Don Quixote's song, or ballad, with a better voice than Cervantes himself. (Obviously Cervantes regretted this quotation more than once, as soon as Avellaneda's novel appeared: Cervantes had openly invited someone else, anyone else, to continue his novel, and Avellaneda had accepted the challenge.)

Considering the results of Part I having been left open at the end it is not surprising, and on the contrary it is totally predictable, that Cervantes would take great pains to close Part II of his novel as tightly as possible, with Don Quixote's last will and testament, his death, and the admonition to any future novelist that Don Quixote was created by Cervantes and no one else should attempt to write anything on this subject.

Our first conclusion must be that Cervantes learns from the picaresque novels the art of leaving his novels open-ended. Not only *Don Quixote, Part I,* also *Rinconete y Cortadillo,* another work by

Cervantes in which the picaresque elements are paramount, remains open at the end, against the best Aristotelian advice.

Which does not mean, of course, that Cervantes approves the picaresque attitude, philosophy, and character creation (or should we say character deformation). On the contrary. He makes use of fragments, materials taken from the picaresque quarry, without building a picaresque house for his own characters. Since he does not reject picaresque materials, for he finds them useful and much in demand among his contemporary readers, and yet he considers them ultimately unacceptable, debasing, even abhorrent, he is forced to neutralize them the best way he can. One of the devices he uses is to take away the sting of the "pícaro" by turning him into an artificial character, a masked figure worthy of a carnival ball. This is what happens in the short novel (or long short story, or "novella") *La Ilustre fregona.*

The tale is relatively simple: two young men belonging to noble families leave home, pretending to go to Flanders to fight in the war, and actually disguise themselves as "Pícaros." They are eager to live the adventurous life of the "Pícaros," but Cervantes underlines that they are the sons of noble and rich gentlemen, and under their rags they hide bags of gold doubloons. These young men, Carriazo and Avendaña, are playing the picaresque game, just as much as Don Quixote plays the game of chivalry, but they only resemble Don Quixote in his moments of lucidity in Part II and are in any case much less complex than the "Ingenioso Hidalgo" of Cervantes's great novel. Their role is often that of "voyeurs," taking part in picaresque life without being totally submerged in it, always aware of the possibility of getting out of the picaresque atmosphere, a privilege that is not given to any true "Pícaro" by the authors of true picaresque novels. Yet they are reluctant to leave the Toledo inn they have reached because one of them, Avendaño, has fallen in love with a beautiful girl, Constanza, who works at the inn polishing silver. The young men accept to work at the inn, one of them taking care of horses, the other one of water supplies, and as love develops, Avendaño serenades Constanza and writes love poems for her (which will be discovered by the innkeeper among a list of supplies for the inn's horses) while a rich tapestry of picaresque life unfolds before the eyes of Cervantes's readers.

We examine the ceaseless activity of many rogues, guided by the attraction of money or sex, plotting swindles or rehearsing erotic dances, yet it is all a spectacle, a game, a show that our young heroes enjoy from the outside without being actually full partners of the picaresque game. The end is predictably both happy and contrived, since Constanza turns out to be the daughter of a noble lady, our young men's parents finally reach the inn looking for them, and Constanza and Avendaño get married in the final pages and fade into the sunset of wedded bliss.

Angel Valbuena Prat classifies *La Ilustre fregona* as "realistic-idealistic," in an oxymoronic definition that means that realistic observations about everyday life are mingled with a Platonic conception of love. *La Gitanilla* is, according to Valbuena Prat, another example of this mixture. I agree that the mixture exists, and I suspect such a mixture points to the core of Cervantes's approach to the art of fiction, as a generous effort to embrace and transcend opposites and contradictions. Cervantes does not deny the existence of picaresque situations and characters, yet does his best to redeem or go beyond them through wit, irony, or love, and if it is not possible to turn the picaresque into something made of nobler ingredients Cervantes will always create a door or a window through which his characters can escape the picaresque prison if they really wish to do so, for Cervantes truly believes in freedom, and through this belief, which he infuses into each one of the characters he creates, he subverts or destroys the very foundation of the picaresque world.

I would now hazard a guess, or perhaps a hypothesis, not susceptible of complete proof, yet a plausible hypothesis. It is this: of all the characters created by him, Cervantes must have felt closer to someone like the young heroes of *La Ilustre fregona.* He must have, in any case, envied them, he must have wished his life had been like theirs. Cervantes, the son of a "shabby-genteel" family, had been too close to the picaresque atmosphere from the very beginning of his life. Poverty, debts, hasty displacements in order to avoid debtors, were very much a part of his childhood memories. Later on, once more poverty, debts, together with long months spent in jail, wanderings in southern Spain staying at country or city inns that attracted thieves and pimps: Cervantes's adventurous existence brought him in and out of the picaresque milieu, too close for comfort and at the same time looking at it from his own protected, fortress-like inner self, a mixture of ironic detachment and amused curiosity. Perhaps, when we are trying to define the relationship between Cervantes and the picaresque characters offered in abundance by his society and his contemporary novelists, the key word is "curiosity," which implies both interest and detachment, sympathy and superiority.

As a novelist, Cervantes is an active member of what Marshall McLuhan has called "the Gutenberg Galaxy." A consequence can be easily deduced from the very bulk of many Renaissance novels (*Guzmán de Alfarache* and *Don Quixote* come easily to mind), as opposed to the much more slender appearance of a book of poetry, and that is the role that technology, in the specific shape of Gutenberg's printing press, played in the development of the novel in modern times. A lengthy novel seems to demand the presence of a printer who with his printing press will make the novel available to a large public; copying a long novel by hand is exceedingly tedious and will result in a small number of expensive copies. The novel was from the beginning a democratic genre and was written for the masses of readers, young and old, but especially young, that the schools of the Late Middle Ages and early Renaissance were beginning to mass-produce.

Another distinctive feature of the modern European novel, born at the crossroads between medieval and Renaissance times, is that it was born not only democratic but also Christian. In his brilliant book of critical essays on realism in Western literatures, *Mimesis,* published first in German in 1946 and translated into English in 1953, Erich Auerbach shows how Christianity's strong belief that the souls of all sorts and conditions of men are potentially of equal value produced a narrative tradition very different from the classical literary theory of the separation of styles, according to which serious treatment was restricted to "noble" subject matter, while everyday reality and humble people were considered appropriate only for comic or satiric treatment. We find servant women treated with the utmost interest and respect in great Western novels, from Joanot Martorell's *Tirant lo Blanc* to Benito Pérez Galdós's *Misericordia,* in which the servant Benina often takes center stage and at the end forgives her mistress with words that remind us of the New Testament. Tolstoy, Balzac, and Proust will write some of their best pages about characters that we might consider socially unimportant.

A small masterpiece close to the picaresque genre is the novelette *Rinconete y Cortadillo*. It allows us a close-up of the underworld of Seville in the late sixteenth century, as seen through the eyes of two runaways who hope to find an easy life in it. What they find is initially astonishing: a picaresque organization that is run like a successful corporation, with a first-rate chairman of the board whose name is Monipodio and who supervises everybody's transgressions. Policemen are bribed, even saints and heavenly patrons are duly appeased. Members help each other. The inescapable conclusion is that on the whole the underworld is better run, more harmonious, even more productive, than the "normal" society around it.

We feel almost from the first page the honesty and accuracy of Cervantes's portrait of the Seville mafia. He had been there, both inside and outside the jails of Seville, and his firsthand contact is obvious in the way he handles the rogue's language and describes the situations in which they develop their tricks.

Yet there are noteworthy differences between Cervantes's text and the most typical picaresque novels. Perhaps the most outstanding difference is that Cervantes's novelette is not written in the first person, as Juan Luis Alborg underlines: the very existence of a dialogue between the two main characters separates Cervantes's novelette from the picaresque literary norm.[4]

What Rinconete and Cortadillo achieve is exactly the opposite of what Lázaro or Guzmán do: the young heroes of Cervantes's novelette observe, judge, compare; finally one of them abandons the picaresque life, which he has found wanting, and goes home, while his friend, who has taken a liking to his new existence, remains in Seville and will become with time a full-fledged *pícaro*. Decisions such as the ones taken by these boys imply a high degree of inner freedom, which is always lacking in the true picaresque hero. This has been remarked by Joaquín Casalduero, for whom the essential fact is that the two lads depicted by Cervantes have not lost control over their own destinies.[5] Both critics agree thus with Menéndez y Pelayo, who in "Cultura literaria de Miguel

de Cervantes y elaboración del Quijote" points out the independence of Cervantes's art vis-à-vis the picaresque viewpoints:
Cervantes is a "genre painter," inspired by real-life models, not by
a fixed ideology such as the picaresque literature assumes.[6]

The psychological traits that allow Cervantes to turn mud into
gold in his narrative are above all a stubborn optimism, a faith in
himself and also in mankind in general, a great deal of tolerance,
bordering on cynicism, and above all a spirit of forgiveness that
excuses vice when it is a by-product of the general corruption of
society. Perhaps Monipodio and his gangsters are not only pic-
turesque but mirror, as would a distorting convex mirror, the corruption of the so-called normal society.

Another neutralizing agent that destroys or eliminates the
acids of the picaresque is humor, especially when combined with
irony and farce, which are the main ingredients of *El casamiento engañoso*. Lieutenant Campuzano is not only a rogue who marries
doña Estefanía de Caicedo because he falls in love with the contents of her hope chest, which he estimates is at least two thousand
five hundred gold ducats, but also a "miles gloriosus" that Plautus
would have applauded, a braggart such as the one Cervantes
paints in one of his satirical sonnets. The whole plot of this
"novella" would have pleased Boccaccio. After the wedding doña
Estefanía disappears, taking with her Camnpuzano's meager
earthly goods. The deceiver has been deceived, and on top of this
misadventure he is now infected with a sexually transmitted disease that he is trying to get rid of through a sweating cure at the
hospital.

Closer to the traditional picaresque fiction is the second part of
this "novella," *El coloquio de los perros*, since one of the dogs,
Berganza, narrates his adventures in the first-person singular, and
the other dog, Cipión, plays the role of enlightened and judicious
listener. Much like Lázaro or Guzmán, Berganza has served many
masters and traveled a great deal. He is now in a position to reveal
the cheating and lying that permeate Spanish society. Most probably Cervantes wrote this "novella" soon after settling in Valladolid, when his memories of the Seville jail and its inmates were
still fresh in his mind. Satire and social criticism are perhaps more
biting in this text than in any other by Cervantes. Yet the effect is

one of unreality. Time and time again we are reminded that it is two dogs that are speaking, and the fact that Campuzano is feverish and has taken strong medicine may indicate to the reader that probably he has imagined the dogs' dialogue. This in turn means that the criticism of Spanish society is not backed up by the direct experience of the narrator, if we assume Campuzano imagines the tale, or, if the dogs really speak, how much do dogs understand about the human world, how well can they judge it? The sting remains, yet the problem of who speaks and who has lived through the fascinating adventures told in the dialogue softens some of the sharp edges of Cervantes's satire.

For if the dogs speak we are dealing with a miracle, and like any miracle it is quite inexplicable. The very tale that unfolds supposedly picaresque situations "falls under the category of those things they call miracles," as Cervantes puts it. We are now beginning to suspect that Cervantes's tale, instead of being a picaresque text, is on the contrary a satire of all picaresque literature. As Carlos Blanco Aguinaga points out, "It is not difficult to see the jest implied in the fact that the attempts at moralizing are put in the mouth of a dog who, because he can miraculously speak, thinks that he is more intelligent than he is and that he has the right to judge" (144).

Berganza thinks he knows so much that he can judge everything and everybody (just as Guzmán de Alfarache had been doing all through the pages of the novel that bears his name), but Cipión corrects him and tries to instill in him some humility: "Just look at your paws," he says to him, "and you'll stop playing the dandy, Berganza. What I mean is that you should realize that you are an animal lacking in reason, and if for the moment you show some reason, we have already settled between the two of us that it is a supernatural and unprecedented thing." Cipión's final advice to Berganza is also an appeal to moderation and humility, reminding him that our knowledge is relative and our place in this world a modest one: "You see, Berganza, no one should intrude where he is not invited, nor should he ever undertake anything not within his competence." "It would seem, then, that the Colloquy is hardly a burlesque of the pastoral novel; it is rather a parody of the picaresque novel as a dogmatic and self-complacent form. In its formal and thematic 'realism' the picaresque is as ideal, absolute and fixed as the chivalric novel is in its: the naturalistic novel and the idealistic novel thus stand in contrast to the objective realism of Cervantes whose spirit does not allow, either in theme or form, any fixity. At the ultimate bottom of the box of several bottoms that is the *Deceitful Marriage* and *Colloquy of the Dogs* (in the Prologue Cervantes himself calls his novels 'a game of billiards') we encounter, among other things, a frontal critique of the way of writing novels [the picaresque way] which Cervantes *seems* to have followed" (Blanco Aguinaga 144–45).

There is no doubt that Cervantes acknowledged the existence, the power, the influence of picaresque novels. He read them and understood their message, and his admiration for a text that may have inspired them, *La Celestina,* he stated clearly.

The picaresque novels had sharpened the vision of Cervantes's contemporaries by describing characters and situations that had remained previously beyond the pale of Literature. Once more we should acknowledge that the Renaissance was a culture, whether in Italy, in France, in Spain, or elsewhere, given to extreme ideal-izations, class distinctions, and basic all-encompassing snobbery —and inasmuch as the picaresque novels introduce a new subject, the life of the humble, the poor, the oppressed, even if they are painted as debased criminals, these novels are bound to enlarge our sensitivity and our awareness of a complex world in which even the picaroons have a role to play. They are a counterweight to the excessive idealizations of the pastoral genre and courtly love.

It is possible, therefore, to state in conclusion that the pi-caresque texts that Cervantes read were both necessary to his cre-ative endeavors and also insufficient. Much of what he found in them must have excited his sensitivity and his imagination, yet many of the situations, literary techniques, and characters in the picaresque novels must have seemed to him deficient, incomplete, one-sided. Two important recent books dealing with Spanish pi-caresque fiction are helpful in delineating Cervantes's debt to the picaresque mode and also point out the many ways in which Cervantes's art transcends the picaresque tradition.

Peter N. Dunn's *Spanish Picaresque Fiction: A New Literary History* attempts to soften, even blur, the contrast between Cervantes's art and the picaresque tradition, underlining instead the complexity of the picaresque texts, the divergent strains in picaresque writing, and ultimately the important influence they exerted upon Cervantes: "without *Lazarillo* and *Guzmán* he could not have written *Rinconete y Cortadillo* or the *Coloquio de los perros* or *La ilustre fregona*" (219). Dunn is harshly critical of Carlos Blanco Aguinaga's 1957 article in which he identifies the picaresque completely with Alemán, since, according to Dunn, *Guzmán* "is not the determinist tract that it is often represented to be; the protagonist's message to his readers is 'If I could break free from my inheritance and my circumstance, so can you'" (208–9). Yet, in spite of his efforts to find picaresque elements in Cervantes's works, he is compelled to admit the basic divergence between Cervantes's art and the picaresque as seen in Alemán: "It is likely that Cervantes found *Guzmán* objectionable for its preaching and for its direct haranguing of the reader, two procedures that he never employed without irony, or without the mediation of a different voice" (218). Dunn goes on to point out that one of the triumphs of Cervantes's art is the play of many voices, a polyphony to which the voice of the narrator is subtly responsive, varying its own tone and distance. "With his vocation for theater, Cervantes was not inclined to allow a single voice either to define the imagined world or to hold uncontested sway over it" (219). It is therefore not surprising that Cervantes did not follow *Lazarillo* and *Guzmán* in adopting the first-person narration throughout, "for to have done so would have deprived him of the opportunity for multiple perspectives and narratorial comment" (219). The influence of the picaresque is ultimately felt with anxiety by Cervantes, yet wittily sublimated: Dunn quotes with approval Joaquín Casalduero's phrase, "Cervantes skirts the picaresque without wanting to plunge right in" (219).

Finally, in *Celestina's Brood: Continuities of the Baroque in Spanish and Latin American Literature*, Roberto González Echevarría devotes a long chapter (pages 45–65) to the relationship between Cervantes and the picaresque. His point of departure is Harry Sieber's interpretation of *Lazarillo*. Sieber, in *Language and Society in La Vida de Lazarillo de Tormes*, sees in young Lázaro a lad trying (and succeeding) to survive by means of adjusting to social pressures and changes by mastering the codes of language and society. The greatest value in Sieber's book, González Echevarría points out, is the way in which he underlines the major preoccupation in the picaresque: the emergence of writing and its relation to authority. Lázaro subverts and preserves authority at the same time. He learns enough from the blindman to blind him, but his own authority at the end is based on his own willed blindness to his wife's infidelity (González Echevarría 53). González Echevarría goes on to state: "though Cervantes never wrote a picaresque following Alemán's model, he did leave a complex critique of how this new literature was changing the rules of the game" (53–54). In *El casamiento engañoso* and *El coloquio de los perros* Cervantes "reveals how the picaresque has an inner connectedness provided by the way in which the turning points of a picaresque *vida* allude, through appeal to a metaphoric field drawn for sexuality, to the origin and disposition of writing" (57). By uncovering the metaphoric stratum in the picaresque text, Cervantes lays bare a contradiction at the core of this new form of writing: it pretends to be a legal document, related to truth and authority, yet its inner connections remit us to literature, not to the outside world of power and authority. Thus Cervantes has reached a sort of "metapicaresque." Whether his attitude may be described as parody or metapicaresque, both González Echevarría's conclusions and those of other critics seem to validate Casalduero's basic idea: Cervantes surveys the picaresque, goes around it, inspects it, but never fully plunges into its core, its system of values, its technical and ethical approach to literature, and to the description of man's relationship to society and the cosmos.

Looking back to the beginning of this essay, to the role of the discovery and conquest of the Americas by Columbus, Cortés, Pizarro, and so many others, a process that can be described also as an "encounter of cultures" in which both sides fight each other but also learn from each other, groping toward a synthesis that has eluded us yet tantalizes us and appeals to us from the future, we can place the picaresque novels on the side of the fight and the conquest of a new space, a new awareness. Conquests do not take place without bloodshed and destruction. The picaresque novels created a new space for literature, yet the realism they defined was only part of what realism could be. Ideology was a hidden luggage that picaresque writers carried into literature. Sometimes the target of their ideology was the establishment, the status quo, the very fabric of society with its centers of power and oppression. A strong attraction for utopias of all kinds is a characteristic trait of Renaissance thought. The picaresque novel may have produced the shadow image of the many positive Utopias created in Renaissance times, a negative Utopia that in its humble way attempted to validate the positive Renaissance utopias that never came to life. If the world as the picaresque authors describe is so bad, so corrupted, it is perhaps because it is the mirror image, inverted and distorted, of a much better world, the opposite world of Platonic ideas and Christian principles. It offers us a clear-cut choice, a smooth flat image, a "yes-or-no" approach to our view of the world.

Cervantes, on the other hand, gives us an ambiguous multifaceted presentation of lives coming into being, influencing each other, coming to terms with each other, coexisting, evolving before our eyes. Realism is not absolute truth versus false illusion, but rather uncertain, free, unforeseeable life unfolding in time, without a single point of view presented in advance, accepting doubt and uncertainty, giving ugliness, physical and moral ugliness, its place besides idealized Platonic beauty and integrating both in an overview that could be called a synthesis but is too fluid and changing to admit of a single definition. Cervantes is thus not Columbus, discovering uncharted land, which is precisely what the writers of picaresque novels had already achieved, but Cortés, subduing the new lands, bringing them closer to the old metropolis, and transforming them in an enduring way. His conquest and transformation of the picaresque lands will be acknowledged later by Fielding, Stendhal, Flaubert, Galdós, and many other great novelists. The empire created by him in the lands of the novel has turned out to be more durable even than the empire conquered by Cortés: it has lasted almost four centuries and it remains even today prosperous and expanding.

Notes

1. Quoted by Timothy Forte, *The World of Bruegel* (New York: Time-Life Books, 1968) 99.

2. Forte 99.

3. Forte 17.

4. "Por su ambiente y protagonistas bien se ve que *Rinconete y Cortadillo* pertenecen al mundo de la novela picaresca. En líneas generales, así es. Pero Cervantes, que tantos préstamos tomó de todos los moldes literarios de su tiempo, los rompía cada vez al henchirlos con su propia fuerza y medida. De la narración picaresca habitual se diferencia el *Rinconete* en aspectos formales, o de técnica más bien diríamos: estos pícaros cernantinos no cuentan su propia vida, según norma creada por el *Lazarillo* y seguida por todos los demás" (Alborg 91).

5. "Parece que nos encontramos en el mundo de la picaresca, pero observamos que Rincón y Cortado no son pacientes, sino agentes de la acción. En la picaresca se nos presenta siempre al hombre en su choque con la vida, adquiriendo una experiencia a costa de su dolor. Indefenso, en su salida al mundo, en su nacer, la vida le despierta y abre los ojos para que, echando una mirada a su alrededor, contemple la bajeza y villanía humana" (Casalduero 103–4).

6. "La novela picaresca es independiente de él [Cervantes], se desarrolló antes que él, camina por otros rumbos: Cervantes no la imita nunca, ni siquiera en *Rinconete y Cortadillo,* que es un cuadro de género tomado directamente del natural, no una idealización de la astucia famélica como *Lazarillo de Tormes,* ni una profunda psicología de la vida extrasocial como *Guzmán de Alfarache.* Corre por las páginas de *Rinconete* una intensa alegría, un regocijo luminoso, una especia de indulgencia estética que depura todo lo que hay de feo y de criminal en el modelo" (Menéndez y Pelayo I: 398–399).

Works Cited

Alborg, Juan Luis. *Cervantes.* Madrid: Gredos, 1966.

Blanco Aguinaga, Carlos. "Cervantes and the Picaresque Mode." *Cervantes: A Collection of Critical Essays.* Ed. Lowry Nelson Jr. Englewood Cliffs, N.J.: Prentice-Hall, 1969.

Casalduero, Joaquín. *Sentido y forma de las Novelas Ejemplares.* Buenos Aires: Imprenta y Casa Editora Coni, 1943.

Castro, Américo. *El pensamiento de Cervantes.* Madrid, 1925.

Dunn, Peter N. *Spanish Picaresque Fiction: A New Literary History.* Ithaca and New York: Cornell Univ. Press, 1993.

González Echevarría, Roberto. *Celestina's Brood: Continuities of the Baroque in Spanish and Latin American Literature.* Durham and London: Duke Univ. Press, 1993.

Menéndez y Pelayo, Marcelino. "Cultura literaria de Miguel de Cervantes y elaboración del Quijote." In *Obras completas.* Santander: Edición Nacional. 1941.

Sieber, Harry. *Language and Society in La Vida de Lazarillo de Tormes.* Baltimore: Johns Hopkins Univ. Press, 1978.

◆ Chapter 9

Sonnes of the Rogue: Picaresque Relations in England and Spain

Anne J. Cruz

Emerging during times of similar economic crises, the fictional narratives of early modern Europe—in Spain, the picaresque novel and in England, rogue tales—presaged the modern novel in their retelling of a subaltern's immoral and illegal activities, enticing the reader through their opposing exemplary powers of social degeneration and spiritual redemption (Davis 126).[1] As the narratives gained rhetorical mastery, the mixture of the historical and the poetic, of *fabula* and *historia,* shifted (dis)continuously to offer differing levels of signs and their meanings. While anticipating the break in prose style, the rhetorical strategies of the narratives, as they developed in the various European contexts, incorporated varying literary traditions even as they claimed individual experience.[2] Indeed, it is no longer possible to state as unequivocally as Alexander Parker that "the modern novel is born when realism supplants the fanciful idealistic romance . . . the pastoral novel and the pseudo-historical romances" (5–6), since the trajectories of national literatures have been discovered to wend through highly uneven representational terrain.

The differences distinguishing the precursors of the European model are worth noting, since through them we may discern both the literary and historical reconfigurations that permitted and manipulated such a perception of "realism" by their readers. While the narrator-*pícaro* of the Spanish picaresque novels early on assumed a self-reflexive, ironic stance, English rogue tales developed from such straightforward narratives as John Awdeley's *The*

Fraternity of Vacabondes and Robert Greene's conny-catching pamphlets, to Thomas Nashe's far more complex *Unfortunate Traveller; or, The Life of Jack Wilton,* printed in 1594, whose discourse, recently analyzed by Robert Weimann, moves between "topos and topicality, rhetoric and experience" (17). The narratives' differences, moreover, are reflected in and affect the varying critical approaches to each narrative form.

Critical definitions of the Spanish picaresque novel tend to separate into two camps: one adopts a generically "purist" concern with the narrative's formal aspects, such as its autobiographical voice, its episodic structure, and, in its so-called realism, its opposition to such idealistic narratives as the epic and chivalric romances. The other, more sociohistorical approach focuses mainly on the novel as social and ideological critique.[3] While the former privileges the Golden Age Spanish picaresque canon even to the point of its restriction to two works (Rico), the latter views the picaresque as a literary barometer for social crisis and change, regardless of geographical location or time period. Like the English rogues, then, the Spanish picaresque novel's literary protagonists function as unevenly "realistic" representations of the growing numbers of disenfranchised poor that made their way from the countryside to the cities during the sixteenth and seventeenth centuries (Redondo, "Pauperismo"; Cruz, "Discourses").

The sheer number and extent of the Spanish genre's translations throughout Europe—in France, for instance, from as early as the elusive 1560 Lyon translation of the *Lazarillo* (Rumeau) to Lesage's version of the *Guzmán de Alfarache* in 1732—give concrete evidence of the interrelations of the genres transnationally. As Harry Sieber (38) has pointed out, however, not all picaresque novels gained equal popularity, since many were not so much translations as blends of Spanish originals with already existing "native" traditions. Stories of trickery and fraud were common to Italian literature at least since Boccaccio, for instance, and Germany's *liber vagatorum* easily adapted the Spanish specifics of wine and *germanía* to beer and *Rotwelsch,* or German thieves' cant.

Yet the differences that remained among the various translations of the Spanish picaresque and other national rogue tales contributed to the critical confusion surrounding the new genre

(Wicks 26–27). And since the genre was so closely tied to the changing social and economic factors in each country, these differences also served to differentiate the proliferating rogue tales. For Sieber, the European rogues who populate both the translations of the Spanish and their own anatomies of roguery are set apart from the Spanish *pícaro* in that they rise above their lower-class background to a higher social status:

> Even though some of them were unaware of their "advantages" at the beginning, they usually discovered their "middle-class" or "noble" ancestry. At the end of their lives, far from being hunted fugitives or social outcasts, they had improved their situations considerably. Whether country gentlemen, prosperous planters or pilgrim-hermits, they had advanced beyond the level of mere survival. (55)

When the vagabonds come from the lower classes, however, there is no such social mobility. If, unlike their Spanish counterparts, the other European protagonists of picaresque narrative oftentimes descended from the nobility, the vagrants listed in the German *liber vagatorum* and the English beggars' books are described solely in terms of baseness, deviancy, and deceit.

In conforming to specific historical and cultural conditions, contemporary translators and imitators took into account the differences among various European versions of the picaresque by stressing the text's representation of national characteristics. The title of the 1561 French translation of the *Lazarillo*, for instance, states that its contents expose the "meurs, vie et conditions des Espagnolz," while the English translation by David Rowland calls attention to the fact that it narrates the "Pleasaunt Historie" of Lazarillo, whom he is quick to identify as a "Spaniarde." Sieber cites a passage from the anonymous 1680 novel, *Don Tomaso; or, The Juvenile Rambles of Thomas Dangerfield*, that distinguishes between the Spanish *pícaro* Guzmán and the English rogue Tomaso: "the one pursuing a poor hungry plot upon his penurious master's bread and cheese, the other designing to grasp the riches of the fourth part of the world by the ruin of the national commerce." This distinction, Sieber notes, sets apart the mercantile interests of the former from the precapitalist concerns of the latter: "Because he operated within an hierarchical society in which honour and status were defined by birth and lineage, by 'blood,' the Spanish *pícaro* had no recourse to commerce as a means of achieving his goals" (52).

Most studies of European rogue tales nevertheless continue to define the genre's variants by the same literary standards set by the Spanish models. In his discussion of Nashe's *The Unfortunate Traveller*, printed in 1594, Ulrich Wicks admits that the controversy as to whether this book should be considered a picaresque novel is symptomatic of "the failure of theory to come to terms with a universally acceptable concept of the picaresque" (344). Rather than attempting to fit the European picaresque into the strictures of the classical Spanish canon, therefore, it may be more fruitful to see how two variants of this protean literary form respond to different cultural, social, and historical conditions.

The increase in vagrants and vagabonds due to the economic malaise of sixteenth-century Spain is documented in the *Lazarillo de Tormes*, which reflects the growing concerns about poor relief and the poor (Herrero; Redondo, "Pauperismo"; Cruz, "*Lazarillo*"). The third *tratado* in particular points to the conflict between the townspeople's feelings of charity toward the young beggar and their incipient work ethic; he is given a handout only while he recuperates from the wounds inflicted by the priest in the previous *tratado*. Once he is cured, the townspeople call him a good-for-nothing and exhort him to go find work. Lazarillo's position "at the height of all good fortune" ("en la cumbre de toda buena fortuna") ironically uncovers the double bind in which the poor are caught: in order to survive, they are forced to break God's law and the local poor regulations, thus transgressing both social and religious rules.

Published in 1554, the *Lazarillo* depicts the ambivalent social attitudes directed toward the poor, as the *pícaro* exemplifies in his own experience the historical conflicts that arose between secular and religious values.[4] The traditional Christian charity of the Middle Ages, whereby individual donors succored the poor for their own spiritual salvation, was inadequate to meet the demands of the increasing numbers of disenfranchised in the sixteenth century, and much confusion ensued regarding poor relief and who constituted the poor (Redondo, "Pauperismo" 704–6;

Cruz, "Lazarillo" 64). The debates between the Dominican Domingo de Soto and the Benedictine Juan de Robles in particular polarized the issue; the former maintained the traditional view of the poor and granted them the right to beg, while the latter hoped to improve their condition through social reform (Márquez Villanueva 115–18; Flynn 90–98; Cruz, "Lazarillo" 68).

By the beginning of the seventeenth century, ambiguity toward the poor was replaced by the increasingly hardened attitudes of a society no longer willing to accept social change. The *casas de misericordia* supported by such reformers as Miguel Giginta and Cristóbal Pérez de Herrera ultimately failed in their intents to integrate the poor through job training (Cavillac 54–55). The shift in the meaning of the term *pícaro* from a kitchen scullion in the early 1500s to that of a delinquent by the middle of the century may serve as an index of the changing social perceptions of poor youths. Cautioning that philologists are still not agreed on the word's etymology, Alexander Parker points out that the word *pícaro* was first documented in 1525 to mean "kitchen boy," but twenty years later it already was synonymous with "evil living" (4). It is therefore not coincidental that in both the *Guzmán de Alfarache* and the *Buscón*, written during Philip III's reign of growing aristocratization—and despite the differing ideological positions of their respective authors—the *pícaro*'s image was devalued from that of a poor lad victimized by society to one of social reprobate. As in the *Lazarillo*, however, pauperism in Spain continued to elicit conflicting responses from both the church and the state, responses that varied from the ongoing charities supplied by the broad range of confraternities to the harsh penalties imposed on poor criminals (Flynn 44–74; Perry 163–89; Pike).

Social mobility in England during the early modern period has still to be examined thoroughly, as Lawrence Stone has readily admitted (Stone, "Social Mobility"). Nonetheless, his own pioneering efforts have helped illuminate the complex changes taking place in the status and occupational hierarchies of urban and rural society.[5] Stone addresses the "unprecedented" upward and downward mobility of the period among several of these groups, yet he notes that the bottom rung, that of the dependents on charity, apprentices, and living-in servants, remained relatively unchanged, since its only mobility was horizontal, one of geographical shift from rural areas to towns. In fact, he concludes that the redistribution in population may have augmented the numbers of poor: "Many of these wanderers failed to find a permanent home either on the wastes and forests or in the towns, and there is plenty of evidence—if of a non-quantitative character—for a serious increase of vagabondage ("Social Mobility" 40).

The influx into towns was, according to Stone, even greater than the high urban death rates; both the rapid urban growth and the dwindling food supplies of the late sixteenth century spurred fears of social disorder. John Pound identifies two active periods—at the beginning and the end of the sixteenth century—when enclosure of common land in the English Midlands uprooted several thousand agricultural workers, a phenomenon that contributed significantly to the numbers of poor (11). For Joel Samaha, the famine of the 1590s fostered a "new attitude toward crime, especially the lawlessness of the growing number of landless laborers" (66). An example of this attitudinal change can readily be seen in Essex, where the reporting of crimes, jury behavior, and the judicial machinery in general had to adapt to the growing demand for law and order.

The rising number of poor, most of whom would eventually be forced to steal, had already been noted in Robert Copland's poem, "The Hyeway to the Spyttell Hous," dated 1535. In its dialogue between Copland and the hospital porter, most probably of St. Bartholomew's, the poem graphically describes both the many kinds of people that were given lodging and those who were refused. The porter's reply to Copland's query ("Syr, I pray you, who hath of you relefe?" [13]) transmits the general negative attitudes toward the deceptively mendicant:

> PORTER:
> And they walke to eche market, and fayre,
> And to all places where folke do repayre,
> By day on styltes, or stoupyng on crowches,
> And so dyssymule as fals lewtryng flowches,
> with bloody clowtes all about theyr legge,
> And playsters on theyr skyn, whan they go beg;
> Some countrefayt lepry, and other some
> Put sope in theyr mouth to make it scome
>
> . . . .

> And whan they be in theyr owne company,
> They be as hole as eyther you or I:
> But at the last, whan sekenes cometh in dede,
> Than to the spytell hous must they come nede. (16)

William Harrison's *Description of England,* first published in 1577, continues to distinguish between "beggars through other mens occasion" and "beggars through their own default." While the former were considered deserving recipients of public charity, the latter were meted harsh punishment:

> For their idle roging about the countrie, the law ordeineth this maner of correction. The roge being apprehended, committed to prison, and tried in the next assise . . . he is then immediatelie adiugded to be greeuouslie whipped and burned through the gristle of the right eare, with an hot iron of the compass of an inch about, as a manifestation of his wicked life, and due punishment received for the same. . . . If he be taken the second time . . . he shall then be whipped againe, bored likewise through the other eare and set to seruice: from whence if he depart before a yeare be expired, and happen afterward to be attached againe, he is condemned to suffer paines of death as a fellon. (Awdeley xiii)

Harrison's description of "idle vagabonds" is based on Thomas Harman's *A Caveat or Warening for Common Cursetors vulgarely called Vagabones,* printed in 1567, which is itself taken from *The Fraternitye of Vacabondes,* a compilation of vagrant types, both "rufling and beggerly," first printed by John Awdeley most probably in 1561.

Harman's *Caveat* was so popular that it was pirated several times throughout the seventeenth century, and such texts as *The Groundworke of Conny-catching* (1592) and Thomas Dekker's *Bellman of London* (1608) copied whole sections of the *Caveat* (Awdeley xiv).[6] Painfully aware of his status as a disenfranchised gentleman, Harman states that he writes the tract, which he dedicates to the Countess of Shrewsbury, in order to warn others of what he calls "the rowsey, ragged rabblement of rakehells that—under the pretense of great misery, dyseases, and other innumerable calamities"—attempt to deceive "good givers," who through their misdirected charity become their victims. He set about interviewing as many of the vagabonds as would talk to him until he composed an anatomy of roguery with an accompanying dictionary of thieves' cant. What probably drew attention to the tract, however, was not so much its didactic intent to caution "the country" about the dangerous group in their midst, as Harman's ability to turn what had been a mere list of the strange titles given the fraternity of vagabonds into a major storytelling event.

Despite Harman's disclaimer that he writes "in plain termes— and not so playnly as truely"—about a social crisis that was to grow ever more threatening, his alliterative style anticipates Nashe's *The Unfortunate Traveller* in its admixture of hyperbole and attention to realist detail that nevertheless offers an engaging view of the English underworld. Although it does not fully suc- ceed in converting its denizens into agreeable folk, it reduces their threat considerably by exposing their language and tricks. The vagabonds are listed according to their rank: as soldiers returned from the wars, the "rufflers," are the "first in degre of this odious order." Harman discloses that "some wyll shew you some out- ward wounde, whiche he gotte at some dronken fraye." The ruffl- ers are followed in importance by "upright men," rogues, and "pallyards," all described in great detail; about the latter, Harman specifically warns:

> Vnderstand for trouth that the worst and wickedst of all this
> beastly generation are scarse comparable to these prating
> Pallyardes. All for the most part will either lay to their legs
> an herb called Sperewort, eyther Arsnicke, which is called
> Ratesbane. The nature of this Spereworte wiyll rayse a great
> blister in a night vpon the soundest part of his body; and if
> the same be taken away, it wyl dry vp againe and no harme.
> But this Arsknicke will so poyson the same legge or sore,
> that it will euer after be incurable: this do they for gaine and
> to be pitied. (44)

The descriptions of vagabonds are accompanied by short stories and anecdotes that highlight the beggars' cunning at stealing the townspeople's money and belongings, and their riotous con- frontations with constables and other law officers. Harman even includes an alphabetical list of "upright men," "roges," and "pallyards" by first name, some with aliases, and others followed by a short description; the "upright man" Iohn Horwood, for example, is listed under "I" as "a maker of wels; he wyll take halfe his bargayne in hand, and when hee hath wrought ii or iii, dais, he runneth away with his earnest" (79).

While its purpose is to serve as warning, as its title indicates, the *Caveat* nevertheless defangs its message by devalorizing the rogues through its emphasis on their seriocomic adventures, as well as by its righteous belief in having uncovered all there is to know about them. Harman's ending poem, while insisting upon his reformist ideals, belies their unlikely realization:

> Thus I conclude my bolde Beggars booke,
> That all estates most playnely maye see,
> As in a glasse well pollyshed to looke,
> Their double demeaner in eche degree.
> Their lyues, their language, their names as they be,
> That with this warning their myndes may be warmed,
> To amend their mysdeedes, and so lyue vnharmed. (91)

Yet while Harman's poem fails to redeem the rogues, it succeeds in conventionalizing them. As in Spain, where picaresque literature was taken up by the small literate middle class and the aristocracy, it was not, of course, the beggars who read Harman's book, but the middle and upper classes, just as it was not the mendicants or the other "knaves" mentioned who read Copland's poem. Weimann has called attention to the untidiness of the poetical and historiographical functions in these sorts of writings, where fiction and history cease to be diametrical opposites (16). Despite Harman's intent to individuate the rogues and expose them to an unsuspecting public, they had already become literary figures by their frequent appearances in the earlier texts exploited by Harman, and their repeated modes of deception were by then mere commonplaces. In underscoring the false beggars' faults and the likelihood of divine retribution, both Copland and Harman, whose warning was directed as well to the "cursetors," intended a moral corrective that went unheeded, precisely due to the discourses' instability.

But the texts' preference for the poetical must also be understood within its historical, and more specifically, its religious context. Although varying substantially from one text to another, the distance established between the assorted collection of vagrants wittily denounced by these writers and so-called moral society was significantly, and what is more, easily measurable by the attitudes of the middle and upper classes toward the poor. The "exhortation" that ends Copland's preface expresses the need for Christian charity, not so much for the receivers' welfare as for the donors' spiritual benefit:

> I pray all you, which hauve ynough with grace,
> For the loue of God to do your charyte,
> And fro the poore neuer turne your face;
> For Chryst sayth, what euer that he be
> That to the least of myne dooth in the name of me,
> Vnto myself I do accept the dede,
> And for rewarde my realme they shall possede. (8)

When, in the poem, Copland worries about giving to the undeserving poor, the porter reminds him that "Where ony gyveth almesse with good entent, / The rewarde can not be nowyse mysspent" (14). The author's attitude reflects upon the concerns of a society in the midst of a religious revolution, one that would irreversibly alter not only the country's spiritual beliefs but its social structure as well.

Copland's poem coincided both with the 1534 Act of Supremacy and with the English publication in 1535 of the reforms at Ypres, modeled after Vives's influential treatise *De subventione pauperum*. Writing for the Flemish city of Bruges, the reformer puts forth his sweeping new ideas of poor relief, reforms that would result in the establishment in England of a series of enactments that culminated in the English Poor Law of 1601.[7] In Spain, reformist ideas such as Vives's were viewed with suspicion by the Mendicant Orders, who preached the virtues of poverty, as well as by church prelates who traditionally controlled the monies collected for the poor (Martz 7–8). In England, however, the dissolution of the monasteries in 1536, and thus curtailed monastic charity, apparently added to the number of poor, although Pound admits that it is difficult to gauge to what extent. He cites Robert Aske, leader of the Yorkshire rebellion, who affirms that at least in the north, "much of the relief of the commons was by succour of abbeys" (Pound 23).

Therefore, while the various movements to secularize poor relief and curtail vagrancy spread throughout Europe at approximately the same time in the early sixteenth century, they prevailed longest in England.[8] The changes introduced by the English Reformation were enforced through the Act of Supremacy that confirmed and protected the king's leadership of the Church of England. After Henry VIII, the Anglican church stressed justification by faith alone; the Thirty Nine Articles of 1571, revised from earlier articles published in 1553, have this as their most important doctrine.

Unlike Luther, who prefaced the *Liber Vagatorum* by warning about the false poor but believed in assisting the "local" poor according to Catholic doctrine, the Anglican church, influenced by Zwingli and Calvin, did not consider charitable acts necessary for salvation.[9] The early Poor Laws that relied upon voluntary contributions (and which provided poor treatment at St. Bartholomew's Hospital, among others) proved a failure even in London. During the following decade, therefore, secular and religious leaders attempted to form an organization that would assume the responsibility for all of London's poor. The Common Council resolved in 1547 that "citizens and inhabitants of the said City shall further contribute and pay towards the sustentation and maintaining of the said poor personages the moiety or half-deal of one whole fifteenth" (qtd. in Webb 48). In 1555, the Common Council established an institution that would set "idle and lewd people" to work, and care for the "poor, sick and weak, and sore people of the city." In particular, the "thriftless poor"—defined as the "rioter that consumeth all," "the vagabond that will abide in no place," and "the idle person as the strumpet"—were to be compelled to work in hospitals that would later serve as models for the houses of correction (Webb 49–50).[10]

The enforcement of "poor rates" throughout England, made compulsory by Parliament in 1563 and codified in 1572, which taxed the inhabitants and imprisoned them for nonpayment, reveals the continuing efforts to make mandatory what had been considered Christian duty under medieval Catholic doctrine.

Lady Jane Grey's "A Certain Communication" with a Master Feckenham shortly before her beheading in 1554, in response to an apparent attempt on Feckenham's part to convert the young girl to Catholicism, documents her defense of the Anglican creed on the diminished role of charity and reflects the general religious ideology of the period:

> FECKENHAM: Why then is it necessary to salvation to do good works and it is not sufficient to believe?
> JANE: I deny that and I affirm that faith only [alone] saves. But it is meet for Christians, in token that they follow their master Christ, to do good works, yet may we not say that they profit to salvation. For, although we have all done all that we can, yet we be unprofitable servants, and the faith only in Christ's blood saveth. (Spitz 170)

By the time Harman's *Caveat* appeared in print, the Elizabethan Poor Laws had already gone into effect in London, Norwich, and York. The imposition of a compulsory rate and institutional treatment for the poor according to certain categorizations effectively broke with the medieval Catholic view of charity as a religious obligation as parishes were turned into "units of obligation" through which both state and church arranged for essential collective welfare services (S. and B. Webb, 5 ff.).[11] Funds were provided for abandoned children, the aged, the sick, and those unable to work, while the able-bodied were assigned employment. Fears of rebellion by vagrants would not be quelled, however, and resulted in the approval of severe legislation: the 1572 Act ordained whipping and boring through the ear for the first offense, condemnation as felon for the second, and death for the third (Pound 47).

The unemployed were increasingly perceived as potential criminals, and indeed, many of them were; Samaha points out that the economic crises of the late 1500s drove greater numbers of destitute people to steal in order to survive (36). He notes, however, that shifting popular opinion against the poor may have strengthened the perception that poverty was a matter of criminality. In rejecting charity and obedience of the Poor Laws as a means of salvation, Anglicans judged crime, no matter how petty, as deserving of stricter punishment. Rogue literature reflects little of these conflicts, however. The rogue tales that follow Harman's *Caveat* and Awdeley's *Fraternity of Vacabondes* demonstrate less a desire for the didactic representation of social reality than a burgeoning interest in fictional narrative. Neither these anatomies of roguery nor the translations of the Spanish picaresque espouse the moral and spiritual cause identified with the latter. Thus, the *Lazarillo*, translated in 1568 but extant only in the 1586 edition, is prefaced by the translator as containing "strange and mery reports, very recreative & pleasant" (cited in Sieber 51). While the translator goes on to insist that the novel illustrates the "nature and disposition of sundrie Spaniards," his view of what constitutes a picaresque tale corroborates, I believe, my argument that, in their admixture of historiography and fiction, the English rogue narratives fail to achieve the same degree of moralization as their Spanish counterparts.

Rather, the rogues are continually refashioned into fictive characters, their codified language made public through the dictionaries appended to the texts and appropriated in popular ballads.[12] Even Robert Greene, who barely escaped with his life for his disclosures of the conny-catchers' (card-sharps) names and tricks, interweaves factual reporting with fictional episodes in his popular pamphlets, which quickly became best-sellers. In response to Greene's pamphlets, the *Defence of Conny-Catching,* written in 1592 by the pseudonymous Cuthbert Conny-Catcher, excoriates him for wasting his time on such supposedly innocuous foes while ignoring the truly important criminals:

> Why should you be so spitefull maiser Robert Greene to poore Conny-catchers above all the rest? . . . But you play like the spider that makes her webbe to intrap and snare little flies, but weaves it so slenderly, that the great ones breake through without damage. You straine Gnats, and passe over Elephants, you scour the ponde of a few croaking Frogges, and leave behinde an infinite number of most venomous Scorpiones.

Ironically, though, the *Defence* itself does not hesitate to disclose certain types—gentlemen, actors, brokers—all equally deserving of the title of conny-catcher, yet whose occupations marked them as socially more acceptable. Each description generates a "pleasant tale" in which the author intends to prove that "there is no estate, trade, occupation, nor mistery, but lives by conny-catching" (64). Again, the value of these stories, like the pamphlets their anonymous author inveighs against, lies not so much in their moralistic premise as in their narrative focus—stories that Greene, himself a bit of a literary conny-catcher, then borrowed and retold in his last pamphlet, *The Black Bookes Messenger; or, the Life and Death of Ned Browne.*

The varying levels of historiography and representation exhibited in rogue tales are, as Weimann convincingly points out, most noticeable in Nashe's *The Unfortunate Traveller.* Although often compared to the Spanish picaresque (Albertini; Ferguson; Jones), Nashe's tale, while narrated in the first person, shares few of the formal characteristics we have come to identify with the Spanish narratives: there is no "prehistory," since the story begins when Jack, already a young page, is stationed at a military post in France with Henry VIII's army. Through the course of his adventures, he anachronistically meets up with Luther, Thomas More, and Erasmus. He has only one master, and he keeps company with a rich widow with whom he travels to Rome, finally ending his adventures at another military post in France. The reason he gives for telling his story, moreover, convincingly privileges its *dulce* over its *utile:*

> And so as my story began with the king at Turney and
> Turwin, I think meet here to end it with the King at Ardes
> and Guines. All the conclusive epilogue I will make is this:
> that if herein I have pleased any, it shall animate me to more
> pains in this kind. Otherwise I will swear upon an English
> chronicle never to be outlandish chronicler more while I
> live. (149)

Weimann calls the blend of reality and fantasy in Nashe a "crisis of the 'universalle consideration'" since the idealism of Sidney's classical term clashes with particularized history as it combines with it to form a hybridized "fantastical historiography" (18). If Nashe's penchant for fiction over historical material allows the text to go beyond both chronicle and poetry, however, it also redirects the narrative away from the chronicle's didactic and truth-telling purpose.

For Wicks, the differences between the Spanish picaresque and Nashe's tale are attributable to the genre's literary history, since the English author's satirical bent more closely follows that of Petronius and Apuleius than the *Lazarillo*'s anonymous author, Mateo Alemán, or even Quevedo (346). Satirical though the *Unfortunate Traveller* may be, as Wicks concedes, the continuing argument over its relation to the Spanish picaresque "complicat[es] the problem of conceptual inadequacies with the historical reality of the apparent misreadings of the Spanish picaresque works at the time they were being translated" (346).

In his assessment of Nashe's narrative as producing "the vision of disorder that underlies all picaresques," Stuart Miller misses the point when he calls it "a narrative that refuses to get on with the business of narration . . . [b]ecause the narrator quite gratuitously refuses to tell his story straight" (qtd. in Wicks 347). For although the text's incongruities—its jumps from one type of discourse to another and its "dilations" on specific narrative events—may remind us of the *Guzmán*'s various rhetorical strategies, they also admit to its lack of any moral teleology, as Ann Rosalind Jones rightfully asserts (65). Yet, while Jones goes on to include Nashe's narrative within the canon of the picaresque genre, in its open-ended discourse, *The Unfortunate Traveller* rejects both the formal and the moral closure of the Spanish picaresque.

But if Jack Wilton is not a *pícaro*, neither is he a rogue. As narrator, the *Unfortunate Traveller*'s protagonist exposes what Jones calls "his novelistic undertakings" (76). In other words, his is a narrative that reveals itself by admitting its fictionality, by acknowledging the narrator's awareness of his task as well as his reader's reception. In discussing the qualities of his master, the Earl of Surrey, as a poet, Jack stops his hyperbole in time, ironically recognizing the need to advance the story: "Let me not speak any more of his accomplishments, for fear I spend all my spirits in praising him, and leave myself no vigor of wit or effects of a soul to go forward with my history" (65). Moreover, as Weimann reminds us (21), although Nashe condemns the chronicles for their unadorned "historie," he also imbues his narrative with a sense of social history. The Anabaptist episode may be criticized for its ambivalent attitude regarding artistic free speech and censorship (Ferguson 176–177), but the narrator's ambivalence is contextualized within the moral struggles for right religion. Openly anti-Puritan, anti-Semitic, and anti-Papist throughout his *peregrinatio,* and playfully derisive of Luther's debating skills, Jack also seems to doubt Anglican reliance on faith alone as opposed to good works:

> Yet this I must say to the shame of us Protestants; if good works may merit heaven, they do them, we talk about them. Whether superstition or no makes them unprofitable servants, that let pulpits decide; but there you shall have the bravest ladies, in gowns of beaten gold, washing pilgrims' & poor soldiers' feet, and doing nothing they and their waiting maids, all the year long, but making shirts and bands for them against they come by in distress. Their hospitals are more like noblemen's houses than otherwise . . . that a soldier would think it a sufficient recompense for all his travail and his wounds, to have such a heavenly retiring place. (108)

Jack Wilton's rhetoric separates him from the rogues we have seen in Harman's and Greene's texts, but in the final analysis, his narrative is at least as socially instructive as the rogue tales. In the text's rhetorical inconsistencies, then, we read the social inconsistencies of narrative: Nashe's book offers the amoral pleasures of a knave, but Jack Wilton is not, like the rogues, representative of a group. Instead, his is a particularized self and rhetorical figure that stands for the narrative itself. And in contrast to the unreliable narrators of the Spanish picaresque, whose first-person narrative draws us as readers into the text and with whom we develop some sort of sympathy or antipathy, Nashe's duplicitously ironic protagonist treads lightly through a realistic landscape, and is as removed from his social contemporaries, and from his readers, as are Harman's devalorized and distanced rogues.

Whether through the diverting stories of figuralized conny-catchers or Jack Wilton'narratively complex misadventures, English rogue tales refuse to reinscribe the psychological tensions that build between the narrator and the reader of the Spanish picaresque, tensions caused by the reader's fear, either conscious or unconscious, of being subsumed into the figure of the *pícaro*. Despite the fact that Spanish social categories, which had earlier been more permeable, became increasingly closed through stricter criteria for social change in the mid-sixteenth century, *pícaros* continued to speak to the multiple religious and social fears of the community. Historian Jaime Contreras explains that the exclusionary campaign unleashed against such heretics as Protestants and crypto-Jews wished to transform them into scapegoats for the monarchy's continued economic malaise that occasioned three bankruptcies (93–123). The Spanish picaresque, with the *pícaro* a constant reminder of the *converso* and the criminal, echoes the disquietude of a xenophobic society that nonetheless suspected the presence of the "other" in itself. Whether or not the authors intend social reform, their novels' protagonists reenact the precarious position of the readers, who, as members of the incipient middle class and the lower nobility, are only too aware of the concerns over purity of blood.

A clear example of this "return of the repressed" is Francisco de Quevedo, whose satirical works relentlessly attack all sorts of outcasts and social climbers, in particular those who, like the *conversos*, could afford to purchase titles of nobility. That the *converso* Mateo Alemán would ridicule subaltern groups through his satirical portrait of the *pícaro* Guzmán de Alfarache in an ineffectual attempt to distance himself from the taint of his origins is understandable (Friedman 229). What might be less easily perceived is Quevedo's projections of his fears and hatred onto the abject protagonist; Quevedo, after all, would never admit to any similarity between himself and his abject protagonist. Indeed, the *pícaro* Pablos, son of a *converso* thief and a *conversa* witch-prostitute, incarnates the most hated elements of early modern Spain (Domínguez Ortiz 8). Victimized by his own creator, however, the protagonist assumes a paradoxically Christ-like role.[13] The rhetorical representation of the many ills besetting Spain through the *Buscón*'s scatological excesses thus ensures the novel's moral tenor. Nashe's Doctor Zachary shares with Quevedo's dómine Cabra the same descriptive hyperboles: "He was Dame Niggardize's sole heir & executor. A number of old books had he, eaten with the moths and worms: now all day would not he study a dodkin, but pick those worms and moths out of his library, and of their mixture make a preservative against the plague" (128). Yet, quite unlike Zachary and Jack, the underlying connections that are drawn between Cabra and the *pícaro* serve to render their insepa-rability, as when Cabra's bones sound like *tablillas de san Lázaro* (91), and in the baleful description of his bedroom, which echoes the emptiness of the squire's rented premise in the *Lazarillo:* "aun arañas no había en él. Conjuraba los ratones de miedo que no le royesen algunos mendrugos que guardaba. La cama tenía en el suelo y dormía siempre de un lado para no gastar las sábanas. Al fin, él era archipobre y protomiseria" (92).

In the *Unfortunate Traveller,* there is never any doubt that as a Jew, Zachary fully deserves the trick played on him by Juliana that precipitates the Pope's edict of expulsion. Nashe's graphic de-scription detailing the gruesome tortures of Zachary's execution illustrates the "hold of the body" so well noted by Michel Foucault in his study of the birth of the prison. The decline of the spectacle, of "theatrical representation of pain," amounted, according to Foucault, to the end of "a certain kind of tragedy; comedy began" (17). Instead, Quevedo's high praise for the exemplary character of the earlier *Lazarillo* (Roncero López 108), which surely served as a foil for his own text, demonstrates that he took seriously the pi-caresque's moral didacticism. The *Buscón's* dark irony, Pablos's in-ability to shake off his past, the shame attached to his birthright, remind us of how closely the Spanish bourgeoisie and the upper classes were socially and morally bound to the figure of the *pícaro.* While Nashe's Jack Wilton assumes the Earl of Surrey's persona without serious threat to the social order, Lazarillo can only at-tempt a parody of knighthood as he quits his job as water-carrier to strut about in secondhand clothes that link him metonymically to his third master, the impoverished squire. Similarly, Pablos falls into a trap set by his earlier master, don Diego, when he tries to pass himself off as his relative: "y dame dos palos en las piernas, y derríbame en el suelo; y llega el otro y dame un trasquilón de oreja a oreja, y quítanme la capa y déjanme en el suelo, diciendo: —Así pagan los pícaros embustidores mal nacidos" (231). The irony, of course, is that don Diego is himself a *converso;* in their efforts to es-tablish difference, they have more in common than either margin-alized figure admits to the other.

Since England's social structures were divided by class rather than caste, they lacked the obsession with *limpieza de sangre* that characterized Spanish social relations. Economic gain allowed certain social mobility among the various groups mentioned: tradesmen-craftsmen, husbandmen and yeomen, up through the gentry's lower rungs. Groups closed ranks, however, during periods of economic hardship. The expanding population in the cities and the bad harvests of the 1590s contributed directly to the crime rate unchecked even by the Poor Laws (Samaha 36). Of the nonmobile groups, it was the landless laborers who most suffered for lack of secure work, yet they were stigmatized as vagabonds or beggars and blamed for their idleness. J. C. K. Cornwall charts the growth of the laboring class from 1475 to 1700, with laborers closing the gap between them and the landholding class by 1590:

> Faced with the growth of the landless element, the "establishment" feared the imminent collapse of the social order. The peasantry, in whose midst the crisis was maturing, descried an ominous portent of their own fate and readily believed the worst. . . . The upshot was that the labourer could not be allowed a place in the commonweath. Society rejected him, branded him (sometimes physically) a vagabond, and tried to ignore his very existence. (214–15)

Criminal records show that of all social groups, the numbers of laborers accused of stealing doubled during the famines from 1593 to 1597 (Samaha 64–65). Hunger brought on by lack of work was, therefore, one of the main causes of criminal activity; the other social groups reacted by not seeing themselves in this position, since the religious tenets of the Anglican church and Calvinism rejected poverty as either willingly brought on or as punishment divinely assigned. Rather, they isolated the criminal even more through higher rates of prosecution and punishment. In this, the rogues' tales anticipate the change in punishment that was to occur in the eighteenth century whereby its public ceremonial aspects were replaced by closed judicial practices:

> The execution itself is like an additional shame that justice is ashamed to impose on the condemned man; so it keeps its distance from the act, tending always to entrust it to others, under the seal of secrecy. (Foucault 9–10)

While Spain and England both experienced an inordinate growth in poverty that urban authorities were unable to check, and although their national literatures reflect the sentiments of the middle classes and the aristocracy against the impoverished, the English rogue tale is psychologically distanced from the poor, reacting against their physical proximity by attempting their control through full disclosure and maintaining the reader's moral distance through the narrative's lack of serious moral concern.[14] The Spanish picaresque, on the other hand, uncovers the collusion of the *pícaro* and his social superiors in a caste system that keeps the social classes bound to each other through the fearful recognition of their similitude. Unlike the rogue, who is singled out, isolated, and diminished by the same social groups that would disclose his presence and make known his language, the Spanish *pícaro* embodies in his self-conscious discourse the tensions, fears, and hatreds of a society obsessed.

The failure to fully isolate the impoverished from the rest of society by means of *casas de misericordia*, as well as the continually failed desire to expel the perceived "other," as in the *estatutos de sangre* and the expulsion of the *moriscos*, proves Spain's profoundly ambivalent relationship to its disorderly members as it exemplifies the difficulties in applying exclusionary methods to the same groups that for so long had functioned significantly from within. In the narrative's self-generating impulse, the Spanish picaresque assumed the concerns of the historical *pícaro*. In contrast to their English rogue cousins, who were to lose their narrative appeal through their fictionalization, the sons of Lazarillo, despite constant authorial efforts aimed at their control and containment, refuse marginalization or redemption, spilling instead onto the proliferating pages of the genre they engendered.

Notes

1. Davis draws an incisive analogy between the seventeenth-century English novels of criminals and the criminality inherent in literary production and in literature itself: "It is difficult to escape the conclusion that something about the literary trade was considered illicit, disreputable, and even criminal. . . . The habit of reading novels was a sure sign that a young man or woman was on the way down" (125).

2. In his influential *The Rise of the Novel*, Ian Watt attributes the modern novel's

origins to the philosophical realism of Descartes, Locke, and, later, Thomas Reid, thereby limiting his discussion to English texts.

3. Generic approaches to the picaresque include Parker, Guillén, and Alter. Positivist criticism of the picaresque began with De Haan and Chandler; later sociohistorical approaches include Maravall, Cros, Cavillac, and Redondo. Ulrich Wicks has succinctly addressed the complexities of both approaches in his "Part 1: A Theory of Picaresque Narrative" (3–84). For a discussion of the difficulties of classifying picaresque narratives, see Dunn.

4. It is most likely that the novel itself was written close to its publishing date; Marcel Bataillon has shown that the *Lazarillo* makes mention of the laws against the "foreign" poor in Toledo, which were published in 1540 in Madrid and in 1544 in Medina del Campo (see Márquez Villanueva 115–21).

5. Stone divides status into six groups: (1) dependents on charity, apprentices, and live-in servants; (2) live-out laborers, both agricultural and industrial; (3) husbandmen, yeomen, artisans, and shopkeepers; (4) lesser gentry; (5) county elite such as squires, knights, and baronets; and (6) the peers: barons, viscounts, earls, marquises, and dukes. These are compared with four semi-independent occupational hierarchies: (1) merchants; (2) lawyers; (3) clergy; and (4) administrators for the crown ("Social Mobility," 28–30). A contemporary survey, Sir Thomas Smith's 1550 *De Republica Anglorum*, identifies four sorts—gentlemen, citizens or burgesses, yeomen, and artificers or laborers—adding that there were besides "great swarms of idle servingmen" and quoted the proverb, "[y]oung servingmen, old beggars" (cited by Cornwall, 8–10).

6. Harman lists more than twenty-four classes of vagrants; following Harman's lead in warning others of rogues' habits, Dekker describes a rogue as "known to all men by his name, but not to all men by his conditions . . . he will speak in a lamentable tune and crawl along the streets . . . his head shall be bound about with linen, loathsome to behold; and as filthy in colour as the complexion of his face; his apparel is all tattered, his bosom naked, and most commonly no shirt on, not that they are driven to this misery by mere want, but that if they had better clothes given them, they would rather sell them . . . and move people to compassion, and to be relieved with money, which being gotten, at night is spent as merrily and as lewdly as in the day it was won by counterfeit villainy. Another sect there be of these, and they are called STURDY ROGUES; these walk from county to county under colour of travelling to their friends or to find out some kinsman or else to deliver a letter to one gentleman or other . . . others use this shift to carry a Certificate or passport about them, with the nad or seal of some Justice to it . . . all these writings are but counterfeit, they having amongst them (of their own RANK), that can write and read, who are their secretaries in this business" (cited by Pound, 98).

7. Henry VIII visited Bruges in 1521, where he met Vives; according to S. and B. Webb (36), Vives may have alternated between London and Oxford, Bruges and Louvain through 1528. Vives's policy was apparently not adopted by Bruges, but he most likely advised the smaller town of Ypres as to which regulations to enforce: begging was prohibited, indigent relief was carried out by the municipality, the needy were registered, the able-bodied were given employment, and the impotent were cared for in institutions. William Marshall's translation of the Ypres reforms, *The Forme and Maner of Subvention or Helping for pore people devysed and practised in the Cytie of Hypres in Flanders,* was modeled also on Spengler's reforms adopted at

Nurenberg in 1522 (Webb 39). Although Vives's treatise had tremendous impact throughout Europe in pointing out the need for social welfare reform, each country responded according to its particular situation. For an excellent introduction to welfare in Spain, see Martz.

8. The multiple complex causes during the early sixteenth century of England's "special economic stress" are given by S. and B. Webb as "the agrarian revolution that was dislocating the manorial organisation, or the growth of manufactures in the towns, involving the production of an urban proletariat; or the rapid increase of commerce with its unsettlement of one national industry after another" (43).

9. Luther's concerns initiated systematic measures against vagrancy in Germany; his "Ordinance for a Common Chest" attempted to do away with begging by offering loans from the Common Chest, "its income composed from the revenues of ecclesiastical estates, free contributions and . . . *if necessary, of an assessment upon resident citizens* (qtd. in Webb 31; their emphasis). Yet his statement in the *Liber Vagatorum* reflects as well his continuing belief in the importance of good acts: "But the right understanding and true meaning of the book is, after all, this, viz. that princes, lords, counsellors of state, and everybody should be prudent, and cautious in dealing with beggars, and learn that, whereas people will not give and help honest paupers and needy neighbors, *as ordained by God,* they give, by the persuasion of the devil, and contrary to God's judgment, ten times as much to Vagabonds and desperate rogues—in like manner as we have hitherto done to monasteries, cloister, churches, chapels, and mendicant friars, forsaking all the time the truly poor" (qtd. in Wicks, 242; my emphasis).

10. Space does not allow me to address in this essay the extremely complex issue of poor women and their consequent prostitution. It is important to note, however, that rather than place "strumpets" to work in hospitals as in England, Spanish moralists encouraged their confinement in state-controlled brothels. Spanish female picaresque novels play against this enclosure; see my "Sexual Enclosure." Carlos Blanco Aguinaga's comparison of English female rogues with Spanish *pícaras*, though useful, remains chronologically inaccurate, since he restricts the English text to *Moll Flanders* ("Picaresca española"). In Renaissance Spain, redemption of prostitutes was carried out, not unsurprisingly, by a remarkable religious woman, Magdalena de san Jerónimo. See Barbeito; also Perry, "Magdalens."

11. Although ecclesiastical parishes levied taxes upon the parishioners, they also had other sources of revenue, such as livestock, and Church Ales, parish feasts where parishioners would spend their money on food and drink, and which became less profitable with the growth of Puritanism (Webb 11–14).

12. Unlike Spanish *germanía,* whose viability as a means of communication depended upon its marginality and hermetic character, and was largely unknown before the seventeenth century, English thieves' cant appeared in print concurrently with its oral usage. For a study of *germanía* appearing in Baroque literature, see Alonso Hernández.

13. For several perceptive studies on carnavalization and the grotesque in the *Buscón,* see Cros and Iffland.

14. Maureen Flynn distinguishes between two different codes in Spain and the rest of Europe, but attributes Spain's attachment to traditional methods of poor relief to continued belief in Catholicism (111–13).

Works Cited

Albertini, Stefania. "Personaggi a confronto: Lazarillo de Tormes e Jack Wilton." *Quaderni di Filologia e Lingue Romanze* (1985): 33–51.

Alonso Hernández, José Luis. "Le monde de voleurs dans la littérature espagnole des xvie. et xviie. siècles (Structures sociales révélées par l'étude du lexique)." *Culture et Marginalités au XVIe. Siècle.* Ed. J. L. Alonso Hernández et al. Paris: Librairie C. Klincksieck, 1973. 11–42.

Awdeley, John. *The Fraternitye of Vacabondes.* 1898. Ed. E. Viles and F. J. Furnivall. London: Oxford Univ. Press, 1937.

Barbeito, Isabel, ed. *Cárceles y mujeres en el siglo XVII. Razón y forma de la Galera. Proceso inquisitorial de san Plácido.* Madrid: Castalia, Instituto de la Mujer, 1991.

Blanco Aguinaga, Carlos. "Picaresca española, picaresca inglesa: sobre las determinaciones del género." *Edad de Oro,* II 2 (1983): 49–65.

Cavillac, Michel. "L'enfermement des pauvres, en Espagne, a la fin du XVIeme siècle." *Actes Picaresque Européenne.* Montpellier: Etudes Sociocritiques, Université Paul Valéry, 1976. 45–57.

Contreras, Jaime. "Aldermen and Judaizers: Cryptojudaism, Counter-Reformation, and Local Power," in Cruz and Perry, 93–123.

Copland, Robert. "The Hyeway to the Spyttell Hous." *Select Pieces of Early Popular Poetry: Republished Principally from Early Printed Copies, in the Black Letter.* Vol. ll. London, 1817.

Cornwall, J. C. K. *Wealth and Society in Early Sixteenth Century England.* London: Routledge & Kegan Paul, 1988.

Cros, Edmond. *Ideología y genética textual: El caso del "Buscón."* Madrid: Cupsa, 1980.

———. *L'aristocraté et le carnaval des gueux: Etude sur le "Buscón" de Quevedo.* Montpellier: Etudes Sociocritiques, Centre d'Etudes Sociocritiques U.E.R. II, Université Paul Valery, 1975.

Cruz, Anne J., and Mary Elizabeth Perry, eds. *Culture and Control in Counter-Reformation Spain.* Hispanic Issues 7. Minneapolis: Univ. of Minnesota Press, 1992.

———. "Lazarillo de Tormes as Social Redemptor." *Marginated Groups in Spanish and Portuguese History: Proceedings of the Seventeenth Annual Meeting of the Society for Spanish and Portuguese Historical Studies.* Ed. William D. Phillips and Carla Rhan Phillips. Minneapolis: Society for Spanish and Portuguese Historical Studies, 1989. 61–70.

———. "The Picaresque as Discourse of Poverty." *Ideologies and Literature* 1.3 (1985): 74–97.

———. "Sexual Enclosure, Textual Escape: The *pícara* as Prostitute in the Spanish Female Picaresque Novel." *Seeking the Woman in Late Medieval and Renaissance Writings: Essays in Feminist Contextual Criticism.* Ed. Sheila Fisher and Janet E. Halley. Knoxville: Univ. of Tennessee Press, 1989. 135–59.

Davis, Lennard J. *Factual Fictions: The Origins of the English Novel.* New York: Columbia Univ. Press, 1983.

Domínguez Ortíz, Antonio. *La clase social de los conversos en Castilla en la Edad Moderna.* Granada: Universidad de Granada, 1991.

Dunn, Peter N. "Spanish Picaresque Fiction as a Problem of Genre." *Dispositio* 39 (1986):1–15.

Ferguson, Margaret. "Nashe's The Unfortunate Traveller: The 'Newes of the Maker' Game." *English Literary Renaissance* 11 (1981): 165–82.

Flynn, Maureen. *Sacred Charity: Confraternities and Social Welfare in Spain, 1400–1700.* Ithaca: Cornell Univ. Press, 1988.

Foucault, Michel. *Discipline and Punish: The Birth of the Prison.* Trans. Alan Sheridan. New York: Vintage Books, 1977.

Friedman, Edward H. "Narcissus's Echo: *La vida del buscón* and the Question of Authority in the Baroque." *Indiana Journal of Hispanic Literatures* 1 (1992): 213–60.

Greene, Robert. *The Blacke Bookes Messenger, 1592. Cuthbert Conny-Catcher. The Defence of Conny-Catching, 1592.* Elizabethan and Jacobean Quartos. Ed. G. B. Harrison. New York: Barnes and Noble, 1966.

Grey, Lady Jane. "A Certain Communication," in Spitz, 169–72.

Harman, Thomas. *A Caveat or Warning for Common Cursetors, vulgarly called Vagabonds.* London, 1814.

Iffland, James. *Quevedo and the Grotesque.* 2 vols. London: Tamesis, 1978 and 1982.

Jones, Ann Rosalind. "Inside the Outsider: Nashe's *Unfortunate Traveller* and Bakhtin's Polyphonic Novel." *English Literary History* 50 (1983): 61–81.

Lazarillo de Tormes. Ed. Francisco Rico. 2nd ed. Madrid: Cátedra, 1987.

Márquez Villanueva, Francisco. *Espiritualidad y literatura en el siglo XVI.* Madrid: Alfaguara, 1968.

Martz, Linda. *Poverty and Welfare in Hapsburg Spain: The Example of Toledo.* Cambridge: Cambridge Univ. Press, 1983.

Nashe, Thomas. *The Unfortunate Traveller; or, The Life of Jack Wilton.* Ed. John Berryman. New York: Capricorn Books, 1960.

Parker, Alexander A. *Literature and the Delinquent: The Picaresque Novel in Spain and Europe 1599–1753.* Edinburgh: Edinburgh Univ. Press, 1967.

Perry, Mary Elizabeth. *Crime and Society in Early Modern Seville.* Hanover, N.H.: Univ. Press of New England, 1980.

——— . "Magdalens and Jezebels in Counter-Reformation Spain," in Cruz and Perry. 125–144.

Pike, Ruth. *Penal Servitude in Early Modern Spain.* Madison: Univ. of Wisconsin Press, 1983.

Pound, John. *Poverty and Vagrancy in Tudor England.* Seminar Studies in History. Ed. Patrick Richardson. London: Longman, 1971.

Quevedo, Francisco de. *El buscón.* Ed. Pablo Jauralde Pou. Madrid: Clásicos Castalia, 1990.

Redondo, Augustin. "Pauperismo y mendicidad en Toledo en época del *Lazarillo.*" *Hommage des Hispanistes Français à Noel Salomon.* Barcelona: Laia, 1979. 703–24.

Rico, Francisco. *La novela picaresca.* Barcelona: Planeta, 1970.

Roncero López, Victoriano. *Historia y política en la obra de Quevedo.* Madrid: Editorial Pliegos, 1991.

Rumeau, A. "La première traduction du "Lazarillo": Les éditions de 1560 et 1561." *Bulletin Hispanique* 82.3–4 (1980): 362–79.

Samaha, Joel. *Law and Order in Historical Perspective: The Case of Elizabethan Essex.* New York; London: Academic Press, 1974.

Sieber, Harry. *The Picaresque*. London: Methuen, 1977.

Spitz, Lewis W., ed. *The Protestant Reformation*. Englewood Cliffs, N.J.: Prentice-Hall, 1966.

Stone, Lawrence. "Social Mobility in England, 1500–1700." *Seventeenth Century England: Society in an Age of Revolution*. Ed. Paul S. Seaver. New York, London: New Viewpoints, A Division of Franklin Watts, 1976. 25–70.

Watt, Ian. *The Rise of the Novel: Studies in Defoe, Richardson and Fielding*. Berkeley and Los Angeles: Univ. of California Press, 1962.

Webb, Sidney and Beatrice. *English Poor Law History, Part 1: The Old Poor Law*. 1927. English Local Government Volume 7. Hamden, Conn.: Archon Books, The Shoe String Press, Inc., 1963.

Weimann, Robert. "*Fabula* and *Historia:* The Crisis of the "Universall Consideration" in *The Unfortunate Traveller*." *Representations* 8 (1984): 14–29.

Wicks, Ulrich. *Picaresque Narrative, Picaresque Fictions: A Theory and Research Guide*. New York: Greenwood Press, 1989.

◆ **Chapter 10**

The Protean Picaresque

Howard Mancing

Proteus and Menelaos

In Book IV of the *Odyssey*, Menelaos, searching for the way to return home, talks with Eidothea, daughter of Proteus, the ancient god of the sea. Eidothea assures Menelaos that her father can provide the needed information, indicates where the old man might be found, and describes the manner by which he can be subdued and questioned. She says:

> Next, as soon as you see that he is asleep, that will be
> the time for all of you to use your strength and your vigor,
> and hold him there while he strives and struggles hard to
>   escape you.
> And he will try you by taking the form of all creatures that
>   come forth
> and move on the earth, he will be water and magical fire.
> You must hold stiffly on to him and squeeze him the harder.
> But when at last he himself, speaking in words, questions
>   you,
> being now in the same form he was in when you saw him
>   sleeping,
> then, hero, you must give over your force and let the old
>   man
> go free, and ask him which one of the gods is angry with
>   you,
> and ask him how to make your way home on the sea where
>   the fish swarm. (76)

273

The next day Menelaos and three stalwart warriors wait until
Proteus lies down to rest; then he describes what happens:

> We with a cry sprang up and rushed upon him, locking him
> in our arms, but the Old Man did not forget the subtlety
> of his arts. First he turned into a great bearded lion,
> and then to a serpent, then to a leopard, then to a great
> boar,
> and he turned into fluid water, to a tree with towering
> branches, but we held stiffly on to him with enduring
> spirit.
> But when the Old Man versed in devious ways grew weary
> of all this, he spoke to me in words and questioned me:
> "Which of the gods now, son of Artreus, has been advising
> you
> to capture me from ambush against my will. What do you
> want?" (77)

The old man goes on to tell Menelaos what he and his men need to
know in order to be on their way. Cleverness, daring, and perse-
verance were required to wrest from Proteus the secret of the path
that led home.

Scholars who have tried to define the picaresque novel can be
likened to Menelaos struggling with Proteus.[1] The adversary is
slippery and constantly changing; at any given moment it may assume the shape, not of a lion, running water, or a tree, but of a comic
biography, a fictional autobiography, or a realistic or satiric novel; it
may center on a protagonist who is a servant to many masters, a
delinquent, a beggar, or a social climber; it may consist of a study in
moral ambiguity, decadence, or honor. Whenever a critic perceives
clearly some version of the picaresque novel and tries to seize and
describe it, it turns into something else entirely. Lacking the perse-
verance of Menelaos, we have not been able to follow Eidothea's
advice: "You must hold stiffly on to him and squeeze him the
harder." The picaresque novel has inevitably eluded the grasp of
its pursuers and has never been forced to reveal its secrets.

The purpose of this essay is to challenge Proteus again. By attempting to recognize both the partial accomplishments and the
ultimate shortcomings of my predecessors, I hope to "hold stiffly"
and get the wily *pícaro* to yield his secret. I propose first to review

briefly some of the major trends in twentieth-century genre studies of the picaresque novel. Then I will draw from the best of these attempts, together with several aspects of recent literary theory, especially genre theory, in order to offer a new definition of the genre and to identify a canon of the Spanish picaresque novel.

Concepts of Genre

Modern scholarly study of the picaresque novel begins in 1899 with the publication of Frank Wadleigh Chandler's *Romances of Roguery*. Chandler defines the genre with admirable clarity and brevity as "a rogue relating his adventures" (45). He then goes on to expand his definition by describing the *pícaro* as follows:

> He is born of poor and dishonest parents, who are not often troubled with gracing their union by a ceremony, nor particularly pleased at his advent. He comes up by hook or crook as he may. Either he enters the world with an innate love of the goods of others, or he is innocent and learns by hard raps that he must take care of himself or go to the wall. In either case the result is much the same; in order to live he must serve somebody, and the gains of service he finds himself obliged to augment with the gains of roguery. So he flits from one master to another, all of whom he outwits in his career, and describes to satirize in his narrative. Finally, having run through a variety of strange vicissitudes, measuring by his rule of roguery the vanity of human estates, he brings his story to a close. (45–46)

Chandler continues in this vein at great length, describing impressionistically the characters, adventures, and social satire found in the picaresque novels. The problem is that many of the specific works Chandler cites as picaresque simply do not conform to many aspects of his description. The author seems to be unconcerned with his inconsistencies and self-contradictions.

Little, if any, improvement is made on Chandler's traditional and impressionistic definition through the first six decades of the twentieth century. I will not list the dozens of essays and books that essentially reproduce or, at best, modify only slightly the major elements of this type of definition. A perusal of any standard manual of literature will illustrate the degree to which the traditional definition has become institutionalized.

The major studies of the picaresque novels of the 1960s, 1970s, and 1980s, however, are characterized by a series of attempts to achieve greater methodological rigor and to offer some original concepts with regard to the problem of a generic definition. There are two major trends that we can identify in this period. The first is the tendency to choose a single criterion as the basis for identifying picaresque novels. Often this standard is sociological in orientation and focuses on the figure of the *pícaro*. Thus, for Alexander A. Parker the picaresque novel is—specifically and exclusively—a study in delinquency; for Maurice Molho the key is begging; for Enrique Tierno Galván, Jenaro Talens, and José Antonio Maravall the picaresque novel reflects the economic struggle of the oppressed social classes. For others the criterion is more or less thematic: for Marcel Bataillon the picaresque novel is characterized by a preoccupation with honor and reputation; for Christine J. Whitbourn the central issue is moral ambiguity; for Carlos Blanco Aguinaga the religious dogmatism of *Guzmán* is the entire genre's defining characteristic; for Alán Francis the picaresque novel is a study in decadence. Meanwhile, for Francisco Rico the single criterion is formalist: the picaresque novel is a fictional autobiography. Another group of formalist critics, including Stuart Miller, Oldrich Belic, and Gustavo A. Alfaro, use multiple criteria, rather than a single one in defining the genre.

Without doubt three names stand out in the past three decades: Claudio Guillén, Fernando Lázaro Carreter, and Ulrich Wicks. Guillén initiated the new phase in picaresque genre studies with his essay "Toward a Definition of the Picaresque," probably the most prestigious and most frequently cited study of the subject. Guillén identifies eight characteristics of the picaresque novel in the strict sense; of these, the two most important are the protagonist as orphan and the autobiographical form. Then he goes on to discuss novels that meet some but not all of his criteria, novels that he calls picaresque in a looser sense. Finally he considers an even broader and more generalized picaresque myth. Wicks prefers to think of the picaresque not as a genre but as a mode. He too lists eight elements that tend to characterize the picaresque mode, with stress on the *pícaro* as a solipsistic individual confronted with a disordered universe. Lázaro Carreter's approach is less prescriptive and more original. Basing his observations on the secondary works as well as the acknowledged masterpieces of the genre (*Lazarillo, Guzmán,* and *Buscón*), Lázaro maintains that the authors of picaresque novels were aware of an unwritten poetics of the genre and could modify literally any of the formal and thematic conventions associated with the tradition and still write what they and their readers considered picaresque novels.

The various scholars I have just cited very briefly tend toward one of two positions with regard to the picaresque canon. These positions are exclusivist and mediated. The exclusivist, usually single-criterion, critics seem to take an almost perverse delight in pointing out that certain texts, because they do not meet the standard of their unique and arbitrary criterion, are obviously not picaresque novels. Thus, for example, Parker excludes Lazarillo because he is not a juvenile delinquent; Molho denies admission to Marcos de Obregón because he is not a beggar; and Rico banishes Elena because *La hija de Celestina* is not a fictional autobiography. The second group recognizes that only a limited number of texts meet their criteria but that several others lurk somehow near the boundaries they have established, so they create various mediated categories of the picaresque novel. Thus it is that we have references to works called pseudo-picaresque, anti-picaresque, digressive picaresque, bourgeois picaresque, problematic picaresque, thematic picaresque, picaresque novels without *pícaros,* and more. A related problem is that generic concepts of the picaresque are frequently set forth on the basis of grossly inadequate evidence. Even many Hispanic scholars discuss the picaresque solely on the basis of the three canonical texts, *Lazarillo, Guzmán,* and *Buscón.* Meanwhile, many non-Hispanic scholars who barely know *Lazarillo* and most often are completely ignorant of *Guzmán* (see Wicks, *Picaresque Narrative*) begin and end with generic ideas based largely on post-seventeenth-century and non-Spanish models. It is largely because they look beyond the three classic texts that Guillén, Wicks, and Lázaro Carreter are more insightful in their assessments.

The inevitable reaction to this proliferation of definitions and diffusion of the genre came about in the late 1970s. I refer now to a series of excellent books on the picaresque in which the authors choose to evade the problem of generic definition. Specifically I am thinking of the works of Richard Bjornson, Harry Sieber, Alexander Blackburn, Peter N. Dunn, Walter L. Reed, and Edward H. Friedman. Most of these scholars review previous definitions, discuss the complexity of the generic problem, lament that past generic models have often confused or misled critics and general readers, call for a new and more precise concept, and then go on to analyze specific works and the history of the genre without committing themselves to a precise definition. Perhaps because they avoid the problem and are unencumbered by a generic concept that might limit their subsequent observations, these books are among the very best literary studies we have of the picaresque novel. Finally, it is but a single step from evasion to denial, and this step has been taken by Daniel Eisenberg, in a 1979 essay that asks rhetorically "Does the Picaresque Novel Exist?" Not surprisingly, Eisenberg concludes that it is impossible to use the term in any meaningful way and suggests that we would do better to reject it.

The current field of genre studies with respect to the picaresque novel appears to be in complete disarray. The vaguely impressionistic concept inherited from Chandler and his descendants still competes with jealous exclusion, apologetic fragmentation, coy evasion, and aggressive denial and deconstruction. Proteus would seem to have defied all attempts to pin him down and has yet to surrender his secrets. Richard Bjornson's conclusion, after surveying the problem, is that we need

> not an inductively established list of picaresque elements, but a dynamic model sufficiently flexible to encompass the unique individual works and their historical contexts while clearly identifying shared elements which justify their inclusion in the same category. (5)

Definition and Canon

Few scholars have agonized so acutely over the act of defining a literary genre as has Andrew V. Ettin. He states the problem succinctly: "Writing about a literary kind always means mediating between the description too inclusive to be a definition and the definition too exclusive to be a description." Where and how to begin is not the least of the difficulties: "It is, after all, hard to find the starting point in an interpretative circle: to describe pastoral literature, one needs to define the canon; to define the canon one needs a description of the category" (2). Later, Ettin affirms the inevitability of formulating a definition: "To study a genre is to make definitions and distinctions, to draw similarities and differences that will enhance our comprehension of a text and deepen our understanding of the ways and functions of literature" (74).

As Ettin says, a literary genre can—indeed, must—be defined if we are to study it in any significant way. Modern notions of literary history and literary theory allow us to conceptualize rather specifically how to go about constructing a generic definition. Since literary genres are changing historical entities, any useful definition should be flexible enough to accommodate the different texts that comprise the genre. One way to comprehend the options available to authors for the modification of generic conventions is to take into consideration what Renato Poggioli calls the unwritten poetics of a genre. Just as authors know what they are doing when they consciously write a literary text as part of a specific genre, so do readers know what they are doing when they read and react to specific texts. Thus, the techniques of reception theory as expounded by Hans Robert Jauss and others can be important in appreciating the historical, social, and cultural realities of literary genres. If authors are aware of the poetics of the genre within which they work, they are equally aware of the literary traditions of the same genre. All previous writers are the rivals of any given author. W. Jackson Bate refers to this as the "burden of the past"; Harold Bloom talks in terms of the "anxiety of influence"; less exotically, Roger Sale considers it simply in terms of "literary inheritance." This literary inheritance, especially that of the immediately preceding generations, may be a blessing or a curse, but it is a reality to be confronted. Narrative conventions employed by authors and presupposed by readers are, as Peter J. Rabinowitz and Helen H. Reed have demonstrated, crucial in determining how a text will be read. Literature is often based on life, but—as Michael Riffaterre, Gian Biagio Conte, and others have assured us—literature always invokes previous literature. The inclusive concept of intertextuality allows us to establish generic links among works by a variety of techniques. The fictional texts themselves are usually the best means of detecting the realities of genre, but they should be supplemented by the extrafictional apparatus that can be equally important in establishing a literary tradition.

Alastair Fowler's *Kinds of Literature* is our most complete, thorough, and convincing extended essay on genre theory (but see also Bakhtin, Cohen, Colie, Dubrow, Fussell, Kent, Schwartz, and Todorov). If it is possible to reduce this complex and subtle book to a single precept, it is the following: literary genres change and evolve. Genres constantly expand and contract; all literary texts modify the concept of the genres of which they form a part; the variations and modifications introduced by new texts are always significant; each new text expands the concept of its genre. According to Fowler the evidence we have for the existence of genres includes authors' statements, contemporary practice, readers' comments, and indirect inference. Among the generic signals or markers that Fowler identifies are generic allusion, references to previous writers and texts, and literary titles that evoke past practices.

Of the previously mentioned critics of the picaresque, the one whose work is most obviously recalled by the theories of Fowler and others just cited is that of Fernando Lázaro Carreter, who spoke of an unwritten poetics and the freedom of authors to eliminate or modify specific aspects that characterized previous practice. The problem with Lázaro Carreter's essay is that he did not pursue with much rigor his very suggestive thesis: he did not hold on to Proteus long enough or hard enough; he did not demonstrate in detail how the secondary works expanded the generic concept of the picaresque novel.

Genre definition must result from a hermeneutical process that takes into consideration the original texts and the several critical and theoretical processes I have already outlined. I believe that we can take the two basic constituents of most approaches to the picaresque novel—the figure of the *pícaro* and the form of fictional autobiography—and combine them with the concepts of generic change and unwritten poetics of Fowler and Lázaro Carreter in order to devise the sort of dynamic yet flexible definition called for by Bjornson. I propose the following definition of the picaresque novel:

> A picaresque novel is a text in which a major character is a *pícaro* who usually tells the story of his or her own life; the text always displays some degree of generic self-consciousness; it is a protean form.

In order to determine what a *pícaro* was in sixteenth- and seventeenth-century Spain, we can examine how the word and its synonyms were used and discussed at that time (see Mancing). These texts include a variety of (mostly anonymous) poems and essays dealing with the life of the *pícaro; comedias* and *entremeses* by Lope de Vega, Cervantes, Quevedo, and others that deal with *pícaros;* and novels by Mateo Alemán, Cervantes, Juan de Luna, and others. In addition, we can utilize the work of linguists who have studied the various possible etymologies of the word *pícaro* and historians who have written about *pícaros* in that epoch.

As a result, we find that the protean term *pícaro* can have a wide variety of connotations (see also Cañedo). Literary *pícaros* are usually orphans, whether literally or figuratively, of necessity or by choice, either permanently or temporarily. Very often they are servants, jacks-of-all-trades who may hold any number of menial jobs such as kitchen scullion (*pícaro de cocina*), stableboy, page, valet, jester or buffoon, or blindman's guide. Because they can function in so many capacities, they frequently serve a series of masters (*mozo de muchos amos*). Very frequently *pícaros* are self-sufficient, working independently or in concert with others as carriers (*ganapán* or *esportillero*). Often their activities are criminal; again, they may work alone or with others in delinquent or roguish activities such as petty thief, cutpurse, cape stealer, swindler, gambler, card shark, pimp, or confidence artist. At other times *pícaros* are unemployed and travel freely at their leisure as vagabonds, drifters, tramps, or vagrants. This frequently leads to another characteristic picaresque activity: begging. *Pícaros* often act alone as beggars, but also frequently join organizations of professional beggars. *Pícaros* are often some sort of trickster (*burlador, embustero, embelecador, tacaño, buscón*). In such activities *pícaros* are capable of assuming whatever disguise may be required by the situation. Thus we have *pícaros* who pose as wealthy noblemen (*galanes*), merchants, soldiers, hermits, actors, and many more. The female *pícara* is usually either a prostitute or confidence artist who uses her charms to deceive her way into the hearts and pocketbooks of wealthy noblemen; she, too, may work alone or with a pimp or other accomplices.

Although *pícaros* are often thought of as being alone and abandoned in the world—as indeed they frequently are—it is probably more common to see them in the company of a variety of other people. These others often represent some aspect of the criminal world: organized crime, ruffians, the beggars' guild, prison inmates, pimps and prostitutes, gamblers, and swindlers. But *pícaros* also associate with soldiers (braggart types, regiments traveling to or from wars, and so forth); students (especially as tricksters or participating in the life of boarding houses); acting troupes (as actors, writers, or mere hangers-on); people involved with transportation, travel, and tourism (muleteers and transporters, travelers, innkeepers and their guests, prostitutes); and the genuinely poor and needy (authentic beggars, blindmen, other *pícaros*, and so forth). *Pícaros* are often found in large urban centers such as Madrid, Sevilla, or Toledo, where they are seen near the city entrances, on the streets and boulevards, in the plazas and theaters, at the stockyards and shipping and fishing docks, or in the inns and taverns. Since they travel a great deal they are frequently observed on the road and at highway inns, especially on the main highways such as that between Madrid and Toledo. No university, especially the major ones of Salamanca and Alcalá de Henares, is complete without its complement of *pícaros*. Another favorite haunt is the tuna fishing industry based in southern Spain, especially around Cádiz and Sanlúcar.

Perhaps the major characteristic of the lifestyle of *pícaros* is their sense of freedom, independence, and nonconformity. *Pícaros* tend to rejoice in their antisocial lack of responsibility and accountability. Their preferred activities tend to be eating and drinking, singing and dancing. But with the joy of independence come also the hardships of having to make long journeys on foot, suffering from inclement weather, sleeping out of doors, lacking personal hygiene, dressing poorly, and lacking economic security and material comfort. In order to gain the latter, *pícaros* tend to devote much of their time and energy to rising in the social and economic order. They seek status, honor, and money, not often by dint of hard work and application, but through deception and dishonesty, often by means of marriage into a wealthy family.

Any novel that contains a major character (usually the protagonist, but occasionally an important secondary character) who can be described by a substantial subset of the aforementioned qualities is likely to be a picaresque novel. The characters who inhabit other types of fiction written at the same time—romances of chivalry, pastoral and sentimental romances, historical tales, Byzantine romances, adventure stories, Italianate or courtly fiction—simply cannot be described (except occasionally and briefly, in passing) in these terms.

The second key element in the definition is related to the practice of life-telling. I have chosen with care the phrase "who usually tells the story of his or her own life," because this standard should be more inclusive than the full-fledged autobiographical form frequently cited—especially by Rico—as an identifying characteristic of the genre. It is true that the majority of picaresque novels are written from start to finish in the form of a first-person autobiographical narration. But a substantial subset of the texts in question do not have this form. And yet all picaresque novels display at least some of a complex of autobiographical conventions that are related to the telling of one's own life.

The first of these conventions is the use of the word *vida* in the title. Harold Jones has shown that before the publication of *La vida de Lazarillo de Tormes* in 1554 no work of fiction ever contained that word in its title. The only *lives* written were those of saints, soldiers, and illustrious historical figures; thus we have the *Vida* of Teresa de Jesús, the *Discursos de la vida* of Alonso de Contreras, and others. After *Lazarillo de Tormes* the only works of fiction that used the term *vida* as part of their titles were picaresque novels: *Segunda parte de la vida del pícaro Guzmán de Alfarache*, *Relaciones de la vida del escudero Marcos de Obregón*, *Vida y hechos de Estebanillo González*, and so forth. Other types of fiction were called *libros*, *historias*, or *novelas*, but never *vidas*.

The second important convention is that the picaresque character will either volunteer or be asked to *contar su vida*. This first-person narration may be the work's major mode (as it is in *Lazarillo de Tormes, Guzmán de Alfarache,* or *Teresa de Manzanares*); it may be embedded in a third-person narration (as in the case of Elena in Salas Barbadillo's *La hija de Celestina,* Rinconete and Cortadillo in Cervantes's story, or Andrés in Carlos García's *Desordenada codicia de bienes ajenos*); or it may be used indirectly: occasionally the author of a third-person narration states that he is going to *contar la vida* of his protagonist (as does Castillo Solórzano in *El bachiller Trapaza* and *La garduña de Sevilla* and Francisco Santos in *Periquillo el de las gallineras*). Again it is worth noting that in other types of fiction of the period—chivalric, sentimental, pastoral, and so forth—the characters virtually never offer or are asked to *contar su vida*. Instead they will *contar su historia, contar sus desgracias,* or simply *descubrirse*. The picaresque novel is clearly unique in its conception that its characters have *lives,* rather than stories or misfortunes, that are interesting and worth recounting (see Rico, Spadaccini, and Talens, and Friedman "Story and History"). Narrative's "inward turn" that Erich Kahler has shown to be characteristic of the Renaissance is nowhere more manifest than in the Spanish picaresque novel, where the individual attained a new and characteristically modern status.

Often overlooked completely or, at best, commented on only very briefly (as it is, for example, by Wicks), is the generic self-consciousness that for me is the third major identifying characteristic of the picaresque novel. No picaresque novel fails to evoke consciously the literary tradition with which it is associated. The generic evocations are most frequently found in the texts' extrafictional apparatus. Here I draw upon Susan S. Lancer's excellent book *The Narrative Act,* in which she describes an authoritative extrafictional voice, a voice that creates a reader's generic expectations through the book's title, preface, foreword, dedication, epigraphs, chapter titles, and so forth. Thus there can be no question that a reader knows what to expect when encountering the following typical circumstances: the publication together in a single volume of *Guzmán de Alfarache* and *Lazarillo de Tormes;* the use in titles of synonyms of the word *pícaro,* such as *guitón* and *buscón;* titles containing stock phrases like *mozo de muchos amos* and *niña de los embustes;* a frontispiece that consists of an engraving showing Justina and Guzmán together in a boat of picaresque life, guided by Lazarillo in a rowboat; an editor's preface in which *Lazarillo de Tormes* and *Guzmán de Alfarache* are evoked; a prologue in which Justina says that she will eventually marry Guzmán; or the various sequels to *Lazarillo* and *Guzmán.*

Similarly, within the fictional texts, characters and narrators occasionally compare themselves specifically to previous literary *pícaros,* or cite episodes from, or the titles of, other picaresque novels. The cumulative effect of these allusions, of the constant intertextual play, is overwhelming. The authors of the Spanish picaresque novels clearly knew the literary tradition in which they were writing. And their contemporary readers clearly knew what sort of book they had in hand. Lázaro Carreter is absolutely correct in asserting that the literary community of the age recognized a poetics at work—unwritten, yes, but clearly identifiable and readily perceived.

The fourth and final element in the definition is more an observation about the genre than part of the definition per se: the picaresque novel is a protean form. By this I mean that, like Proteus, the picaresque novel can take literally any shape. A picaresque novel can be a short story (as short as about 15,000 words: *Rinconete y Cortadillo*) or a very long novel (up to 250,000 words in length: *Guzmán de Alfarache*). It can be in the form of a dialogue or narrated either in the first or the third person. Its structure may be completely open, with a sequel promised, or closed, ending with the death of the protagonist. It may be constructed in a tight, logical, and causal way, or it may be loose, arbitrary, and episodic. It may contain no embedded material or it may consist primarily of interpolations, rather like a collage. The embedded material may be short fictions (usually courtly tales, but also Moorish, Byzantine, or picaresque stories), discursive digressions (on moral, social, or literary themes), anecdotes (fables, apologues, emblems, or folk tales), poems, and even one-act plays. It is even possible for a picaresque novel to be an interpolation within another work (as is *La vida de Gregorio Guadaña* in *El siglo pitagórico*). The elements of essay, moral discourse, or social satire may be as important as or even more important than the picaresque narration. The work's tone may be deadly serious, completely frivolous, or anywhere in between. The *pícaro* may be the protagonist (whether or not the narrator) or an important secondary character, but not a mere walk-on, as is the *pícaro* Ginés de Pasamonte in *Don Quijote*. There may be one, two, or more *pícaros* in a single work, and they can be any type of *pícaro* described previously. The *pícaro* may be a man, a woman, a dog, or even a tuna. There is literally no end to the variety of character, theme, style, structure, or narrative technique that can be—and is—found in the Spanish picaresque novel. Many *pícaros*, such as those of Obregón, Castillo Solórzano, and Gómez, are so bourgeois that they are nearly indistinguishable from the standard *galán* (see Thacker). In spite of some shared generic characteristics, works such as *Lazarillo*, *Guzmán*, and *Buscón* are much more fundamentally different from than they are similar to each other (see Dunn, *Picaresque Fiction*, and Ife). The range of individuality and difference becomes even greater yet when we look at texts such as *Justina*, *Trapaza*, or *Periquillo*.

It should be stressed that there is no characteristic ideology of the picaresque novel. If *Lazarillo* and *Estebanillo* are radically critical of the religious and political norms of society, *Buscón* and the novels of Salas Barbadillo are as conformist as possible. Although the concept of "marginality" has frequently been considered central to the picaresque enterprise, characters like Marcos de Obregón are at best only marginally marginal; and the marginal spaces occupied by *pícaros* as different as Lazarillo, Justina, and Periquillo have relatively little in common. It is important to base our concept of genre on the texts as they are and not to force our readings of the texts to correspond to our previously formed concepts of genre.

If we apply carefully each of the four elements in the proposed definition to the dozens of sixteenth- and seventeenth-century Spanish texts that have been called picaresque at one time or another, we can construct an inclusive canon that contains between twenty-five and thirty titles published between 1554 (*Lazarillo de Tormes*) and 1688 (*Periquillo, el de las gallineras*). The Appendix that follows lists all the Spanish texts of the sixteenth and seventeenth centuries that I have been able to identify as picaresque, according to the definition offered in this essay.

Although it is common to speak of the permutations through which the picaresque novel passes as it is adapted to the French Enlightenment, the age of existentialism, or the postmodern era, we have already seen that protean change and adaptation are essential features of the genre from the start. There is no single, sustaining, or controlling theme, worldview, tone, philosophy, or attitude that characterizes the genre. It is my contention that the picaresque novel cannot be traced *only* through a study of its formal characteristics, *only* by the nature of its protagonists, or *only* as seen in certain themes. Rather, it is the presence of all these elements, plus the crucial generic self-consciousness, that makes it possible for us to identify a picaresque novel, no matter how many forms it may assume.

Appendix: The Picaresque Canon

1554	*La vida de Lazarillo de Tormes y de sus fortunas y adversidades*
1555	*Segunda parte del Lazarillo de Tormes y de sus fortunas y adversidades*
(ca. 1595?)	*Diálogo intitulado el Capón*
1599	M. Alemán. *Primera parte de Guzmán de Alfarache*
1602	J. Martí. *Segunda parte de la vida del pícaro Guzmán de Alfarache*
1604	M. Alemán. *Segunda parte de la vida de Guzmán de Alfarache, atalaya de la vida humana*
(ca. 1604?)	G. González. *El guitón Honofre*
1605	F. López de Ubeda. *Libro de entretenimiento de la pícara Justina*
1612	A. J. de Salas Barbadillo. *La hija de Celestina*
1613	M. de Cervantes. *Novelas ejemplares.* *Rinconete y Cortadillo; La ilustre fregona; Coloquio de los perros*
1618	V. Espinel. *Relaciones de la vida del escudero Marcos de Obregón*
1619	C. García. *La desordenada codicia de los bienes ajenos*
1620	J. Cortés de Tolosa. *Lazarillo de Manzanares*

1620	J. de Luna. *Segunda parte de Lazarillo de Tormes, sacada de las crónicas antiguas de Toledo*
1621	A. J. de Salas Barbadillo. *El necio bien afortunado*
1624	J. de Alcalá Yáñez. *Alonso, mozo de muchos amos*
1626	J. de Alcalá Yáñez. *Segunda parte de Alonso, mozo de muchos amos*
1626	F. de Quevedo. *Historia de la vida del buscón, llamado don Pablos, exemplo de vagamundos y espejo de tacaños*
1632	A. de Castillo Solórzano. *La niña de los embustes, Teresa de Manzanares*
1637	A. de Castillo Solórzano. *Aventuras del Bachiller Trapaza, quinta esencia de embusteros y maestro de emb-elecadores*
1642	A. de Castillo Solórzano. *La garduña de Sevilla y anzuelo de bolsas*
1644	A. Enríquez Gómez. *Vida de don Gregorio Guadaña*
1646	*Vida y hechos de Estebanillo González, hombre de buen humor, compuesto por él mismo*
(ca. 1650?)	*Vida y costumbres de la Madre Andrea*
(ca. 1655?)	A. F. Machado de Silva. *Tercera parte de Guzmán de Alfarache*
1688	F. Santos. *Periquillo el de las gallineras*

Notes

1. It seems especially appropriate to evoke the figure of Proteus in this context. A. Bartlett Giamatti has written on the extensive presence of the shape-changing god of the sea in Renaissance literature in general. In his book on the picaresque novel Stuart Miller devotes a chapter to "The Protean Form" (70–77), on the characteristic ability of the *pícaro* to assume any new role or adopt any social identity. Edmond Cros, in his massive study of Alemán's novel, takes Proteus as the governing image of Guzmán de Alfarache. In an earlier essay on the picaresque genre I employed the term "protean form." Proteus may indeed stand as the patron saint both of the *pícaro* and of the picaresque novel.

Works Cited

Alfaro, Gustavo A. *La estructura de la novela picaresca.* Bogotá: Instituto Caro y Cuervo, 1977.

Bataillon, Marcel. *Pícaros y picaresca: La pícara Justina.* Trans. Francisco Rodríguez Vadillo. Madrid: Taurus, 1982.

Bakhtin, M. M. *The Dialogic Imagination: Four Essays.* Ed. Michael Holquist. Trans. Caryl Emerson and Michael Holquist. Austin: Univ. of Texas Press, 1981.

Bate, W. Jackson. *The Burden of the Past and the English Poet*. Cambridge: Belknap Press, 1970.

Belic, Oldrich. "La novela picaresca y el realismo." *Romanistica Pragensia* (Acta Universitatis Carolinae). *Philologica* 2 (1961): 5–15.

Bjornson, Richard. *The Picaresque Hero in European Fiction*. Madison: Univ. of Wisconsin Press, 1977.

Blackburn, Alexander. *The Myth of the Picaro: Continuity and Transformation of the Picaresque Novel 1554–1954*. Chapel Hill: Univ. of North Carolina Press, 1979.

Blanco Aguinaga, Carlos. "Cervantes y la picaresca: Notas sobre dos tipos de realismo." *Nueva Revista de Filologa Hispánica* 11 (1957): 314–42.

Bloom, Harold. *The Anxiety of Influence: A Theory of Poetry*. Oxford: Oxford Univ. Press, 1973.

Cañedo, Jesús. "El 'curriculum vitae' del pícaro." *Revista de Filología Española* 49 (1966): 125–80.

Chandler, Frank Wadleigh. *Romance of Roguery, an Episode in the History of the Novel I: The Picaresque Novel in Spain*. New York: Macmillan, 1899.

Cohen, Ralph. "History and Genre." *New Literary History* 17 (1986): 203–17.

Colie, Rosalie L. *The Resources of Kind: Genre-Theory in the Renaissance*. Ed. B. K. Lewalski. Berkeley: Univ. of California Press, 1973.

Conte, Gian Biagio. *The Rhetoric of Imitation: Genre and Poetic Memory in Virgil and Other Latin Poets*. Trans. from Italian. Ed. and foreword by Charles Segal. Ithaca: Cornell Univ. Press, 1986.

Cros, Edmond. *Protée et le Gueux: Recherches sur les origines et la nature du récit picaresque dans "Guzmán de Alfarache."* Paris: Didier, 1967.

Dubrow, Heather. *Genre*. London: Methuen, 1982.

Dunn, Peter N. *Spanish Picaresque Fiction: A New Literary History*. Ithaca: Cornell Univ. Press, 1993.

———. *The Spanish Picaresque Novel*. Boston: Twayne, 1979.

Eisenberg, Daniel. "Does the Picaresque Novel Exist?" *Kentucky Romance Quarterly* 26 (1979): 203–19.

Ettin, Andrew V. *Literature and the Pastoral*. New Haven: Yale Univ. Press, 1984.

Fowler, Alastair. *Kinds of Literature: An Introduction to the Theory of Genres and Modes*. Cambridge: Harvard Univ. Press, 1982.

Francis, Alán. *Picaresca, decadencia, historia: Aproximación a una realidad histórico-literaria*. Madrid: Gredos, 1978.

Friedman, Edward H. *The Antiheroine's Voice: Narrative Discourse and Transformation of the Picaresque*. Columbia: Univ. of Missouri Press, 1987.

———. "The Picaresque as Autobiography: Story and History." In Spadaccini and Talens 119–27.

Fussell, Paul, Jr. "Writing as Imitation: Observations on the Literary Process." *The Rarer Action: Essays in Honor of Francis Furgusson*. Eds. Alan Cheuse and Richard Koffler. New Brunswick: Rutgers Univ. Press, 1970. 218–39.

Giamatti, A. Bartlett. "Proteus Unbound: Some Versions of the Sea God in the Renaissance." In *The Disciplines of Criticism: Essays in Literary Theory, Interpretation and History*. Eds. Peter Demetz, Thomas Greene, and Lowry Nelson Jr. New Haven: Yale Univ. Press, 1968. 437–75.

Guillén, Claudio. "Toward a Definition of the Picaresque." *Literature as System: Essays toward the Theory of Literary History*. Princeton: Princeton Univ. Press, 1971. 71–106.

Homer. *The Odyssey.* Trans. Richmond Lattimore. New York: Harper Perennial, 1991.

Ife, B. W. *Reading and Fiction in Golden-Age Spain: A Platonist Critique and Some Picaresque Replies.* Cambridge: Cambridge Univ. Press, 1985.

Jauss, Hans Robert. *Toward an Aesthetic of Reception.* Trans. Timothy Bahti. Minneapolis: Univ. of Minnesota Press, 1982.

Kahler, Erich. *The Inward Turn of Narrative.* Trans. Richard and Clara Winston. Foreword by Joseph Frank. Princeton: Princeton Univ. Press, 1973.

Kent, Thomas. *Interpretation and Genre: The Role of Generic Perception in the Study of Narrative Texts.* Lewisburg: Bucknell Univ. Press, 1986.

Jones, Harold G. "La *vida* de Lazarillo de Tormes." *La picaresca: Orígenes, textos y estructuras. Actas del I Congreso Internacional sobre la Picaresca.* Ed. Manual Criado de Val. Madrid: Fundación Universitaria Española, 1979. 449–58.

Lanser, Susan Sniader. *The Narrative Act: Point of View in Prose Fiction.* Princeton: Princeton Univ. Press, 1981.

Lázaro Carreter, Fernando. "Para una revisión del concepto 'Novela Picaresca.'" *"Lazarillo de Tormes" en la picaresca.* Barcelona: Ariel, 1972. 195–229.

Mancing, Howard. "The Picaresque Novel: A Protean Form." *College Literature* 6 (1979): 182–204.

Maravall, José Antonio. *La literatura picaresca desde la historia social (siglos XVI y XVII).* Madrid: Taurus, 1986.

Miller, Stuart. *The Picaresque Novel.* Cleveland: Press of the Case Western Reserve University, 1967.

Molho, Maurice. *Introducción al pensamiento picaresco.* Trans. Augusto Gálvez-Cañero y Pidal. Salamanca: Anaya, 1972.

Parker, Alexander A. *Literature and the Delinquent: The Picaresque Novel in Spain and Europe, 1599–1753.* Edinburgh: Edinburgh Univ. Press, 1967.

Poggioli, Renato. "Poetics and Metrics." *The Spirit of the Letter: Essays in European Literature.* Cambridge: Harvard Univ. Press, 1965. 343–54.

Rabinowitz, Peter J. *Before Reading: Narrative Conventions and the Politics of Interpretation.* Ithaca: Cornell Univ. Press, 1987.

Reed, Helen H. *The Reader in the Picaresque Novel.* London: Tamesis, 1984.

Reed, Walter L. *An Exemplary History of the Novel: The Quixotic versus the Picaresque.* Chicago: Univ. of Chicago Press, 1981.

Rico, Francisco. *The Spanish Picaresque Novel and the Point of View.* Trans. Charles Davis with Harry Sieber. Cambridge: Cambridge Univ. Press, 1984.

Riffaterre, Michael. *Semiotics of Poetry.* Bloomington: Indiana Univ. Press, 1978.

Sale, Roger. *Literary Inheritance.* Amherst: Univ. of Massachusetts Press, 1984.

Schwartz, Elias. *The Forms of Feeling: Toward a Mimetic Theory of Literature.* Port Washington, N.Y.: Kennikat Press, 1972.

Sieber, Harry. *The Picaresque.* London: Methuen, 1977.

Spadaccini, Nicholas, and Jenaro Talens, eds. *Autobiography in Early Modern Spain.* Minneapolis: Prisma Institute, 1988.

———. "The Construction of the Self. Notes on Autobiography in Early Modern Spain." In Spadaccini and Talens 9–40.

Talens, Jenaro. *Novela picaresca y práctica de la transgresión.* Madrid: Júcar, 1975.

Thacker, M. J. "Gregorio Guadaña: *pícaro francés* or *pícaro-galán?*" *Hispanic Studies in Honour of Frank Pierce.* Ed. John England. Sheffield: Department of Hispanic Studies, Univ. of Sheffield, 1980. 149–68.

Tierno Galván, Enrique. "Sobre la novela picaresca." *La novela picaresca y otros escritos.* Madrid: Tecnos, 1974. 9–135.

Todorov, Tzvetan. *Genres in Discourse.* Trans. Catherine Porter. Cambridge: Cambridge Univ. Press, 1990.

Whitbourn, Christine J. "Moral Ambiguity in the Spanish Picaresque Tradition." *Knaves and Swindlers: Essays on the Picaresque Novel in Europe.* Ed. Christine J. Whitbourn. London: Oxford Univ. Press, 1974. 1–24.

Wicks, Ulrich. *Picaresque Narrative, Picaresque Fictions: A Theory and Research Guide.* New York: Greenwood Press, 1989.

Revisiting the Picaresque in Postmodern Times

Francisco J. Sánchez and Nicholas Spadaccini

The present volume of Hispanic Issues touches upon one of the most canonical of genres, the picaresque, a type of fiction that, since its invention in Spain at the turn of the seventeenth century (Guillén), has drawn the interest of readers in Spain and Europe and, more recently, in modern times, has even found a privileged locus in a variety of institutional settings: literary histories, university course catalogues, and symposia on both sides of the Atlantic. Moreover, it is safe to say that only Cervantes's *Don Quijote* has been accorded more critical attention as books and essays on picaresque literature continue to be printed at a breathtaking pace. The question, then, is why yet another volume on this subject, especially at the present juncture in literary and cultural studies. A possible explanation may be found in the peculiar character of the picaresque, which, even while retaining its canonical status, allows us to enter into a consideration of the related issues of diversity, difference, periphery, and marginality, issues that have a prominent place in a debate that ultimately deals with the role of traditions and the possibility of alternatives to them.

Most of the essays included in this volume constitute an attempt to uncover areas in the field of representation that have not been sufficiently studied in the past, areas such as sexual repression, the relationship between authorship and property in the discursive domain, the connection between linguistic and social alienation, the synchrony of marginality in relation to its own center (a synchrony that allows for a consideration of marginality at the same moral level of centrality), the emergence of new models of subjectivity, and an attempt to integrate different means of representation at the intersection of political writing, picaresque narratives, painting, and iconography.

In his introductory essay Giancarlo Maiorino suggests that contemporary critical and theoretical interest in the "marginal," the unheroic, the everyday, can be brought to bear fruitfully upon the reexamination of the picaresque, a literature dealing with social nobodies that, from the mid-sixteenth century to the present day, has captured the imagination and experience of readers. *Lazarillo,* he concludes, "initiated a novelistic discourse" that was to "change the very notion of canonicity and marginality." Maiorino deals with the impact of economics on the cultural syncretism of the age, arguing that wealth affected what he calls econopoetics, that is, the description of "deficient negotiations between economic signs and noneconomic verbal signifiers." Thus, "From food and lodging to fashion, money, and manners, econopoetics brings together an array of different languages, which are reciprocally paraliterary and paraeconomic." Maiorino's analysis of *Lazarillo* goes on to concentrate on the waterseller chapter, which he compares to Velázquez's painting of the same subject. The old waterseller in Velázquez is said to display personal pride in a job that gives him identity and social respectability whereas for Lázaro the selling of water is strictly an economic task.

In focusing on econopoetics, Maiorino seeks to move away from traditional formalist readings of picaresque narratives, especially those that tended to stress unity and theme alone; he also professes a distrust for totalizing social approaches to these same texts, arguing that to limit one's interpretation to class struggle or to overemphasize tensions resulting from caste differences is no longer sufficient. Thus, his own focus on econopoetics entails a semiotic approach centering on the representation of the distribution of wealth as an indicator of changing values in early modern Spain. Implicit in this approach is the idea that the *pícaro*'s lot is never disconnected from the concrete organization of society; that the actual distribution of wealth, as seen from the perspective of this econopoetics, refers to that very organization at the level of values and symbols (honor, status, clothes, language, etc.), what Bourdieu would call symbolic capital.

Viewing the picaresque as a cultural artifact seems to us to be more productive than what has recently been proposed by Peter N. Dunn, who argues for an anthropological perspective against any kind of sociological explanation—especially Maravall's (*La picaresca*)—of the conflicts to which an individual is exposed in his or her attempts at integration into society. Dunn borrows from Victor Turner's investigations of "the intermediate 'liminal' phase"—as earlier proposed by Arnold van Gennep in his classic *Rites de passage*—to conclude that the different phenomena of marginality are related to a self-imposed constant state of transition. According to Dunn, "Those that live in a state of permanent liminality are all who choose to occupy a place apart in observance of other rulers and 'alternative lifestyles'" (309). One could argue that a conception anchored in the notion of ritual minimizes the potential for tensions between the individual and society within specific historical coordinates, forgetting that baroque society encompasses a whole range of social and economic spaces in which the marginalized individual and the dominant segments of society are likely to collide.

From our perspective, the question of picaresque marginality is dealt with imaginatively and productively by Maravall, who characterizes the *pícaro* as "desvinculado" ("uncoupled") precisely because of a realization that no amount of work will gain him access to privileges; such perceived impossibility of "medro" leads the *pícaro* to adopt a position of anomie and deviation vis-à-vis society and its norms (*La picaresca* 105). The *pícaro's* "desvinculación," which manifests itself in a rupture with traditional social binders such as place of origin, family, political community, and church, is ultimately related to his or her individualism, solitude, and a newfound freedom from social restraints and responsibilities. What ultimately matters for the *pícaro* are the external signs of honor, what Maravall calls "visible social esteem" ("la social estimación visible") (*La picaresca* 536). Honor, therefore, cannot be disconnected from wealth.[1]

Maiorino's "econopoetics," coupled with Maravall's sociopolitical explanation of the picaresque as yet another manifestation of the culture of crisis of baroque Spain, could be used to analyze the canon of picaresque literature, keeping in mind, of course, that

the "deficient negotiations between economic signs and noneconomic verbal signifiers" (44) function within a specific historical
context and within different models of representation of subjectivity as we move from the Erasmian *Lazarillo* to the baroque texts of
the early 1600s such as *Guzmán, La pícara Justina,* and *Buscón,* to
Cervantes's excursion into the picaresque, and later to *Estebanillo
González* (1646).[2]

The type of sociological approach to the picaresque proposed
by Maravall brings into focus the idea that, from the time of his
emergence as a fictional "hero," the *pícaro* represents one of the
major breaks in the mental and social order of the medieval period. In this respect, picaresque literature participates in the concerns shown by many writers of early modern Spain toward the
phenomena of poverty, vagrancy, and the diverse proposals that
emerge for the implementation of a system to help and control the
poor.

Anne J. Cruz in this volume deals with the position of picaresque narratives vis-à-vis these same concerns in England, focusing on the literary manifestations of the rogue in English literature, as well as on the ordinances and debates regarding the
proper remedy for vagrancy, a social cancer that was seen as posing a threat to the social order. Following a comparative approach,
Cruz argues that while the English "rogue is isolated and diminished by the same social groups that would disclose his presence
and make known his language," the Spanish picaresque "uncovers the collusion of the *pícaro* and his social superiors in a caste system that keeps the social classes bound to each other through the
fearful recognition of their similitude." This fearful recognition,
one might add, is an acknowledgment of the potential for subversion of the status quo.

Cruz seems to assume that the socioeconomic structure of Spain
is that of a "caste system," a conception that achieved common
currency through the work of Américo Castro and his school, especially at U.S. universities. Yet, Maravall has argued (*Poder, honor
y élites*) that the determinant factor in Spanish society as well as in
other societies of Europe is stratification by wealth rather than by
ethnicity. For what moves the *pícaro* toward the usurpation of
codes and symbols traditionally assigned to the nobility is an

awareness of the lack of possibilities for social mobility. Hence the *pícaro*'s propensity for knowingly seeking to be what she or he is not: a member of the idle segments of Spanish society. It is for this reason that the more privileged elements of society tend to see the *pícaro* as a shameless usurper capable of turning upside down any semblance of difference between individuals. Thus, from the perspective of those privileged groups that support the status quo, the *pícaro*'s aspiration to "medro" brings with it the potential for social chaos. Within this context, Cruz is right when she affirms that "the Spanish *pícaro* embodies in his self-conscious discourse the tensions, fears, and hatreds of a society obsessed."

The questions of poverty and marginality are, then, related to phenomena that are normally associated with modernity (the individual subject, the idea of progress and socioeconomic growth, the emergence of the state and its institutions, and so on). It could be argued that *Lazarillo de Tormes* is part of a wide-ranging debate on the discourse of marginality in Spain and Europe—a discourse that touches both on the problem of charity and vagrancy in the Old World and on the marginality of the Amerindians in the fourth terrestrial continent.[3] In other words, the notions of "progress" and "growth," which have been advanced until very recently as the framing attributes of the Renaissance, now need to be examined in conjunction with many other issues that were part of the social and cultural reality of the time (Maravall, "Prólogo," *Antiguos y modernos*).[4] For the notions of "progress" and "growth" may well have blinded us to the symptoms of crisis that are inherent to modernity. Those symptoms may be said to manifest themselves not only at the level of social stratification but also in that of representation (in the visual arts, in writing, etc.), which, in turn, allows for the possibility of dealing with subjectivity in terms of the social and individual dimensions of the self.

It can be argued that an analysis of picaresque literature cannot be separated from a consideration of the question of social marginality. For the cultural meaning of this type of literature lies in the description of the *pícaro*'s interaction with an urban world and in the development of a modern mentality. It may be said that the *pícaro* now replaces the knight errant as mediator of knowledge as his wanderings in an urban setting gives the reader access to a variety of experiences that invariably represent differing degrees of social interactions undertaken in pursuit of some of the symbols of wealth. It is, in fact, through Lazarillo's eyes that the reader of the mid-1500s is made to see the extent of the *pícaro*'s marginalization in the solitude of the city, roaming among other individuals, engaged in various processes of adaptation and survival. In other words, the reader is likely to experience the cultural event of the city through the gaze of the marginalized. The city is seen as a process involving relations between different individuals; it is viewed as a field of conflict and struggle in which the Other refuses to be reduced to the same.

The reader's experience is also mediated by the depiction of the *pícaro*'s social behavior, which includes the representation of the erotic body. Such a body is alluded to ironically in *Lazarillo* but comes to the fore explicitly in those picaresque texts in which the protagonist is a woman. Thus, *La Lozana andaluza* and *La pícara Justina*, for example, allow us to expand the concept of marginality to include prostitution and, in a broader sense, the exchange value of sexuality as it connects with the corruption of the institution of marriage.

Virtually every picaresque narrative touches upon the related issues of "love," marriage, and sexual deception. Thus, the sexual body, the institution of marriage, the corruption of that institution, and the broader phenomena of economic pragmatism are related elements of the same discourse. Moreover the values deformed through the sexual body project an inverted image of courtly society in the sense that the *pícara*'s transactions involve the pragmatic use of established moral values such as virginity. From Fernando de Rojas's *La Celestina* (1500) onward, virginity becomes a commodity as well as a means of social deception. Such is the case with López de Ubeda's Justina, Salas Barbadillo's Elena (*La hija de Celestina*), Castillo Solórzano's female characters (*Las harpías en Madrid*) and Cervantes's Estefanía (*El casamiento engañoso*), to mention some of the salient examples.

Several important picaresque narratives force modern readers to reflect upon the status of marginalized women in a male-dominated culture. Nina Cox Davis, in this volume, remarks that in *La pícara Justina* there emerges "a feminine engendered counterpart" to *Lazarillo, Guzmán,* and *Buscón,* novels in which women do not have a voice. Focusing on the narrative of Ubeda's *pícara* as structured by the discourse of the body, and relying on Butler (*Gender Trouble*), Cox Davis concludes that "the writing that conveys this protagonist's narrative is distinctly 'feminized,' in its engendered response to the elitist masculine literary and cultural models that it ridicules." Ubeda is said to "enhance the political potential of the picaresque" as the *pícara's* words are freed "from the tradition of referentiality that privileges discourse over the body and material existence." Cox Davis also highlights the deconstruction of the figure of Perlícaro and through it, "the position of male readers—from their places in society to their very bodies." From this analysis one can surmise that the reader's mediated experience of female marginality or repression is drawn from the novel's representation of the conflict between male gaze and female sexuality.

The question of marginality in the guise of sexual transgression is highlighted in two other essays in this volume. George A. Shipley argues that the fourth chapter of *Lazarillo* "is layered with inherited erotic signifiers and suggestions of illicit behavior." The suppression of those signifiers in the reception of the novel is attributed by Shipley to a lack of appreciation for "the rhythms of orality" that govern the written word, to an oral prose that "beguiles the ear, excites the mind's eye." His conclusion is that "sex is one of the common denominators he [Lázaro] uses to reduce us from judges of his behavior to participation in the demeanor he describes and to equivalence with his neighbors in Toledo."

Shipley's suggestive reading of *Lazarillo's* elliptical fourth chapter challenges the contemporary reader to go beyond the stated purposes of the narrator, to shed his or her own prejudices and taboos about sex and to understand that he or she is ultimately implicated in the very construction of perversion.

Marginality and sexual transgression are also the focus of Janis A. Tomlinson and Marcia L. Welles's intertextual reading of *Lazarillo de Tormes* and Luis Murillo's *Four Figures on a Step,* a painting for which *Lazarillo* served as textual background. The authors argue that the recent critical inquiries that have helped to fill the gaps and silences in *Lazarillo* also "serve to fill in the narrative gaps left by the painter [Murillo]." They then go on to conclude that "like the picaresque novel, Murillo's composition is . . . transgressive . . . as these characters usurp an illusionistic space usually reserved for devotional imagery." Following Paul Julian Smith's (118) view of the picaresque novel as the portrait of an "unholy family," they claim that "so, too, is Murillo's painting an irreverent icon of the Unholy." Moreover, in line with Shipley's reading of *Lazarillo*, they argue that the viewer's complacency is shattered, in both Murillo's painting and the novel, "as we are caught in the act of looking, willing witnesses to the display of transgressive sexuality. Dislodged from a position of sole control, we cannot help but experience discomfort as our shameless scrutiny is discovered—both by the figures within the painting and by the prologuist of the *Lazarillo*."

By analyzing these two means of representation (painting and text) we become privy to a different and more comprehensive discourse "as the looks outward and the scrutiny inward meet at the boundary line between propriety and impropriety." That wider discourse is created largely through a conflict of perspectives, by different subject positions, and, above all, by a radical awareness that a relativization of values and codes of conduct is taking place. This intertextual dimension of the discourse of marginality can be said to have those features that Kristeva has proposed in her interpretation of Bahktin's dialogism: the superseding of the (monological) sign by the "double"; the ongoing transposition of a dominant meaning into its other.[5]

The Tomlinson and Welles essay provides an interesting example of the relationship between various art forms in early modern Spain, especially in the period of the baroque, when the monarcho-seigniorial segments of society used all means at their disposal—from repression to sociopolitical propaganda (Maravall, *La cultura*)—to preserve their privileges. It must also be said that Murillo's painting fits into a whole range of discursive practices that manage simultaneously to display official values as well as the symptoms of their corruption. Thus, the broadening of the discourse of marginality to include the sphere of the visual arts allows us to examine the relationship between image and idea. Such a dialectics is not a discovery of modern research—as well-known studies by Panofsky, Praz, and Argan have shown—but is one of the major factors in the creation of perspectivism as a compositional element of artistic illusion. For perspectivism may be said to entail the opening of a discursive locus where the individual subject may be posited and, possibly, subjected to the rhetorical devices that stage the composition. At the same time, the illusionistic character of perspectivism is revealed through the gap that is created between the canvas and the world outside of it. Velázquez and Cervantes are two outstanding examples of baroque artists who portray the illusionistic trappings of baroque culture for what they are.[6]

Another issue touching on the relationship between idea and image is the question of iconography or, more precisely, the ideological value of imagery that combines verbal and nonverbal signifiers. Luis Beltrán's essay on Francisco Delicado's *La Lozana andaluza* analyzes typographical signs in relation to the position accorded to the author-character and his diagetic relationship with the narrator. Using a facsimile of the only extant copy of the princeps, Beltrán provides a detailed analysis of the fourteenth "sketch" (*mamotreto*) of the novel, arguing that the typographical signs, vignettes, and illustrations with which the author experiments are "transmitters operational as both text and context." Beltrán concludes that "there are two Delicados but two—and here is where the phrase author's author comes in—who have much in common," so that a written author becomes indistinguishable from the writing one as reality is translated into the text (234).

From our perspective what is interesting about Delicado's novel is the timing of the appearance of the *auctor* in the fourteenth *mamotreto* in the middle of a lovemaking session between the grotesque Lozana and Rampín. It is then, precisely at the moment when passionate sex propels the characters into silence, that the *auctor* makes an appearance to report that the two lovers are waking up from their snoring. While the *auctor* is an entity who reports on what he hears and sees, it is Lozana's blow-by-blow description of the copulation that creates the visual image of an erotic encounter.

Lozana is actor, director, and writer of a pornographic scene, while the *auctor* assumes his own voice only to describe her silence after the sexual exchange. It is in this pornographic sequence, when Lozana becomes a sexual icon, a purely sexual body, that she acquires an independence of her own. The attributes that the author had previously given to her—by characterizing her as a syphilitic, noseless prostitute with many monstrous features—become unimportant at the moment of the sexual encounter. The plasticity of Lozana's description of the pleasurable sexual act counters the author's portrait of an ugly, marginalized woman. In this and other instances the discourse of marginality makes possible a critical debate on authority as well as on the social and political relevance of the act of reading.

As Carroll B. Johnson observes in his essay on *Guzmán*, the implicit relation between authorship and authority thematizes the material relationships between discourse and property. Johnson continues a polemic initiated by Paul Julian Smith (*Writing in the Margin*), who had argued that most critical approaches to the picaresque are based on "unexamined preconceptions concerning the nature of representation in literature" (79). Those preconceptions, according to Smith, are derived from what he calls "pictorialism," an "appeal . . . to the visual arts or the visual imagination as a privileged model for writing" (79). Smith suggested that both traditional and heretical critics of Guzmán (Rico and Johnson exemplifying tradition and heresy, respectively) tend to render readings that are at once idealist and empiricist: idealist in that they posit an eternal and unchanging subjectivity, and empiricist in that they suppose a concrete and discrete object, divorced from, yet freely accessible to, the critical gaze (102). Smith's alternative is "a revised model of literary representation, which, unlike pictorialism, does not suppress the contradictions inherent in the picaresque" (79).

For Smith, "if the textual register of the *Guzmán* seems inconsistent, it is because its author juxtaposes the individual and deficient testimony of the character with the universal and authoritative commentary of the narrator, with no concern for illusionistic pictorialism or empiricist evaluation. Hence, the site of unification (if one were needed) is not in the author or narrator, but in the reader. The *Guzmán* contains within itself a constant and ever-changing projection and representation of the public to whom it is addressed. But the readership is shown to be as multiple and fragmented as the narrator. Divided initially and uncompromisingly into the common and the disabused reader ('vulgar' and 'discreto'), it is unceasingly imagined throughout the narration" (105).

Johnson takes issue with Smith's antihumanist reading of *Guzmán* and seeks to rescue the author (or at least his created alter ego *Guzmán*) from the oblivion to which he has been relegated by Smith's poststructuralist reading. For Johnson, "what is at stake is deciding who has the power to call speech or discourse into existence, and who has the power to shut it off." While attributing that power to Mateo Alemán's alter ego, Guzmán, who, as commentator, "is a writer, an 'auctor', an authority [who] possesses the power of the pen," Johnson ultimately concludes that "the real owner of the discourse is now located in that fiction that is always the writer's audience," so that there is a "struggle for authority, for ownership of the discourse, between the writing I and the inscribed reader." Finally, for Johnson, if the writing "I" is not an integrated whole it is because it is profoundly human.

In a curious way, despite the polemic, the respective positions of Smith and Johnson seem to converge on the notion of a fragmented readership. Now such a readership can be dealt with by addressing the far-reaching, political question of the position that individual subjects acquire within the process of constructing a hierarchized distribution of wealth and values. To this extent Edward H. Friedman's brilliant analysis of the "double agency" in the artistic composition of *El buscón* allows for a rigorous articulation of the linguistic and social alienation that the individual subject suffers through the imposition of authority and order.

In commenting on Iffland's Freudian reading of Quevedo's novel, Friedman distinguishes between the reception that might have been accorded to Pablos's story in the seventeenth century and the possibility that, in our own times, greater credence may be given to the underdog and those factors that position him at the margins of society. In our days the underdog or marginalized individual may become a new center while the institutions of the state "may become decentered images." This turn of fortunes is attributed to poststructuralism's penchant for "teaching us how to operate in the subtextual realm, how to produce counterreadings."

Moving away from traditional formalist readings of *Buscón* (Rico's, for example), Friedman concentrates on the text's "unique and mystifying engagement of narrator and author," stressing the significant changes in the linguistic directions of the novel in chapter 4 where the reader can clearly "differentiate between Pablos's voice (and authority) and Quevedo's." In undermining the authority of the speaker by "metaphorically dislodging Pablos from the center of story and discourse," Quevedo is said to re-shape the autobiographical format of first-person picaresque narratives. In so doing, he ensures the victory of the state's discourse (Godzich and Spadaccini).

Friedman's essay, which focuses on a close analysis of Pablos's discourse, concludes with a political reading, namely, that the *Buscón* "may be about the need to respect the forces that supersede the individual, that stabilize society, and that perpetuate the status quo." His interpretation fits nicely within Maravall's definition of baroque culture as the culture of those groups (the monarcho-seigniorial segments of society) who deployed all means at their disposal (in Quevedo's case a corrosive wit) to preserve a system of privileges, understanding of course that Maravall views this type of literature as directed to the middle segments of society ("grupos intermedios"), those who had the most to lose from the *pícaro*'s lawlessness, vagabondage, and general affront to the no-biliary values to which those very groups aspired. In a way, Fried-man's reading also comes near to Talens's affirmation of Pablos's final fall into delinquency as the only real way out for the *pícaro*, in a world that does not allow the lower segments of society to share in the nobility's privileges, since the other two modes of "integra-tion"—Lázaro's and Guzmán's—were both false, as they were based upon dishonor and "religious conversion," respectively. At the same time Friedman seems to hint that today's reader may fo-cus more on the miseries and social alienation of Pablos the un-derdog, whose destiny is sealed at birth, than on Quevedo's bril-liant attempts to deprive him of a voice.

This textual tension between authority and transgression in pi-caresque narratives opens an implicit debate between, on the one hand, a naturalistic conception of the causes and reasons of mar-ginality and, on the other, a social interpretation. For it is a deep conviction of the unchangeable nature of individual behavior that propels Quevedo to reduce the *pícaro* to a moral condition barely above animality. In the same vein, female rogues and criminals such as Elena (*La hija de Celestina*) are marked from birth by their celestinesque origins, which in turn refer us to questions of prostitution, robbery, and ethnic domination (Moorish infamy).

In the pages of picaresque narratives these individuals' attempts to gain economic and social privileges are doomed to failure. And if some of them finally do manage to eke out a living, it is because they either willingly accept immorality (Lazarillo) or they radicalize a pragmatic conduct to the extreme (Estebanillo). Yet, even in these two cases, their human condition appears to be downgraded by cuckoldry and cowardice, respectively.

Along this naturalistic and conservative view, the textual tension between authority and transgression also posits a perspective that allows for a reflection upon the social conditions that affect the existence of disruptive conduct. The display of repressed subjectivity within an authoritarian system of values is after all an indication of the existence of an awareness that seigniorial stratification and the lack of access to wealth and privileges by certain social groups contribute to the production of a socially aggressive behavior.

The collection is rounded out with essays by Manuel Durán and Howard Mancing. The first establishes a suggestive analogy between the travels of exploration and conquest of the so-called New World and Cervantes's rethinking of the picaresque to construct an entire literary continent;[7] the second reviews the various attempts at defining the picaresque to conclude that "there is no single, sustaining or controlling theme, worldview, tone, philosophy, or attitude that characterizes the genre,"[8] providing an appendix titled "The Picaresque Canon" that includes some twenty-eight Spanish novels published between 1554 and 1688.

From our perspective, if picaresque narratives and the whole phenomenon that we have called here the discourse of marginality in early modern Spain may still appeal to us today, it is precisely because they reveal a deep doubt at the heart of modernity, a doubt that refers to the questioning of the universal validity of the social structure that comes with this modernity. The emergence of modern subjectivity is a contradictory phenomenon in which one can detect the hints of social and political domination;

moreover, it is also a dialogical structure of meaning that comes to light when we observe that moral transgression and social aggression are embedded in the same idea of cultural homogeneity.

To have access to this array of conflicts is also to expand the implicit debate that the picaresque developed along with its own creation. For there is a political need to enlarge social discourses to include the voices and experiences of those individuals and groups that have not had the privilege of feeling that the culture into whose midst they have been thrown is also their own. This political need must be fulfilled if socioeconomic changes aspire to arrive at an ethical justification; otherwise, as picaresque marginality clearly testifies, the compulsion for aggression and the choice of a radically pragmatic morality may result in a social order that is in a permanent state of fear. As Fernando de Rojas's *La Celestina* makes clear around 1500, the expectations for a better future (in love, in friendship, and in business) are dangerously filled with the by-products of universal insolidarity.

We can find here the answer to the question posed at the beginning of these pages: why the interest in the picaresque at this time? The shift in scholarship from traditional approaches to a more comprehensive cultural view forces us to deal with literary works not just as "monuments," but as "documents" where processes of institutionalization, political misreading, the marginalization of discourses, and so on are inscribed. As a writing expression of the multiple and contradictory reality of sixteenth- and seventeenth-century Spain, the picaresque appears now as a challenging panorama from which to rethink the origins of modernity.

Notes

1. Taking issue with Castro and others who would give absolute importance to blood statutes, Maravall argues that the *pícaro* is fully cognizant of the practical dependence of honor upon wealth, and vice versa: "there is no pícaro, as far as I can recall, who limits his pretensions to being an hidalgo without being rich" ("no nay ningún pícaro que yo recuerde, que se reduzca en su pretensión a ser hidalgo sin ser rico") (536).

2. Curiously, Dunn seeks to disconnect *Estebanillo* from the genre, as he focuses on "Estebanillo's relentless facetiousness" (285), downplaying the *pícaro*-buffoon's constant struggle for survival through any means, including humor and wit, as a buffoon of Ottavio Piccolomini and other personalities of the Spanish and Austrian wings of the Hapsburg Empire. Estebanillo, like all other *pícaros*, is a mar-

ginalized individual who lacks a fixed profession or occupation. Moreover, his drunkenness is tied to a melancholy that results from his experiences as a servant within the brutal context of the Thirty Years War, a conflict fought for economic self-interest by major European powers. In 1967 the novelist Juan Goytisolo was to call *Estebanillo* the most important novel of the Spanish Golden Age after *Don Quijote*. Goytisolo had read *Estebanillo* as an antiwar novel. Ironically, *Estebanillo* also condenses the features of the marginalized individual as represented in many of the texts of the baroque period: antiheroism, drunkenness, pragmatism, lack of a fixed occupation, a lack of honor and access to privileges, and, therefore, a permanent need to find a master.

3. See Martz, especially 7–91, where she touches upon the different positions regarding the debates on poverty. See also Maravall, "De la misericordia a la justicia social en la economía del trabajo: La obra de Fray Juan de Robles."

4. In the "Prologue" to his most recent edition of *Antiguos y modernos* Maravall even suggests the need to get rid of the mythical conception of linearity in history and argues for the recuperation of a relativized idea of progress.

5. "Dialogue and ambivalence lead me to conclude that, within the interior space of the text as well as within the space of *texts,* poetic language is a 'double'" (69).

6. Velázquez, for example, manages to bridge art and reality in *Las Meninas* by "confounding the barriers of space and matter in order to allow the real and the artificial to intermingle" (Brown 98).

7. An interesting connection between the chronicles of exploration and conquest, the picaresque, Cervantes, and the origins of the modern novel is made by González Echevarría, who speaks of the "pervasiveness of legal rhetoric" in various types of narratives in sixteenth- and seventeenth-century Spain as well as "in early American historiography" (10). Durán's observations could be expanded further by focusing on the role assigned by Cervantes to the printing press in the dissemination of printed narratives.

8. Mancing reduces Tierno Galván's and Maravall's use of the picaresque as a historical and cultural "document" and Talens's semiotic approach to narrative structure to a similar discussion about class struggle, a concept that in Maravall, for instance, never appears as such.

Works Cited

Argan, Giulio Carlo. "Ideology and Iconology." *The Language of Images.* Ed. W. J. T. Mitchel. Chicago: Univ. of Chicago Press, 1980. 15–23.

Bourdieu, Pierre. *Ce que parler veut dire: L'économie des échanges linguistiques.* Paris: Fayard, 1982.

Brown, Jonathan. *Images and Ideas in Seventeenth-Century Spanish Painting.* Princeton: Princeton Univ. Press, 1978.

Butler, Judith. *Gender Trouble: Feminism and the Subversion of Identity.* New York: Routledge, 1990.

Dunn, Peter N. *Spanish Picaresque Fiction: A New Literary History.* Ithaca: Cornell Univ. Press, 1993.

Godzich, Wlad, and Nicholas Spadaccini. "Popular Culture and Spanish Literary

History." *Literature among Discourses: The Spanish Golden Age.* Ed. Wlad Godzich and Nicholas Spadaccini. Minneapolis: Univ. of Minnesota Press, 1986.

González Echevarría, Roberto. *Myth and Archive: Toward a Theory of Latin-American Narrative.* New York: Cambridge Univ. Press, 1990.

Goytisolo, Juan. "Estebanillo González, hombre de buen humor." *El furgón de cola.* Paris: Editions Ruedo Ibérico, 1967. 59–76.

Guillén, Claudio. "Luis Sánchez, Ginés de Pasamonte y los inventores del género picaresco." *Homenaje a Rodríguez Moñino.* Madrid: Castalia, 1966. 221–31.

Iffland, James. *Quevedo and the Grotesque.* London: Tamesis Books, 1978–82.

Kristeva, Julia. "World, Dialogue and Novel." *Desire in Language: A Semiotic Approach to Literature and Art.* Ed. Leon S. Roudiez. New York: Columbia Univ. Press, 1980.

Maravall, José Antonio. "De la misericordia a la justicia social en la economía del trabajo: La obra de Fray Juan de Robles." *Utopía y reformismo en la España de los Austrias.* Madrid: Siglo XXI, 1982.

———. *La literatura picaresca desde la historia social.* Madrid: Taurus, 1986.

———. "Prólogo." *Antiguos y modernos.* Madrid: Alianza, 1986.

Martz, Linda. *Poverty and Welfare in Hapsburg Spain.* Cambridge: Cambridge Univ. Press, 1983.

Panofsky, Erwin. *Perspective as a Symbolic Form.* Trans. Christopher S. Wood. New York: Zone Books, 1991.

———. *Studies in Iconology.* New York: Icon, 1972.

Praz, Mario. *Studies in Seventeenth Century Iconography.* Rome: Edizioni di Storia e Letteratura, 1964.

Smith, Paul Julian. *Writing in the Margin.* Oxford: Oxford Univ. Press, 1988.

Talens, Jenaro. *Novela picaresca y práctica de la transgresión.* Madrid: Jucar, 1975.

Turner, Victor. *The Ritual Process: Structure and Antistructure.* Ithaca: Cornell Univ. Press, 1969.

Contributors

Luis Beltrán. Professor of Spanish and Comparative Literature at Indiana University, Bloomington. He has written studies on Western European medieval topics and on Spanish lyric poetry. His books include *Razones de Buen Amor, La arquitectura del humo: Una reconstrucción del Romancero gitano* and *Las cantigas de loor de Alfonso el Sabio.* He was for sometime a contributor to the Madrid newspaper *Ya* and has published a novel and several collections of poetry.

Anne J. Cruz. Professor of Portuguese and Spanish at the University of Illinois-Chicago Circle. She is the author of *Imitación y transformación: El petrarquismo en la poesía de Boscán y Garcilaso de la Vega* (1988) and is coeditor of three anthologies on Renaissance and baroque literature and culture. Currently, she is finishing a study of Golden Age picaresque novels.

Nina Cox Davis. Associate Professor of Spanish at Washington University in St. Louis. She is the author of *Autobiography as "Burla" in the "Guzmán de Alfarache"* and has published articles on the picaresque novel, Cervantes, and early Renaissance Spanish theater. Her recent investigations include preparation of a book-length study on gender and authority in development of the picaresque and essays on the problem of national consciousness in the Golden Age *novelas.*

Manuel Durán. Professor of Spanish at Yale University. He is the author or editor of more than forty books of criticism and anthologies. Among his titles are *La ambigüedad en el Quijote,* the Twayne *Cervantes,* and books on Quevedo, Luis de León, and Calderón, as well as more than 150 articles of literary criticism.

Edward H. Friedman. Professor of Spanish and Portuguese at Indiana University, Bloomington. His primary field of research is Spanish Golden Age literature. His publications include *The Unifying Concept: Approaches to Cervantes's Comedias* and *The Antiheroine's Voice: Narrative Discourse and Transformations of the Picaresque.*

Carroll B. Johnson. Professor of Spanish Literature and Chair of Spanish and Portuguese at UCLA. His principal research interest is sixteenth- and seventeenth-century narrative, which he has studied from both psychoanalytic and historical-materialist perspectives. He is the author of *Matías de los Reyes and the Craft of Fiction, Inside Guzmán de Alfarache, Madness and Lust: A Psychoanalytical Approach to Don Quixote,* and *Don Quixote: The Quest for Modern Fiction.* He is at work on a book about power, gender, and discourse in the *Novelas ejemplares,* as well as an anthology of letters to the Dean.

Giancarlo Maiorino. Professor of Comparative Literature and Director of Renaissance Studies at Indiana University, Bloomington. His area of interest is Renaissance interdisciplinarity with a particular emphasis on literature and the visual arts. He is the author of *Adam, "New Born and Perfect": The Renaissance Promise of Eternity, The Cornucopian Mind and the Baroque Unity of the Arts, The Portrait of Eccentricity: Arcimboldo and the Mannerist Grotesque,* and *Leonardo da Vinci: The Daedalian Myth-Maker.* He is currently working on the relationship between literature and the poetics of affluence-indigence.

Howard Mancing. Professor of Spanish at Purdue University. He is the author of *The Chivalric World of Don Quijote* (1982) and editor (with Charles Ganelin) of *Text, Theory, and Performance: Golden Age Comedia Studies* (1994), and has written numerous articles on Cervantes, the picaresque novel, and academic administration. He is currently studying the relationships between cognitive science and literary theory.

Francisco J. Sánchez. Assistant Professor of Spanish at the University of Iowa. He has published several essays on Spanish literary and cultural history and is the author of a recently published book, *Lectura y representación: Análisis cultural de las "Novelas ejemplares" de Cervantes* (1994).

George A. Shipley. Associate Professor of Spanish at the University of Washington. He has published half a dozen studies of *Lazarillo de Tormes* and as many of Fernando de Rojas's *La Celestina.*

Recently he has focused his attention principally on Cervantes's *Don Quixote* and especially on Sancho Panza and the episode of the fulling mill.

Nicholas Spadaccini. Professor of Hispanic Studies and Comparative Literature at the University of Minnesota. He has written on the Spanish Golden Age and colonial cultures, and has edited a number of Spanish classics and several volumes of literary theory and criticism. His most recent book (coauthored) is *Through the Shattering Glass: Cervantes and the Self-Made World* (1993).

Janis A. Tomlinson. Associate Professor of Art History at Columbia University. Her publications include *Francisco Goya, Goya in the Twilight of Enlightenment,* and *Graphic Evolutions: The Print Series of Francisco Goya.*

Marcia L. Welles. Professor of Spanish at Barnard College. She is the author of *Style and Structure in Gracián's "El Criticón"* and *Arachne's Tapestry: The Transformation of Myth in Seventeenth-Century Spain,* and the coeditor of *From Fiction to Metafiction: Essays in Honor of Carmen Martín Gaite.* The relationship between verbal and visual art in both contemporary and Golden Age texts has been the subject of several of her articles.

Index

313